AUSTRIAN STUDIES
VOLUME 17
2009

VOL. 17   2009

AUSTRIAN STUDIES

Editors
JUDITH BENISTON, GEOFFREY CHEW
and ROBERT VILAIN

Reviews Editor
JON HUGHES

Words and Music

Modern Humanities Research Association

INTERNATIONAL ADVISORY BOARD

Professor Andrew Barker, *University of Edinburgh*
Dr Steven Beller, *Washington, USA*
Dr Gilbert J. Carr, *Trinity College Dublin*
Professor Geoffrey Chew, *Royal Holloway, University of London*
Professor Gary B. Cohen, *Center for Austrian Studies, University of Minnesota, Twin Cities*
Professor R. J. W. Evans, *Oriel College, Oxford*
Professor Allyson Fiddler, *Lancaster University*
Professor Konstanze Fliedl, *Universität Wien*
Professor Sander L. Gilman, *Emory University*
Professor Hans Höller, *Universität Salzburg*
Professor Florian Krobb, *National University of Ireland, Maynooth*
Professor Jacques Le Rider, *École Pratique des Hautes Études, Paris*

Mr Peter Mikl, *Austrian Cultural Forum, London*
Dr Helga Mitterbauer, *Universität Graz*
Professor Robert Pynsent, *SSEES, University College London*
Professor Jens Rieckmann, *University of California, Irvine*
Professor Ritchie Robertson, *St John's College, Oxford*
Professor Eda Sagarra, *Trinity College Dublin*
Professor Sigurd Paul Scheichl, *Universität Innsbruck*
Professor Carl E. Schorske, *Princeton University*
Dr Janet Stewart, *University of Aberdeen*
Professor Edward Timms, *University of Sussex*
Dr Andrew Webber, *Churchill College, Cambridge*
Professor W. E. Yates, *University of Exeter*

Contributions for volume 18: *Austria and the Alps: Landscape, Culture and National Identity* have already been commissioned. A call for papers for *Austrian Studies* 19, *The Austrian 'Noughties': Texts, Films and Debates 2000–09*, together with Notes for Contributors giving guidance on the form in which to submit papers, can be found at:

http://www.austrian.mhra.org.uk/

Copies of *Austrian Studies* may be ordered from Subscriptions Department, Maney Publishing, Suite 1C, Joseph's Well, Hanover Walk, Leeds LS3 1AB, UK; email mhra@maney.co.uk. The journal is also available to individual members of the Modern Humanities Research Association in return for a composite membership subscription payable in advance. Further information about the activities of the MHRA and individual membership can be obtained from the Honorary Secretary, Prof. David Gillespie, School of European Studies and Modern Languages, University of Bath, Bath BA2 7AY, UK, or from the website at www.mhra.org.uk.

Parts of this work may be reproduced as permitted under legal provisions for fair dealing (or fair use) for the purposes of research, private study, criticism, or review, or when a relevant collective licensing agreement is in place. All other reproduction requires the written permission of the copyright holder who may be contacted at rights@mhra.org.uk.

ISSN 1350-7532
ISBN 978-1-907322-08-2

© 2010 The Modern Humanities Research Association

Contents

Introduction
By ROBERT VILAIN 1

ARTICLES

Setting the Tone: Austria's National Anthems from Haydn to Haider
By ANDREW BARKER 12

Mozart's Words, Mozart's Music: Untangling an Encounter with a Fortepiano and its Remarkable Consequences
By JOHN IRVING 29

'Ausgleichs-Abende': The First Viennese Performances of Smetana's *The Bartered Bride*
By DAVID BRODBECK 43

Arnold Schoenberg's Wounded Work: 'Litanei' from The String Quartet in F sharp minor, Op. 10
By DARLA M. CRISPIN 62

Mahler's Farewell or The Earth's Song? Death, Orientalism and 'Der Abschied'
By ANDREW DERUCHIE 75

Leo Golowski as Minor Key in Schnitzler's *Der Weg ins Freie*: Musical Theory, Political Behaviour and Ethical Action
By FELIX W. TWERASER 98

The Adventures of *The Cunning Little Vixen*: Leoš Janáček, Max Brod and their Predecessors
By GEOFFREY CHEW 113

'Meine Not ist zu Ende und all meine Qual': Erich Zeisl's Setting of Alfons Petzold's 'Der tote Arbeiter'
By KARIN WAGNER 133

'Das Erdorchester bedienen': Epiphany, Enchantment and the Sonorous World of Peter Handke
By MARTON MARKO 164

'Schreiben und Komponieren': Elfriede Jelinek's *Rosamunde*
By GILLIAN PYE AND SIOBHÁN DONOVAN 179

REVIEWS

Derek Beales, *Joseph II*. Volume II: *Against the World 1780–1790* (TIM HOCHSTRASSER) 194

Deborah Coen, *Vienna in the Age of Uncertainty. Science, Liberalism and Private Life* (DEBORAH HOLMES) 195

Wien und die jüdische Erfahrung 1900–1938. Akkulturation — Antisemitismus — Zionismus, ed. by Frank Stern and Barbara Eichinger (LARS FISCHER) . . 197

Marc Lacheny, *Pour une autre vision de l'histoire littéraire et théâtrale. Karl Kraus lecteur de Johann Nestroy* (W. E. YATES) 199

Aus großer Nähe. Karl Kraus in Berichten von Weggefährten und Widersachern, ed. by Friedrich Pfäfflin (GILBERT J. CARR) 200

Rainer Maria Rilke / Norbert von Hellingrath. Briefe und Dokumente, ed. by Klaus E. Bohnenkamp (HELEN BRIDGE) 202

Stimmen zur Unterhaltung. Operette und Revue in der publizistischen Debatte (1906–1933), ed. by Marion Linhardt (JUDITH BENISTON) 204

Wilhelm von Sternburg, *Joseph Roth. Eine Biographie* and Heinz Lunzer, *Joseph Roth. Im Exil in Paris 1933 bis 1939* (JON HUGHES) 206

Kati Tonkin, *Joseph Roth's March into History. From the Early Novels to 'Radetzkymarsch' and 'Die Kapuzinergruft'* (ISABEL DOS SANTOS) 208

Hildegard Atzinger, *Gina Kaus. Schriftstellerin und Öffentlichkeit. Zur Stellung einer Schriftstellerin in der literarischen Öffentlichkeit der Zwischenkriegszeit in Österreich und Deutschland* (GODELA WEISS-SUSSEX) 210

Anthony Bushell, *Poetry in a Provisional State. The Austrian Lyric 1945–1955* (HEIDE KUNZELMANN) 213

Michael Hammerschmid and Helmut Neundlinger, *'von einen sprachen'. Poetologische Untersuchungen zum Werk Ernst Jandls* (JOHN J. WHITE) . . . 215

Bärbel Lücke, *Elfriede Jelinek. Eine Einführung in das Werk* (REBECCA BRAUN) 217

Obituary: Peter Branscombe (1929–2008) By W. E. YATES 220

ABSTRACTS OF ARTICLES. 223

Words and Music

Introduction

ROBERT VILAIN

Amongst the various literary works that bear the title *Words and Music*, one film and one radio play suggest between them both the more straightforward and the more esoteric aesthetic possibilities offered by combining the two elements of their titles. The film, made in 1948, directed by Norman Taurog, and starring Mickey Rooney and Tom Drake, is a somewhat bowdlerized version of the collaboration between Lorenz Hart and Richard Rodgers, 'the words' and 'the music' respectively in a long-lasting partnership that produced nearly thirty musicals and hundreds of songs. It was a successful cooperation, aesthetically and commercially ('nine hits in ten tries', as one historian remarks[1]). However, the paradigm the film offers for the integration of light verse and melodious music is relatively simple: one partner writes the words, the other the music, and the two (the products, not necessarily the artists) interact in an essentially harmonious and mutually completing manner. This is not to condemn this mode of writing — such a stance would fail to do justice to a whole series of critically respected partnerships from Gilbert and Sullivan to Hofmannsthal and Strauss[2] — and it is not intended as a snobbish comment on the relative merits of so-called 'high' and 'low' (or 'lower') art. It means only that the film does not begin to exhaust the potential ways in which the linguistic, or the textual, and the musical interact.

Another work with that title, Samuel Beckett's play, first broadcast by the BBC in November 1962, gives a more challenging and altogether more troubling insight into this potential. Here Words and Music are characters, the servants Joe and Bob, who are enjoined to entertain their frail and irritable old master, Croak, with joint illustrations of the concepts of 'Love', 'Age' and 'Face'. If we read *Words and Music* as in some sense allegorical of the creative act, with Croak as the artist, and Joe and Bob as the dual media in which he creates, then it is clear that these media are to some degree independent of their shaping spirit; they can ignore him and they exist when he is not present. Croak demands that they represent his chosen themes, but they 'have to stumble by roundabout ways to reach the desired epiphany', which reflects both

---

[1] Geoffrey Holden Block, *The Richard Rodgers Reader* (Oxford, 2002), p. 4.
[2] It also includes works in which both elements stem from the same pen, of course, such as Noël Coward's *Words and Music*, a musical from 1932 (in which 'Mad Dogs and Englishmen' first featured).

on the instability of this partnership and on its necessity.[3] The servants' own relationship is more than a little fraught. They are told 'be friends' by Croak,[4] but argue and irritate each other most of the time, as the 'dialogue' prompted by Croak's demand for the representation of 'Age' shows:

> CROAK: Bob. (*Pause.*) Age. (*Pause. Violent thump of club.*) Age!
> MUSIC: *Rap of baton. Age music, soon interrupted by violent thump.*
> CROAK: Together. (*Pause. Thump.*) Together! (*Pause. Violent thump.*) Together, dogs!
> MUSIC: *Long la.*
> WORDS: (*Imploring.*) No!
> (*Violent thump.*) (pp. 129–30)

The dialogue is such that Bob answers Joe's verbal prompts with musical responses. Music's 'speeches' (in italics but without parentheses, to distinguish them from the stage directions) are Samuel Beckett's shorthand for actual music, which in the original production only was provided by his cousin, John Beckett. When Katharine Worth proposed a production in 1973, she approached John Beckett for permission to re-use his music but this was denied. Her score was written by Humphrey Searle; subsequent versions use music by Morton Feldman, written in 1986–87.[5] The difficulty that a reader of the printed text will have in conceiving of the sounds suggested by Beckett's very laconic descriptions in Music's 'speeches' is thus compounded by the fact that there is not even an authorized score for musicians to interpret. The reader has virtually no idea what one half of the dialogue is, although this indeterminacy does not seem to be acknowledged by the text itself, which proposes 'humble muted adsum', 'Age music', 'suggestion for following', 'air', 'warm suggestion from above' or 'irrepressible burst of spreading and subsiding music' at various points. Worth notes how the author was not interested in meeting the new composer in 1973, which suggests that the *actual* music, as it would sound to an audience, was of little importance to him.[6] 'Music seems to be treated as if it will be and mean the same in any realisation — as a pure idea, indivisible and unchanging in essence from one manifestation to another, or as "pure

---

[3] Katharine Worth, 'Words for Music Perhaps', in *Samuel Beckett and Music*, ed. by Mary Bryden (Oxford, 1998), pp. 9–20 (p. 10).

[4] Samuel Beckett, *Words and Music*, in *Collected Shorter Plays of Samuel Beckett* (London, 1984), pp. 125–34 (p. 127). References to this play are given by page number in parentheses in the text.

[5] See Catherine Laws, 'Music in *Words and Music*: Feldman's Response to Beckett's Play', in *Samuel Beckett Today / Aujourd'hui*, 11: *Samuel Beckett. Endlessness in the Year 2000 / Samuel Beckett, fin sans fin en l'an 2000*, ed. by Angela Moorjani and Carola Veit (Amsterdam, 2001), pp. 279–90.

[6] Worth, 'Words for Music Perhaps', p. 13. *Words for Music Perhaps* was the title of a sequence of twenty-five poems by W. B. Yeats published in 1932 and soon taken into *The Winding Stair* (1933); it includes the 'Crazy Jane' poems.

spirit".[7] It is as if the idea of music is being tested to see whether it can release dimensions of the imagination that words alone cannot touch or trigger.

From the point of view of the history of words and music in Austria, the antagonistic situation staged in Beckett's play is strangely reminiscent of that in Richard Strauss's and Hugo von Hofmannsthal's play-opera *Ariadne auf Naxos*, where Zerbinetta's troupe of actors is required by the Major Domo to perform simultaneously with the opera company's production of their mythologically inspired music-drama, such that the apparently incompatible are ultimately fused to the audience's aesthetic satisfaction. No such fusion emerges from Beckett's play. The relationship there between Words and Music is always uncertain or conflictual: Music's more confident outbursts are met with 'Peace!', 'No!' or 'Please!' from Words; the more tentative 'discreet suggestion[s]' have Words 'trying to sing', which implies failure or at least dissatisfaction. The play ends with Croak shuffling off into the distance, Words pleading for more music — 'Again. [...] Again!' — a pause, and then Words' emission of a 'deep sigh' (p. 134).

Beckett apparently told Theodor Adorno that the play 'ends unequivocally with the victory of the music',[8] but it is hard to reconcile such a judgement with the equivocations of the play itself, which are characteristic of Beckett's 'endless wandering to find an elusive home', as Catherine Laws puts it, and demonstrate 'a groping through language for a true expression of self and experience'. *Words and Music*, she suggests, 'hold[s] out for the possibility of language finding, perhaps through the example of music, a way towards this point'.[9] This is a more positive assessment than Jonathan Kalb's, who sees music in this play as 'confine[d] to a function very similar to that of a filmic signature score'.[10] We are a long way from the confidence in the relationship of words and music that I suggested was implied emblematically by the 1948 film of that title. Beckett explicitly rejects that degree of confidence in terms that prefigure the contrast of the two works considered here. His *Words and Music* has been called 'the closest thing there is in the Beckett canon to an opera',[11] but Beckett disliked both operas and the opera: 'By definition, opera is a hideous corruption of this most immaterial of all the arts: the words of a libretto are to the musical phrase that they particularise what the Vendôme Column, for example, is to the ideal perpendicular. From this point of view opera is less complete than vaudeville, which at least inaugurates the comedy of an exhaustive enumeration'.[12]

---

[7] Laws, 'Music in *Words and Music*', p. 279.
[8] Quoted in Clas Zilliacus, *Beckett and Broadcasting* (Åbo, 1976), p. 114; quoted in Jonathan Kalb, 'The Mediated Quixote: The Radio and Television Plays, and *Film*', in *The Cambridge Companion to Beckett*, ed. by John Pilling (Cambridge, 1994), pp. 124–44 (p. 132). The statement seems to have been repeated to Worth (see 'Words for Music Perhaps', p. 16).
[9] Laws, 'Music in *Words and Music*', pp. 288–89.
[10] Kalb, 'The Mediated Quixote', p. 132.
[11] Zilliacus, *Beckett and Broadcasting*, p. 103.
[12] Samuel Beckett, 'Proust', in *Proust and Three Dialogues* (London, 1987), p. 92.

The conceptual axis that the juxtaposition of the 1948 film and the 1962 radio broadcast seeks to establish might be summarized as the tension between easy success and strained failure, or in reverse, and more suggestively, in lines from the fifth of Rilke's *Duineser Elegien* [*Duino Elegies*] conveying 'die unsägliche Stelle, wo sich das reine Zuwenig | unbegreiflich verwandelt —, umspringt | in jenes leere Zuviel' [the ineffable place where pure too-little is incomprehensibly transformed — where it flips over into an empty too-much].[13] But these works also highlight the factor of control, the artist's (lack of) control over the medium, or media, in which s/he 'composes' — in the extended sense of that word. The pole represented by the film implies a high degree of mutual control: the two parties concerned, 'the words' and 'the music', can expect to arrive at a satisfying reciprocity. The pole represented by the play suggests the opposite, that frustration and antagonism are the norm, such that meaning is generated by a failure straightforwardly to map the one onto the other.

It is important to retain a sense that failure in this respect can also be a creative bonus, since it is all too tempting to see the interaction of words and music sentimentally as mysterious but ultimately of guaranteed significance. George Steiner has reflected at length on the subject, here in the context of translation:

> The composer who sets a text to music is engaged in the same sequence of intuitive and technical motions which obtain in translation proper. His initial trust in the significance of the verbal sign system is followed by interpretative appropriation, a 'transfer into' the musical matrix and, finally, the establishment of a new whole which neither devalues nor eclipses its linguistic source.[14]

This account presupposes a high degree of confidence in the controlling capacity of the composer and takes a good deal for granted. Discussing at first multiple musical settings of canonical poems by a variety of composers, Steiner asks:

> Has the composer read his poem accurately? Which individual syllables or words, which phrases or prosodic units, does he select for instrumental or vocal emphasis? Does this selection or its converse, the understatement of certain units, fairly enact the poet's intention (is Schubert right, in setting Schmidt von Lübeck's 'Der Wanderer', when he concentrates the whole meaning of the song on the word *nicht* in the last line, making the word come on a poignant appoggiatura over a strange chord of the sixth)? In what ways are Schumann's, Liszt's and Rubinstein's settings of Heine's 'Du bist wie eine Blume' successive but also divergent commentaries on a deceptively naïve text? [...]
> There are numerous cases in which the composer simply misreads

---

[13] Rainer Maria Rilke, *Werke*, Kommentierte Ausgabe, ed. by Manfed Engel et al., 5 vols (Frankfurt a. M. and Leipzig, 1996), II, 216.

[14] George Steiner, *After Babel. Aspects of Language and Translation* (Oxford, pbk. 1976), pp. 415–16.

his text. In all his six settings of Heine, Schubert misconstrues the poet's covert but mordant irony. Often the musician will tamper with the words, altering, omitting or 'improving' on the poem to suit his personal gloss or formal programme [...]. Mozart tacks on an extra verse to Goethe's 'Veilchen'; wishing to obtain a rise of a full octave on the word, Schubert elides the *e* in *Vögelein* in Goethe's 'Ueber allen Gipfeln'; in Schumann's opus 90, the composer alters Lenau's text, changing words, leaving out several, inserting some of his own (being the most verbally-perceptive [*sic*] of songwriters, Hugo Wolf almost never modifies the lyric). In musical translation, no less than in linguistic there are problems of surpassing. In both *Die Schöne Müllerin* and *Die Winterreise*, Schubert utterly transfigures the feeble poems of Wilhelm Müller, making of them a searching statement on the griefs and doubts of human existence.[15]

The quotation could be continued, but is interrupted here both because its gist is already perfectly apparent and because this section ends with a series of references to Austrian poets and musicians and thus begins to lead neatly back to the theme of this volume. Leaving aside the problematic assumptions made by value-judgements such as 'accurately', 'fairly', 'misreads' and 'surpassing', the relationships of power and control that this rather traditional account of aspects of the interrelations of words and music presupposes are useful as a foil against which to judge the more ambitious and exciting accounts of this relationship that this volume offers.

Some of the studies encompassed by this volume undertake the kind of analysis that Steiner adumbrates here — that of one composer's settings of a particular poet's work — albeit with rather more critical rigour. Others trace the ways in which a literary text is modified and adapted before and as it develops as one of the principal components of an opera. Several share new insights into the complex relationships of individual works with the literary and musical traditions out of which they emerge (or which they transform and renew) — or set such works in the political contexts of their genesis or reception, often using a key historical moment, a turning-point or a 'snapshot', as the starting-point for a wide-ranging investigation. In some cases the words and the music are those of the same 'composer', the relationship here shedding light on the process of composition itself. Literary works are often scrutinized for the light they shed on a musician's creative processes, but the importance of music to writers — as audiences, but also as amateur or even semi-professional practitioners — is no less important as an investigative standpoint.

The chronological range covered by the individual essays is more than two hundred years, from the Classical Enlightenment to the early twenty-first century. In his study of the Austrian national anthem that opens the volume, Andrew Barker single-handedly spans the same period, as he traces the shifting paths taken by the anthem's words and music as they were used at various times and in a multitude of different combinations as expressions of social, political

[15] Ibid., pp. 416–17.

and patriotic identity, under both Empire and Republic. Haydn's tune for 'Gott erhalte Franz den Kaiser' [God preserve our Emperor Francis] to words by Lorenz Leopold Haschka emerged during the Napoleonic wars. The need for an anthem seems to have been triggered by the recognition of the unifying role played by England's 'God Save the King', to another melody that has been 'recycled' in a variety of different, and often implicitly contradictory, national contexts (including Prussia and then most, but not all, of the united Germany until 1918). New words were sometimes substituted during the lifetime of Haydn's melody, and some of Austria's most distinguished writers, such as Adalbert Stifter, Franz Grillparzer and Hugo von Hofmannsthal, were approached for a definitive text. After the end of the First World War, other composers, too, had a shot at providing a lasting melody, but Haydn's was reinstated after the *Anschluss* in 1938, since it was, ironically, the one used for the infamous 'Deutschland, Deutschland, über alles' [Germany, Germany, above all else], and indeed for the current German national anthem 'Einigkeit und Recht und Freiheit' [Unity, laws and liberty].

The current Austrian anthem is sung to a tune attributed to Mozart, although the essay on Mozart in this volume approaches the relationship of words and music from an entirely different perspective. John Irving looks as Mozart's encounter with the renowned fortepiano maker Johann Andreas Stein in October 1777, which was documented in a compelling series of letters between Mozart and his father over the next few weeks. Stein's development of the escapement action provided the technical basis for a touch-sensitive instrument and thus a more sophisticated range of possibilities for dynamic, articulation, expression, register and texture, of which Mozart made full use in his sonatas KV284 and KV309. The letters chart father and son's excited realization of how important this was for Mozart's compositional potential, the texts both recording and anticipating the musical developments that Irving explores in detail, convincingly illustrating his claim that 'neither Mozart's words nor his music make full sense without the other'.

In the first of two contributions on Czech opera, David Brodbeck's study of the first Viennese performances of Bedřich Smetana's *The Bartered Bride* opens with a historical moment similarly rich with potential significance for European music, the eagerly anticipated (and politically sensitive) arrival in Vienna on 31 May 1892 of a train carrying members of the Czech National Theatre for a programme of five Czech operas as part of the Viennese Exhibition of Music and Theatre. Music here served to articulate the growing cultural independence of a Slavic component of the Habsburg Empire at a point when tensions between its German and Czech nationalities were coming to a head. Analysing the responses of the German liberal and nationalist press, Brodbeck documents the complexities and tensions that underlie the surprisingly warm reception of an ambitious and contentious repertoire. Some critics sought to deploy the German-speaking Mozart's relationship with Prague and Smetana's affinity for

Wagner as well as other musical rapprochements between the Germanic and the Slavic to explain the phenomenon of the first performance of *The Bartered Bride* in Czech, which one of them, alluding to the 'Böhmischer Ausgleich' [Bohemian Compromise] of 1890, described as a musical 'Ausgleichs-Abend' [evening of compromise]. Others by contrast stressed the uniquely Czech nature of Smetana's opera or chided the Germans for not defending their native musical tradition as vociferously as the Czech visitors supported theirs. A more extraordinary 'Ausgleich nach Noten' [musical compromise], which must be a *hapax legomenon* amongst the multifarious possible relationships of words and music, was a series of four performances of *The Bartered Bride* in German but with one performer singing in Czech! Unfortunately the musical model for harmony and healing was not to prove replicable on the streets of Prague.

The closing of wounds is overtly the theme of the next essay in the volume. A decade and half after the premiere in Vienna of Smetana's *Bartered Bride* in German, another premiere, that of Schoenberg's Second String Quartet in F sharp minor, Op. 10, met with a markedly different response. Darla Crispin explores both the scandal prompted by this work — whose third and fourth movements each set a poem, most unusually for a genre in which words habitually play no role at all — and the relationship it embodies between Schoenberg's chamber music and the music dramas of Wagner. Crispin also draws some telling parallels between Schoenberg's hatred of what he felt to be many contemporaries' dishonest use of the language of music and Karl Kraus's campaign against an equivalent tendency to pervert the written word in journalism and literature. It was the words in this concert that prompted the most furious hostility, embodying as they did an empirical articulateness felt to be transgressive within a genre traditionally associated with the abstract. Superimposed on this tension is another that derives from Schoenberg's determination to use the strictness of variation form to control the inherent romantic emotionality and drama of the text he chose to set in the third movement, Stefan George's 'Litanei' [Litany], which itself displays intertextual links with the libretto of Wagner's *Parsifal* that parallel the musical referencing of Kundry's laughter at Christ on the cross in Schoenberg's setting of the word 'Liebe' [love] with a similarly 'deformed' octave leap. Furthermore, Crispin shows how the two poems by George, especially 'Entrückung' [Transport] in the fourth movement, actually have a commentating and explanatory function in relation to the music itself.

Crispin's concluding paragraphs speculate eloquently on the implications the order of the last two movements (and of the texts they set) has for our understanding of Schoenberg's views on the theme of redemption in music, given their respective relationships with the antithetical pairing of Wagner's *Parsifal* and *Tristan und Isolde*. The importance of appreciating the response to *Tristan* articulated by Gustav Mahler's *Lied von der Erde* [*Song of the Earth*] provides the starting point for Andrew Deruchie's exploration of the treatment of the theme of death in its last movement, 'Der Abschied' [The Farewell]. Deruchie challenges the traditional subjectivist view that this work enacts the process of an individual death (much less the composer's own, which his illness made more imminent) and proposes that it explores an alternative epistemology, an exotic, oriental and anti-subjectivist alternative to late-nineteenth-century attitudes to death, one mediated via the poetry that inspired the work, Hans Bethge's *Die chinesische Flöte* [*The Chinese Flute*]. Deruchie offers a rich tour of the anthropological and cultural history of death in the nineteenth century that ranges from the ecstatic Wagnerian 'Liebestod' [love-death] on the stage to the less alluring medicalization and commercialization of death in what one might paradoxically call 'real life'. But it is the combination of the brutally real and the ideal that emerges from Rilke's novel *Die Aufzeichnungen des Malte Laurids Brigge* [*The Notebooks of Malte Laurids Brigge*], his conception of the mutual relationship of life and death in a form of 'Doppelbereich' [double realm], that provides the closest link to Mahler's 'Der Abschied' and the Taoist background mediated, albeit tenuously, via Bethge's reworkings of German translations of French paraphrases of Chinese originals. Deruchie concludes by exploring in detail how the music *and* the textual narration of the finale to *Das Lied* interdependently work through the Taoist solution in grammar, texture and gesture, moving from being 'drama *of* to discourse *on* death'.

Mahler's *Lied von der Erde* is perhaps the first song-cycle with ambitions towards being a symphony (in ways distinct from, for example, Hector Berlioz's *Les Nuits d'été* [*Summer Nights*] or Richard Wagner's *Wesendonck-Lieder*), and as such it is an important landmark in the otherwise shifting terrain of the relationship of words and music. It was begun in 1908, the same year in which Arthur Schnitzler's novel *Der Weg ins Freie* [*The Road into the Open*] was completed and published. Mahler's work is the product of a series of personal crises (his resignation as the principal conductor at the Opera House, his daughter's death and the diagnosis of his own serious heart condition). As Felix Tweraser points out in the opening paragraph of his essay, Schnitzler's novel depicts a whole culture in crisis. Mahler's resignation from the Opera House was partly prompted by the anti-Semitism he encountered, a phenomenon that forms one of the main themes of *Der Weg ins Freie*, whose principal character, Georg von Wergenthin, attends a performance of Wagner's *Tristan und Isolde* conducted by Mahler. Tweraser presents a reading of the novel's demystification of social constructions including, but not limited to, those affecting the Jewish population of Austria in the early twentieth century, that draws out the extent to which music is not only thematized (Wergenthin is a composer and conductor) but pervades both its structural and conceptual architecture. The latter emerges most elaborately in the musical theories of one of Wergenthin's most important interlocutors, the Zionist Leo Golowski, who exposes the sentimentality and self-indulgence of his friend's music and thereby of his politics and ethics.

1908 was also the year in which *Schloß Nornepygge* [*Nornepygge Castle*] was published, a hugely successful first novel by Max Brod, who would later become an influential champion of the operas of Leoš Janáček. The uneasy relationship between German and Czech explored by David Brodbeck in the context of the performance of late-nineteenth-century opera in Vienna manifests itself on a different plane in Geoffrey Chew's investigation of Max Brod's 'Umdichtung' of Janáček's opera *The Cunning Little Vixen*, which was completed in 1923. The origins of the story lie in a series of drawings of animals by Stanislav Lolek and texts provided by Rudolf Těsnohlídek when they were serialized in a Brno newspaper before being drawn together into a novel, where they acquired a satirical-political dimension, and thence into the opera, where they represent a broader vision of humanity without in a narrow sense being allegorically anthropomorphic. Thus the material undergoes an unusually varied trajectory from the entirely wordless images, via Těsnohlídek's expanded narrative, into a pared-down verbal partnership with Janáček's music. Chew shows how the text is defamiliarized in various ways and how the music takes on the narrative function. Brod's attempts to intervene when shown the work in 1923 demonstrate his failure to grasp the full extent of Janáček's originality in the handling of the text–music relationship, as does the freedom he proposed to exercise when translating it in 1925, rendering the animal–human relationships mutually symbolic in a more overt and less sophisticated way. Chew argues that Brod's version reflects concerns he developed in his own work on religion and cultural history at the expense of Janáček's musical achievements, and that the tendency to use or study the German translation of the libretto rather than the Czech original similarly masks or even distorts Janáček's unique realignment of the relationship of words and music in the genre usually known as *Literaturoper*.

Despite a certain chronological proximity, there is a considerable contrast between the delicately experimental animal world of *The Cunning Little Vixen* and the world inhabited by the poet Alfons Petzold, settings of whose socially aware, often highly politicized 'workers' poetry' by Erich Zeisl are the subject of Karin Wagner's essay, the only contribution to this volume that focuses directly on the tradition of the *Lied*, so important in Austria. Looking first at Zeisl's origins, his studies first with 'out-and-out romantics' and then with more innovative, more Modernist teachers, Wagner argues that Zeisl's miniatures were intimately linked to the times and circumstances that inspired them and focuses on the period after 1931 (his 'Liederjahr' [year of songs]) when his choice of texts shifted away from works largely by Romantic or Neo-Romantic authors. In 1932, against a background of increasing political unrest, Zeisl expressed his solidarity with the Social Democratic movement via his settings of four poems by Petzold. Adopting a musical style free of ornament and artifice — at some remove from his Romantic origins, therefore — Zeisl even sharpens the political focus of some of Petzold's poems by omitting their more redemptive elements or by setting up contrasts between more optimistic sounding passages of text and settings that emphasize the transience of hope. In 'Der tote Arbeiter' [The Dead Worker], for example, words and music both in different but cooperative ways establish a tension between the harsh world of labour and an optimism suggested by youthful purity, their subtle interrelationship itself a form of optimism that no longer obtains in the more overtly melancholy 'Komm süsser Tod' [Come Sweet Death] that in January 1938 clearly anticipates the threat of National Socialism in Austria.

The last two essays in this volume mark a shift to a much later period in Austria's history. The subject of Marton Marko's essay, Peter Handke, was born in 1942, four years after Zeisl left Austria, first for France and then for the United States, and nearly two decades after Petzold's death. And the music with which he became most familiar as a young man — pop, rock, folk and blues — is at some little remove from the tradition of the German *Lied*, opera, the concerto or the symphony, as is the jukebox that features in *Der kurze Brief zum langen Abschied* [*Short Letter, Long Farewell*] and in the long essay *Versuch über die Jukebox* [*Essay on the Jukebox*]. It is tellingly alien to the world of the symphony orchestra, the chamber ensemble or the live accompanied voice that is inhabited by other essays in this volume. Marko argues that music functions in Handke's works, and for Handke personally, as the vehicle of moments of 'recurring epiphanic enchantment' that are desirable and necessary as antidotes to his intense experience of cultural and subjective fragmentation — with the whistle of a steam boat in *Der kurze Brief*, for example, acting as the epicentre of a volcanic experience of music, myth and the collective. From his earliest works on — including *Publikumsbeschimpfung* [*Offending the Audience*] — the capacity of rhythm in music and language to impact on and change emotional states is systematically exploited, and Handke's texts contain performance guidance akin to that of a musical score (and not unlike Croak's structuring 'thumps' and pauses in Beckett's *Words and Music*). Marko uses the work of Roland Barthes and Walter Benjamin to suggest deeper affinities between the practice of music and the expanding concept of the text — text and music are both 'composed', as Barthes points out — in an era of mass culture and mechanically reproducible cultural products, in which both the authenticity of the work of art and its unique auratic character are under threat.

In doing so, Marko returns to a question raised by a number of the other essays in this volume, that of the relationship of the modern to Romanticism, which is also the starting-point of the examination of Elfriede Jelinek's dramolet *Rosamunde* by Gillian Pye and Siobhán Donovan. In a satisfyingly indirect way, this essay makes good what would otherwise have been a near-incomprehensible lacuna in a volume on words and music in Austria, by acknowledging the presence of Franz Schubert in this tradition. Schubert's incidental music to Helmina von Chézy's drama *Rosamunde* has all but smothered the play itself — and there is a further ironic refinement of the complexities of musico-verbal interrelation in the fact that Jelinek's play was written to 'accompany' a performance of Schubert's *incidental* music. His reworking of his own setting of 'Der Tod und das Mädchen' [Death and the Maiden] by Matthias Claudius as a string quartet is virtually a one-work definition of the term 'canonical'. That it provides the title for Jelinek's much less obviously canonical quintet of dramas is an irony clearly intended by their author, who describes her *Rosamunde* as 'autobiographically' and 'parasitically' 'abusing' Chézy's original. Musically, too, Jelinek's drama productively 'abuses' its Romantic intertexts, producing a cacophonous mix of discourses to enact the drowning out of the female voice by generations of male voices in a post-dramatic drama whose full realization requires its 'recipients' (actors and audience) to 'play' it as they might play music. In a sophisticated deployment of concepts developed by Barthes and modified by him in response to the work of Julia Kristeva, the 'pheno-song' and the 'geno-song', Pye and Donovan take the notion of the 'grain of the voice' as the starting-point for their analysis of Jelinek's text as one that 'skirts the fringe of contact between words and music' and works with the 'friction' that their mutual engagement produces. The idea of virtuosity in musical performance is mapped onto the inability of the female voice to express itself in Jelinek's *Rosamunde* where the 'geno-song' is allowed to emerge above the disrupted 'pheno-song', effectively parodying or debunking its Romantic intertext by 'playing it out of tune'.

★ ★ ★

In accordance with the usual practice of *Austrian Studies*, German quotations are also given in English translation, usually by the authors of the respective contributions or by the editors. Titles of German works are translated upon their first appearance. Karin Wagner's essay was translated by Robert Vilain and Geoffrey Chew.

Setting the Tone:
Austria's National Anthems from Haydn to Haider

ANDREW BARKER

University of Edinburgh

'Classical' music may be the most abstract of the arts, but it has played a very tangible role in the politics of modern Europe. During the *Risorgimento*, for example, revolutionary crowds expressed support for a country free from Austrian rule by chanting the name of Giuseppe Verdi, composer of the inspirational 'Chorus of the Hebrew Slaves' from Act 3 of *Nabucco* (1842). Everyone knew, however, that Verdi also stood for Vittore Emmanuele Re d'Italia [Victor Emanuel King of Italy]. Half a century later, Jean Sibelius's tone-poem *Finlandia* (1900) came to symbolize the nation itself during the struggle for independence from Tsarist Russia. Neither Verdi nor Sibelius, however, provided the music for their new nation's anthem. Perhaps their works lacked the folksong quality common to the three best-known, and longest-lived, European anthems: 'God save the King/Queen', 'La Marseillaise' and Haydn's tune for a Holy Roman Emperor in times of war, 'Gott erhalte Franz den Kaiser', which the composer himself referred to as his 'Volck's Lied'.[1] Following the Empire's demise, even the caustic Karl Kraus acknowledged the power of what he called Haydn's 'Volksgesang' [folksong], whose 'Genialität [...] imstande war, den niedersten Schranzensinn auf seine Flügel zu nehmen' [genius could make the lowliest imperial lickspittle's fantasies take flight].[2]

The notion of the national anthem as music encapsulating national self-awareness developed from the eighteenth century onwards, when 'God Save the King' gained widespread popularity among the Hanoverian section of the

---

[1] See Franz Grasberger, *Die Hymnen Österreichs* (Tutzing, 1968), p. 6. Grasberger's study proved a rich factual source for this essay, as did also *Joseph Haydn — Gott erhalte. Schicksal einer Hymne*, ed. by Thomas Leibnitz (Vienna, 2008). This is the illustrated catalogue of an exhibition held at the Austrian National Library (from November 2008 to February 2009). The texts of Haschka's anthem and of the Austrian anthem in other major guises are collected in the appendix to this essay.

[2] Karl Kraus, *Die Fackel*, 554–56 (1920), 58–59. Although Kraus did not admire Heine, there is an embedded reference here to 'Auf Flügeln des Gesanges' [On wings of song] from the *Buch der Lieder* (*Lyrisches Intermezzo*, IX). Not surprisingly, Haydn's melody often evoked a negative reaction in non-Germanic parts of the Empire. Franz Joseph's decree during World War I that all public concerts begin with the Austrian anthem so angered the composer Josef Suk, a member of the Czech String Quartet, that he arranged the ancient Czech hymn to Saint Wenceslas for the quartet to play alongside Haydn's melody.

United Kingdom during and after the Jacobite rebellion of 1745–46. It has been commonly called the 'National Anthem' since the beginning of the nineteenth century.[3] It was quickly recognized that such works are potent expressions of music's secular power, and the practical significance of a song associated with successful statehood and political might was not lost on the rest of the world. Even if not composed by Georg Friedrich Händel, as Adalbert Stifter erroneously believed,[4] the British melody was eventually adopted at one time or another by such diverse countries as the USA, Sweden, Russia, Switzerland and Liechtenstein.[5] Evidence has recently re-emerged that an anthem was briefly sung to this tune in Vienna early in 1797.[6]

During the last decade of the eighteenth century, Haydn twice visited London (1791–92 and 1794–95), observing at first hand the rallying effect singing 'God save great George our King' had on the people. As H. E. Jacob remarks:

> The populace of London was not noted for respecting persons or institutions, but whenever the anthem [...] rang out, the critics of the House of Hanover fell silent. At the time, national anthems were not a matter of course. It was a novel experience for people to feel in such music the kind of inner force which only religious hymns conveyed.[7]

Returning to a Vienna unsettled by Napoleon's rapid advance, the traditionally minded Haydn decided to compose a work which, like the British anthem, would celebrate continuity not change, and strengthen popular feeling towards the Emperor and the Habsburg dynasty in their defence of the Empire.[8] According to Anton Schmid, Haydn's aristocratic friend and collaborator Baron van Swieten (1733–1803) passed on Haydn's idea to Franz Joseph Graf Saurau (1760–1832), the reactionary Governor of Lower Austria and a figure very close to the Emperor.[9] Writing in 1820, however, Saurau credited himself as the now-famous anthem's instigator:

---

[3] For a discussion of the complex musical origins of the British anthem, see Percy A. Scholes, *God save the Queen! The History and Romance of the World's First National Anthem* (Oxford, 1954), pp. 92–103.

[4] See Grasberger, *Die Hymnen Österreichs*, p. 73. See also Otto Erich Deutsch, 'Haydn's hymn and Burney's translation', *The Music Review*, 8 (1943), 157–62 (p. 159).

[5] It was heard, for example, at the inauguration of US President Barack Obama on 20 January 2009, sung to the words 'My Country, 'tis of thee' by the so-called 'Queen of American soul', Aretha Franklin.

[6] See Wien Museum Inv. Nr. 54.737. The item is a snuff box on whose lid is printed a version of the song (cf. Deutsch, 'Haydn's hymn', pp. 157–58).

[7] H. E. Jacob, *Joseph Haydn. His Art, Times and Glory*, trans. by Richard and Clara Winston (London, 1950), p. 246.

[8] Ibid.

[9] See Anton Schmid, 'Etwas über die österreichische Volkshymne von Joseph Haydn', *Allgemeine Wiener Musikzeitung*, 2 (1842), 126 and 510–11. See also Anton Schmid, 'Die Entstehung der österreichischen Volks-Hymne "Gott erhalte Franz den Kaiser"', *Caecilia*, 22 (1843), 152–64. Schmid (1787–1857) was the music librarian of the Hofbibliothek in Vienna, the forerunner of the Austrian National Library.

Oft habe ich bedauert, daß wir nicht gleich den Engländern ein Nazionallied hatten, das geeignet wäre die treue Anhänglichkeit des Volkes an seinen guten und gerechten Landesvater vor aller Welt kund zu thun, und in den Herzen aller guten Österreicher jenen edlen Nazionalstolz zu wecken der zur energischen Ausführung jeder von dem Landesfürsten als nützlich erkannten Maßregel unentbehrlich ist. Dieß schien mir besonders in dem Zeitpunkte nothwendig wo die Revoluzion in Frankreich am heftigsten wüthete und wo die Jakobiner sich mit der vergeblichen Hoffnung schmeichelten, unter den guten Wienern Anhänger und Theilnehmer ihrer verbrecherischen Anschläge zu finden.

Ich habe von dem verdienstvollen Dichter Haschka den Text machen laßen, und um es in Musik zu setzen, mich an unseren unsterblichen Landsmann Haydn gewendet, den ich allein fähig hielt, etwas zu machen, das dem englischen god save the King gleichkäme; so entstand unser Volkslied![10]

[I often regretted that we had not, like the English, a national air calculated to display to all the world the loyal devotion of our people to the kind and upright ruler of our Fatherland, and to awaken within the hearts of all good Austrians that noble national pride so indispensable to the energetic fulfilment of all the beneficial measures of the sovereign. This seemed to me more urgent at a period when the French Revolution was raging most furiously and when the Jacobins cherished the idle hope of finding among the worthy Viennese partisans and participators in their criminal designs. I caused that meritorious poet Haschka to write the words and applied to our immortal countryman Haydn to set them to music, for I considered him alone capable of writing anything approaching in merit to the English *God save the King*. Such was the origin of our national hymn.][11]

Saurau was no closet democrat: in 1796, with the Chief of the Vienna Police, Count Johann Anton Pergen (1725–1814), he had organized show-trials resulting in the execution or incarceration of many so-called 'Viennese Jacobins'. Saurau's chosen poet, Lorenz Leopold Haschka (1749–1827), also acted as a police informer. A man of no fixed principles, poetic or political, Haschka had been a Jesuit until the Order's dissolution in 1773, becoming a Freemason in 1780. During the reign of Joseph II he composed anti-clerical and even anti-monarchical verse, but in the 1790s wrote exclusively patriotic, anti-revolutionary odes in an antiquated style reminiscent of Klopstock. Goethe and Schiller disparaged them in the penultimate epigram (No. 413) of their *Xenien* (1796), a petulant attack on contemporary German letters, composed

---

[10] Quoted in Grasberger, *Die Hymnen Österreichs*, pp. 13–14. See also Karl Hafner, 'Franz Joseph Graf von Saurau', *Zeitschrift des historischen Vereins für Steiermark*, 7 (1909), 24–94. By 1820 the term 'Volkslied' was used to denote both the national anthem and a folksong. The Austrian anthem itself appeared in Friedrich Karl Erlach, *Die Volkslieder der Deutschen. Eine vollständige Sammlung der vorzüglichen deutschen Volkslieder von der Mitte des fünfzehnten bis in die erste Hälfte des neunzehnten Jahrhunderts*, 5 vols (Mannheim, 1834–36), IV, 472–73.

[11] Translation from J. Cuthbert Hadden, *Haydn*, rev. and ed. by Eric Blom (London, 1934), pp. 112–13.

after the failure of Schiller's journal *Die Horen*: 'Aber jetzt rat' ich euch, geht, sonst kommt noch gar der Gorgona | Fratze oder ein Band Oden von Haschka hervor' [But now I advise you, go, otherwise the Gorgon's grimace or a volume of Haschka's odes will appear].[12] As G. H. Lewes wryly remarked, when reading these epigrams, 'all the bad writers in the kingdom, and they were many, felt themselves personally aggrieved'.[13]

Haschka's unexceptional text immediately reveals its indebtedness to the British anthem which had provided him with a direct model. Indeed, when first published in 1797, the title page was entitled simply 'Gott, erhalte den Kaiser' [God, save the Emperor].[14] Compared with either the British anthem or 'La Marseillaise', however, Haschka's poem is almost entirely lacking martial fervour,[15] the only lines betraying its provenance in times of war being 'Laß von seiner Fahne Spitzen | Strahlen Sieg und Fruchtbarkeit!'. Haschka sent Saurau his verses on 11 October 1796, and by January 1797 Haydn had set them to music, the first performance taking place in Vienna on the Emperor's birthday, 12 February 1797. The mood in Vienna was anxious. Napoleon's troops had reached Styria, and to maintain public morale, as well as to celebrate the birthday of Franz II, part of Karl Ditters von Dittersdorf's comic opera *Der Apotheker und der Doktor* [*The Apothecary and the Doctor*, 1786] had been scheduled at the K. K. Hoftheater nächst der Burg [Royal and Imperial Court Theatre by the Castle]. Jacobs reports how, before the performance,

> Leaflets bearing the text of Haydn's anthem were distributed among the audience. The anthem was to be sung as soon as the emperor entered his box. But Francis [...] disliked being acclaimed in public. Therefore he deliberately came late. But this did not help matters; the director of the Court Theatre simply postponed the singing of the imperial anthem until the first intermission. After the music had been played once by the orchestra, the entire audience suddenly rose and sang the words to the monarch, who stood listening with deep emotion and embarrassment. Enthusiasm broke all bounds, and it was a long while before the company could continue the operetta.[16]

Having met with Franz's approval, the anthem rapidly achieved the popularity Haydn hoped for, and he rapidly reused the melody for the second movement of his Opus 76, No. 3, the so-called 'Kaiserquartett' [Emperor Quartet, 1797].[17] Haydn's lasting attachment to his tune is recounted in the account given by the actor Wilhelm Iffland, who visited the ageing composer in September 1808:

---

[12] Johann Wolfgang von Goethe, *Werke. Hamburger Ausgabe*, ed. by Erich Trunz, 14 vols (Munich, 1999), I: *Gedichte und Epen 1*, p. 221.
[13] G. H. Lewes, *The Life and Works of Goethe* (London, 1965), p. 405.
[14] See *Joseph Haydn — Gott erhalte*, ed. by Leibnitz, pp. 15–17 and 21.
[15] There is no trace of the animus towards other parts of the Empire found in the British anthem's invitation to crush rebellious Scots.
[16] Jacobs, *Joseph Haydn*, p. 249.
[17] *Grove's Dictionary of Music and Musicians*, ed. by Eric Blom, 10 vols, 5th edn (London, 1954–61), IV, 159.

> Er [Haydn] stand auf, reichte dem Bedienten den Arm. Wir geleiteten ihn [...] zum Pianoforte. — Er setzte sich daran nieder und sagte: Das Lied heißt 'Gott erhalte Franz den Kaiser'! — Er spielte hierauf die Melodie ganz durch, und zwar mit unerklärbarem Ausdruck [...] — Nach Endigung des Liedes blieb er noch eine Weile vor dem Instrument stehen, legte beide Hände darauf und sagte mit dem Ton eines ehrwürdigen Patriarchen: 'Ich spiele dieses Lied an jedem Morgen und oft habe ich Trost und Erhebung daraus genommen in den Tagen der Unruhe. — Ich kann auch nicht anders, ich muß es alle Tage einmal spielen.'[18]
>
> [Haydn stood up, giving his servant his arm. We accompanied him to the piano. — He sat down at it and said: 'The song is called "God save Emperor Franz"!' Whereupon he played the melody through with inexpressible feeling. — After concluding the song he remained standing for a while in front of the instrument, placed both hands on it and said in the tones of a venerable patriarch: 'I play this song every morning and it has often consoled and uplifted me during the days of unrest. — I can't help myself, I have to play it once a day'.]

Even during the bombardment of Vienna in May 1809 he continued playing it every morning, and on 26 May, five days before his death, rendered it three times in succession 'with a degree of expression that astonished himself'.[19] The anthem's text would change many times over the coming years, but the melody remained constant until the Habsburgs' abdication in 1918.

Like 'God save the King', Haydn's melody has undergone considerable scrutiny, not just because it is a fine tune, but also because its use (and later abuse in the twentieth century) extended far beyond its intended purpose. One of the first composers to draw on the melody was Haydn's contemporary, Antonio Salieri, the reputed poisoner of Mozart, who quoted it (along with the 'La Marseillaise') in the overture to his patriotic cantata *Der Tyroler Landsturm* [*The Tyrolese Home Guard*, 1799]. Musicians far removed from the Austro-German tradition were equally happy to incorporate it in their own works: it crops up in Rossini's opera *Il viaggio a Reims* [*The Journey to Rheims*, 1825], commissioned to celebrate the coronation of the French King Charles X; three years later Paganini used it as the basis for his variations for violin and orchestra *Maestosa Sonata Sentimentale* (1828). In 1876 Tchaikovsky, better known as an ardent Mozartian, prepared an arrangement of Haydn's work for full orchestra before incorporating the Russian national anthem 'God save the Tsar!' into his patriotic *1812 Overture*, first performed in 1882.

Following the Croatian nationalist scholar Franjo Kuhač, the nineteenth-century British musicologist Sir William H. Hadow suggested that the melody may betray Haydn's origins in the village of Rohrau, whose Croatian-speaking population knew it as Trstnik.[20] The music of the first two bars ('Gott erhalte

---

[18] *Joseph Haydn — Gott erhalte*, ed. by Leibnitz, p. 33.
[19] Hadden, *Haydn*, p. 113.
[20] William H. Hadow, *A Croatian Composer. Notes towards the Study of Joseph Haydn*

Franz den Kaiser') is indeed identical to that of a Croatian folksong 'Žalostna zaručnica' [The Sad Bride] sung around Eisenstadt, where Haydn had spent many years serving the Esterhazy family. If this was indeed the source of Haydn's inspiration, it was transformed by his lengthening of the cadence at the end of the fourth bar to accommodate the line 'Unser'n guten Kaiser Franz'. Thereafter, the setting bears no relationship whatsoever to the folk melody.

Like the British anthem, Haydn's melody has had multiple ownership, and not only within German-speaking lands. By 1802, the tune known to Anglophone hymn singers as 'Austria' had been attached to the text 'Glorious things of thee are spoken, Zion, city of our God', written in 1779 by John Newton (1725–1807), an erstwhile slave-trader turned minister of religion.[21] The Austrian text also soon became known in Britain, thanks to its translation by the English musical writer Charles Burney in an adaptation beginning 'God preserve our Emp'rer Francis!'.[22] Already on friendly terms with the composer, Burney greeted his arrival in London in 1791 with some 'Verses on the Arrival in England of the Great Musician Haydn'. He later kept Haydn abreast of developments, noting in a letter in English, dated 19 August 1799, how he had provided 'rather a paraphrase than a close translation'.[23] In his diary for 5 September 1799, Burney records a private performance at Walmer Castle, Kent, attended by the Prime Minister, William Pitt the Younger: 'I not only played this hymn of Haydn's setting, but Suwarrow's March to the great minister: and though Mr. Pitt never knows or cares one farthing for flutes and fiddles, he was very attentive.'[24]

The subsequent application of Haydn's work for political purposes reveals much about the nature of Austrian and German identities. Indeed, the expressly political function of the 'Kaiserhymne' melody may well inaugurate the link between music and politics which would prove so contentious in the German-speaking world over the next 150 years. Interestingly, when German unity arrived in 1871 (minus the Habsburg lands), Hoffmann von Fallersleben's 'Lied der Deutschen' [Song of the Germans] of 1841 ('Deutschland, Deutschland, über alles' [Germany, Germany, above all else]), written with Haydn's melody in mind, was not adopted as the anthem for the Second German Empire. In view perhaps of the recent war with Austria, and the ongoing association of Haydn's tune with the Habsburgs, whose defeat had been crucial in shaping the new Germany, the work chosen was the Prussian anthem. Like the British

(London, 1897; repr. New York, 1972). Despite many attempts to make Haydn a Croat, *The New Grove* seems to have settled beyond doubt Haydn's Germanic lineage.
[21] For further examples of English settings of Haydn's tune, see Deutsch, 'Haydn's hymn', p. 158.
[22] Ibid., p. 159.
[23] Ibid.
[24] Frances Burney, *Memoirs of Doctor Burney. Arranged from his own Manuscripts, from Family Papers, and from Personal Recollections, by his Daughter, Madame d'Arblay*, 3 vols (London, 1832), III, 274–75.

anthem, whose melody it employs, 'Heil dir im Siegerkranz' [Hail to Thee in Victor's Crown] never achieved official status. Nevertheless, it was Britain, disparaged in Germany as the 'land without music',[25] that provided directly the melody for the new empire's quasi-official anthem, and more circuitously, for that of its popular rival, the 'Lied der Deutschen'. That Haydn's tune may also have partly Slavic origins is an irony which, presumably, would have been lost both then and in later, still more strenuously nationalistic times.

On 1 October 1826, at the height of the Metternich era, with the Emperor newly recovered from a grave illness, an imperial decree saw Haschka's verses (apart from the opening lines) replaced by a new anthem by an anonymous hand. At the same time, an instrumental version of Haydn's melody, arranged by the Moravian-born court composer Franz Krommer (1759–1831),[26] was adopted for ceremonial use by the imperial army, thereby sidestepping the linguistic problems posed for an institution whose members were mostly non-German speakers. The fourth stanza elevates the monarch's role in the defeat of France — 'Er zerbrach der Knechtschaft Bande, / hob zur Freiheit uns empor' [He broke the bonds of subservience, | lifted us up to freedom] — which may have consoled the erstwhile Franz II, who, beaten by Napoleon, had become Emperor Franz I of Austria in 1804, the Holy Roman Empire itself being finally dissolved in 1806. This 1826 anthem remained in use until 1835, when a further anthem was required for the new Emperor Ferdinand I.

Between April 1835 and January 1836 the favoured text was by the Silesian Karl von Holtei (1798–1880), whose Prussian origins rendered his work unacceptable to popular Viennese taste. Hence his anthem was quickly replaced with one by Joseph Christian Freiherr von Zedlitz (1790–1862), a schoolfriend of Joseph von Eichendorff. This remained in use from 1836 until 1854. For the first time, the word 'Österreich' appeared in the anthem, and indeed in prime position: 'Segen Östreichs hohem Sohne | Unserm Kaiser Ferdinand' [Bless'd be Austria's noble son | Our emperor Ferdinand]. Throughout this period, however, Haschka's original text remained lodged in popular consciousness, remaining *de facto* the anthem of choice for most German-speaking Austrians.[27] As Grillparzer recalled in a poem of 1853, 'Als ich noch ein Knabe war, | Rein und ohne Falte, | Klang das Lied mir wunderbar, | Jenes "Gott erhalte"' [When I was but a laddie, | Pure and wrinkle-free, | The strains of 'Gott erhalte' | Sounded wonderful to me].[28]

In 1848 Franz Joseph I succeeded his uncle, the slow-witted, dumpling-

---

[25] Oscar A. H. Schmitz, *Das Land ohne Musik. Englische Gesellschaftsprobleme* (Munich, 1904). The origins of the term can be found in Carl Engel, *An Introduction to the Study of National Music* (London, 1866).
[26] Krommer was baptised František Vincenc Kramář.
[27] From 1797 onwards, translations of the anthems had appeared in all the empire's major languages as well as Aramaic, Hebrew and Modern Greek.
[28] Franz Grillparzer, 'Als ich noch ein Knabe war', *Sämtliche Werke*, ed. by August Sauer and Reinhold Backmann, 42 vols (Vienna, 1909–48), I. Abt., x: *Gedichte 1*, p. 247.

loving Ferdinand I. No new anthem accompanied the change of monarch; indeed, several versions were now in circulation. Even 'Gott erhalte Franz den Kaiser' was still heard long after Franz Joseph had become emperor. The move towards a single alternative was led by the Upper Austrian *Statthalterei* [provincial administration] in Linz, who based their appeal on a document solicited from Adalbert Stifter. Dated 16 September 1853, this notes the absence of 'ein gesezlich eingeführter Text der österreichischen Staatshymne' [legally sanctioned text of the Austrian national anthem] and bemoans the mediocre texts currently circulating. However, Stifter felt he knew the answer to the problem. Haydn's tune — 'ein Meisterwerk der Tonkunst' [a musical masterpiece] — needed a great poet to do it justice. Who better, then, than 'der erste der jetzt lebenden Dichter in deutscher Sprache [...] Franz Grillparzer' [the foremost living poet writing in German, Franz Grillparzer].[29] Unbeknown to Stifter, in March and April 1835 Grillparzer had already written a version beginning 'Gott erhalte unsern Kaiser, | Unsern guten Ferdinand!' [God save our dear Emperor Ferdinand],[30] and then again, at the instigation of Count Schwarzenberg, a version celebrating the succession of Franz Joseph I in 1848 beginning 'Gott erhalte unsern Kaiser | Und in ihm das Vaterland' [God save our Emperor and in him our fatherland]. With the recently failed revolution still fresh in mind, the poet prefaced this text with the words 'Schirm ihn, Herr, mit starker Hand!' [Defend him, Lord, with Thy mighty hand!]. However, Grillparzer's second anthem, like its predecessor, never saw service.[31] In April 1853, at the behest of the Emperor himself, Grillparzer was invited officially to submit a text to the Interior Minister, Alexander Freiherr von Bach. On 24 April 1853 Grillparzer handed in the poem of 1848, expressing reservations about the quality of the work and in a draft letter to Bach distancing himself from it: 'Ich habe [die versprochenen Textworte] schon vor drei Jahren auf Aufforderung des Fürsten Schwarzenberg geschrieben, aber nicht abgegeben, weil ich sie nicht für gut halte' [I wrote (the promised words) three years ago at the instigation of Prince Schwarzenberg but didn't hand them over because I don't think they are any good]. Claiming to lack the ability to match new words to a pre-existing piece, he stressed his affection for the anthem of his childhood, whose echoes could still be heard in his own 'verfehlte Arbeit' [failed version].[32] In this instance, Grillparzer's dissatisfaction was probably justified, for words and music provide a far from ideal match. It is a further indication, however, of the status the old anthem had by now assumed that

---

[29] Quoted in Grasberger, *Die Hymnen Österreichs*, pp. 72–73.
[30] Franz Grillparzer, 'Die österreichische Volkshymne, umgearbeitet bei der Thronbesteigung Kaiser Ferdinands' [The Austrian Anthem, reworked upon the accession of Emperor Ferdinand], *Sämtliche Werke*, I. Abt., XI: *Gedichte 2*, p. 124.
[31] 'Die österreichische Volkshymne, umgearbeitet nach der Thronbesteigung Kaiser Franz Josephs I [The Austrian Anthem, reworked after the accession of Emperor Franz Joseph I]: Grillparzer, *Sämtliche Werke*, I. Abt., XI: *Gedichte 2*, p. 227.
[32] Grillparzer, *Sämtliche Werke*, III. Abt., III: *Briefe und Dokumente 3*, p. 115.

Grillparzer refers to Haschka's text as 'das Volkslied aus meinen Kinderjahren' [the folksong / national anthem of my childhood]. It was as if for him too the original 'Kaiserhymne' had taken on a life of its own.[33]

The need for a new, official anthem had become pressing given the Emperor's forthcoming marriage to the Bavarian Duchess Elisabeth on 24 April 1854. Thus on 27 March 1854, Franz Joseph decreed a fresh text, by the writer, publisher and numaticist Johann Gabriel Seidl (1804–1875), to be the new anthem. This was specifically designated as a 'Volkshymne'. Except for changes wrought by circumstances — the suicide of Crown Prince Rudolf in 1889 and the assassination of his mother in 1898 — this text, augmented by a stanza written after Rudolf's birth in 1858, remained in use until the end of the Empire itself.

Following Franz Joseph's death in 1916, the minister of the interior Count von Toggenburg invited several prominent writers, among them Hugo von Hofmannsthal and Anton Wildgans, to write a new final stanza, acknowledging the accession of Karl I.[34] Both declined. On 11 May 1918, however, Franz Karl Ginzkey came up with a version of the old anthem with a stanza tailored to the new emperor, but historical events meant it was never used. Long after Karl's death in exile in 1922, supporters of the monarchy continued to adapt the anthem in the hope of seeing the Habsburgs restored in the figure of Karl's son Otto von Habsburg.[35] The Francisco-Josephinian anthem was heard in Vienna as late as 1989, at the funeral of Karl's widow, the Empress Zita, and it is still played each year on 18 August in Bad Ischl, at a mass celebrating Franz Joseph's birthday.

In 1920 a new, albeit unofficial, anthem was adopted for the First Republic, the text of 'Deutsch-Österreich, du herrliches Land, wir lieben dich!' [German-Austria, you splendid land, we love you!], stemming from the Socialist Chancellor Karl Renner. Haydn's imperial melody was dropped (it would not have fitted the words anyway), replaced with a tune by Renner's friend Wilhelm Kienzl (1857–1941), best remembered today for his folk-opera *Der Evangelimann* [*The Preacher Man*, 1895]. Karl Kraus responded with a long article in *Die Fackel* [*The Torch*] which quotes the imperial text before presenting a savage reworking of it, giving full vent to his contempt for the Habsburgs. Equally, however, the republican anthem, which never gained popularity, failed to move the satirist. Lamenting the loss of Haydn's 'erhabene Melodie' [sublime melody], now appropriated by German nationalists, Kraus noted: 'Renner und Johann Gabriel Seidl [haben] doch wenigstens das Gemeinsame, daß sie beide keine Dichter sind' [Renner and Johann Gabriel Seidl have at least one thing

---

[33] Ibid.
[34] Grasberger, *Die Hymnen Österreichs*, p. 93.
[35] See: http://www.twschwarzer.de/ottohymne.htm [accessed 5 February 2009].

in common: neither is a poet].³⁶ As Kraus indicates in a detailed analysis of the poem, his reworking of Seidl's verses, imparting a meaning diametrically opposed to the original, retains not just all the rhymes of the originals, but nearly all the rhyming words too. Haydn's posthumous permission to use his tune 'steht über allem Zweifel' [stands beyond all doubt], given that the composer had never sanctioned its use in Seidl's text for Franz Joseph.³⁷ What had been a 'Kaiserhymne' now becomes a hymn for the people:

Volkshymne

Gott erhalte, Gott beschütze
vor dem Kaiser unser Land!
Mächtig ohne seine Stütze,
sicher ohne seine Hand!
Ungeschirmt von seiner Krone,
stehn wir gegen diesen Feind:
Nimmer sei mit Habsburgs Throne
Österreichs Geschick vereint!

Fromm und bieder? Wahr und offen
laßt für Recht und Pflicht uns stehn!
Nimmermehr, so laßt uns hoffen,
werden in den Kampf wir gehn!
Eingeheizt die Lorbeerreiser,
die das Heer so oft sich wand!
Gut und Blut für keinen Kaiser!
Friede für das Vaterland!

Was des Bürgers Fleiß geschaffen,
schützet keines Kriegers Kraft!
Nicht dem Geist verfluchter Waffen
diene Kunst und Wissenschaft!
Segen sei dem Land beschieden;
Ruhm und Wahn, sie gelten gleich:
Gottes Sonne strahl' in Frieden
auf ein glücklich Österreich!

Laßt uns fest zusammenhalten,
in der Eintracht liegt die Macht!
Mit vereinter Kräfte Walten
wird das Schwerste leicht vollbracht.
Laßt uns, eins durch Brüderbande,
gleichem Ziel entgegengehn:
Ohne Kaiser glückts dem Lande —
dann wird Österreich ewig stehn!

---

³⁶ Karl Kraus, *Die Fackel*, 554–56 (1920), 57.
³⁷ Ibid., pp. 59–60.

Uns gehört, was Gott verwaltet,
uns im allerhöchsten Sinn,
reich an Reiz, der nie veraltet —
Reich der Huld, arm an Gewinn!
Was an Glück zuhöchst gepriesen,
gab Natur mit holder Hand.
Heil den Wäldern, Heil den Wiesen,
Segen diesem schönen Land!

[*People's Anthem*: God save, God defend our land from the Emperor! Powerful without his support, safe without his hand! Unprotected by his crown we stand against the foe: Nevermore let Austria's fate united be with Habsburg's throne!

Pious and proper? True and open let us stand for justice and duty! Nevermore, let us hope, shall we go into battle! Burned are the laurels the army so often bound for itself! No more goods and blood for the emperor! Peace for the fatherland!

No warrior's force protects the citizen's hard-won gains! Art and science should not serve the spirit of accursed weapons! Blessings be on the land; fame and delusion count for the same: May God's sun shine in peace on a happy Austria!

Let's hold firm together, in unity lies power! With our efforts united the hardest things will be easily done. United through bonds of brotherhood, let us work towards the same goal: The land will prosper without the emperor — then will Austria last forever!

To us belongs what God looks after, to us in the highest sense. Rich with ageless appeal — rich in favour, poor in profit! What counts as the highest fortune nature gave with its fair hand. Hail to the forests, hail to the meadows, blessings be on this lovely land!]

In 1929 the Renner/Kienzl anthem was replaced by 'Sei gesegnet ohne Ende, | Heimaterde wunderhold!', written in 1920 by the Styrian poet-priest Ottokar Kernstock (1848–1928), a man of a firm German national persuasion.[38] Not coincidentally, his words fitted the metre of Haydn's reinstated melody, and this anthem remained in use until the *Anschluss* of 1938, its pan-German sentiments reflecting views widely held by Left and Right alike. Given that Haydn's melody had already been adopted by the Weimar Republic in 1922, its reappearance in Austria suited both monarchists and those actively seeking political union with Germany. Still sung to the words 'Deutschland, Deutschland über alles', the Weimar anthem was retained after the Nazis took power in Germany in 1933. Thus after 1938, Fallersleben's text with Haydn's tune (now often played as a bombastic *marche militaire*), became the anthem of what had once been Austria and was now the Ostmark of the Third Reich.

The degradation of Haydn's melody was complete, and after 1945 the use of

---

[38] In 1923 Kernstock wrote his 'Hakenkreuzlied' [Swastika song] for the Fürstenfelder Ortsgruppe of the NSDAP. He later protested against its propagandistic use by the National Socialists.

Fallersleben's anthem was vetoed, along with all the other symbols of National Socialism. After the establishment of the FRG and the GDR in 1949, the question of anthems again loomed large, but understandably, nowhere were the words 'Deutschland, Deutschland über alles' deemed appropriate. Eventually, the third stanza of Fallersleben's 'Lied der Deutschen' was adopted in West Germany, still sung to Haydn's tune, despite its now world-wide association with Nazi Germany rather than Imperial Austria. Following reunification in 1990, this remains the official German anthem. Not by coincidence, Johannes R. Becher's text for the GDR anthem 'Auferstanden aus Ruinen' [Arisen from Ruins] was also perfectly suited for singing to Haydn's melody. In the event, the tune adopted in the GDR was by Schoenberg's pupil and Brecht's collaborator Hanns Eisler (1898–1962), who had served as a front-line soldier in the Austro-Hungarian army in World War I.[39] Eisler's melody is worthy to stand alongside Haydn's, and some regret it was not adopted by the new Federal Republic.

When the Second Republic sought a replacement for the Nazi anthem, it faced a dilemma: a melody once so much Austria's own was now indelibly associated with a nation from which it was desperate to disassociate itself. Convinced (unlike West Germany) that Haydn's melody was now untenable in the wake of the Third Reich, Austria once more required fresh words and music. So, on 9 April 1946, the government announced a competition to find a new anthem, and on 22 October of that year a tune attributed to Mozart was announced the clear winner. This was the 'Bundeslied' [song of union], found in the 'Freimaurerkantate' [Freemasons' Cantata, KV623] of 1791. Sung to the words 'Brüder reicht die Hand zum Bunde' [Brothers, give your hands in union], a version had been often used by choral societies and student fraternities in Germany and Austria in the nineteenth century. A reworked version of Kernstock's anthem would have been the popular choice for a text, but this was metrically incompatible with Mozart's melody. It also, perhaps inconveniently, emphasized Austria's German heritage. Felix Hurdes, the Education Minister, therefore announced a further competition for a suitable text to accompany Mozart's melody. The response was considerable, with around 1,800 submissions, including texts from Alexander Lernet-Holenia, Rudolf Henz and Franz Theodor Csokor, but the winner was Paula von Preradović (1887–1951), granddaughter of the Croatian poet Petar Preradović, and mother of the publisher Fritz Molden. In Krausian fashion, he promptly wrote a parody of his mother's work.[40] On 25 February 1947, almost exactly

---

[39] Brecht's poem 'Kinderlied' [Children's Song] is also designed to be sung to Haydn's melody.

[40] 'Land der Erbsen, Land der Bohnen, | Land der vier alliierten Zonen, | Wir verkaufen Dich im Schleich, | Viel geliebtes Österreich! | Und droben überm Hermannskogel | Flattert froh der Bundesvogel!' [Country of peas, country of beans, | Country of the four Occupied Zones, | We sell you on the black market, | Well-beloved Austria! | And high above the Hermannskogel | The Federal Bird flutters with glee!]. See Fritz Molden, *Fepolinski & Waschlapski auf dem berstenden Stern* (Vienna, 1976), pp. 445–46.

150 years after the first performance of 'Gott erhalte', 'Land der Berge, Land am Strome' officially became the new Austrian anthem.

With its references to the Danube, mountains and hammers, Preradović's simple text clearly sought to establish parallels with Renner's first republican anthem of 1920. Again like Renner's anthem, Preradović's work proved slow to find favour in the Second Republic. When the 150th anniversary of the composer's death was celebrated in 1959, attempts were again made to reinstate Haydn's melody with a suitable republican text.[41] For many, the quite complex melody of the new anthem lacked the instant appeal of Haydn's, a defect made worse when it emerged that the tune was probably not even by Mozart at all, but by a fellow-freemason, the Viennese vocal composer Johann Baptist Holzer (1753–1818).[42] With the demise of the GDR, modern Germany's remains the only national anthem with a melody 'written by a master'.[43]

As the Second Republic established itself as a viable state, able to call on the loyalty of a population increasingly perceiving and defining itself as Austrian rather than German, so 'Land der Berge' became an accepted fact of Austrian civic and political life. However, the susceptibility of the Austrian anthem to change, observable over more than two centuries, again became apparent late in the twentieth century, when women not just in Austria but across Europe began objecting to the phallocentricity evident in so many of the continent's anthems. Eventually in 2005, Austria's conservative Minister for Health and for Women's Issues, Maria Rauch-Kallat (ÖVP), suggested replacing such locutions as 'Heimat bist du großer Söhne' and even 'Vaterland' by less gender-specific terms ('Heimat großer Töchter, Söhne' and 'Heimatland'). However, nothing has so far come of this, and the Austrian anthem has now remained unaltered for sixty-two years. This sets a record, which despite two troubled decades dominated by Waldheim and Haider, has been made possible by the longest period of unbroken peace and stability in the nation's modern history. In the year when the world marks the bicentenary of the composer's death, it would appear that Haydn's 'Volck's Lied' has been consigned finally to Austria's political history.[44]

---

[41] See Otto Erich Deutsch, 'Zur Wahl unserer Volkshymne', *Österreichische Musikzeitschrift*, 14 (1959), 47–48.
[42] See Alexander Weinmann, 'Ein Streit mit untauglichen Mitteln. Zur Frage nach der Autorenschaft der österreichischen Bundeshymne', in *Musik und Verlag. Karl Vötterle zum 65. Geburtstag* (Kassel, 1968), pp. 581–85.
[43] Deutsch, 'Haydn's Hymn', p. 157.
[44] Haydn's melody was last heard in an official capacity in Vienna on 16 June 2008 when sung by the German football team prior to the match against Austria in the European Championship. Austria lost 0–1.

Appendix

(1). Haschka/Haydn (1797)

Gott! erhalte Franz den Kaiser,
Unsern guten Kaiser Franz!
Lange lebe Franz der Kaiser,
In des Glückes hellstem Glanz!
Ihm erblühen Lorbeer-Reiser,
Wo er geht, zum Ehren-Kranz!
Gott! erhalte Franz den Kaiser,
Unsern guten Kaiser Franz!

Laß von Seiner Fahnen Spitzen
Strahlen Sieg und Fruchtbarkeit!
Laß in Seinem Rathe sitzen
Weisheit, Klugheit, Redlichkeit;
Und mit Seiner Hoheit Blitzen
Schalten nur Gerechtigkeit!
Gott! erhalte Franz den Kaiser,
Unsern guten Kaiser Franz!

Ströme Deiner Gaben Fülle
Über Ihn, Sein Haus und Reich!
Brich der Bosheit Macht; enthülle
Jeden Schelm- und Bubenstreich!
Dein Gesetz sey stets Sein Wille,
Dieser uns Gesetzen gleich!
Gott! erhalte Franz den Kaiser,
Unsern guten Kaiser Franz!

Froh erleb' Er Seiner Lande,
Seiner Völker höchsten Flor!
Seh' sie, Eins durch Bruder-Bande,
Ragen allen andern vor;
Und vernehme noch am Rande
Später Gruft der Enkel Chor:
Gott! erhalte Franz den Kaiser,
Unsern guten Kaiser Franz!

[God save Emperor Francis, | Our good Emperor Francis! | Long live Emperor Francis, | In the brightest glow of happiness! | May sprigs of laurel bloom for him | As a garland of honour, wherever he goes. | God save Emperor Francis, | Our good Emperor Francis!

From the tip of his standard | May victory and fruitfulness shine! | In his council | May knowledge, wisdom and honesty sit! | And through his Majesty's dazzling insights | May only justice prevail! | God save Emperor Francis, | Our good Emperor Francis!

May the abundance of thy gifts | Pour over him, his house and realm! | Break the power of wickedness, and reveal | Every trick of rogues and knaves! | May thy law always be his will, | And this be like laws to us. | God save Emperor Francis, | Our good Emperor Francis!

May he enjoy the highest bloom | Of his land and of his peoples! | May he see them, united by brotherly bonds, | Tower over all others! | And may he hear at the edge | Of his future tomb his grandchildren's chorus: | God save Emperor Francis, | Our good Emperor Francis!]

(2). Renner/Kienzl (1920)

Deutsch-Österreich, du herrliches Land, wir lieben dich!
Hoch von der Alm unter'm Gletscherdom
stürzen die Wasser zum Donaustrom:
Tränken im Hochland Hirten und Lämmer,
treiben am Absturz Mühlen und Hämmer,
grüßen viel' Dörfer, viel' Städte und ziehn
jauchzend zum Ziel, unserm einzigen Wien!
Du herrliches Land, unser Heimatland,
wir lieben dich, wir schirmen dich.

Deutsch-Österreich, du tüchtiges Volk, wir lieben dich!
Hart ist dein Boden und karg dein Brot,
Stark doch macht dich und klug die Not.
Seelen, die gleich wie Berge beständig,
Sinne, die gleich wie Wasser lebendig,
Herzen so sonnig, mitteilsamer Gunst
Schaffen sich selber ihr Glück, ihre Kunst.
Du tüchtiges Volk, unser Muttervolk,
Wir lieben dich, wir schirmen dich.

Deutsch-Österreich, du treusinnig Volk, wir lieben dich!
Dienende Treu' schuf dir Not und Reu' ...
Sei nun in Freiheit dir selber treu!
Gibt es ein Schlachtfeld rings in den Reichen,
Wo deiner Söhne Knochen nicht bleichen?
Endlich brachst du die Ketten entzwei.
Diene dir selber, sei dein! Sei frei!
Du treusinnig Volk, unser Duldervolk,
Wir lieben dich, wir schirmen dich.

Deutsch-Österreich, du Bergländerbund, wir lieben dich!
Frei durch die Tat und vereint durch Wahl,
eins durch Geschick und durch Blut zumal.
Einig auf ewig, Ostalpenlande!
Treu unserm Volkstum, treu dem Verbande!
Friede dem Freund, doch dem Feinde, der droht,
wehrhaften Trotz in Kampf und Not!
Du Bergländerbund, unser Ostalpenbund,
wir lieben dich, wir schirmen dich.

[German-Austria, you splendid land, we love you! | From the high meadow beneath the glacier's dome | Waters cascade to the Danube below: | To lambs and shepherds they give drink in the highlands, | At the cascades they drive mill-wheels and hammers, | Greet many villages, many towns and journey | Rejoicing to their goal, our one and only Vienna! | You wonderful land, our native land, | We love and protect you.

German-Austria, you staunch folk, we love you! | Your ground is hard and your bread is meagre, | But want makes you clever and strong. | Souls solid as mountain rock, | Senses lively as water, | Hearts so radiant, sharing and kind, | Create their own happiness and art. | You staunch folk, our native folk, | We love and protect you.

German-Austria, you faithful folk, we love you! | Faithful service brought you want and regret ... | Now in freedom be true to yourself! | Is there a battlefield anywhere in the realms, | Where your sons' bones are not bleaching? | Finally you broke your bonds. | Be your own master, be yours! Be free! | You faithful folk, our suffering folk, | We love and protect you.

German-Austria, league of mountain lands, we love you! | Free through deeds and united through choice, | A community of fate and blood. | As one for ever, East Alpine land! | True to our nation, true to our union! | Peace to our friends, but to the threatening foe, | Doughty defiance in battle whatever the odds! | You league of mountain lands, our East Alpine league, | We love and protect you.]

(3). Kernstock/Haydn (1929)

Sei gesegnet ohne Ende,
Heimaterde wunderhold!
Freundlich schmücken dein Gelände
Tannengrün und Ährengold.
Deutsche Arbeit ernst und redlich,
Deutsche Liebe zart und weich —
Vaterland, wie bist du herrlich,
Gott mit dir, mein Österreich!

Keine Willkür, keine Knechte,
Off'ne Bahn für jede Kraft!
Gleiche Pflichten, gleiche Rechte,
Frei die Kunst und Wissenschaft!
Starken Mutes, festen Blickes,
Trotzend jedem Schicksalsstreich
Steig empor den Pfad des Glückes,
Gott mit dir, mein Österreich!

Laßt, durch keinen Zwist geschieden,
Uns nach einem Ziele schau'n,
Laßt in Eintracht und in Frieden
Uns am Heil der Zukunft bau'n!
Uns'res Volkes starke Jugend
Werde ihren Ahnen gleich,
Sei gesegnet, Heimaterde,
Gott mit dir, mein Österreich!

[Endless blessings upon you, | Wondrous native soil! | Friendly green firs and golden | Crops adorn your lands. | Earnest, honest German toil, | Soft and tender German love — | Fatherland, how marvellous you are, | God be with you, my Austria!

No tyranny, no serfs, | The way open for all! | Equal duties, equal rights, | Art and science free! | Strong of heart, firm of gaze, | Defying every trick of fate | Ascend the path of happiness, | God be with you, my Austria!

Through no discord divided, | Let us have but one aim, | In unity and peace | Let us build for future well-being! | May our nation's sturdy youth | Grow like their forebears, | Blessings upon you, native soil, | God be with you, my Austria!]

(4). Preradović/Holzer (1947)

Land der Berge, Land am Strome,
Land der Äcker, Land der Dome,
Land der Hämmer, zukunftsreich!
Heimat bist du großer Söhne,
Volk, begnadet für das Schöne,
vielgerühmtes Österreich,
vielgerühmtes Österreich!

Heiß umfehdet, wild umstritten
liegst dem Erdteil du inmitten,
einem starken Herzen gleich.
Hast seit frühen Ahnentagen
hoher Sendung Last getragen,
vielgeprüftes Österreich,
vielgeprüftes Österreich!

Mutig in die neuen Zeiten,
frei und gläubig sieh uns schreiten,
arbeitsfroh und hoffnungsreich.
Einig laß in Brüderchören,
Vaterland, dir Treue schwören,
vielgeliebtes Österreich,
vielgeliebtes Österreich!

[Land of mountains, land beside the river, | land of fields, land of cathedrals, | land of hammers, with a bright future! | You are home to great sons, | nation with a gift for beauty, | much-lauded Austria, | much-lauded Austria!

Hotly fought for, fiercely contested, | you lie at the continent's core, | like a strong heart. | Since time immemorial | you have borne a great mission's burden, | sorely tried Austria, | sorely tried Austria!

Boldly into a new age, | free and devout watch us stride, | working happily and filled with hope. | United in fraternal chorus, | Fatherland, let us swear our allegiance to you, | dearly beloved Austria, | dearly beloved Austria!]

Mozart's Words, Mozart's Music: Untangling an Encounter with a Fortepiano and its Remarkable Consequences

JOHN IRVING

Institute of Musical Research, School of Advanced Study, University of London

In October 1777 Mozart visited his father's home town of Augsburg. Among his first ports of call was the workshop of the instrument maker, Johann Andreas Stein (1728–1792).[1] It was an encounter that would change the composer's life, for from that moment flowed a realization that a truly expressive style of keyboard playing now lay within his grasp, a realization that was to bear rich fruit in a torrent of keyboard sonatas and, most important, concertos, that flowed from his pen almost continuously until the end of his life. Mozart's encounter with Stein's fortepianos maps onto the idiomatic style of keyboard writing found in the C major sonata, KV309, that he wrote during the next three weeks for his pupil, Rosa Cannabich, in Mannheim.[2] So powerful was this circumstance that Mozart was compelled to document it in a succession of letters to his father in the weeks immediately following. These letters form the backbone of this essay, which attempts to probe a quite remarkable synchrony between Mozart's words and his music. In this synchrony, neither Mozart's words nor his music make full sense without the other. Instead, they

---

[1] Stein was one of the most inspired and renowned manufacturers of keyboard instruments in the eighteenth century. His firm continued to produce instruments until 1896, his fame living on after his death through his daughter, Maria Anna (Nanette) Stein (1769–1833), a close friend of Beethoven whose appreciation of her pianos is attested in his letters. In 1794 Nanette Stein married the composer Johann Anton Streicher. Her piano company was founded in 1802, the instruments bearing the designation 'Nanette Streicher *née* Stein'. Their son, Johann Baptist Streicher (1796–1871), further developed the Viennese action in instruments built during the 1830s and 1840s, and his pianos were much admired by Brahms. Stein's technical innovations contributed greatly to the early development of the piano. See Michael R. Latcham, 'The Pianos of Johann Andreas Stein', in *Zur Geschichte des Hammerklaviers: 14. Musikinstrumentenbau-Symposium in Michaelstein am 12. und 13. November 1993*, ed. by Monika Lustig (Michaelstein, 1996); repr. in *The Galpin Society Journal*, 51 (1998), 114–53.

[2] Rosa was the eldest daughter of Christian Cannabich (1731–1798), leader of the Mannheim orchestra from 1759 and director of instrumental music from 1774. Rosa was evidently a talented keyboard player, as Mozart's remarks suggest. On 13 February 1778, aged just fourteen, she performed Mozart's B flat major concerto, KV238, in a concert at her father's house; see Otto Erich Deutsch, *Mozart. A Documentary Biography*, trans. by Eric Blom, Peter Branscombe and Jeremy Noble (London, 1965; repr. 1990), pp. 172–73.

combine to form a kind of meta-text that is about the sudden empowerment of expressivity in his keyboard sonatas.

I

Compared to the fortepianos previously experienced by Mozart, which were uneven in touch, whose keys jammed and jangled and whose dampers did not work reliably, the Augsburg instruments suited his ideal playing style completely. Presented with such mechanical capabilities, Mozart lost no time in translating them into previously unimagined technical and, consequently, expressive possibilities in the C major sonata, KV309. The story begins in a letter from Mozart to his father of 17 October 1777 from Augsburg:

> Nun muß ich gleich bey die steinischen Piano forte anfangen. Ehe ich noch vom stein seiner arbeit etwas gesehen habe, waren mir die spättischen Clavier die liebsten; Nun muß ich aber den steinischen den vorzug lassen; denn sie dämpfen noch viell besser, als die Regensburger. wenn ich starck anschlage, ich mag den finger liegen lassen, oder aufheben, so ist halt der ton in dem augenblick vorbey, da ich ihn hören ließ. ich mag an die Claves kommen wie ich will, so wird der ton immer gleich seyn. er wird nicht schebern, er wird nicht stärcker, nicht schwächer gehen, oder gar ausbleiben; mit einem wort, es ist alles gleich. es ist wahr, er giebt so ein Piano forte nicht unter 300 f: aber seine Mühe und fleiß die er anwendet, ist nicht zu bezahlen. seine instrumente haben besonders das vor andern eigen, daß sie mit auslösung gemacht sind. da giebt sich der hunderteste nicht damit ab. aber ohne auslösung ist es halt nicht möglich daß ein Piano forte nicht schebere oder nachklinge; seine hämmerl, wen man die Claves anspielt, fallen, in den augenblick da sie an die saiten hinauf springen, wieder herab, man mag den Claves liegen lassen oder auslassen. wen er ein solch Clavier fertig hat, |: wie er mir selbst sagte :| so sezt er sich erst hin, un Probirt allerley Passagen, läuffe und springe, und schabt und arbeitet so lange bis das Clavier alles thut.

> [This time I shall begin at once with Stein's pianofortes. Before I had seen any of his make, Späth's claviers had always been my favourites. But now I much prefer Stein's, for they damp ever so much better than the Regensburg instruments. When I strike hard, I can keep my finger on the note or raise it, but the sound ceases the moment I have produced it. In whatever way I touch the keys, the sound is always even. It never jars, it is never stronger or weaker or entirely absent; in a word, it is always even. It is true that he does not sell a pianoforte of this kind for less than three hundred gulden, but the trouble and the labour which Stein puts into the making of it cannot be paid for. His instruments have this special advantage over others that they are made with escape action. Only one maker in a hundred bothers about this. But without an escapement it is impossible to avoid jangling and vibration after the note is struck. When you touch the keys, the hammers fall back again the moment after they have struck the strings, whether you hold down the keys or release them.[3] He himself told

---

[3] The escapement action went through subtle developments in Stein's instruments. The

me that when he has finished making one of these claviers, he sits down to it and tries all kinds of passages, runs and jumps, and he shaves and works away until it can do anything.]⁴

Later in the same letter, Mozart records that 'die lezte ex D kommt auf die Pianforte vom *stein* unvergleichlich heraus. die Machine wo man mit dem knie drückt, ist auch bey ihm besser gemacht, als bey den andern. ich darf es kaum anrühren, so geht es schon; und so bald man das knie nur ein wenig wegthut, so hört man nicht den mindesten nachklang' [The last (sonata) in D (KV284), sounds exquisite on Stein's pianoforte. The device too which you work with your knee is better on his than on other instruments. I have only to touch it and it works; and when you shift your knee the slightest bit, you do not hear the least reverberation] (*Briefe*, 352: 49–53; Anderson, 225).⁵

KV284 in D major, composed in February–March 1775 in Munich for Baron Thaddeus von Dürnitz, is the last of a set of six solo keyboard sonatas (KV279–84) written in winter-spring 1774–75. The autograph score — actually Mozart's composing score, rather than a fair copy — contains a large number of dynamic markings as well as very precise indications for the articulation, and obviously sounds to best effect on a touch-sensitive fortepiano, rather than a harpsichord.⁶

most developed, further adapted as the 'Viennese' action in due course by the rival maker Anton Walther from *c.* 1785, is not seen in surviving Stein instruments dating from before 1781. This may mean that the version that impressed Mozart in 1777 was a prototype. For detailed information, see Latcham, 'Mozart and the Pianos of Johann Andreas Stein', and his liner notes to the recording, *Mozart am Stein Vis-a-Vis*, played by Andreas Staier and Christina Schornsheim (Harmonia Mundi HMC 901941 [2007]). A detailed organological examination of the state of development of Stein's fortepianos at the time Mozart encountered them in 1777 is given in Latcham's forthcoming paper, 'Johann Andreas Stein and the search for the expressive *Clavier*'. I am grateful to Mr Latcham for sharing this work with me before publication. The gist of Mr Latcham's research, and a taste of its wonderful result in sound, may be had by consulting the liner notes to the CD referred to above.

⁴ German original from *Mozart. Briefe und Aufzeichnungen. Gesamtausgabe*, ed. by Wilhelm A. Bauer and Otto Erich Deutsch, Internationale Stiftung Mozarteum, Salzburg, 7 vols (Kassel, 1962–75), II: 1777–1779, no. 352, lines 1–19 (henceforth *Briefe*); English translation from *The Letters of Mozart and His Family*, ed. by Emily Anderson, 3rd rev. edn, ed. by Stanley Sadie and Fiona Smart (London, 1985), no. 225 (henceforth Anderson).

⁵ Leopold Mozart's laconic response to Wolfgang's exuberant comments appears in his reply of 23 October: 'Mir ist lieb, daß H: Steins Pianforte so gut sind. Sie sind aber freilich auch theuer' [I am glad that Herr Stein's pianofortes are so good, but indeed they are expensive] (*Briefe*, 354: 46–47; Anderson, 227).

⁶ Kraków, Uniwersytet Jagiellońska, ms. V, 5, inw. no. 5995. The autograph of the six sonatas, KV279, 280, 281, 282, 283 and 284, contains all but the first movement of the first sonata in C. For that movement, the text of the *Neue Mozart-Ausgabe* (ed. by Wolfgang Plath and Wolfgang Rehm) is taken substantially from an 1841 edition issued by the firm of Johann Anton André (Offenbach am Main) which they claim was closely modelled on the (now lost) autograph. One enigma regarding these sonatas is the fact that, at the time of their composition, Mozart is not known to have encountered the fortepiano. In Munich in the winter of 1774–75, he may have played on a fortepiano and, compared to Ignaz von Beecke, appeared to one commentator to have been rather inexperienced on the

There are many places in KV284 where the attack of a harpsichord, in which the strings are plucked and the player has no possibility of controlling the dynamic, would ruin the contrasts of articulation, register, texture and idiom — all of which are essential to the character of this music. Obvious examples from the first movement include the entry of the secondary theme in bar 22 and the intervention of the delicate *piano* phrase at bars 34–40, sandwiched between *forte* passages and strongly suggestive of an orchestral layout contrasting upper strings with the full *tutti*. A more subtle illustration is the two-bar *piano* insertion, bars 46–47; the second bar repeats the material of this first a little higher and with a slight harmonic intensification (a diminished-7th chord), leading towards the climactic re-entry of the (implied) *tutti* for the cadence.

While no dynamic differentiation between bars 46 and 47 is notated, the slightly higher register and slightly more intense harmony of bar 47 can be effectively conveyed by a subtle gradation of the degree of *piano* from bar to bar, as well as by 'voicing' the texture (that is, making a minuscule crescendo in the right hand, proceeding from bar 46 to bar 47, while retaining exactly the same dynamic level for the left-hand chords at the beginning of each bar, the effect being to enhance the degree of separation between the two strands of the texture in bar 47 relative to bar 46). The musical reason for such a strategy is to avoid making bar 47 seem to be merely an echo of the preceding bar, of lesser intensity, after which the *forte* of bar 48 arrives as a jarring shock. Clearly Mozart had dynamic contrast between this two-bar *piano* insertion and the following cadential climax in mind; but the register and harmony of bar 47 are clues that he envisaged bar 47 as being at least equal in intensity to bar 46, and if the opposite effect (of tailing off) in performance is to be avoided, some sort of creative intervention by the player is required. A touch-sensitive instrument allows the player to capture what Mozart's notation does not explicitly convey without having to adapt other aspects of the narrative (for instance, the articulation, as would be necessary on a harpsichord).

Perhaps it was passages such as these that sounded 'exquisite' to Mozart when he played on Stein's instruments, and which he could render far more suitably than had previously been possible for him on harpsichords or on other fortepianos (including those of Späth). In all the respects he lists in his letter (sensitivity and evenness of touch, effective escapement action and dampers, operated by a knee-lever), Stein's fortepianos would have allowed him to render passages such as bars 34–43 exactly as notated (including, no doubt, 'voicing'

---

instrument. See John Irving, *Mozart's Piano Sonatas. Contexts, Sources, Style* (Cambridge, 1997), p. 56, for further details. Evidently between 1775 and 1777 he gained in experience to the point where he could make a detailed qualitative comparison of the characteristics of a Späth *versus* a Stein. Nevertheless, the precise notation of dynamics throughout KV279–84 is a little puzzling. The Mozarts had a clavichord at home, and the sonatas may have been conceived on that instrument. In a letter of 24 October 1777 (*Briefe*, 355; Anderson, 228b), he implies that on 19 October he had played one of these sonatas on a clavichord in Augsburg.

bars 34–36 in such a way as to make a subtle dynamic distinction between the repeated e' quavers and the inner melodic line in the left hand),[7] and thereby to achieve a carefully designed expressive effect, not just locally, but in the context of the surrounding textures.

What Stein's instruments made possible for Mozart was the full realization of a truly expressive style of keyboard playing which — to judge from the notation of the six sonatas, KV279–84 — he had aspired towards since at least late 1774–75, but which he could only imperfectly grasp on fortepianos by Späth and others because of mechanical inadequacies. If Mozart's own testimony is to be believed, it would seem that he recognized an advance in his own fortepiano playing at this time. In his letter of 24 October 1777, he explains to his father that

> [Stein] war in den Becché völlig vernarrt. nun sieht und hört er, daß ich mehr spielle als Becché; daß ich keine grimaßen mache, und doch so expreßive spielle, daß noch keiner, nach seinen bekenntniss, seine Piano forte so gut zu tractiren gewust hat. daß ich immer accurat im tact bleybe. über das verwundern sie sich alle. Das Tempo rubato in einem Adagio, daß die lincke hand nichts darum weiß, können sie gar nicht begreifen. bey ihnen giebt die lincke hand nach. graf Wolfeck und mehrere, die ganz Paßionirt für Beché sind, sagten neülich öfentlich im Concert, daß ich den Becché im sack scheibe. graf wolfeck lief immer im saal herum, und sagte. so hab ich mein lebetag nichts gehört. er sagte zu mir. ich muß ihnen sagen, daß ich sie niemahlen so spiellen gehört, wie heüte. (*Briefe*, 355: 89–100)

> [(Stein) used to be quite crazy about Beecke;[8] but now he sees and hears that I am the better player, that I do not make grimaces, and yet play with such expression that, as he himself confesses, no one up to the present has been able to get such good results out of his pianofortes. Everyone is amazed that I can always keep strict time. What these people cannot grasp is that in tempo rubato in an Adagio, the left hand should go on playing in strict time. With them the left hand always follows suit. Count Wolfegg and several other passionate admirers of Beecke, publicly admitted at a concert the other day that I had wiped the floor with him. The Count kept running about in the hall, exclaiming: 'I have never heard anything like this in my life'. And he said to me: 'I really must tell you, I have never heard you play as you played today'.] (Anderson, 228b)

While certain of the technical bases for such expressive playing will have ripened gradually over the years (for instance, on Späth's instruments), such fulsome praise from Stein himself may have confirmed Mozart's belief that his fortepianos now offered him the opportunity to make a decisive advance in the expressive potential of the solo keyboard sonata. Having discovered what

---

[7] Voicing the *piano* chords at the end of bars 40 and 43 so as to maintain the treble line's thirds in adequate focus above the left-hand octaves is another textural subtlety that can be rendered effectively only on a touch-sensitive keyboard.

[8] Ignaz von Beecke (1733–1803) was Kapellmeister at the Oettingen-Wallerstein court and a fine keyboard player.

a difference they could make to the execution of KV284 (at that time, Mozart's most extended and technically demanding sonata), he immediately seized an opportunity to compose a new sonata that would show off the Augsburg instruments to the full.

II

Mozart's first reference to his Sonata in C major, KV309, appears in a letter to his father of 4 November from Mannheim, his next port of call:

> [I]ch bin alle tage bey Canabich. [...] er hat eine tochter die ganz artig clavier spiellt,[9] und damit ich ihn mir recht zum freünde mache, so arbeite ich iezt an einer Sonata für seine Mad:^{selle} tochter, welche schon bis auf das Rondeau fertig ist. ich habe wie ich das erste Allegro, und Andante geendiget hatte selbe hingebracht und gespiellt; der Papa kann sich nicht vorstellen was die sonata für einen beyfall hat. (*Briefe*, 363: 10–17)

> [I am with Cannabich every day. He has taken a great fancy to me. He has a daughter who plays the clavier quite nicely; and in order to make a real friend of him I am now working at a sonata for her, which is almost finished save for the Rondeau. When I had composed the opening Allegro and the Andante I took them to their house and played both to them. Papa cannot imagine the applause which this sonata won.] (Anderson, 235)

Four days later, Mozart notes the completion of the Rondeau finale: 'Ich habe heute vormittag bey H: kanabich das Rondeau zur Sonata für seine Mad:^{selle} tochter geschrieben, folglich haben sie mich nicht mehr weggelassen' [I wrote out at Cannabich's this morning the Rondeau to the sonata for his daughter, with the result that they refused to let me go] (*Briefe*, 366: 41–42; Anderson, 238a) — a point reiterated on 13 November (*Briefe*, 370: 79–80; Anderson, 241). The new sonata clearly aroused Leopold's attention and curiosity. In his next letter to Wolfgang, of 10 November, he writes: 'Ich hoffe du wirst die *Sonata, so du der Mdsle: Canabich gemacht, auf klein Papier Copierter auch deiner Schwester schicken*' [I hope that you will send *your sister the sonata, which you have composed for Mlle Cannabich, copied out on small paper*] (*Briefe*, 367: 14–16; Anderson, 239). Mozart duly obliged, although it was almost three weeks before he enclosed the autograph of the first two movements of KV309 in a letter of 29 November, and the Rondeau finale in a further letter of 3 December (*Briefe*, 381: 87–91; 95–98 and 383: 47–48; 92–95; Anderson, 251 and 253).[10] Meanwhile, in a letter of 14 November, he offers a foretaste of its character, in the context of his tutelage of

---

[9] See note 2 above.

[10] In the first of these, Mozart is careful to note that he is sending the autograph, rather than a copy, since the price of music copying was four times as expensive in Mannheim than in Salzburg. The cost of postage was also a factor, and after he had made a copy (which still survives in a private Swiss collection) Leopold returned the autograph manuscript page by page in successive letters (see *Briefe*, 389, 403, 406 and 417; Anderson, 259, 272, 274 and 282a).

Kapellmeister Cannabich's daughter, Rosa:

> [D]ie sonaten die ich für die Mad:^selle^ Canabich geschrieben habe, werde ich so bald es möglich auf klein Papier abschreiben lassen, und meiner schwester schicken. vor 3 tägen habe ich angefangen der Mad:^selle^ Rose die sonate zu lehren; heüte sind wir mit dem ersten Allegro fertig. das Andante wird uns am meisten mühe machen; den das ist voll expreßion, und muß accurat mit den gusto, forte und piano, wie es steht, gespiellt werden. sie ist sehr geschickt, und lernt sehr leicht. die Rechte hand ist sehr gut, aber die lincke ist leider ganz verdorben. ich kann sagen daß ich oft sehr mitleiden mit ihr habe, wenn ich sehe, wie sie sich oft bemühen muß, daß sie völlig schnauft, und nicht aus ungeschichtlichkeit, sondern weil sie nicht anderst kan, weil sie es schon so gewohnt ist, indemm man ihr es nie anderst gezeügt hat. ich habe auch zu ihrer Mutter und zu ihr selbst gesagt, daß wenn ich iezt ihr förmlicher meister wär, so sperrte ich ihr alle Musikalien ein, deckete ihr das Clavier mit einem schnupftuch zu, und liesse ihr so lang mit der rechten und lincken hand, anfangs ganz langsam, lauter Pasagen, Triller, Mordanten Ecetra: exerciren, bis die hand völlig eingericht wäre, denn hernach getrauete ich mir eine rechte Clavieristin aus ihr zu machen. denn es ist schade. sie hat so viell genie, sie liest ganz Paßable, sie hat sehr viel natürliche leichtigkeit, und spiellt mir sehr viel empfindung. (*Briefe*, 373: 33–51)

> [As soon as I can, I shall have the sonata which I have written for Mlle Cannabich copied out on small paper and shall send it to my sister (in fact, Mozart eventually sent the autograph). I began to teach it to Mlle Rosa three days ago. We finished the opening Allegro today. The Andante will give us most trouble, for it is full of expression and must be played accurately and with the exact shades of forte and piano, precisely as they are marked. She is smart and learns very easily. Her right hand is very good, but her left, unfortunately, is completely ruined. I can honestly say that I often feel quite sorry for her when I see her struggling, as she so often does, until she really gets quite out of breath, not from lack of skill but simply because she cannot help it. For she has got into the habit of doing what she does, because no one has ever shown her any other way. I have told her mother and I have told her too that if I were her regular teacher, I would lock up all her music, cover the keys with a handkerchief and make her practise, first with the right hand and then with the left, nothing but passages, trills, mordents and so forth, very slowly at first, until each hand should be thoroughly trained. I would then undertake to turn her into a first-rate clavierist. For it's a great pity. She has so much talent, reads quite passably, possesses so much natural facility and plays with plenty of feeling.] (Anderson, 243a)

On 6 December Mozart amplifies his earlier point about the expressive character of the *Andante*:

> seine tochter welche 15 jahr alt, aber das Älteste kind ist, — ist ein sehr schönes artiges mädl. sie hat für ihr alter viell vernunft und gesetztes weesen; sie ist serios, redet nicht viell, was sie aber redet —— geschieht mit anmuth und freündlichkeit. gestern hat sie mir wieder ein recht unbeschreibliches

vergnügen gemacht, sie hat Meine sonata ganz —— fortreflich gespiellt. das Andante | welches *nicht geschwind* gehen muß | spiellt sie mit aller möglichen empfindung. sie spiellt es aber auch recht gern. sie wissen daß ich den 2:^{ten} tag als ich hier war, schon das erste allegro fertig hatte, folglich die Mad^{selle} Cannabich nur einmahl gesehen hatte. da fragte mich der junge danner, wie ich das andante zu machen in sinn habe; ich will es ganz nach den Caractére der Mad:^{selle} Rose machen. als ich spiellte, gefiele es halt ausserordentlich. der junge danner erzehlte es hernach. es ist auch so. wie das andante, so ist sie. ich hoffe sie werden die sonata richtig erhalten haben? (*Briefe*, 386: 27–40)

'[Cannabich's] daughter who is fifteen, his eldest child, is a very pretty and charming girl. She is very intelligent and steady for her age. She is serious, does not say much, but when she does speak, she is pleasant and amiable. Yesterday she again gave me indescribable pleasure; she played the whole of my sonata — excellently. The Andante (which must *not be taken too quickly*) she plays with the utmost expression. Moreover, she likes playing it. I had already finished the Allegro, as you know, on the day after my arrival, and thus had only seen Mlle Cannabich once. Young Danner asked me how I thought of composing the Andante. I said that I would make it fit closely the character of Mlle Rosa. When I played it, it was an extraordinary success. Young Danner told me so afterwards. It really is a fact. She is exactly like the Andante. I hope that you received the sonata safely.] (Anderson, 256)

A few days later, on 10 December, Mozart notes that, on hearing of his imminent departure from Mannheim, '[Rosa] spiellte darauf ganz serieuse meine sonate; hören sie, ich konnte mich des weinens nicht enthalten. [...] denn sie spiellte just die sonata, und das ist das favorit vom ganzen haus' [Thereupon Mlle Rosa played my sonata very seriously. I assure you, I couldn't keep from weeping, [...] for she had been playing my sonata, which is the favourite of the whole house] (*Briefe*, 388: 36–40; Anderson, 258).

Once KV309 had arrived in Salzburg, Nannerl began exploring it enthusiastically. On 8 December she wrote to her brother, 'ich danke dir für das erste stuk und andante der Sonaten, ich habe es schon durchgespielt das Andante braucht schon eine starke aufmerksamkeit und nettigkeit. mir gefählt sie recht gut, man kennet es, das du sie in Manheim componirt hast' [Thanks for the first movement and Andante of your sonata which I have already played through. The Andante requires indeed great concentration and exactness in playing. But I like the sonata very much. One can see from its style that you composed it in Mannheim] (*Briefe*, 387: 106–09; Anderson, 257a). Nannerl's point about a specific 'Mannheim' style is reinforced by Leopold on 11 December: 'Die Nannerl spielt deine ganze Son[a]te recht gut und mit aller Expreßion. [...] Die Sonate ist sonderbar? Sie hat was vom *vermanierierten* Manheimmer goût darinne, doch nur so wenig, daß deine gute Art nicht dadurch verdorben wird' [Nannerl plays your whole sonata excellently and with great expression. [...] Your sonata is a strange composition. It has something in it of the *rather artificial* Mannheim style, but so very little that your own good style is not spoilt thereby] (*Briefe*, 389: 8–18; Anderson, 259). Nannerl's expressive playing is singled out twice more in Leopold's correspondence touching on KV309, on 22 December and again on 26 January 1778 (*Briefe*, 395: 112 and 410: 78–87; Anderson, 265 and 276). The second of these refers in penetrating detail both to Nannerl's performance and to Wolfgang's sonata:

> Die 2 H: von Wallerstein wollte absolute die Nannerl spielen hören, sie liessen es sich entwischen, daß es ihnen nur darum zu thun war aus ihrem gusto auf deine Spielart zu schlüssen, so wie sehr darauf drangen etwas von deiner Composition zu hören. Sie spielte deine Sonate von Manheim recht treflich mit aller Expression. Sie waren über ihr spielen und über die Composition sehr verwundert, sagten, sie hätten niemals etwas von dir gehört, Sie sagten es wären lauter neue und besondere gedanken: und Reicha der Violozellist, der recht gut das Clavier spielt, [...] sagte öfter, *das heist recht gründlich Componiert!*
>
> [The two gentlemen from Wallerstein insisted on hearing Nannerl play. It emerged that their sole object in so doing was that they might guess from her style of playing what yours was like; and they were particularly anxious to hear one of your compositions. She played your Mannheim sonata most excellently and with all the necessary expression. They were amazed at her performance and at the composition, saying that they had never heard any of your works and that this one had some entirely new and original ideas; and Reicha, the cellist, who is an excellent clavierist [...], remarked several times that *it was a very sound composition*.]

The common factor in all these quotations is the expressive nature of KV309. For Leopold and Nannerl, Mozart's autograph was confirmation of what he had prepared them for in his earlier letters. Both are quite clear that the expressivity is central to the Andante, both visually (that is, in reading and forming an impression of the notated score) and in its realization in performance. Nannerl refers to the fact that it 'requires indeed great concentration and exactness in playing', whereas Leopold comments on the 'necessary expression' that had characterized Nannerl's playing of it. The implication also is that Nannerl was able to play it on an instrument that enabled such expression to be suitably conveyed. That was not, of course, a Stein fortepiano, at least not in the Mozart household, though they did own a Stein clavichord, which Leopold had bought in Augsburg in 1763,[11] and which allowed dynamic gradation over a limited range. Despite this, and the fact that he was only otherwise familiar with Späth's instruments, Leopold may have been able to imagine something of the effect that KV309 might make on a Stein, as the following report of a meeting with Countess Lodron, in his letter to Wolfgang of 1–2 November hints:

---

[11] This is referred to in a letter from Leopold Mozart to Lorenz Hagenauer of 20 August 1763 (*Briefe*, 63: 76–78; Anderson, 16).

38　John Irving

> Sie sagte mir eine Menge und fragte mich eine Menge wegen der Piano-Forte vom Stein, und ich erzehlte ihr was du mir davon geschrieben, sie gab dir aus dem Beyfahl der Gräfin Schönborn recht, die ihr erzehlt hätte, daß sie wegen den Steinischen Instrumenten über Augsp: gegangen, solche unendlich besser als die Spätischen gefunden, und für sich eines zu 700 fl angefrümmt hatte. (*Briefe*, 362: 68–73)
>
> [She talked a great deal and, upon her asking me about Stein's pianoforte, I told her what you had written to me about it. She said that you were right, judging by the approval of Countess Schönborn [both Countess Lodron and Schönborn were sisters of the Salzburg Archbishop, Arco], who had told her that she had travelled through Augsburg on purpose in order to see these instruments and, finding them infinitely better than Späth's, had ordered one for herself at the cost of 700 gulden.] (Anderson, 234)

Imagination is one thing; experience another. What Mozart had literally at his fingertips towards the end of 1777 was the new-found ability to work with sound at the keyboard in a way hitherto beyond his grasp. In what ways do Stein's mechanically unrivalled fortepianos leave their trace within the pages of KV309? We may usefully approach this question under three headings: Technique, Expression and Sound.

Technique

Repeated notes
- Themes: Allegro con spirito, subsidiary themes at bars 15–19; 27–28; 110–11. Rondeau finale, opening theme (specifically bars 1–2; 3–4; 5–6; 6–7).
- Accompaniments: repeated chords (Allegro con spirito, bars 21–26; 50; 116–21; 144).
- Virtuosity: extended rapid tremolando octaves (Rondeau, bars 55–61; 69–74; 111–14; 162–65; 173–78; 221–27); see example 1.
- Decoration: embellished restatements of themes (Allegro con spirito, bars 65; 69. Andante un poco adagio, bars 17–19; 36–37; 37–38; 56–57; 57–58; 72–74. Finale, bars 32–35; 55; 108–09; 159; 197; 199).
- More subtle melodic/rhythmic repercussions (Allegro con spirito, bars 60–61; 87–88; 91–92. Rondeau, bars 42–43; 46–47; 149–50; 153–54; 250–51).

Evenness of touch
- Semiquaver or demisemiquaver passagework (Allegro con spirito, bars 43–47; 56–58; 84–85; 137–41; 150–51; 153–56. Rondeau, bars 40–52; 116–31; 143–57; 179–86; 204–10).
- Decoration (Andante un poco adagio, bars 27–30; 53–56, 60–62, 67–68).

Effective damping
- Cleanness in exposed intervallic patterns (Allegro con spirito, bars 21–32; 43–47; 103–07; 116–26; 137–41. Andante un poco adagio, bars 33–36. Rondeau, bars 139–43; 207–10; 228–32).

Example 1. Rondeau, bars 55–61

- Clarity in melody/accompaniment textures (Allegro con spirito, bars 33–42; 127–36) and in contrapuntal textures (Andante un poco adagio, bars 40–44; 60–64).
- Rapid, usually chromatic, melody or chord shifts (Allegro con spirito, bars 103–08. Andante un poco adagio, bars 64; 69–71. Rondeau, bars 225–27).

Expression

The following is not a comprehensive list, but cites examples where the expressive quality of the music depends wholly upon the ability reliably to control and shade dynamics:

Dynamic contrast
- Allegro con spirito, bars 1–2/ 3–7; 8–9/ 10–14; 48–49; 54–56/ 56–58; 59–62; 67–72; 82–93; 101–07; 142–43; 148 to the end. This feature is essential to the entire Andante un poco adagio, and may be observed on both local and general levels. A small selection:
- Local: The opening theme, bars 1–4; the first paragraph more generally, bars 1–16; the secondary theme, bars 33–36; its continuation, bars 36–40; the Coda, bars 76 to the end.
- General: Compare the subtly different dynamic placements of the analogous bars 4 (upbeat)-8 and 20 (upbeat)-24; bars 14 (upbeat)-16 and 30 (upbeat)-32; and bars 49 (upbeat)-52 and 72 (upbeat)-76. In each case, the second phrase is an embellishment of the first, retaining the harmonic and phrase outlines, yet expressively different because of the contrasting dynamics.
- Rondeau, bars 37–48; 66–69; 85–93; 131–35; 142–57; 170–73; 179–87; 213–17; 244 to the end.

Dynamic gradations
- Allegro con spirito, bars 33–34; 108–09; 127–28. Andante un poco adagio, bars 15; 50–51. Rondeau, bars 55–57; 159–60; 210–12; 228–30.

Example 2. Andante, (a) bars 9–12; (b) bars 25–28

Chord and texture balance
- Allegro con spirito, bars 54–56; 59–62; 82–84; 86–93; 129–32; 148–50. Once again, the whole of the Andante un poco adagio depends on the ability to manage subtle dynamic shadings so as to give the effect of balance, or 'voicing' of the chords or textures. Frequently, the hands are wide enough apart for this quality to manage itself simply by dint of register contrast, but careful gradation by the player is certainly needed to clarify the textures at just about every cadence point, and also at bars 5–6; 21–22; 36 (upbeat)-44; 56 (upbeat)-64. Rondeau, bars 42–43; 46–47; 53–56; 66–69; 131–37; 145–46; 149–50; 153–54; 157–61; 170–72; 244 to the end.

Articulation
Articulations (principally staccatos and slurs) are a vital aspect of this sonata's expressive impact in performance. All three movements apply them precisely (representative examples include bars 103–09 of the Allegro con spirito and bars 131–36 of the Rondeau). But it is in the Andante un poco adagio that Mozart employs these articulations with especial refinement. Two examples:

- Compare, for instance, the articulation marks to the right-hand upbeats: at the end of bar 4, four staccato semiquavers; the end of bar 5, four semiquavers under a single slur; at the end of bar 6 two pairs of slurred semiquavers. But at the end of bars 20, 21 and 22, all the embellished versions of these upbeats are the same (eight demisemiquavers under a single slur).
- The restatement of the opening theme beginning at bar 9 retains the slurred pairs of the opening (beginning dotted semiquaver, demisemiquaver, and giving a distinctive scansion of quaver, quaver, crotchet, crotchet; quaver,

Example 3. Allegro con spirito, bars 73–82

quaver, crotchet, crotchet; quaver, quaver, quaver, quaver, quaver, quaver; crotchet, crotchet, crotchet). But by the time these bars are embellished at bars 25–28, the original pairings have been sacrificed for longer slurs (uniformly in crotchet beat lengths, and with markedly different scansion); see example 2.

Sound

Could Mozart have been inspired by the mechanical possibilities of Stein's instruments to attempt to capture an 'orchestral' sound in his keyboard writing, given that he was in Mannheim and exposed to the sound-world of the famous Mannheim orchestra? Its textures are quasi-orchestral, especially in the first movement, Allegro con spirito, with its opening 'Mannheim rocket' figure, its driving chordal accompaniment textures featuring repeated chords in the left hand, and 'busy' Alberti bass patterns. Also the textures are quite varied in the Allegro con spirito. The secondary theme (bar 35) suggestive perhaps of a reduction, in orchestral terms, to upper strings; the opening of the development (which in this case actually *is* a development) perhaps a dialogue between tutti (bars 59–60) and a pair of flutes or oboes (bars 61–62). Dialogue textures animate this movement, most obviously in the *forte* — *piano* disposition of the opening theme, but also from bars 73–93, at first tutti (to bar 81) thereafter alternating between brief *piano* or *pianissimo* phrases (wind pairs, or upper strings) and *forte* tutti interjections. Dialogue animates the development section to a large extent, providing a kind of 'counterpoint' to the tonal course of this section and the ongoing process of thematic development, involving fragmentation of the opening theme (bars 61–62) along with intervallic adaptation of the entire opening phrase and sequential repetition (bar 73 foll.). The return of the dialogue texture of bars 59–62 at bars 86–93 creates a peculiar sense of reprise within the development and simultaneously reinforces the (temporary) sense of tonal arrival at A minor (bar 86). Arguably, the dialogue texture also sets up the recapitulation of the opening theme in bar 94, making its entry (on C) seem a climactic point of arrival after two successive upward steps, A (bar 86), B (bar 90) and C, a stature it might not naturally enjoy coming after such a turbulent textural and harmonic passage as bars 73–82 (see example 3).

In many ways KV309 is a special piece, unlike any keyboard work Mozart had penned previously. As so often in his music, a decisive innovation in his language, moving from the known toward the unknown, was driven by an external stimulus. (Other examples include dramatic characterization in the operas, inspired by particular singers and their vocal capabilities, and the related drama of the piano concerto, which exploits a specifically public concert setting in 1780s Vienna.) Leopold, in his letter to Wolfgang of 11 December 1777, already quoted above, had called this sonata a 'strange composition'; indeed it is, for KV309 is a crucial turning point in the evolution of the language of a genius.

'Ausgleichs-Abende': The First Viennese Performances of Smetana's *The Bartered Bride*

DAVID BRODBECK

University of California, Irvine

I

On the afternoon of 31 May 1892, a specially chartered train pulled into Vienna's Franz Josef Station after making the six-hour journey from Prague. On board were the operatic personnel of the Czech Landes- und Nationaltheater [National Theatre], who had come to the Austrian capital in order to perform in the city's Internationale Ausstellung für Musik- und Theaterwesen [International Exhibition of Music and Theatre], held in the Prater from 7 May to 9 October 1892. The Czechs, who were scheduled to appear during the first week of June, had announced an ambitious programme centred on five operas by native composers, comprising Bedřich Smetana's *Prodaná nevěsta* [*The Bartered Bride*] and *Dalibor*, Antonín Dvořák's *Dimitrij*, Karel Benda's *Lejla* and Karel Šebor's *Nevěsta husitská* [*The Hussite Bride*]. Rounding out the bill were Zdeněk Fibich's melodrama *Námluvy Pelopovy* [*The Courtship of Pelops*] and two spoken plays, including one by František Adolf Šubert, the National Theatre's general director.[1]

Šubert had been shuttling between Prague and Vienna over the previous few weeks attending to all the final preparations, and he now stood on the station platform awaiting the arrival of his company. There he was joined by

---

[1] The most detailed source on the Czech National Theatre's guest residency remains Fr[antišek] Ad[olf] Šubert, *Das Böhmische National-Theater in der ersten internationalen Musik- und Theater-Ausstellung zu Wien im Jahre 1892* (Prague, 1892); my description of events in this and the following paragraph is based on that account (pp. 8–14). The guest residency is discussed briefly in Vlasta Reittererová and Hubert Reitterer, *Vier Dutzend rothe Strümpfe .... Zur Rezeptionsgeschichte der 'Verkauften Braut' von Bedřich Smetana in Wien am Ende des 19. Jahrhunderts* (Vienna, 2004), pp. 54–63; Martina Nußbaumer, 'Identity on Display: (Re-)Präsentationen des Eigenen und des Fremden auf der Internationalen Ausstellung für Musik- und Theaterwesen in Wien 1892', *Historische Anthropologie. Kultur, Gesellschaft, Alltag*, 13 (2005), 45–60 (52–55); Oscar Teuber, 'Das Ausstellungs-Theater und seine Thaten', in *Die internationale Ausstellung für Musik- und Theaterwesen Wien 1892*, ed. by Siegmund Schneider (Vienna, 1894), pp. 305–09; and Oskar Fleischer, *Die Bedeutung der internationalen Musik- und Theater-Ausstellung in Wien für Kunst und Wissenschaft der Musik* (Leipzig and New York, [1894]), pp. 65–66.

Franz von Jauner, co-director of the Theater an der Wien and artistic director of the Exhibition Theatre, as well as by a delegation of Czech representatives to the *Reichsrat* [Imperial Council] and the leaders of several Czech voluntary organizations in Vienna, all of whom had turned out to greet their Bohemian compatriots, some 270 persons altogether, including soloists, choir, orchestra, ballet, administrative personnel and technical staff. The festivities continued the following morning, when the group assembled in the Exhibition Theatre for a well-attended public rehearsal for that evening's sold-out, opening night performance of *Prodaná nevěsta*. After thanking the Exhibition Commission for its invitation, Šubert called upon Jauner to speak. Knowing that Šubert was sceptical about the prospects for a favourable reception in Vienna, Jauner began by acknowledging his own admiration for the Czechs' work and then added his assurances that they would be greeted in Vienna with the same sympathy with which so many Viennese artists had been greeted in Prague in the past.[2] In response, Šubert invited his troupe — first in Czech, then in German — to hail the Exhibition Commission with a three-fold 'Sláva!' [Hurrah!], whereupon he turned to his players once more and exclaimed:

> Wir werden in Wien von allen Seiten freundlich, ja herzlich aufgenommen, das wird für Sie gewiß ein Ansporn sein, mit freudigem Muthe an Ihre Aufgabe zu schreiten. Rufen wir ein *Na zdar!* auf das Gelingen des großen Unternehmens, welches uns zum erstenmale Gelegenheit bietet, außerhalb Prags in unseren nationalen dramatischen und musikalischen Leistungen hervortreten zu können.[3]

> [We are received by all sides in Vienna in a friendly, indeed cordial manner, which will certainly be an incentive to you to take up your task with joyous courage. Let us make a toast to the success of the great undertaking, which gives us the opportunity to display our national dramatic and musical products for the first time outside Prague.]

The National Theatre's appearance in Vienna, then, was a political act, and it invited a politicized response. On the one hand, performance on an international stage of compelling Czech-language theatrical works symbolized the emergence of the Czechs as a modern nation of European standard. Prague now looked not towards Vienna in a state of cultural subservience, but towards Berlin and Paris as cultural equals.[4] On the other hand, in Vienna, capital of

---

[2] Šubert's doubts are reported in Guido Adler, *Wollen und Wirken. Aus dem Leben eines Musikhistorikers* (Vienna, 1935), p. 64. Adler was in charge of the music-historical division of the Exhibition but also played a role in administering the artistic productions in the Exhibition Theatre and Concert Hall.

[3] Šubert is quoted in 'Die Musik- und Theater-Ausstellung', *Neue Freie Presse, Abendblatt*, 1 June 1892, p. 2.

[4] It was only fitting, therefore, that the Czechs' week in the Exhibition Theatre was sandwiched between similar residencies by Berlin's Deutsches Theater and the Théâtre National de l'Odéon from Paris. See also Katherine David-Fox, 'Prague–Vienna, Prague–Berlin: The Hidden Geography of Czech Modernism', *Slavic Review*, 59 (2000), 735–60, and

the multi-national Austrian (Habsburg) state, this public display of cultural independence by one of the Monarchy's Slavic nationalities could only be viewed against the background of traditional assumptions of German cultural superiority. Here I shall be interested less in what the Czechs' appearance at the Exhibition represented for the Czech nation than with how the Germans in Vienna attempted to come to terms with it. To be more precise, I shall focus on the critical reception in the German liberal and German-nationalist press, and home in especially on the week's runaway hit, Smetana's *The Bartered Bride*.[5]

The cultural politics that were embedded in the Czech National Theatre's Viennese performances formed but a part of a broader political battleground involving ongoing tensions between the Monarchy's German and Czech nationalities, tensions that were coming to a new head at that very moment. The *Neue Freie Presse*, the voice of Austria's traditional liberal establishment, spoke unmistakably to those tensions — and to the potential for the International Exhibition to help to ameliorate them — in its leading article for 8 May 1892, written to mark the Exhibition's opening:

> Für uns Oesterreicher hat das Wort international eine umfassendere Bedeutung als für alle Anderen, für uns verbindet es nicht blos Nation mit Nation, sondern auch Nationalität mit Nationalität. Da wir keine Nation sind und unser Reich selbst schon eine Versammlung von Nationalitäten darstellt, so schließt jedes Werk, welches den Absonderungstrieb der Völker überwinden hilft und sie zu einem gemeinschaftlichen Ziele vereinigt, für uns einen doppelten Segen ein: es einigt uns mit den anderen Nationen und einigt uns in uns selbst. Je tiefer und schmerzlicher wir es täglich empfinden, wie sehr vor Allem das Letztere uns nothhut, desto höher müssen wir es schätzen, daß die Wiener Musik- und Theater-Ausstellung auch in diesem Sinne ein internationales Unternehmen ist und auf dem Gebiete der Kunst zwischen den oft trotzig und feindselig sich von einander abkehrenden Völkerschaften des eigenen Staates Berührungen schafft, welche sie wenigstens in Einer [sic] Beziehung einander näher bringen und vielleicht auch auf viele andere Beziehungen segensreich fortwirken werden.[6]

> [For us Austrians, the word 'international' has a more comprehensive meaning than for all others; for us it does not merely bind nation to nation but also nationality to nationality. Since we are not a nation, and our empire itself is made up of a collection of nationalities, every project that helps to overcome the separatist impulse of the peoples and unite them in pursuit of

Christopher P. Storck, *Kulturnation und Nationalkunst. Strategien und Mechanismen tschechischer Nationsbildung von 1860 bis 1914* (Cologne, 2001).

[5] For two excellent guides to Vienna's *fin-de-siècle* music critics and the newspapers for which they wrote, see Sandra McColl, *Music Criticism in Vienna 1896–1897. Critically Moving Forms* (Oxford, 1996), pp. 11–32; and Reittererová and Reitter, *Vier Dutzend rothe Strümpfe ...*, pp. 407–38. Margaret Notley, *Lateness and Brahms. Music and Culture in the Twilight of Viennese Liberalism* (Oxford and New York, 2006), *passim*, offers a thoughtful engagement with the politicized work of many of the critics with whom I shall be concerned here.

[6] 'Wien, 7. Mai', *Neue Freie Presse*, Morgenblatt, 8 May 1892, p. 1.

a common goal brings a double blessing: it unites us with the other nations and unites us with ourselves. The more deeply and painfully we feel every day how very much the latter above all is necessary for us, the more we must appreciate that the Viennese Exhibition of Music and Theatre is also an international undertaking in this sense, one that creates contacts in the realm of art between peoples within our own state who often turn their backs on one another in a hostile and confrontational manner. In one respect at least they are brought closer together, an experience that will perhaps have a positive effect on many other areas of interaction.]

This might have seemed a naïve hope. Only a few months earlier, as reported by the music critic Theodor Helm in the *Deutsche Zeitung*, Vienna's oldest German-nationalist daily, the Vienna Philharmonic's performance of Dvořák's *Hussite Overture* had sparked a minor contretemps along national lines among those in attendance at the Musikverein on 21 February 1892.[7] Yet nothing of the kind seems to have occurred that June in the Exhibition Theatre. Not surprisingly, Czechs and other Slavs were disproportionately represented in the audiences; prominent by their presence were the Czech and Polish members of the Cabinet, large numbers of delegates to the *Reichsrat* from Bohemia, Moravia, Slovenia and Croatia, members of the Bohemian and Moravian nobility and large land-owning classes, as well as representatives of Vienna's many Slavic voluntary associations and, of course, members of the Czech press. Clearly, Slavic pride was in full display throughout the week. But, if only out of an initial curiosity, large numbers of bourgeois Germans attended the performances as well — and were no less won over by them. As Helm described matters this time:

> Die Prager tschechische Oper [...] errang [heute] einen vollen *künstlerischen* Erfolg. Wir betonen das Wort 'künstlerisch', denn [...] das reizende, ebenso volksthümliche als fein gearbeitete Werk und seine vortreffliche Aufführung hätte in dem gastfreundlichen Wien auch vor einem nicht slavischen Publicum seine Wirkung nicht verfehlen können.[8]
>
> [Today the Czech Opera from Prague achieved complete *artistic* success. We stress the word 'artistic', since the delightfully folk-like as well as finely developed work and its outstanding performance could not have failed in hospitable Vienna to have an effect even on a non-Slavic audience.]

[7] h — m [Theodor Helm], 'Theater, Kunst und Literatur', *Deutsche Zeitung*, 25 February 1892, p. 6; for a discussion, see David Brodbeck, 'Dvořák's Reception in Liberal Vienna: Language Ordinances, National Property, and the Rhetoric of *Deutschtum*', *Journal of the American Musicological Society*, 60 (2007), 71–132 (pp. 116–17).

[8] h — m [Theodor Helm], 'Ausstellungs-Theater', *Deutsche Zeitung*, 2 June 1892, p. 5, emphasis in original. In fact, the public response to both of Smetana's works was so favourable that the scheduled operas by Benda and Šebor were set aside to allow *The Bartered Bride* and *Dalibor* to be repeated. And even those additions proved insufficient to meet the demand: in the end, the troupe stayed on for an extra day to give an unscheduled final performance of *The Bartered Bride*, thereby causing a one-day postponement of the opening performance by the Théâtre National de l'Odéon.

In view of the Czechs' subaltern status within the Austro-Hungarian Monarchy — and nowhere was this status more evident than with respect to language and high culture — it comes as no surprise that many Viennese had read the National Theatre's ambitious prospectus of works with some incredulity. In his report for the *Allgemeine Kunst-Chronik*, Max Dietz suggested that, while the notion of Czech opera might seem as outlandish as an Indian flute concert, the public had nevertheless been won over:

> Die Tschechen sind allerorts als gute Musiker geschätzt, schöpferische Leistungen auf dem Gebiete der Tonkunst jedoch hat man ihnen nicht zugetraut, am wenigsten in der Oper. Die Gesangstruppe des verdienten Direktors Šubert hat uns eines Besseren belehrt.[9]
>
> [The Czechs are valued everywhere as good musicians. They have not, however, been thought capable of creative achievements in the realm of musical composition, least of all in opera. The vocal ensemble of the excellent Director Šubert has set us straight.]

To make sense of this sudden turnabout in attitude and understanding, it will be necessary first to provide some historical context. Pieter M. Judson's succinct description of liberal ideology provides a good point of departure:

> German [liberal] nationalists in Habsburg Central Europe had traditionally conceived of their own nation in universal, non-territorial and largely cultural terms. To them, the German nation represented a positive force for the progressive transformation of all the region's inhabitants, a universal culture of education that offered opportunities for social and economic advancement [to] all ambitious Austrians.[10]

Yet the Czech bourgeoisie resisted the German liberal imperative, claiming ethnicity, not culture, as the basis of its social identity, and despite common interests with the German-speaking bourgeoisie, this group, represented after 1860 by the Czech National Party, focused on winning autonomy from the powerful central bureaucracy in Vienna. To this extent, the party's interests coincided with those of the Czechophile Bohemian nobility (the so-called Feudal Conservatives), who favoured decentralized, federalist government. To the German liberal nationalists, then, Czech nationalism came to be seen as a reactionary threat to liberal ideals of progress and civilization.

This fear became all too real in 1879, when the Monarchy's last German Liberal cabinet was dissolved, and the Czech National Party (known by now as the Old Czechs, and led by František Rieger) ended its lengthy boycott of the *Reichsrat* and entered a new conservative-clerical government headed by Count Eduard von Taaffe. In the ensuing decades the Czechs were gradually able to

---

[9] Max Dietz, 'Die tschechische Oper', *Allgemeine Kunst-Chronik*, 16 (1892), 308–12 (pp. 308–09).
[10] Pieter M. Judson, *Guardians of the Nation. Activists on the Language Frontiers of Imperial Austria* (Cambridge, MA, 2006), p. 15.

advance their interests. In 1880, Czech was introduced as a second language, alongside German, in which the public in Bohemia and Moravia was permitted to communicate with the governmental bureaucracy. Two years later, the University of Prague was divided into separate German and Czech divisions. And in 1885 the Czechs benefited further when voting rights were extended to lower-middle-class men. By the end of the decade, frustrated German Liberals had undertaken a boycott of their own of the Bohemian Diet.

In January 1890, Taaffe sought to defuse tension between the two nationalities by inviting leading representatives of the German Liberals and Old Czechs to negotiate a set of agreements that were designed to divide the Crown Land into separate German- and Czech-speaking administrative zones. To the more radical Young Czechs (who had broken from the Old Czechs some years earlier and were not invited to take part in the negotiations), this so-called *Böhmischer Ausgleich* [Bohemian Compromise] constituted an unacceptable infringement on Bohemian state right, which asserted the territorial integrity of the Crown Land as well as its intrinsic Czech character. In March 1891 German–Czech relations took a decided turn towards greater confrontation when the Young Czechs, led by outspoken radicals such as Julius and Eduard Grégr and Jan Vašatý, won nearly all the Czech seats in the elections to the *Reichsrat* on a platform of outright opposition to Taaffe's proposed *Ausgleich*. In April 1892, the increasingly irrelevant Old Czechs acknowledged the direction in which the winds were blowing by withdrawing their support of the very Compromise with the Germans that they had helped to negotiate.

None of this recent political history was lost on the unnamed author of an article entitled 'Czechen in Wien' [Czechs in Vienna], which appeared in the liberal *Wiener Allgemeine Zeitung* on 5 June 1892. Here the Czechs in question were not political figures, but rather the members of Šubert's National Theatre, who had dispelled years of bad feeling through 'eine Großthat auf dem Felde der Kunst, die auch nicht ohne Folgen auf anderen Gebieten bleiben kann' [a great deed in the field of art that cannot remain without consequences in other areas].[11]

As the author continues, he follows a time-honoured tradition by placing the blame for the current 'bad feeling' between Austria's Germans and Czechs on fear rooted in simple ignorance, indicting those who erect unnecessary barriers between them while concealing 'das Güte und Schöne, das sich wie ein himmlisch-leuchtend Band um alle Nationen schlingt' [the goodness and beauty that is entwined around all nations like a heavenly gleaming ribbon]. 'Da kommt auf einmal' — the reference is to the recent première of *Prodaná nevěsta* — 'entweder ein Mann oder ein Ereigniß, und die Blinden werden sehend' [Then, all of a sudden, a man or an event comes along, and the blind are given

---

[11] D., 'Czechen in Wien', *Wiener Allgemeine Zeitung*, 5 June 1892, p. 2, from which several of the following quotations are also taken. A portion of this article is cited (with the incorrect date of 4 June 1892) in Nußbaumer, 'Identity on Display', p. 54.

sight]. Directing his attention to the Czechs as a whole, he continues:

> Dieser Volksstamm, nächst dem deutschen der tüchtigste, fleißigste, sparsamste und wirthschaftlich fortgeschrittenste in Oesterreich, hat sich jetzt auf dem Gebiete der Kunst dem deutschen durchaus ebenbürtig gezeigt. Was könnten diese beiden Volksstämme für die Gesammtheit leisten, wenn sie einträchtig zusammenstünden im Dienste des staatlichen Gemeinwesens!
>
> [This people, after the Germans the most competent, industrious, canny and economically progressive in Austria, has now shown itself the absolute equal of the Germans in terms of its artistic production. Imagine what these two peoples could achieve for the benefit of the whole, if they worked together harmoniously in the service of the commonwealth!]

On the face of it, this appears to be a call for what nowadays would be described as multiculturalism. Yet the well-defined cultural hierarchy that had always been part and parcel of liberal ideology lies scarcely hidden beneath the surface:

> Das mit der hussitischen Tradition versetzte Czechenthum ist seiner ganzen historischen Entwicklung gemäß durchtränkt mit freisinnigen Ideen, wie sie das deutsche Bürgerthum durchziehen [...]. Daß sich die Czechen jetzt auf dem Gebiete der Kunst so sehr hervorthun, rückt sie wieder vollends in die vorderste Reihe der Culturvölker, denn die aus vorurtheilslosem Denken resultirende Bildung und die nach dem Höchsten strebende Kunst sind die besten Schutzmittel gegen Rückfälle in veraltete und überlebte Doctrinen.
>
> [Tempered with Hussite tradition, Czechdom is saturated in its historical development with free-thinking ideas, such as pervade the German bourgeoisie. That the Czechs are now excelling so greatly in the realm of art places them once more fully amongst the civilized nations of the first rank, for cultivation that results from unbiased thinking and art that strives towards excellence are the best defence against backsliding into obsolete and outdated doctrines.]

The author applauds the Czechs for successfully transcending reactionary, feudal conservatism (with its clericalism); here, in other words, the old aspirations of German liberalism have been realized.

This political commentator was no music or theatre critic, however, and he does not explain why *Prodaná nevěsta* warranted the place he accords it alongside the artistic products of the 'civilized nations'. More than one critic found that explanation in Mozart. For example, Oscar Teuber, writing in the *Fremden-Blatt*, cites Prague's historic importance as a Mozart city, and then argues that the composer had, long after his death, remained a living inspiration among Bohemian musicians, whether they identified themselves as German or Czech. While Teuber conceded that *Prodaná nevěsta* was 'erfüllt mit dem frischen, ursprünglichen Leben eines jungen Volkes, sie wurzelt tief im Volkscharakter, sie ist national durch und durch' [filled with the fresh, unspoilt vitality of a young people, deeply rooted in its folk character, national through and through], he attributes the work's outstanding quality to 'die wohlthätige Verschmelzung deutschen und slavischen Geistes, die glückliche Befruchtung slavischer Volkskraft durch die deutsche Kunst' [the beneficent fusion of the Slavic and German spirits, the happy fertilization of the Slavic energy by German art]. It is no wonder, then, that earlier in the same review Teuber had borrowed from contemporary political discourse by pointedly describing the night of the first performance as an 'Ausgleichs-Abend', an evening of compromise, conceived 'um die feindlichen Brüder auf musikalischem Gebiete friedlich zusammenzubringen' [in order to unite the fraternal enemies peaceably in the domain of music].[12]

Albert Kauders, the Prague-born music critic of the *Wiener Allgemeine Zeitung*, takes this line of reasoning even further.[13] He acknowledges that the Czechs celebrate Smetana as the founder of their national music and recognizes that Smetana's operas are Czech by virtue of their texts, their plots drawn from Czech history and their local colour. But, for Kauders, 'in ihrem innersten Grundwesen ist aber seine Musik nichtsdestoweniger — deutsch; und über dieses Wort wird sich wohl auch die übertriebenste nationale Eitelkeit nicht gekränkt fühlen, wenn hinzugefügt wird, daß ich zur deutschen Kunst Alles zähle, was sich zum Evangelium Bach's, Mozart's und Beethoven's bekennt' [in its innermost character Smetana's music is nevertheless German; and even the most exaggerated national vanity will probably not be offended by this word, if I add that I count among German art everything that confesses the Gospel of Bach, Mozart and Beethoven]. Moreover, Kauders suggests that Smetana was a 'German' composer before he ever became a 'Czech' one: 'An den Brüsten deutscher Kunst hat Smetana sein vornehmes Talent vollgesogen, und erfüllt von deutschem Kunstgeiste ging er daran, den Producten seiner Erfindung nationale Färbung zu geben' [Smetana's fine talent suckled at the breasts of German art and, imbued with German artistic spirit, he went on to give national colouring to the products of his invention]. Finally, to those who would argue for a pan-Slavic musical sensibility, he counters that Russian and German music are entirely different in kind and irreconcilable: 'Ohne Zwang lassen sich diese verschiedenartigen Productionen nicht unter einen Hut bringen. Deutscher Geist und russischer Fusel! — Der feinsinnige Künstler Smetana wußte, auf welche Seite er sich zu schlagen habe' [These heterogeneous productions cannot be brought under the same roof unless by force. German spirit and stale Russian liquor! The highly subtle artist Smetana

---

[12] Oscar Teuber, 'Zwei czechische Opern im Ausstellungs-Theater', *Fremden-Blatt*, 4 June 1892, pp. 11–12; this review is erroneously attributed to Albert Kauders in Nußbaumer, 'Identity on Display', p. 54.

[13] K. Anders [Albert Kauders], 'Die böhmische Oper in Wien', *Wiener Allgemeine Zeitung*, 3 June 1892, p. 7; Nußbaumer, 'Identity on Display,' p. 54, erroneously cites the source of this review as the *Wiener Zeitung*.

knew on which side he had to acquit himself]. All this tells us more, of course, about Kauders than about Smetana. But the critic does seem to have got things at least half right: Smetana may not have been the acculturated German liberal whom Kauders describes, but neither was he a pan-Slavicist. What gets lost here, however, is the composer's own identity as a Czech nationalist.

The importance of that identity, by contrast, was not lost on the critics who wrote for Vienna's German-nationalist newspapers. By the early 1890s, the older *Deutsche Zeitung* had been joined by the upstart *Deutsches Volksblatt*, along with the tabloid *Ostdeutsche Rundschau* (the organ of the Pan-German radical fringe), in providing a platform for a new post-liberal music-critical discourse centred on the 'progressive' music of Wagner, Liszt and Bruckner.[14] To a greater degree than reviews in more traditional liberal organs, this body of music criticism reflected the transformation of liberal politics that had been developing over the previous decade at the hands of younger party activists, who reacted to the political gains won by the Czechs at the expense of long-standing German prerogatives by seeking to steer the party away from its traditional loyalty to the *state* and towards a new loyalty to the *nation* — to urge, that is, adoption of an openly German-nationalist, interest-group orientation.[15] A result of this change, as Judson has noted, was the emergence of a new rhetoric of *Nationalbesitzstand* [national property], which was seen to be in need of defence against encroachment by the Monarchy's Slavs (and, increasingly, its Jews). Here political identities and social conflicts were defined in terms of a nationalist discourse that understood Germanness as a matter of ethnicity rather than liberal bourgeois cultural values.[16]

Yet politics makes for strange bedfellows. The Young Czechs, who championed the music of the late Smetana while criticizing that of Dvořák (who was seen as too beholden to German liberal interests in Vienna and too keen on putting international success ahead of national consciousness), shared much ideologically with the German Nationalists; both parties espoused strong anti-clericalism, 'radical' (left-liberal) politics and anti-Semitism (directed, in the case of the Young Czechs, against Bohemia's Germanophile Jews).[17] It is not surprising, then, that among the critics in the German-nationalist press, the Czech nationalist Smetana — in decided contrast to Dvořák — was greatly admired. As much as anything else, this had to do with Smetana's affinities for Wagner's music dramas, as well as for the symphonic poems of Liszt. Dvořák could only suffer by comparison on account of his close association with Brahms and — what was even worse — from his status as a protégé of the musically

---

[14] On the reception of the music of Brahms and Bruckner in this context, see Notley, *Lateness and Brahms*, pp. 27–35.

[15] This, of course, is precisely the kind of attitude that the *Neue Freie Presse* was arguing against in its editorial of 8 May 1892, quoted above.

[16] Pieter M. Judson, ' "Not Another Square Foot!": German Liberalism and the Rhetoric of National Ownership in 19th-Century Austria', *Austrian History Yearbook*, 26 (1995), 83–97.

[17] Steven Beller, *Francis Joseph* (London and New York, 1996), p. 142.

'conservative' (and 'Jewish') critic Eduard Hanslick, of the *Neue Freie Presse*.[18] In other words, it worked to Smetana's advantage that he could be linked, in a way that Dvořák could not at this stage of his career, to the New Germans.

Theodor Helm made this argument in a roundabout way in two pieces that appeared in the *Deutsche Zeitung*. In a brief notice on 2 June, as we have seen, he stressed the appeal of *The Bartered Bride* to Slavic and non-Slavic audiences alike.[19] In a *feuilleton* that appeared two days later, Helm builds on this notion by adopting the now familiar strategy of explicitly linking Smetana to the German tradition (which he clearly associates with the 'fine workmanship' to which he had alluded in his previous notice).[20] He observes how the composer developed the music of *Prodaná nevěsta* from Czech folk-song with good taste and with secure compositional and orchestral technique. In his view, Smetana, basing his technique squarely on the German tradition of Mozart and Beethoven, Mendelssohn, Schumann, Lortzing and Wagner, is not opposed to German music although he is a Slav 'durch und durch' [through and through]. Yet it is only Wagner with whom Smetana is specifically compared, as Helm takes note not only of certain thematic reminiscences but also of what he calls Smetana's 'geistige Verwandschaft' [spiritual kinship] with the German master, whereby the Czech composer consciously adopts Wagner's technique of thematic reminiscence.

But what appeals to the German-nationalist critics are not only Smetana's progressive (i.e. New German) musical credentials, but also his national consciousness. Thus the *Deutsches Volksblatt* pointed to *Prodaná nevěsta* — indeed, to the Czech National Theatre's entire project — as something worthy of emulation at home. Reviewing the Czechs' opening night performance at the Exhibition Theatre, this newspaper's unnamed critic reports that

> Auf der Bühne sah man *durchwegs* Arier, ein seltener Anblick für unser Auge. [...] Die ganze Vorstellung hatte etwas Frisches, Unblasirtes [...]. O, wären doch die Deutschen unserer Ostmark auch solch' frischer nationaler Begeisterung fähig. Wir verließen das Theater [...] mit einem Gefühl [...] der Beschämung, daß wir nicht im Stande sind, eine derartig judenreine, wahrhaft nationale Volksbühne uns zu erringen.[21]

---

[18] Compare, for example, the discussion of *Prodaná nevěsta* with that of Dvořák's *Dimitrij*, performed on the second evening of the National Theatre's Viennese guest residency, in both Theodor Helm, 'Tschechische Oper', *Deutsche Zeitung*, 4 June 1892, pp. 1–3, and the anonymous *feuilleton* 'Tschechische Musik', *Deutsches Volksblatt*, 4 June 1892, pp. 1–3.

[19] Helm, 'Ausstellungs-Theater', p. 5. By contrast, Helm frequently criticized Dvořák's music for what he described as its limited appeal, restricted to those who listened with a 'slavisch-nationales Ohr' [Slavic-national ear]; see Brodbeck, 'Dvořák's Reception in Liberal Vienna', pp. 102–04, 107, 121.

[20] Helm, 'Tschechische Oper', pp. 1–2.

[21] 'Die erste Vorstellung des tschechischen Nationaltheaters', *Deutsches Volksblatt*, Abend-Ausgabe, 2 June 1892, p. 3, emphasis in original. See also the anonymous *feuilleton* 'Das königlich böhmische Landes- und Nationaltheater in Prag', *Deutsches Volksblatt*, Morgen-Ausgabe, 2 June 1892, p. 1: 'Wir können diese Zeilen nicht schließen, ohne nochmals auf das rege [...]

[One *consistently* saw Aryans on the stage, a rare sight for our eyes. The entire production had about it something fresh, unjaded. Oh, if only the Germans of our Ostmark were capable of such fresh national enthusiasm. We left the theatre ashamed that we are not in a position to achieve for ourselves a truly national popular theatre that is equally free of Jewish influence.]

Obviously, we are at a great remove here from the liberal-nationalist rhetoric of a Kauders or a Teuber, with its assumption of Smetana's acculturation to German norms. For the anonymous author of these last-quoted lines, by contrast, the importance of Smetana's work lay precisely in its insistence on its own Czechness.

Thus in Vienna, in the summer of 1892, *Prodaná nevěsta* was all things to all people. As the composer himself would have wished, it was a source of national pride for the Monarchy's Czechs. But for traditional liberal nationalists the opera could be seen as a cultural product of an enduring supranational Austrian state in which German — and German music — remained the *lingua franca*. And for the city's *deutschnational* critics the work represented nothing less than a salutary model of national consciousness, an example of what might be accomplished by properly 'German' composers in *Deutschösterreich*. Each of these groups would soon be heard from again: within a year, *The Bartered Bride* would be staged once more in Vienna — although this time under very difference circumstances.

II

Sparked by the National Theatre's performances in the Prater, Viennese interest in Czech music soon reached an all-time high. In its 1892–93 subscription season, for example, the Vienna Philharmonic included performances of both Fibich's programmatic concert overture *Noc na Karlštejně* [*A Night at Karlstein Castle*], heard on 20 November 1892, and Smetana's symphonic poem *Z českých luhů a hájů* [*From Bohemia's Woods and Fields*], which followed on 29 January 1893. Meanwhile, the Czech String Quartet had conquered the city on 19 January 1893 in an all-Czech debut concert that featured Smetana's First String Quartet *Z mého života* [*From My Life*]. Public enthusiasm for the visitors from Prague was such that three additional performances had to be scheduled —

Nationalgefühl hinzuweisen, das sich in [...] der Leitung des böhmischen Nationaltheaters kundgibt. Wenn in Wien ein Kritiker an eine Bühne, die sich, wenigstens ihrem Namen nach, die Aufgabe stellt, ein deutscher Volkstheater zu sein, die Aufforderung richtet, die französischen Ehebruchs-Dramatiker etwas weniger zu protegiren und dafür mehr das Classische und das Volksstück zu pflegen, dann läuft er Gefahr, ausgelacht zu werden.'
[We cannot conclude without mentioning once again the strong national consciousness shown by those in charge of the Czech National Theatre. If a critic in Vienna challenges a theatre that, at least according to its name, presents itself as a theatre for the German populace to promote French dramas of adultery somewhat less and instead to cultivate the German classics and popular dialect drama, then he runs the danger of being laughed at].

on 24 January (another all-Czech concert, in which the quartet *From My Life* shared the bill with Dvořák's String Quartet in E, B57), and on 10 and 27 February (with additional performances of works by Smetana and Dvořák).[22]

This flurry of activity in the Viennese mainstream led an unnamed critic for the *Ostdeutsche Rundschau* — here sounding very much like the anonymous critic for the *Deutsches Volksblatt* from the previous year — to couple praise for Smetana with a bitter complaint about the willingness of his fellow Viennese to countenance an egregious infringement of *Nationalbesitzstand*:

> Die an den Anschlagsäulen angekündigten Concerte können uns viel eher glauben machen, daß wir uns in Moskau, Paris, Prag oder irgendwo befinden, nur nicht in einer deutschen Musikstadt [...]. Die Verehrung und Begeisterung, mit der die Tschechen für ihren einzigen und wirklich bedeutenden Tondichter Smetana eintreten, sollte für uns Deutsche ein beherzigenswerthes Beispiel sein. Es ist wirklich beschämend, daß das einzige wahre Kunstereignis im Ausstellungstheater die Aufführungen des böhmischen Nationaltheaters waren. Eine solch' künstlerisch vollendete Aufführung, wie die der 'Verkauften Braut' hat unser Hof-Operntheater seit vielen, vielen Jahren nicht zu Stande gebracht.[23]

> [The concerts announced on the advertising pillars would have us believe that we are in Moscow, Paris, Prague, or anywhere but a German city of music. The admiration and enthusiasm with which the Czechs stand up for Smetana as their only truly important composer should be for us Germans an example worth heeding. It is really shameful that the only true artistic successes in the Exhibition Theatre were the performances by the Czech National Theatre. Our Court Opera has not produced a staging of such consummate artistry as that of *The Bartered Bride* for many, many years.]

Šubert, in fact, had already sought to exploit the interest shown in Czech opera the previous summer by requesting permission to stage a series of guest performances in the Court Opera House. The director, Wilhelm Jahn, held out against the idea of opening up his stage to any of the Monarchy's national theatres, but he did at least now begin to consider introducing some of Smetana's operas himself.[24] When negotiations for an immediate German-

---

[22] The popularity of this ensemble in Vienna grew over several years following this to the extent that it soon eclipsed that of the local Hellmesberger and Rosé quartets. See Elizabeth Way Sullivan, 'German Nationalism and the Reception of the Czech String Quartet in Vienna', in *Nineteenth-Century Music. Selected Proceedings of the Tenth International Conference*, ed. by Jim Samson and Bennett Zon (Burlington, VT, 2002), pp. 296–313.

[23] M., *Ostdeutsche Rundschau*, 29 January 1893, p. 5.

[24] In a memorandum to the *Generalintendanz* [management of the Court Theatres] dated 8 December 1892 (quoted in Reittererová and Reitterer, *Vier Dutzend rothe Strümpfe ...*, p. 164), Jahn noted: 'Ebenso würde dies Ansuchen um Überlassung des Hofoperntheaters an die czech. National-Oper gewiß nicht vereinzelt bleiben, da die ungarische und polnische National-Oper sicher nachfolgen dürften' [This request to allow the Czech National Opera residency at the Court Opera House would certainly not be a one-off, since the Hungarian and Polish National Operas would surely follow suit].

language performance of *The Bartered Bride* at the Court Opera fell through, the work was acquired by the Theater an der Wien, the city's leading venue for operettas, where a long and successful run in Max Kalbeck's German translation opened on 2 April 1893.[25]

As with *Prodaná nevěsta* in the Exhibition Theatre, so now with *Die verkaufte Braut* in the Theater an der Wien, the critical response was overwhelmingly enthusiastic.[26] Helm renewed his praise of 'die zahllosen Schönheiten des Werkes, dessen Musik die naive Frische des Volksthümlichen mit wahrer Kunst vereint' [the innumerable beauties of the work, whose music unites the naïve freshness of the folk tradition with true art].[27] Richard Heuberger, in an obvious allusion to Taaffe's still-unratified *Böhmischer Ausgleich*, noted that the work proved the capacity of 'wahre Kunst' [true art] to reconcile those of goodwill 'ohne Ausgleich und Bezirksabgrenzung' [without compromise and demarcation of separate regions].[28] Other critics used the occasion to chide Jahn for programming works by non-Austrian composers such as Mascagni and Massenet at the Court Opera when a work by so fine an 'Austrian' (*oesterreichisch*) or 'patriotic' (*vaterländisch*) composer as Smetana might easily be staged instead.[29] And Albert Kauders picked up from where he had left off the previous year by enthusing that 'Smetana's Musik spricht die gemeinverständliche Sprache der Schönheit und des Gemüthes in so unzweideutiger Weise, daß sie Aller Herzen bezwingen muß, ob nun czechisch oder deutsch oder botokudisch gesungen wird' [Smetana's music speaks the universal language of beauty and feeling so unequivocally that it conquers every heart, whether the text is sung in Czech or German or Botucano].[30]

For Kauders, the German-language production was all the more significant in that it proved wrong all those who had doubted whether the work could survive translation from Czech. Indeed, Kauders praises Kalbeck — here

---

[25] Reittererová and Reitterer, *Vier Dutzend rothe Strümpfe ...*, pp. 66–72.

[26] Reittererová and Reitterer provide transcriptions of 54 reviews or other notices, but without offering any critical commentary; see ibid., pp. 227–92 (from which I have quoted several reviews below).

[27] Theodor Helm, 'Theater, Kunst und Literatur', *Deutsche Zeitung*, 4 April 1893, pp. 3–4 (p. 3).

[28] R. Hr. [Richard Heuberger], 'Die verkaufte Braut', *Wiener Tagblatt*, 4 April 1893, p. 7.

[29] These descriptions are taken, respectively, from reviews by Rob[ert] Hirschfeld, '"Die verkaufte Braut" von Fr. Smetana (Erste Aufführung in deutscher Sprache)', *Die Presse*, 5 April 1893, pp. 1–2; and –n [Albert von Hermann], '"Die verkaufte Braut" von Friedrich Smetana', *Das Vaterland*, 6 April 1893, p. 1. See also the report in the *Illustrirtes Wiener Extrablatt*, 8 April 1893, p. 1. Prompted by the success of *Die verkaufte Braut* (and hounded by the critics), Jahn delayed no longer in introducing Smetana at the Court Opera, where one of the composer's works was staged in German in each of the director's last three seasons: *Der Kuß* [*Hubička* / *The Kiss*, 1894], *Das Geheimnis* [*Tajemství* / *The Secret*, 1895] and *Die verkaufte Braut* itself (on the Emperor's name day in 1896).

[30] k. a. [Albert Kauders], 'Theater an der Wien', *Wiener Allgemeine Zeitung*, 4 April 1893, p. 2. Tucano is the name of a group of languages from the Brazilian Amazon.

traditional assumptions about German cultural superiority are transparent — for having improved on Karel Sabina's original libretto, in part by producing new verse in place of the 'endlose Textwiederholungen' [endless textual repetitions] of the original. The critic acknowledges that Kalbeck, because he did not know Czech, had been unable to reproduce 'das Derb-Volksthümliche' [the hearty, folklike qualities] of Sabina's text, but he quickly adds that 'der urwüchsige Erdgeruch wird an einzelnen Stellen vermißt, allerdings nur von genauen Kennern des Werkes' [the original earthy smell is missed here and there, but only by meticulous cognoscenti of the work], and argues that an unbiased, unschooled listener will enjoy it thoroughly.[31]

The ideology of traditional German liberal nationalism is evident to an even greater degree in Eduard Hanslick's review for the *Neue Freie Presse*. Hanslick had been conspicuous by his silence during the previous summer's residency by the Czech National Theatre — Albert von Hermann had provided coverage for the *Neue Freie Presse* in his place — but he now weighed in at length. Hanslick, the doyen of the Viennese music critics, had already written favourably about Smetana in reviews of the Vienna Philharmonic's recent performances of the opera's overture and of two movements from the orchestral cycle *Má vlast*, and now, in words similar to those employed there, he hails *Die verkaufte Braut* as a model of good taste in comic opera: 'Stets natürlich, volksthümlich und melodiös, wird sie doch niemals ordinär; eine höchst seltene Erscheinung auf diesem Gebiete' [Always natural, folksy and melodious, it never becomes vulgar or common, a highly unusual occurrence in this field].[32]

At the same time, however, Hanslick devotes a good part of his review to the twin projects of cautioning others not to be too easily seduced by the opera's exoticism and convincing them of the necessity of judging the work according to the 'neutral' standards of the German (and Italian) styles:

> Der Werth dieser Oper steht außer Frage; vielleicht ist er unter dem berückenden Eindruck jener czechischen Aufführung im Prater sogar etwas überschätzt worden. 'Mozart's "Figaro" ins Böhmische umgewandelt!' hörte man damals auf Schritt und Tritt. [...] [A]ber [Smetana's] 'Verkaufte Braut' ist noch lange kein Mozart, sie hat nur viel Mozart. [...] Auf dem national-czechischen Grund blühen in Smetana's Oper stellenweise italienische Blümchen und auch deutsche, wie sie in Schubert's, Weber's, Lortzing's Gärten heimisch sind. Und das ist ein Glück für die Oper; wäre sie so ganz urczechisch, daß ihr alle internationalen Verbindungsfäden

---

[31] k. a., 'Theater an der Wien', *Wiener Allgemeine Zeitung*, 5 April 1893, p. 2. For an extended discussion of Kalbeck's adaptation, see Reittererová and Reitterer, *Vier Dutzend rothe Strümpfe ...*, pp. 114–39.

[32] Ed. H. [Eduard Hanslick], 'Oper und Ballet', *Neue Freie Presse, Morgenblatt*, 5 April 1893, pp. 1–2 (from which the next few passages are taken); reprinted in Eduard Hanslick, *Fünf Jahre Musik [1891–1895] (Der 'modernen Oper' VII. Teil)* (Berlin, 1896), pp. 80–84. For a discussion of Hanslick's reception of Smetana's instrumental music, see David Brodbeck, 'Hanslick's Smetana and Hanslick's Prague', *Journal of the Royal Musical Association*, 134/i (2009), 1–36.

fehlten, sie könnte auf deutschem Boden nimmermehr die starke Wirkung üben, wie jetzt in Wien.

[The value of this opera is unquestionable; under the impression of that charming Czech performance in the Prater it may even have become somewhat overrated. 'Mozart's "Figaro" transformed into Czech!' it was said at the time at every turn. (Smetana's) 'Bartered Bride' is far from being worthy of Mozart; but it is very Mozartean. Out of the Czech national soil there bloom here and there in Smetana's opera little Italian flowers and German ones too, such as those native to Schubert's, Weber's and Lortzing's gardens. And that is a good thing for the opera. Were it so utterly Czech that it had no international connections whatever, it could never exert a powerful effect on German soil, as it is now doing in Vienna.]

In Hanslick's view, Smetana stood up to this test — demonstrating his acculturation to German liberalism — in that, as an inheritor of the Prague Mozart tradition, he had been trained as a German musician.[33] Nevertheless — perhaps still smarting over earlier comparisons with *Figaro*, and despite the composer's 'favourable' pedigree — Hanslick found the opera to some degree wanting:

Insbesondere die Kraft und Fülle der musikalischen Erfindung scheint mir [...] nicht so erstaunlich; man muß sie an den rein lyrischen Gesängen prüfen, nicht an den Tänzen, in welchen National-Melodien pulsiren und uns durch exotischen Reiz berücken.

[In particular, the power and fullness of the musical invention do not seem so astonishing to me; one must test it in the purely lyrical songs, not in the dances, in which national airs pulsate and seduce us through their exotic allure.]

Having made these points, Hanslick gets down at last to assessing the work, and here he passes the same favourable judgment that characterizes his reception of Smetana's orchestral music:

Was ein objectives Urtheil begünstigte, war die deutsche Aufführung, da sie frei war von dem bestrickenden Reiz des Fremdartigen und anderen außerordentlichen Einflüssen, welche in der Ausstellungszeit die Gemüther bewegten. [...] Diese Musik gibt sich überall natürlich, bescheiden, unaffectirt, verfällt weder in das Pathos der großen Oper noch in die Trivialitäten der Posse, opfert nie den Gesang dem Orchester, nie die musikalische Form den einseitig dramatischen Prätensionen. [...] Wer jahrelang nur die Keulenschläge 'hochdramatischer' Effecte und die Nadelstiche 'geistreichen' Raffinements erduldet hat, den labt die Musik zur 'Verkauften Braut' wie ein kühlendes Bad. Sie führt uns aus Qualm und Betäubung in die milde, freie Gottesluft.

[What favoured an objective evaluation was the fact that it was staged in German, since it was free of the alluring charm of being foreign and

---

[33] Albert Kauders had made this point in the previous year when, as we have seen, he argued that Smetana was suckled 'at the breasts of German art and [...] went on to give national colouring to the products of his invention'.

> of other extraordinary influences that affected minds at the time of the Exhibition. This music is consistently natural, modest, unaffected, lapses neither into the pathos of grand opera nor into the triviality of burlesque, never sacrifices the voice to the orchestra, nor the musical form in a one-sided way to dramatic pretensions. Anyone who has endured years of nothing but the breast-beating of 'overwrought' dramatic effects and the pinpricks of 'ingenious' refinements, will find the music of *Die verkaufte Braut* as refreshing as a cooling bath. It leads us from fumes and torpidity into the blessed sweetness of fresh air.]

For Hanslick, then, the opera's natural, modest and unaffected style — unlike Helm, he found nothing Wagnerian here — offered a welcome antidote to the more laboured, reflective manner of the day. Yet for all the stress he laid on assessing the work as sung in the 'neutral' German language, the audience in attendance at that evening's performance, the third overall, encountered something altogether different. In the first two performances, the leading role of Marie had been sung by the Viennese soprano Toni Diglas, the understudy who had substituted for Lili Lejo when the latter fell ill following the dress rehearsal. But when Diglas herself became indisposed after the second performance, on 3 April, the theatre hastily replaced *Die verkaufte Braut* on the following evening's bill with Carl Zeller's operetta *Der Vogelhändler* [*The Bird Seller*], while summoning the Prague soprano Anna Veselá from the Bohemian capital to step in for Diglas. Although Veselá had sung Marie to great acclaim in the Czech National Theatre's performances at the Exhibition, she knew the part only in Czech (i.e. as Mařenka), and so for four evenings (5–7 April and 9 April) Smetana's opera was given in curious bilingual performances.[34]

This extraordinary situation did not go unnoticed by the press, of course. On 6 April the liberal *Illustrirtes Wiener Extrablatt* began its report with a wry rhetorical question:

> Was wird der Jungczechenclub dazu sagen? Eine Tochter Libussas hat sich deutschen Künstlern zugesellt und ist einem Wiener Theater zu Hilfe gekommen. In dem Momente, wo der böhmische Landtag eröffnet wird, konnte Derartiges geschehen! Der Ausgleich ist noch nicht zu Stande gekommen und auf musikalischem Gebiete finden bereits Allianzen zwischen Deutschen und Czechen statt.[35]
>
> [What will the Young Czech Club say to that? A daughter of Libuše (the legendary founder of the city of Prague) has joined German artists and come to the aid of a Viennese theatre. Trust such a thing to happen just as the Bohemian Parliament is being opened! The Compromise has not yet come about and already alliances between Germans and Czechs are being formed in the domain of music.]

---

[34] Diglas returned for one performance on 8 April and then, beginning on 10 April, alternated with Lejo until the end of the run; see Reittererová and Reitterer, *Vier Dutzend rothe Strümpfe ...*, pp. 150–51.

[35] -sch [Ludwig Lazar Basch], 'Theater an der Wien', *Illustrirtes Wiener Extrablatt*, 6 April 1893, p. 5.

Not to be outdone, the cover of the satirical Viennese newspaper *Der Floh* [*The Flea*] carried the heading 'Der Ausgleich nach Noten' [The Musical Compromise] over a cartoon showing Veselá and the tenor Georg Streitmann singing to one another before a bemused audience of well-dressed *Bürger*. Here we learn that 'er singt deutsch und sie singt czechisch und sie verstehen einander doch. Ach, Du lieber Sprachen- und Racengott, wenn die Völker im Verkehr untereinander nur singen wollten, anstatt zu sprechen — wie hübsch geschwind man da miteinander in's Reine käme!' [He sings in German and she sings in Czech and yet they understand one another. Ah, thou god of languages and races, if the peoples would only communicate by singing instead of speaking, how quickly they could sort things out with each other!].[36] Less humorous but more noteworthy in some respects were Teuber's comments: 'Das war gestern der dritte Akt des großen musikalischen Ausgleichsschauspieles, und nun sage man noch, der Wiener habe ein Vorurtheil und sei "unversöhnlich". Zuerst das freudenreiche Ausstellungsgastspiel, dann Smetana im Theater an der Wien, und nun unverfälschte czechische Worte auf deutschem Boden!' [Yesterday came the third act of the great musical compromise drama, and now let anyone say that the Viennese are prejudiced and 'irreconcilable'. First the joyous guest performance at the Exhibition, then Smetana at the Theater an der Wien, and now unadulterated Czech words on German soil!].[37] Teuber's readers in the *Fremden-Blatt* could scarcely have missed the ironic allusion made in this last line to *Unverfälschte Deutsche Worte* [*Unadulterated German Words*], the pan-German, anti-Semitic (and anti-Slavic) political organ that had been founded ten years earlier by the notorious Georg Ritter von Schönerer, the older brother of Alexandrine von Schönerer, the owner (and co-director) of the Theater an der Wien.

As *Die verkaufte Braut* neared the end of its run at the Theater an der Wien, the artistic reconciliation to which it had contributed threatened to unravel in the nearby Theater in der Josefstadt. There, on 1 May 1893, the Böhmische Volkstheater-Gesellschaft [Bohemian Popular Theatre Society], directed by Ladislav Chmelenský, opened a six-week guest season of Czech plays. First to be performed was Jan Nepomuk Štěpánek's *Čech a Němec* [*The Czech and the German*], a 'biedermeierliche Romeo-und-Julia Komödie' [Romeo-and-Juliet comedy set in the *Biedermeier* period], as Peter Lotar later described it, that concerns the efforts of a young Czech man and German woman to overcome their parents' animosity towards one another and marry.[38] The

---

[36] 'Der Ausgleich nach Noten', *Der Floh*, 9 April 1893, pp. 1–2.
[37] [Oscar Teuber], 'Theater und Kunst (Theater an der Wien)', *Fremden-Blatt*, 6 April 1893, p. 6.
[38] Peter Lotar, *Eine Krähe war mit mir* (Stuttgart, 1978), p. 205. Dvořák's *Domov můj* [*My Homeland*], in its first Viennese performance, was heard as a prelude; the ballet music from Smetana's comic opera *Dvě vdovy* [*The Two Widows*] and one of Dvořák's *Slavonic Dances* were presented as the entr'actes. See the announcement in 'Theater', *Wiener Zeitung*, 30 April 1893. This announcement erroneously suggests that the play had originally been performed in 1786 under the title *Der Bettelstudent*; in fact, *Čech a Němec* dates from 1816.

play itself may have been an historical comedy from a more innocent time, but in late-nineteenth-century Vienna its subject alone (not to speak of the introduction of the Czech language in a Viennese theatre) was enough to provoke a demonstration by radical *deutschnational* students, who disrupted the performance with hissing and whistling and were eventually removed from the theatre by security personnel.[39] A few days later, an unnamed pan-German critic, writing under the pseudonym Valentin Bröckerl, pointedly described the appearance of the Böhmische Volkstheater-Gesellschaft at the Theater in der Josefstadt as a 'provocation' that justified such protests — even while, in an admiring nod toward the ongoing performances of *Die verkaufte Braut* at the Theater an der Wien, he added: 'Aber ein vorzügliches Werk, ins Deutsche übersetzt und eben damit das Zugeständnis gemacht, wenn mir's bei Deutschen wohl sein soll, dann muß ich auch deutsch reden, ist ganz ein Anderes' [But it is something else again to translate a first-rate work into German and so to concede that, if you want to get on with Germans on their territory, you have to speak their language].[40] But this episode even caused the liberal *Neue Freie Presse* — now questioning the optimism it had shown a year earlier in anticipation of the residency by the Czech National Theatre — to respond with indignation of its own, not to the performances themselves, but to rumours that the press in Prague had urged Vienna's Czech population to respond in kind:

> Man hat es im vorigen Jahre nicht mit Unrecht als einen der schönsten Erfolge der Wiener Musik- und Theater-Ausstellung angesehen, daß es gelungen war, wenigstens auf Einem Gebiete, dem der Kunst, die österreichischen Nationalitäten einander näher zu bringen oder doch von den politischen Kämpfen und Gegensätzen absehen zu machen. [...] Wenn dieser Gewinn wieder verloren geht, so darf sich die czechische Presse rühmen, das Meiste dazu beigetragen zu haben. Man wird in Wien mit der Anerkennung czechischer Kunstleistungen vorsichtiger werden, wenn man befürchten muß, daß hieraus dem deutschen Charakter Wiens abträgliche Schlüsse gezogen werden. Man wird nicht mehr so unbefangen die czechische Sprache auf Wiener Bühnen vernehmen, wenn der Argwohn wachgerufen wird, daß damit nicht künstlerische, sondern nationale Zwecke verfolgt werden.[41]

> [Not without justification, it has been regarded as one of the big successes of last year's Viennese Exhibition of Music and Theatre that it managed, at least in one sphere, that of art, to effect a rapprochement of the national

---

[39] 'Locales (Scandal im Theater in der Josephstadt)', *Wiener Abendpost*, 2 May 1893, p. 6. This account is strikingly similar to those given in newspaper reports of an earlier disturbance by pan-German students of Dvořák's opera *The Cunning Peasant*, when this was given at the Court Opera in November 1886; see Brodbeck, 'Dvořák's Reception in Liberal Vienna', pp. 105–10.

[40] Valentin Bröckerl, *Ostdeutsche Rundschau*, 7 May 1893, pp. 5–6.

[41] 'Wien, 3. Mai', *Neue Freie Presse, Morgenblatt*, 4 May 1893, p. 1; this editorial is erroneously dated 9 May 1893 in Reittererová and Reitterer, *Vier Dutzend rothe Strümpfe ...*, p. 71.

groupings within Austria or rather to persuade them to put aside their political struggles and disagreements. If this gain is again lost, then the Czech press may congratulate itself on being largely responsible. People in Vienna will become more circumspect in praising Czech artistic achievements, if they fear that as a result derogatory conclusions will be drawn as to the German character of the city. People will cease to be quite so relaxed about hearing the Czech language on the Viennese stage if they begin to suspect that national rather than artistic agendas are being pursued.]

Indeed, the political chasm between Germans and Czechs seemed to be growing wider by the day. In the middle of May, Taaffe was forced to close the Bohemian *Landtag* that had opened only a few weeks earlier when the Young Czechs revolted against his efforts to carry out portions of the *Ausgleich* by decree. Weeks of violent street demonstrations followed, leading the government to impose martial law that summer throughout the Bohemian capital.[42] The Viennese performances of *The Bartered Bride* — first in the summer of 1892 and then again in the spring of 1893 — offered something of a respite from these political tensions, and it is no wonder that so many of the city's critics invoked the term *Ausgleich* in connection with them. But music could only go so far, and outside the theatre such compromise remained as elusive as ever.

---

[42] Lothar Höbelt, *Kornblume und Kaiseradler. Die deutschfreiheitlichen Parteien Altösterreichs 1882–1918* (Vienna and Munich, 1993), pp. 61–65.

Arnold Schoenberg's Wounded Work: 'Litanei' from the String Quartet in F sharp minor, Op. 10

DARLA M. CRISPIN

Orpheus Research Centre in Music, Ghent

'Die Wunde ist's, die nie sich schließen will'[1]

When read alongside the furore that greeted the première of Igor Stravinsky's *Le Sacre du Printemps* [*The Rite of Spring*] in 1913, the so-called 'scandal in the Bösendorfer Saal' of 1908 surrounding the première of Schoenberg's Second String Quartet in F sharp minor, Op. 10, has become a kind of complementary cultural signifier of the dysfunctional nature of musical Modernism in surveys of twentieth-century music history.[2] It may be tempting to read into the two incidents a pattern of common underlying discontents, with their origins emerging from similar causes, but this shorthand needs to be evaluated more critically. Newspaper accounts of the Schoenberg *Skandalkonzert* reveal a more complex picture, especially when viewed in the light of Karl Kraus's trenchant critique of the Viennese press of the time.[3] It is necessary therefore to explore more deeply the diverse nature of Schoenberg's Viennese audience and his relationship to it, and to consider again how his own short- and long-term reactions to this particular moment of crisis — in a life riven with crises — reveal ambivalence in his own thinking. Above all, it is important to understand how this work embodies in a very particular and pointed way Schoenberg's complex and often refractory interior dialectic with both the ideas and the musical language of Wagner's music dramas, especially *Parsifal*.

To recount the outward events of the scandal briefly: the Rosé Quartet gave the first performance of Schoenberg's Second String Quartet in F sharp minor on 21 December 1908 in Vienna's Bösendorfer Saal, with the 'Litanei' [Litany] and 'Entrückung' [Transport] movements that incorporate texts by

---

[1] Gurnemanz in Richard Wagner, *Parsifal*, Act I: 'This wound it is that will never close', quoted from the edition in the Dover Full Scores series (New York, 1986), pp. 76–77.

[2] See, for example, one of the 'war-horses' of historical pedagogy, Donald Jay Grout and Claude V. Palisca, *A History of Western Music*, 5th edn (New York and London, 1996), p. 723.

[3] See Edward Timms, *Karl Kraus. Apocalyptic Satirist*, 2 vols (New Haven, CT and London, 1986 and 2005), I: *Culture and Catastrophe in Habsburg Vienna*, in which the social contexts for Kraus's satirical work are explored in depth.

Stefan George sung by the soprano Marie Gutheil-Schoder.[4] While the pro- and contra-Schoenberg claques that had formed prior to the performance maintained an uneasy peace until the end of the first movement (which the daily *Fremden-Blatt* reported the next day as 'für eine Schoenberg-Komposition ziemlich zahm klingend' [sounding rather tame for a Schoenberg composition]), the situation soon deteriorated, with the second movement being punctuated by peals of laughter.[5] It was the vocal movements, however, that generated particular indignation, with the conclusion of 'Litanei' being greeted with calls to stop the performance. These came not only from the apparently non-comprehending 'public', but also from at least one generally accepted member of the cognoscenti, the critic Ludwig Karpath. The performance could only be completed after lengthy hostilities and provoked such unrest that the reviewer Dr Elsa Bienenfeld was led to conclude: 'Es war unmöglich, von dem jüngst aufgeführten Streichquartett Arnold Schoenbergs irgendeinen Eindruck zu gewinnen, da die bübischen Störungen eine zitternde Erregung im ganzen Saal verbreitet hatten, so daß von einem Deutlichwerden und Ausklingen der Stimmungen nicht die Rede sein konnte' [it was impossible to get any impression whatever of Arnold Schoenberg's recently performed String Quartet, for the knavish interruptions had spread a trembling agitation throughout the whole hall, so that there could be no question of the moods becoming clear, and still less of cohesion].[6]

Significantly, the earliest accounts of the concert were to be found not in the review sections of the Viennese press, but in the local daily news reportage. These were then followed by critical commentaries, which appeared sporadically for approximately three weeks after the concert. The *Skandalkonzert* has since been canonized within musicological literature, mainly through early writings by Schoenberg's students, which recall the affair in a manner that, unsurprisingly, articulates a markedly pro-Schoenberg stance.[7] Thus, at each of these stages of presentation, evaluation tends to be clouded by bias. It is helpful to study examples which illustrate how the ostensibly neutral 'news reports' tend to generate a contextual undercurrent of negative criticism, followed a few days later by the 'reviews', in which the commentators generally remain consistent with the critical stance of the earlier accounts (i.e. they adhere to

---

[4] This account is drawn from newspaper columns collated in *Schoenberg, Berg, Webern. Die Streichquartette der Wiener Schule. Eine Dokumentation*, ed. by Ursula von Rauchhaupt (Munich, [1972]) and in the same editor's English version of the volume, *The String Quartets. A Documentary Study* (Hamburg, 1971), abbreviated as SBW/G and SBW/E. While viewpoints about the meaning of the events diverge widely from column to column, accounts of the progression of events themselves remain fairly consistent.

[5] SBW/G, p. 148; SBW/E, p. 142; originally in *Fremden-Blatt*, Vienna, 22 December 1908, headed 'Lärmszenen im Konzertsaal' [Tumult in the Concert Hall].

[6] SBW/G, p. 153; SBW/E, p. 147; originally in the *Neues Wiener Journal*, 25 December 1908.

[7] See, for example, Willi Reich, *Schoenberg. A Critical Biography* (London, 1971), pp. 34–39.

editorial policy). These are then countered later by no less partisan anecdotal remembrances which neatly reinforce the 'fated man' motif of Schoenberg's artistic self-image.

One of the earliest and most vitriolic diatribes against Schoenberg and his Op. 10, in the *Neues Wiener Tagblatt*, is initially presented as 'news':

> Unsere Leser sind gewöhnt, über Ereignisse, die sich im Konzertsaale abspielen, im Kunstteile des Blattes informiert zu werden. Diesmal sind wir gezwungen, den Kammermusikabend des Quartetts Rosé, mindestens was einen Teil des Programms betrifft, an dieser, den lokalen Vorkommnissen gewidmeten Stelle zu besprechen, weil es sich eben nur um einen 'lokalen', nicht künstlerischen Vorfall handelt.

> [Our readers are accustomed to finding reports on events in the concert hall on the arts page of this paper. This time we are forced to discuss the chamber music concert by the Rosé Quartet, at least so far as part of the programme is concerned, here in the local news section, because the incident in question is of a 'local', and not artistic nature.][8]

The objective masking of the 'report' is then completely dropped in favour of a strong denunciation of the Quartet, and of Schoenberg:

> Das, was sich gestern abends zwischen 8 und 9 Uhr im Bösendorfersaale ereignete, *ist einzig in der Geschichte des Wiener Konzertlebens: es kam zu einem regelrechten Skandal während der Aufführung einer Komposition, deren Urheber auch schon mit andern Erzeugnissen öffentliches Ärgernis erregt hatte.* Aber so arg wie gestern hat er es noch nie getrieben. *Man glaubte eine veritable Katzenmusik zu vernehmen.*

> [What occurred between 8 and 9 yesterday evening in the Bösendorfer Saal is unique in the history of concert activities in Vienna: there was a full-fledged scandal during the performance of a composition whose author has already caused a public nuisance with others of his products. But he ha(s) never gone so far as he did yesterday. It sounded like a convocation of all the neighbourhood cats.][9]

Karl Kraus deemed such masking of opinion under the guise of reportage to be ripe for exposure through the means of satire. He saw the formal disguise as being ethically suspect, and demolished it through employing its own devices.[10] He attacked the various excesses of the Viennese press: its insidious insider knowledge, its hypocrisy and its emphasis on middle-class upward mobility. His writing has remarkable similarities to Schoenberg's musical

---

[8] SBW/G, pp. 148–49; SBW/E, pp. 142–43; originally in the *Neues Wiener Tagblatt*, 22 December 1908.

[9] SBW/G, p. 149; SBW/E, p. 143; emphases in the original.

[10] One of Kraus's favourite satirical tactics is to present re-readings of articles in which the editorial voice of the satirized publication is adopted, only to be eroded through a series of asides or 'glosses' which call into question the ethical stance of the original. See Timms, *Karl Kraus*, I, especially the chapter 'Literary Style and Histrionic Temperament: The Paradox of the True Mask', pp. 169–87.

project. Just as Schoenberg reviled habitual, non-discriminating concert-going, Kraus laid bare the daily ritual of reading the paper. Of necessity, both waged their campaigns as outsiders.

In Schoenberg's case, critically charged devices — such as exposing the incongruity of form in the light of unorthodox content, the juxtaposition of traditional genre and progressive musical language, and the inclusion of text in the String Quartet in F sharp minor, Op. 10 — were all marshalled and presented without the ameliorating mask of phantasmagoria.[11] Thus the hostile reaction to the work in a Viennese environment rife with pre-war anxieties begins to reveal deeper social and ethical frailties. In turn, one begins to understand more deeply the affinity that Schoenberg felt with Kraus; he evidently viewed their respective campaigns against their countrymen's misuse of language (whether verbal or musical) as originating in similar moral standpoints.[12]

It is not that the writers of newspaper columns or the other members of the Viennese cultural scene were oblivious to the masks that Kraus so assiduously demolished. In fact, there is an almost morbid sensitivity to the dichotomies revealed; it is not surprising that masking, unmasking and the power of the gaze are important tropes of the visual art of the time.[13] Given this highly sensitized cultural environment, the concert hall itself became a loaded cultural signifier, linking musical propriety and ethical deportment with an idealized and sadly mourned past, as the statement about the conclusion of the *Skandalkonzert* in the *Neues Wiener Tagblatt* reveals: 'Im Foyer stand verzweifelt Ludwig Bösendorfer, der so enorm viel auf Anstand und Würde in seinem Saale hält. Einer seiner Freunde rief ihm zu: "Jetzt wird Beethoven gespielt werden, lassen Sie doch vorher den Saal lüften!"' [In the foyer stood a despairing Ludwig Bösendorfer, for whom proper behaviour and dignity in his concert hall mean such a great deal. One of his friends called out to him, 'They are going to play Beethoven

---

[11] See the chapter 'Phantasmagoria', in Theodor W. Adorno, *In Search of Wagner* (London, 1991), pp. 85–96. Adorno's reading of Schoenberg's atonal music as being devoid of phantasmagorical masking is one of his principal arguments for the ethical validity of this music.

[12] See Nicholas Cook, 'Schenker's Theory of Music as Ethics', originally published in *The Journal of Musicology*, 7 (1989), 415–39, and reprinted in his *Music, Performance, Meaning. Selected Essays* (Aldershot, 2007), pp. 57–81. Cook makes a convincing case that not only Schoenberg, but also Schenker and Loos, were influenced by Kraus's view that given 'the alienation of appearance from reality, personal integrity was the supreme, or even the only possible, ethical goal' (pp. 66–67).

[13] In 1912, Herwarth Walden opened his Berlin art gallery, *Der Sturm*, as an extension of the publishing house of the same name, which he had founded in 1910. *Der Sturm* was important in publicizing European avant-garde trends. The Belgian painter James Ensor, whose canvases feature grotesque faces behind equally grotesque masks, had works exhibited there near the end of 1912. See *Concepts of Modern Art*, ed. by Nikos Stangos (London, 1981), p. 37. Schoenberg's own visual artworks frequently depict 'gazes' or 'stares'; his 1910 painting, 'The Red Stare', is a particularly vivid example. See Carl E. Schorske, *Fin-de-Siècle Vienna. Politics and Culture* (New York, 1981), p. 324 and Plate x.

now. You had better have the hall aired!'].¹⁴ Thus, there is a sense in which the concert hall assumes a sacred aura, with Schoenberg's music heard as desecrating the aural norms and mores of a space such as this, which has been defined quintessentially by the canonical Austro-German composers and their works. In this context, Schoenberg's adaptation of the genre of the string quartet may also be read as a challenge to that which is most sacred in music, in this case, the sacred as epitomized by Beethoven's canonical works in this genre. Whatever the case, the significance of the quip was not lost on Schoenberg, who notes: 'This cry for some air in the Bösendorfer Saal re-echoed through the entire provincial press.'¹⁵

It is not surprising, therefore, that another form of attack by the reviewers was to compare aspects of the performance to perverse rituals; in the *Neues Wiener Tagblatt*, the general description of the work as sounding 'like a convocation of all the neighbourhood cats' is soon followed by an account of the 'Hexentanz des dritten Satzes' [Witches' Sabbath of the third movement].¹⁶ As well as being a sideswipe at Hector Berlioz (and, by extension, at the supposedly inferior world of French music when compared with Austro-German exemplars), this allusion draws attention to the presence of the soprano in the work. By reason of her unauthorized and transgressively articulate presence within the sacred genre of the string quartet (a genre traditionally associated with logic, with the abstract and the absolute, in both compositional and performance terms, and therefore with the 'masculine' realm), Gutheil-Schoder 'embodies' the witch of the critique. Through her insinuation of incongruous verbal language into a traditionally 'absolute' instrumental genre, she casts a degenerating spell. To make matters even more complex, Gutheil-Schoder is portrayed in some of the reviews as being stripped of freedom of choice in this situation; there is a sense in which she is viewed as forfeiting the esteem in which she had previously been held for ignominy: 'Inzwischen war Frau *Gutheil-Schoder* aufs Podium getreten. Ihre Aufgabe war es, den vokalen Teil der Kakophonien auszuführen' [In the meantime, Frau *Gutheil-Schoder* had come on to the stage. It was her task to perform the vocal part of the cacophony].¹⁷ Another review comments that Marie Gutheil-Schoder, 'die die Worte sang, stand auf dem Podium, den Szenen preisgegeben; und sang weinend weiter' [who sang the words, stood on the stage exposed to these scenes, and sang on, weeping].¹⁸ She becomes, like Kundry in *Parsifal*, forced to action through malign enchantment. This points up, albeit in a negative manner, the important possibility of re-reading the vocal movements of Op. 10 in light of the music and ideas of Wagner.

---

¹⁴ SBW/G, p. 149; SBW/E, p. 143.
¹⁵ 'A Legal Question' (1909), in *Style and Idea. Selected Writings of Arnold Schoenberg*, ed. by Leonard Stein with translations by Leo Black (London, 1984), p. 188.
¹⁶ SBW/G, p. 149; SBW/E, p. 143.
¹⁷ Ibid.
¹⁸ SBW/G, p. 147; SBW/E, p. 141; originally in *Arnold Schoenberg zum fünfzigsten Geburtstag*, a special issue of *Musikblätter des Anbruch* (1924), p. 320.

The 'Litanei' movement held a particular fascination for Theodor W. Adorno, who placed it at a seminal point in Schoenberg's musical development. In the final paragraph of his book *In Search of Wagner*, he equates Tristan's dark 'fever music' from Act III with the phantasmagorical rupture which he believes that the Schoenbergian musical language represents. Adorno writes:

> Die Fieberpartien des dritten Aktes Tristan enthalten jene schwarze, schroffe, gezackte Musik, die nicht sowohl die Vision untermalt als demaskiert. Musik, die zauberischste aller Künste, lernt den Zauber brechen, den sie selber um alle ihre Gestalten legt. Die Verfluchung der Minne durch Tristan ist mehr als das ohnmächtige Opfer des Rausches an die Askese: sie ist die sei's auch ganz vergebliche Auflehnung der Musik gegen den eigenen Schicksalszwang, und erst im Angesicht ihrer totalen Determination durch jenen gewinnt sie die Selbstbesinnung wieder. Mit Grund stehen jene Figuren der Tristanpartitur nach den Worten 'der furchtbare Trank' an der Schwelle der Neuen Musik, in deren erstem kanonischen Werk, Schönbergs fis-moll Quartett, die Worte erscheinen: 'Nimm mir die Liebe, gib mir dein Glück!' Sie sagen, daß Liebe und Glück falsch sind in der Welt, in der wir leben, und daß alle Gewalt der Liebe übergegangen ist an ihr Gegenteil. Wer es aber vermöchte, den übertäubenden Wogen des Wagnerschen Orchesters solches Metall zu entreißen, dem vermöchte sein veränderter Klang zu dem Trost zu verhelfen, den es trotz Rausch und Phantasmagorie beharrlich verweigert. Indem es die Angst des hilflosen Menschen ausspricht, könnte es den Hilflosen, wie immer schwach und verstellt, Hilfe bedeuten, und aufs neue versprechen, was der uralte Einspruch der Musik versprach: Ohne Angst Leben.
>
> [The feverish passages in Act III of *Tristan* contain that black, abrupt, jagged music which instead of underlining the vision unmasks it. Music, the most magical of all the arts, learns how to break the spell it casts over the characters. When Tristan curses love, this is more than the impotent sacrifice offered up by rapture to asceticism. It is the rebellion — futile though it may be — of the music against the iron laws that rule it, and only in its total determination by those laws can it regain the power of self-determination. It is not for nothing that those phrases in the *Tristan* score which follow the words, 'Der furchtbare Trank' ('that potion so dread') stand on the threshold of modern music in whose first canonic work, Schoenberg's F♯ minor quartet, we find the words, 'Nimm mir die Liebe, gib mir dein Glück!' (Take love from me, give me your happiness). They mean that love and happiness are false in the world in which we live, and that the whole power of love has passed over into its antithesis. Anyone able to snatch such gold from the deafening surge of the Wagnerian orchestra, would be rewarded by its altered sound, for it would grant him that solace which, for all its rapture and phantasmagoria, it consistently refuses. By voicing the fears of helpless people, it could signal help for the helpless, however feebly and distortedly. In doing so it would renew the promise contained in the age-old protest of music: the promise of a life without fear.][19]

[19] Theodor W. Adorno, 'Versuch über Wagner', in *Gesammelte Schriften*, ed. by Rolf Tiedemann, 20 vols (Frankfurt a. M., 1971–86), XIII: *Die musikalischen Monographien* (1977), ed.

Adorno's reading poses some almost insuperable problems. Does Tristan's experience of truth in delirium, and our experience of the truth content within his chromatic melody, really stand up to the return of Isolde and her final 'star number' — the aforementioned 'Liebestod' [love-death]? And what about Schoenberg's own will to control in 'Litanei'? Schoenberg conceived of variation form as 'a very strict form' in which freedom is 'absolutely to be forbidden'.[20] As it happens, Schoenberg acknowledges his indebtedness to Wagner's leitmotif techniques in his notes on the 'Litanei' movement, even though, by his own admission, his settings tend to be more instinctive:

> In a perfect amalgamation of music with a poem, the form will follow the outline of the text. The Leitmotif technique of Wagner has taught us how to vary such motifs and other phrases, so as to express every change of mood and character in a poem. Thematic unity and logic thus sustained, the finished product will not fail to satisfy a formalist's requirements.[21]

Seemingly in accordance with the above strictures, the 'Litanei' movement opens with the Quartet's principal motivic fragments laid out with surgical precision. The first of these is the work's opening theme, which is now enharmonically recast so that the F sharp minor of the Quartet as a whole becomes G flat major. This transformation to major is remarkable in that the normally affirmative character of the major key is drained away from the music via the increasingly chromatic content and the vicissitudes of the vocal part, not to mention the clash between the major modality and the substance of the poetry, which is unremittingly *Angst*-ridden. This alteration of roles is emphasized by the second motif, the semitone fluctuation, presented in both the first violin and cello parts. This motif acts as a signifier at crucial moments in the music, and is also shorthand for chromaticism itself. The presentation of the 'Litanei' movement as enharmonically linked with the first movement's F sharp minor emphasizes this further.

Schoenberg sets the 'Litanei' movement within the framework of a theme and variations. Though initially hard to perceive as such, this underlying structure does yield to repeated listening and analysis. Of particular interest here is Schoenberg's admonition that in variation form freedom is 'absolutely to be forbidden'. He further elaborates on this idea: 'I was afraid the great dramatic emotionality of the poem might cause me to surpass the borderline of what should be admitted in chamber music. I expected the serious elaboration required by variation would keep me from becoming too dramatic.'[22] There

---

by Gretel Adorno and Rolf Tiedemann, p. 145, translated as *In Search of Wagner*, trans. by Rodney Livingstone (London, 1981), p. 156. See also John Deathridge, 'Wagner and the Post-Modern', *Cambridge Opera Journal*, 4 (1992), 143–61. This reading of Adorno's text necessitates a re-evaluation of its application to Schoenberg's music.

[20] Robert U. Nelson, 'Schoenberg's Variation Seminar', *The Musical Quarterly*, 50 (1964), 141–64 (p. 142).

[21] SBW/G, p. 48; SBW/E, p. 47.

[22] Ibid.

is a peculiar paradox in Schoenberg's employment of variation within this movement, since it is variation at the micro-logical level that makes the large-scale variation form so difficult to discern; thus, the hegemony of the movement's formal diktat is undermined by its own paradigmatic rhetoric. The spare presentation of motivic fragments *as* theme imbues them with an almost iconic character — an iconography which relates not to extramusical content, but to the history of the work as a whole. The motifs escape association with the concrete. Indeed, Schoenberg takes as a *fait accompli* what Wagner appears to strive towards, the escape of the motif from literal meaning through the process of variation within a musical grammar that it saturates.

Given the strength of his post-*Tristan* convictions, Adorno's failure to refer to Wagner's *Parsifal* in connection with the 'Litanei' movement seems odd. Extraordinary twists emerge when the movement is read alongside *Parsifal*, aspects of which Stefan George's text so closely shadows. Wagner highlights the repetition trope in the 'Liebesmahl' [love feast], which culminates in the revelation of the Grail. Repetition of this event is necessary for the preservation of order in a world in which, as Gurnemanz says at the end of Act I, scene 1, 'Zum Raum wird hier die Zeit' [Here time becomes space].[23] This iconization of time may be read as an end to music itself, since music only exists in 'real' time. The world of Monsalvat, in its extolling of stasis, is thereby incompatible with the world of 'real' time. Within this world, it is Amfortas's dereliction of his ritual duties that threatens to expose the Order to the vicissitudes of this 'real' time. Because of this, the already disembodied voice of Titurel is silenced in a kind of musical patricide. Denied the transubstantiative nourishment of the ritual, Titurel expires; his time — and his kind of music — is over. Schoenberg, like Wagner before him, seems fascinated by the negative potential of this iconicized time; variation is one way in which he can explore this idea. It becomes a part of his progressive agenda, the idea that the link between tonal and temporal imperatives might be broken down.

With the first vocal entry in 'Litanei', G flat is fleetingly reconfirmed, linking the affect of the text's 'deep sadness' ('Tief ist die Trauer, die mich umdüstert' [Deep is the sadness that makes me melancholy]) with the movement's core sonority.[24] Taken with the line that follows, 'Ein tret ich wieder, Herr! In dein Haus' [I enter once again, Lord! Into your house],[25] one recalls the despair of Amfortas, both because of the agonies he experiences as a result of his guilt and woundedness, and because of his increasing resistance to the repetitive ritual which brings him face-to-face with his sin at the precise moment of

---

[23] Wagner, *Parsifal*, Act I, p. 144. This is Gurnemanz's attempt to explain the temporality of the world of Monsalvat to Parsifal, who remains disoriented and unable fully to comprehend the import of the statement at this stage in the drama.

[24] Arnold Schoenberg, *String Quartet II, F sharp minor, Op. 10*, 'Litanei', text: Stefan George, quoted from the Universal Edition score (Vienna and London, 1921; new edn Los Angeles, CA, 1940), Bars 14–15, p. 36.

[25] Schoenberg, 'Litanei', Bars 16–17, p. 36.

ritual religious ecstasy. Amfortas's denial of repetition becomes a central point of the drama; his yearning for a freedom beyond ritual is an abnegation of responsibility that brings him into direct conflict with his father's disembodied voice. It also signifies the potential extinction of the old order, and as such is fiercely resisted by its members, who feed on the continuity of the *status quo*.

Amfortas bemoans his losses, as he has previously bemoaned the loss of the spear, having returned to the Order not only wounded, but also empty-handed. In George's 'Litanei', a similar loss is outlined in 'leer sind die Schreine, voll nur die Qual' [empty are the coffers, but full my pain].[26] Implied here is the idea of literal and spiritual bankruptcy. What follows is the longing for the communion feast of wine and bread, an echo of the 'Liebesmahl' of Monsalvat. George again refers the reader to what is remembered; empty-handedness is recalled (literally, 'hohl sind die Hände'), as is the feverishness that results ('fiebernd der Mund'). The references to extremes of hot and cold, to feverishness and coolness, are strikingly evocative of Amfortas's wretchedness; Gurnemanz recounts the event of the wounding: 'doch eine Wunde brannt' ihm in der Seite: die Wunde ist's, die nie sich schließen will' [a wound burned him in his side, this wound it is that will never close].[27] As in George's poem, Amfortas's longing for remedy is linked with the *abnegation* of hope. In Act I (as is also implied in 'Litanei'), his hope is not totally shaken; he does perform the ritual (although under considerable pressure) and prays fervently for remedy and absolution. The irony is, of course, that at the height of religious ecstasy, his woundedness, his fall, is at the very centre of the ritual; the light of the Grail, its very being, forces attention upon the wound at the same instant that it is supposed to exalt purity. Insofar as both the Grail vessel and the wound have lips and are filled with blood, there is a macabre blurring of boundaries between them. If the wound signifies a threat to both Amfortas and the body politic, then the failure of the ritual to heal signifies the infection of the ritual and its impedimenta. The equation of this state with the agonies of love, Parsifal's masterly insight, becomes a resistance to the body, and anything within the ritual that signifies embodiment. Amfortas and Kundry become vocally extinct in the final ritual, and Kundry's otherness, both sexual and ethnic, is expunged through death.

In 'Litanei' the final emphasis is quite different; the problem of woundedness is left unresolved. Adorno's analysis does not expose the significance of this. Though he has referred to the text 'Nimm mir die Liebe, gib mir dein Glück' [Take love from me, give me your happiness], he has omitted the line that George wrote preceding this, which is 'Schliesse die Wunde' [Close the wound].[28] Of course, we hear this same text in Amfortas's Lament in the first Act of *Parsifal*; moreover, the crux of the opera in Act II is the recollection of

---

[26] Ibid., Bars 22–26, p. 37.
[27] Wagner, *Parsifal*, Act I, pp. 76–77.
[28] Schoenberg, 'Litanei', Bars 63–69, p. 43 and Bars 61–62, p. 42.

Amfortas's agony by Parsifal, his specific memory of and identification with Amfortas's woundedness, and his resulting escape from Kundry's seduction and consequent redemption of the Grail Order, which had been weakened by Amfortas's surrender to Kundry. Interestingly, both Amfortas in the opera and George in his poem propose a kind of cosmic bargain: Amfortas cries out 'Nimm mir mein Erbe, schliesse die Wunde' [Take my birthright, close the wound],[29] while George's poem has the text: 'Schliesse die Wunde, nimm mir die Liebe, gib mir dein Glück' [Close the wound, take love from me, give me your happiness].[30] If Adorno's reading of the rupture of the phantasmagorical still holds true, and if we read Parsifal's final healing of Amfortas as a healing of that rupture, then the iteration of the text within Schoenberg's 'Litanei' might well simultaneously recall both rupture and healing, neutralizing somewhat the hope for humanism implicit in Adorno's reading of the truth content, the foregoing of the 'happy ending'. In 'Litanei', solace is proposed, what Adorno goes so far as to call 'the promise of a life without fear'.[31] But promise is not the same as fulfilment.

The continuation of 'Litanei' compounds the interpretative problem. In bars 65 to 66, the soprano's dizzying leap on the word 'Liebe' [love] might imply, as Adorno states, the falsity of love in the abyss-like expanse of the leap. It may also be relevant to recall the disastrous state of Schoenberg's personal life around this time.[32] Yet the soprano actually spans the interval through the process of singing, joining the two distant notes with her breath and voice; thus, her ability to heal the rift is contingent upon virtuosity. Again, this seems to contradict Adorno's reading, both in the implicit vocal healing of the 'truthful woundedness', and of the implication that technique might be the agency of that healing, especially since so much of the phantasmagoric which Adorno decries is also associated with excellent technique. Yet, the vocal leap in question is from C natural to B natural, and thus spans only a semitone, given octave equivalences; however, it is difficult to deny that the vicissitudes of post-Romantic harmony result, in part, from the chromaticism implied by just such a semitone.

There is yet another extraordinary twist to this section.[33] This disjunct setting of 'Liebe' also recalls another pivotal moment in *Parsifal*, that of Kundry's confession that she laughed at Christ on the cross. In the opera, on the word 'lachte', her leap is from B natural to C sharp, so whilst the intervallic complement of the leaps does differ, both are 'deformed' octaves — one shrunk by a

---

[29] Wagner, *Parsifal*, Act I, pp. 189–90.
[30] Schoenberg, 'Litanei', Bars 61–69, pp. 42–43.
[31] Adorno, *In Search of Wagner*, p. 156.
[32] A well-written account of Richard Gerstl's affair with Schoenberg's first wife, Matilde, and Gerstl's eventual suicide, can be found in Jane Kallir, *Arnold Schoenberg's Vienna* (New York, 1984), pp. 24–28.
[33] I am indebted to John Deathridge for pointing out the additional reference to Kundry in this section.

semitone, the other stretched by a tone. The gestural intensity, and associated instrumental silences, of these two moments creates a strong aural link between them.

How does this affect one's hermeneutic strategy? Certainly, the allusion to Kundry at the conceptual core of the String Quartet must completely alter one's focus. Kundry, a Jewess, is condemned to wandering in enslavement until she is redeemed by a pure hero who rejects her. In *Parsifal*, Kundry's fallen state means that even her gesture of penance, the bringing of balsam to Amfortas, fails to heal the wound; she is both wounded, and an agent of woundedness. It is Parsifal who is to redeem Kundry by rejecting her, thereby healing Amfortas. The physical medium of that healing is that same sacred spear which Amfortas lost to Klingsor as a result of Kundry's seduction, and which Klingsor uses to inflict Amfortas's wound. It is the same spear with which Christ was wounded on the cross. Thus Kundry's laughter is inextricably associated with woundedness, while the whole of George's poem as it appears in the Quartet could be read as an analogue to Amfortas's prayer, with its references to the sacrament of bread and wine, and a fervent wish for healing. Its final line encapsulates Kundry's hope of salvation: the obtaining of happiness through the abnegation of love.

How does this relate to Schoenberg? His conversion to Lutheran Protestantism in 1898 meant that he consciously distanced himself from his Jewish origins, associating himself with a doctrine outside the Austrian state religion, Roman Catholicism. The redemption of Kundry is a redemption that he wills for himself, and for which he strives via the mastery of a Wagnerian musical language in a self-directed transmogrification through the medium of German music as manifested in that paradigmatic genre, the string quartet. Furthermore, the final movements of this Quartet move not into the realm of *Lieder*, but into monodrama. They belong to the world of *Erwartung* [*Expectation*, 1909] and *Die glückliche Hand* [*The Fortunate Hand*, 1910–13], in which Schoenberg challenged Wagner on his own hallowed ground — music drama. The connection with *Erwartung* is a literal one: the interval of 'Kundry's laughter' is replicated in the monodrama at the crucial point of the nameless Woman's descent into complete hysteria, with her cry of 'Hilfe!' [Help!]. As with the comparable points in *Parsifal* and Op. 10, the crisis is punctuated by silence.

'Erlösung dem Erlöser' [For the Redeemer redemption] we hear in the massed choruses as *Parsifal* draws to a close.[34] The final repetition of this phrase, high in a disembodied soprano voice, closes with a perfect A flat octave descent, and Kundry's dissonant laugh recedes into memory. Thus redeemed, she sinks down lifeless as Parsifal completes the Grail sacrament; for Schoenberg it could be 'a consummation devoutly to be wished'. Yet, the Quartet movement continues with the setting of 'gib mir dein Glück!', which also generates questions. It is a modified return to material from the opening

---

[34] Wagner, *Parsifal*, Act III, pp. 584–87.

bars of the first movement, creating a sense of large-scale recapitulation. This time, however, the material is heard three semitones lower. There is also a crucial change in the disposition of the parts; the stable tonal centre of the first movement is removed from the cello bass line and replaced by an inversion of material from the viola heard in the opening bar of the first movement, thus creating a descending bass line comprising two pairs of semitones. As a commentary on this and the soprano's 'false leap' discussed above, the vocal line takes over the material of the first violin in the opening of the Quartet, and replaces the violin's whole-tone phrase, ending with a semitone on the words 'dein Glück' (first movement, Bar 2). Given the irony implicit in such a shift, Adorno's reading regains much of its resonance, and Schoenberg's encounter with Wagner remains highly problematic.

One could question Adorno's humanistic reading of the Quartet Op. 10 in the light of the few available sketches for the work. Significantly, these show that the order of the 'Litanei' and 'Entrückung' movements was originally reversed. This makes much more sense programmatically, since the 'Qual' [torment] of 'Litanei' is extinguished in the musical otherworld of 'Entrückung', but it dampens the force of the humanistic reading implied by ending the work with 'Litanei'. However, there may be a more fundamental reading of this change of order; if one regards 'Litanei' as a kind of précis of *Parsifal*, and 'Entrückung' as the same for *Tristan und Isolde*, particularly the 'Liebestod', then Schoenberg's reversal of order becomes a musical challenge to the spiritual or ethical 'solutions' of *Parsifal*. If Schoenberg concluded, as Nietzsche seems to have done, that *Parsifal* and *Tristan* were antithetically related, then the exchange of the world of Monsalvat for a return to Isolde's 'Liebestod', within the string quartet genre, needs to be explored.

Schoenberg reverses the polarity of the Wagnerian *Tristan–Parsifal* relationship. Despite the association of his serial music with completely abstract realms (an association with which he himself vehemently disagreed), Schoenberg seems ultimately mistrustful of a musico-historical solution that posits the renunciation of earthly love for a world of ascetic spiritualism, the premise of *Parsifal*. Indeed, the entire plot of his monodrama *Die glückliche Hand* revolves around an artist figure who wishes to remain within the sphere of human experience and relationships whilst reaching the highest levels of creativity. Most of Schoenberg's works do explore the apparent impossibility of reconciling the two worlds, but the abnegation of human experience is not his solution. Instead, he explores the necessity of the struggle itself.

Instead of overwhelming the singer, the Quartet is given voice by her. That this occurs in a manner that is structurally coherent within the whole work reminds the listener of Schoenberg's (and Adorno's) precepts on musical organicism. But perhaps even more significant is the manner in which the setting of text, particularly in the fourth movement, generates a new generic paradigm. The text here is, in fact, a commentary on the preceding music, heard in the instrumental introduction. The poetry is thus not set to music in the traditional sense of an interpretative act; rather, the words are used as a means of presentation, of representation. The text 'pronounces' the ideas of the music, explains in poetic images what is going on compositionally; the text is a commentary on the music and its historical position: self-reflectivity as a truly modernist stance.[35]

But there is a final twist. In relation to absolute music and the string quartet stands Schoenberg's pride in the hegemony of this mainly Austro-German music, alongside his growing awareness of its imminent demise. Later, he would be forced to grapple with the idea of being rendered both homeless and speechless by the German nation. Already, at the time of the String Quartet, Op. 10, it seems that, for him, the issue of the text or the word goes far beyond a question of linguistic integrity to a Hegelian view in which the absoluteness of music becomes a theological construct: the absolute equals God, a God manifested in the expression of the absolute. Yet Schoenberg's consistent iteration throughout his life and work of the theme of redemption through the exertion and, finally, the denial of the Will actually points to the metaphysics of Schopenhauer. Musically, this tends to create not an arrival at the absolute, but a circular dance with it, culminating in a series of compositional paradoxes and aporias — incomplete works confounded by memory, and works in which, as here in the Quartet, Op. 10, textual content and musical rhetoric appear both interdependent and in conflict with one another.

---

[35] See Reinhold Brinkmann, 'Schoenberg's Quartets and the Viennese Tradition', in *Music of My Future. The Schoenberg Quartets and Trio*, ed. by Reinhold Brinkmann and Christoph Wolff, Isham Library Papers, 5 (Cambridge, MA, and London, 2000), pp. 3–12 (p. 8).

Mahler's Farewell or The Earth's Song?
Death, Orientalism and 'Der Abschied'

ANDREW DERUCHIE

University of Ottawa

The story will be well known to readers familiar with Gustav Mahler's biography: in July 1907, a doctor summoned to tend to his ailing wife also examined the composer and discovered the fatal heart condition that would kill him less than four years later. The distraught Mahler sought solace in *Die chinesische Flöte* [*The Chinese Flute*, 1907], a volume of Chinese poems paraphrased in German by Hans Bethge, and the result was the song-symphony *Das Lied von der Erde* [*The Song of the Earth*, 1908–09]. Composed in the shadow of this terrifying blow, the work sounds a valedictory tone, 'permeated with the bitter taste of mortality', as Deryck Cooke observes.[1] Stephen Hefling has noted that four of its six movements (numbers 1, 2, 5, and 6) deal explicitly with the theme of death.[2] The colossal finale, 'Der Abschied' [The Farewell], with its dirge-like passages, central funeral-march episode, and dark C-minor tonality — the key of the Eroica Symphony's famous funeral march, of Siegfried's funeral music from the third act of Wagner's *Götterdämmerung* [*Twilight of the Gods*] and of the 'Todtenfeier' [Funeral Rites] movement of Mahler's own Second Symphony — has long been understood as a more or less autobiographical farewell to life, the 'gesture of a man ceremonially robing himself for the stately ritual of death', as Egon Gartenberg has put it.[3]

For virtually all writers who have cast a hermeneutic eye on the movement, its final section musically depicts the 'crossing of the doorstep to the beyond' (in Gartenberg's words) or the dissolution of the 'boundaries [...] between the living and the dead' (in Stuart Feder's).[4] Certain commentators, including Cooke and Constantin Floros, maintain that a sense of tragedy and loss continues to haunt here.[5] But the majority of recent critics take Mahler's finale to follow the trajectory from suffering to affirmation that had become virtually axiomatic for the symphonic genre in the nineteenth century: towards the conclusion, a radiant C-major tonality and a soaring, rapturous aria-like

[1] Deryck Cooke, *Gustav Mahler. An Introduction to His Music* (London, 1980), p. 105.
[2] Stephen E. Hefling, *Mahler. Das Lied von der Erde* (Cambridge, 2000), p. 81.
[3] Egon Gartenberg, *Mahler. The Man and His Music* (New York, 1978), p. 345.
[4] Ibid., and Stuart Feder, *Gustav Mahler. A Life in Crisis* (New Haven, CT, 2004), p. 149.
[5] Cooke, *Gustav Mahler*, p. 105; Constantin Floros, *Gustav Mahler. The Symphonies* (Portland, OR, 1997), pp. 262–69.

passage break through the C-minor gloom and dispel the funereal chill, before the texture gradually dissolves and the work ends in dulcet placidity. The final section, this interpretation holds, thereby expresses a vision of an exalted, ecstatic death, one that conforms squarely with the great romantic ethos epitomized by the conclusion of Wagner's *Tristan und Isolde* — and several critics have indeed posited rhetorical parallels between Mahler's radiant C-major passage and Isolde's famous 'Verklärung' [Transfiguration].[6] Hefling, Hermann Danuser, Donald Mitchell and Francesca Draughon have offered sustained readings along these lines.[7] Though the details of their accounts vary, they agree in their broad lines of argument. Mahler's music and the story line of the text are understood to unfold a drama of farewell and death rooted in western culture's archetypal plot of 'subjective becoming'. The final, glowing C-major aria here becomes the reunification or transfiguration of an ego fragmented by the gravest of existential crises and the subject's attainment of a transcendental state: death is conquered — 'death shall be no more; death thou shalt die', as Mitchell puts it — and this triumph marks the climax of the drama and the apotheosis of the subject.[8]

In what follows, I will propose that 'Der Abschied' is more concerned with the very epistemology of death than it is with enacting the death of the protagonist of its story line or expressing any individual's struggle with and triumph over an immanent demise. The piece, I hold, seeks an alternative to the attitudes toward death that prevailed in turn-of-the-century Europe, and it does so by appealing to the mythology of the ancient Chinese culture in which its texts originated, and which its celebrated musical exoticism invokes. The epistemology of death that the work projects, we shall see, is ideologically antithetical to the archetypal plot Hefling, Mitchell, Draughon and others have taken it to articulate. For it is one in which individual identity recedes into an all-encompassing totality of nature. The piece is not ultimately a drama of the subject's transfiguration or transcendence; indeed, it is not a drama of the subject at all. 'Der Abschied' in this respect prefigures Mahler's purely instrumental Ninth Symphony (composed a year after *Das Lied*), which, as Julian Johnson has elegantly shown, 'is not about the journey of any specific subject, but explores the conditions of subjectivity *sui generis*'.[9] In Johnson's

---

[6] See, for example, Hefling, *Mahler. Das Lied*, pp. 117–19; and Benjamin Britten's well-known letter of June 1937 to Henry Boys, in *Letters From a Life. The Selected Letters and Diaries of Benjamin Britten, 1913–1976*, ed. by Donald Mitchell, 3 vols (London, 1991), I, 339–40.

[7] Hefling, *Mahler. Das Lied*, pp. 103–19; Hermann Danuser, *Gustav Mahler. Das Lied von der Erde* (Munich, 1986), pp. 83–110; Donald Mitchell, *Gustav Mahler. Songs and Symphonies of Life and Death*, 2nd edn (Woodbridge, 2002), pp. 339–432; Francesca L. Draughon, 'Mahler and the Music of Fin-de-Siècle Identity' (unpublished doctoral thesis, University of California at Los Angeles, 2002), pp. 199–209.

[8] Mitchell, *Songs and Symphonies*, p. 410.

[9] Julian Johnson, 'The Status of the Subject in Mahler's Ninth Symphony', *19th-Century Music*, 18 (1994), 108–20 (p. 119).

analysis, coloured by Theodor Adorno's reading of Mahler's late style, the Ninth renounces dialectical synthesis of disparate elements and maintains unmediated dualities.[10] Contrary to nineteenth-century practice, musical form here no longer culminates in a *telos* that produces, or affirms the unity of, the intrinsic subject. The piece (especially its first and last movements) unfolds instead as a perpetual cycle: identities (themes, keys, and so on), temporary and fragile, are continually wrested from raw unstructured energies (which Johnson likens to the Nietzschean category of the Dionysian and Kristeva's 'semiotic chora'), which soon reclaim them. Although 'Der Abschied' retains the affirmative, teleological cast of the nineteenth-century symphony, central to the work's affiliation with Eastern thought, we shall see, is that Mahler's musico-poetic apparatus reconfigures the *telos* as the liquidation of the very *notion* of subjectivity. Moreover, and related to this, the work comes to subsume the individual subject's 'journey' — and death — within a broader rhythm of decay and regeneration that it identifies with eternal nature. This rhythm is embodied by a cyclical dimension in the piece's form, which coexists with the linear element and is perhaps even more pronounced here than in the outer movements of the Ninth.

Although it seems evident that *Das Lied* was bound up in the events of Mahler's life — he famously claimed of the work 'ich glaube, daß es wohl das Persönlichste ist, was ich bis jetzt gemacht habe' [I believe that it is the most personal thing I have yet created] — critics have perhaps kept the context too narrow by positioning the work primarily against its composer's biography.[11] Mahler's particular response to the crushing revelation that his days were numbered would also have reflected the social and cultural conditions of its historical moment. We shall therefore begin our account of 'Der Abschied' by taking a tour of the anthropological and cultural history of death in the century preceding its composition, highlighting that by the early twentieth century the act of dying had become alienating in ways it had not been just a few decades earlier. As a result, we shall see, the comforting romantic notions of ecstatic death that have featured so centrally in the reception of 'Der Abschied' came to seem like hopelessly lost ideals. And it was these new challenges to European attitudes and values that mandated Mahler's turn to the East and the thought of ancient China for a new way of coming to terms with death.

The influential historian of death Philippe Ariès calls the first two thirds of the nineteenth century 'The Age of the Beautiful Death'.[12] Although the attitudes, beliefs, and rituals surrounding death varied somewhat according to

---

[10] For Adorno's analysis of late Mahler, see his chapter 'The Long Gaze', in *Mahler. A Musical Physiognomy*, trans. by Edmund Jephcott (Chicago, IL, 1991), pp. 144–67.

[11] Gustav Mahler, *Briefe*, ed. by Herta Blaukopf, 2nd rev. edn (Vienna, 1996), p. 371 (letter of early September 1908 to Bruno Walter).

[12] See Philippe Ariès, *The Hour of Our Death*, trans. by Helen Weaver (New York, 1981), pp. 409–74.

geography, religious sensibilities and social class, Ariès observes a number of generalized cultural tendencies that cut across these categories and characterized the era. Europeans commonly viewed dying as an awesome, transcendental and even sublime act. The prevailing mythology held, as it had for centuries, that death offered repose and a desirable refuge from worldly turmoil. However, new notions of 'fraternal reunion' became folded into traditional Christian eschatology, and these made death a time for sincere happiness and even joy. To die was to enter, in Vladimir Jankélévitch's felicitous formulation, an 'anthropomorphic paradise'.[13] Death in the romantic era, Ariès elaborates, was characteristically viewed as a prelude to a great 'reunion [...] of all those who loved each other on earth, so that they prolong their earthly affections for eternity' in the beyond.[14] The 'Liebestod' [love-death] union of Tristan and Isolde offers a paradigmatic example, and Emily Brontë also articulates this new idea in *Wuthering Heights* (1847). Just before Edgar Linton dies 'blissfully', he kisses his daughter's cheek and recalls his deceased wife: 'I am going to see her'. He even adds 'and you, darling child, shall come to us!'.[15] The allure of an 'anthropomorphic paradise' was evidently powerful enough that a father might fantasize about his daughter's death. Ariès finds remarkably similar sentiments recorded in the memoir of a cosmopolitan family of French aristocrats, seemingly a world away from the Brontës' rural, Protestant Yorkshire. 'She stopped breathing at eight thirty', wrote the family matron in an 1848 letter reporting her daughter's death with great care and in great detail: 'What an angel! She was reunited forever with her Albert [the daughter's husband], with all our dear saints [other deceased family members]'.[16]

A European's relationship with death at this time was relatively uncomplicated. When you became ill, nature would simply take its course: you would either recover or die, although you assumed the former until it became clear that your time had come. A person's final days and hours were typically a deeply dignified time of great intimacy with family, friends and even strangers. In bourgeois and noble circles the deathbed ritual became an elaborate affair, and the dying person typically presided over the whole scene as a figure of authority: he or she received loved ones to bid them farewell, distribute prized possessions, forgive transgressions, dispense wisdom and so on. Death in these circumstances resembled a beautiful production in which the dying man or woman played the roles of the director and the star. As a corollary to these attitudes, death was often characterized as physically beautiful. An excerpt of the memoir cited above recounts in a fashion typical of the era the final hours and death of another young family member in 1843: '[a] radiant expression triumphed over the terrifying alteration of her features. She panted, but like

---

[13] Vladimir Jankélévitch, *La Mort* (Paris, 1966), pp. 380–82.
[14] Ariès, *The Hour of Our Death*, p. 446.
[15] Quoted ibid., p. 436.
[16] Ibid., p. 428.

somebody who is winning a race.' After the woman expired, her beauty only grew: '[t]he most consoling transformation had taken place. All traces of the malady had disappeared. The room had become a chapel in which our angel lay sleeping [...] more beautiful than I had ever seen her in life.'[17] Reunion in the beyond, intimacy, awesome spectacle and beauty: the confluence of these ideas and practices characterized death for a great many nineteenth-century Europeans. As Ariès summarizes:

> Since death is not the end of the loved one [...] death is neither ugly nor fearful. On the contrary, death is beautiful, as the dead body is beautiful. Presence at the deathbed in the nineteenth century is more than a customary participation in a social ritual; it is an opportunity to witness a spectacle that is both comforting and exalting. A visit to the house in which someone has died is a little like a visit to a museum. How beautiful he is! In [...] the most ordinary middle-class western homes, death has come to coincide with beauty.[18]

However, Ariès, Vladimir Jankélévitch, Péter Hanák and others agree that later in the century attitudes towards death changed dramatically, and at a disorienting pace. As hygiene and cleanliness increasingly became bourgeois values, the sight of soiled sheets and the odours of sweat, urine, faeces and gangrene became repugnant, and dying became dirty, revolting and even indecent.[19] Flaubert's merciless depiction of Emma Bovary's death — in 1856, a portent of an attitude that would solidify by the century's end — contrasts sharply with the romantic account cited above:

> [E]lle devenait plus pâle que le drap où s'enfonçaient ses doigts crispés. [...] Des gouttes suintaient sur sa figure bleuâtre [...]. Ses dents claquaient, ses yeux agrandis regardaient vaguement autour d'elle [...]. Peu à peu ses gémissements furent plus forts. Un hurlement sourd lui échappa [...]. Elle ne tarda pas à vomir du sang. Ses lèvres se serrèrent davantage. Elle avait les membres crispés, le corps couvert de taches brunes [...]. Puis elle se mettait à crier, horriblement. [...] Emma, le menton contre sa poitrine, ouvrait démesurément les paupières; et ses pauvres mains se traînaient sur les draps, avec ce geste hideux et doux des agonisants qui semblent vouloir déjà se recouvrir du suaire. [...] Sa poitrine aussitôt se mit à haleter rapidement. La langue tout entière lui sortit hors de la bouche; ses yeux, en roulant, pâlissaient comme deux globes de lampe qui s'éteignent.[20]

> [She became paler than the sheet into which she was digging her clenched fingers. Beads of sweat oozed from her bluish face, her teeth chattered, her wide eyes stared vacuously into space. Little by little her groans became louder. A muffled scream escaped her. She soon vomited blood. Her lips

---

[17] Augustus Craven, *Récit d'une sœur. Souvenirs de famille* (Paris, 1867). Quoted ibid., p. 427.
[18] Ariès, *The Hour of Our Death*, p. 473.
[19] Ibid., pp. 568–69.
[20] Gustave Flaubert, *Madame Bovary*, in *Œuvres*, ed. by Albert Thibaudet and René Dumesnil, 2 vols, Bibliothèque de la Pléiade, 36/37 (Paris, 1951), I, 580–89.

> were drawn, her limbs were contracted, her body was covered with brown spots. Then she began to scream horribly. Emma, her chin against her chest, opened her eyes very wide, and her poor hands grasped at the sheets with that hideous and pathetic gesture of the dying, who seem to want to wrap themselves already in their shrouds. Her chest began to heave rapidly. Her entire tongue protruded from her mouth; her rolling eyes grew as dim as two lamp globes being extinguished.]

Urbanization in the late nineteenth century made life increasingly private. The dead consequently were no longer mourned by the whole community, as they had been for centuries, but only by family and friends.[21] The anonymity of the modern metropolis, moreover, inverted the relationship between the dying and these potential mourners. It brought increased intensity and exclusivity to personal relationships, and as an upshot it became imperative to shield terminally ill loved ones from the true gravity of their condition. To this end speaking to the dying about death became taboo. A dying person, of course, was typically cognizant of his or her condition, but was forced to adhere to the taboo, lest he or she be treated as an invalid and obliged to behave like one. As Ariès points out, dying thus became bound up in a lie: 'The dying person and those around him continue to play a comedy in which "nothing has changed", "life goes on as usual", and "anything is still possible".'[22] Tolstoy vividly captured just how alienating this could be in *The Death of Ivan Ilyich* (1886):

> The worst torment was the lie, this lie that for some reason was accepted by everyone, that he [Ivan] was only sick, and not dying [...]. This lie tormented him. He suffered because no one was willing to admit what everyone, including himself, could see very clearly. He suffered because they lied and forced him to take part in this deception. [...] This lie that degraded the formidable and solemn act of his death [...] had become horribly painful to Ivan Ilyich.[23]

Where earlier in the century the dying man directed and starred in a beautiful production, by the 1880s he was divested of such authority, rendered powerless by and captive to an alienating 'comedy'.

As Hanák shows, creeping bureaucracy also sapped dignity from death. In the Austro-Hungarian Empire, for example, death had to be certified by qualified personnel before burial could take place, and mourning rituals, funeral rites, burial practices and even cemetery etiquette were increasingly subjected to regulation.[24] All of these, moreover, became the commodities of a burgeoning,

---

[21] Péter Hanák, 'The Alienation of Death in Budapest and Vienna at the Turn of the Century', in *The Garden and the Workshop. Essays on the Cultural History of Vienna and Budapest* (Princeton, NJ, 1998), pp. 98–109 (pp. 102–03). See also Ariès, *The Hour of Our Death*, pp. 565–68.
[22] Ariès, *The Hour of Our Death*, p. 562.
[23] Leo Tolstoy, *The Death of Ivan Ilyich and Master and Man*, trans. by Ann Pasternak Slater (New York, 2003), p. 42.
[24] Hanák, 'The Alienation of Death', pp. 99–102.

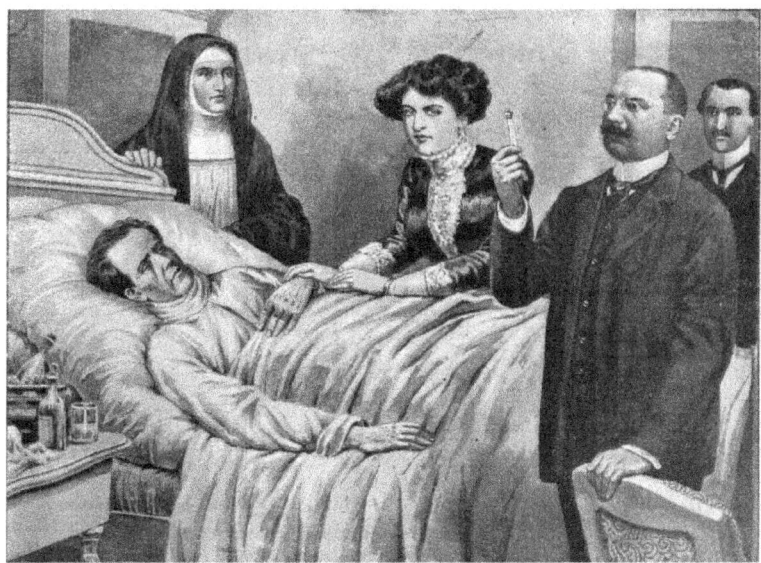

Fig. 1. Mahler's deathbed: anonymous drawing, *Wiener Bilder*, 17 May 1911

capitalist death industry. Everything from the decoration of the dead person's house to funeral rites to the grave itself cost money (a lot of money), and such services were aggressively marketed. 'The body was hardly cold', writes Hanák, 'before sales representatives were calling on the bereaved family, and exploiting their sorrow by offering a wide variety of funeral arrangements'.[25]

Finally, by the 1880s death was becoming 'medicalized'. Doctors, of course, had long tended to the sick. In the late nineteenth century, however, a new scientific outlook came to characterize medical practice, and this fundamentally altered the patient's relationship to illness and death. No longer merely a collection of symptoms, sickness became a clinical 'case' with its own existence and a name. This is significant, for where in earlier times death simply was or was not in nature's course, the patient's destiny now depends on the diagnosis — there are serious, incurable diseases and mild, treatable ones — and his or her death is now mediated by the doctor and the technology of medicine.[26] As a result of these new attitudes and dynamics, death — for the first time ever — became, as Allan Kellehear has put it, 'shameful' and divorced from life itself.[27] 'Modern urban civilization wrenched death out of the integral entity of daily life', summarizes Hanák. 'Death did not belong any more to the man [...]. Man became deprived of his own personal death.'[28]

[25] Ibid., p. 101.
[26] See Ariès, *The Hour of Our Death*, pp. 563–65, and Hanák, 'The Alienation of Death', pp. 103–04.
[27] Allan Kellehear, *A Social History of Dying* (Cambridge, 2007).
[28] Hanák, 'The Alienation of Death', p. 103.

These troubling new realities are naively latent in Figure 1, an anonymous drawing that appeared in the *Wiener Bilder* the day before Mahler died in May 1911.[29] Though the picture does not dwell on dirtiness or elicit disgust, the dying composer looks haggard, very sick and not the least radiant or sublime. But more revealing is that nobody pays him any attention. His wife Alma holds his hand but stares coldly out of the picture. Otherwise, all eyes are on the doctor, including Mahler's and even the nun's. The doctor, authoritatively occupying the foreground of the drawing, does not pay any attention to his patient either, but instead gazes grimly at a thermometer. Here, not only has death become alienated from the dying man, but it has become utterly de-humanized as a scientific instrument holds Mahler's sad fate.

Hanák notes that the Viennese press 'often fulminated against "the outrages of the undertaker-hyenas" and "the depredations of the usurers of death"'.[30] Prominent intellectual figures were also troubled by the fact that death had become ugly, isolating and alienated from life. Rainer Maria Rilke numbered among the most vehement critics, once writing: 'Il y a de la mort dans la vie et cela m'étonne qu'on prétende l'ignorer' [There is death in life, and it astonishes me that we claim not to know it].[31] Elsewhere, he negatively contrasted modern, institutionalized death (Kellehear's 'shameful death') with older times:

> Jetzt wird in 559 Betten gestorben [at the Hôtel-Dieu hospital in Paris]. Natürlich fabrikmäßig. Bei so enormer Produktion ist der einzelne Tod nicht so gut ausgeführt, aber darauf kommt es auch nicht an. Die Masse macht es. Wer giebt heute noch etwas für einen gut ausgearbeiteten Tod? Niemand. [...] Voilà votre mort, monsieur. Man stirbt den Tod, der zu der Krankheit gehört, die man hat (denn seit man alle Krankheiten kennt, weiß man auch, daß die verschiedenen letalen Abschlüsse zu den Krankheiten gehören und nicht zu den Menschen; und der Kranke hat sozusagen nichts zu tun). [...]
>
> Wenn ich nach Hause denke, wo nun niemand mehr ist, dann glaube ich, das muß früher anders gewesen sein. Früher wußte man (oder vielleicht man ahnte es), daß man den Tod *in* sich hatte wie die Frucht den Kern. [...] Die Frauen hatten ihn im Schoß und die Männer in der Brust. Den *hatte* man, und das gab einem eine eigentümliche Würde und einen stillen Stolz.
>
> [They are dying there in 559 beds. Factory-like, of course. Where production is so enormous an individual death is not so nicely carried out but then that doesn't matter. It is quantity that counts. Who cares anything today for a finely-finished death? No one. Voilà, votre mort, monsieur. One dies the death that belongs to the disease one has (for since one has come to know all diseases, one knows, too, that the different lethal

---

[29] *Wiener Bilder*, 17 May 1911.
[30] Hanák, 'The Alienation of Death', p. 102.
[31] Letter to Adelmina 'Mimi' Romanelli, 8 December, 1907, quoted from Rainer Maria Rilke, *Briefe*, ed. by Rilke-Archiv in Weimar with Ruth Sieber-Rilke and Karl Altheim, 2 vols (Wiesbaden, 1950), I, 229.

terminations belong to the diseases and not to the people; and the sick person has so to speak nothing to do). When I think back to my home, where there is nobody left now, I imagine that formerly this must have been otherwise. Formerly one knew (or perhaps one guessed it) that one had one's death within one, as a fruit its kernel. [...] The women had it in their womb and the men in their breast. One *had* it, and that gave one a singular dignity and a quiet pride.][32]

And shortly before Rilke himself succumbed to leukaemia, he further elaborated his views on the individual's relationship with death:

> Der Tod ist die uns abgekehrte, von uns unbeschienene *Seite des Lebens*: wir müssen versuchen, das größeste Bewußtsein unseres Daseins zu leisten, das in *beiden unabgegrenzten Bereichen* zu Hause ist, *aus beiden unerschöpflich genährt* ... Die wahre Lebensgestalt reicht durch *beide* Gebiete, das Blut des größten Kreislaufs treibt durch beide: *es gibt weder ein Diesseits noch Jenseits, sondern die große Einheit.*
>
> [Death is the side of life which is turned away from us, and upon which we shed no light. We must try to widen our consciousness of existence so that it is at home in both spheres, with no dividing-line between them, so that we may draw endless sustenance from both. The true way of life leads through both kingdoms, the great circulation of the blood passes through both: there is neither a here nor a hereafter but a single great unity.][33]

Mahler's 'Der Abschied', as we shall see in the remainder of this essay, seeks to reclaim death's lost beauty by articulating something like the 'great unity' Rilke imagined. It does so, as I have suggested, by drawing upon the ancient Chinese thought that had begun to circulate in the German-speaking world. In this respect, the work represents an early episode in an important Viennese, and more broadly Germanic, intellectual movement that would flourish over several decades to come. As the cultural scholar Susanne Kelley has recently shown, in the early twentieth century Viennese artists and writers increasingly responded to the challenges posed by encroaching modernity by seeking 'philosophical answers to fundamental questions of human existence' in what they viewed as the timeless wisdom of ancient China and Japan. Hofmannsthal, for example, turned to Chinese philosophy (primarily in his speeches and essays, though also in certain literary and dramatic works, notably the fragment *Die beiden Götter* [*The Two Gods*]) for both a political model that could unify a fragmented Europe and a set of values that would foster spiritual growth in individuals. And Klimt partook in the crucial project of re-defining gender

---

[32] Rainer Maria Rilke, *Die Aufzeichnungen des Malte Laurids Brigge*, quoted from *Werke. Kommentierte Ausgabe in vier Bänden*, ed. by Manfred Engel et al. (Frankfurt a. M. and Leipzig, 1996), III: *Prosa und Dramen*, ed. by August Stahl, p. 459; *The Notebooks of Malte Laurids Brigge*, trans. by M. D. Herter Norton (New York, 1964), pp. 17–18.

[33] Letter to Witold Hulewicz, 13 November 1925, in Rilke, *Briefe*, II, 480–81. Translation adapted from *Letters of Rainer Maria Rilke. 1910–1926*, trans. by Jane Bannard Greene and M. D. Herter Norton (New York, 1969), p. 373.

(in a society preoccupied with the so-called *Frauenfrage*) by painting women in fantastic and self-consciously modern Oriental scenes, instead of the domestic spaces traditional to the portrait genre.[34]

Knowledge of ancient Chinese thought was disseminated through a number of channels. These included the research of professional sinologists and orientalists, such as Victor von Strauß, Max Müller and Mahler's friend Friedrich Hirth.[35] Among the Viennese population at large, the World's Fair of 1873 had been an important stimulus of interest in East Asia, and from the 1890s newspapers and magazines regularly featured articles on Chinese culture and traditions.[36] Around the same time there began to appear a series of translations and paraphrases (*Nachdichtungen*) of Tang-era Chinese poetry by literary sinophiles and poets, including Otto Julius ('Ottju') Bierbaum, Richard Dehmel, Hans Heilmann, Otto Hauser, Klabund (Alfred Henscke) and Bethge.[37] There were also periodicals dedicated to *chinoiseries*, such as the monthly *Die Lotosblüten* [*The Lotus Blossom*], founded by Franz Hartmann in 1896, which published translations of classic texts and articles on assorted aspects of culture and also familiarized German-speaking readers with important research by pioneering French and British sinologists.

Among the branches of Chinese thought that found their way into Viennese consciousness was Taoism, a pillar of Chinese philosophy and religion (both broadly defined) that dates back to the fourth century BC and the writings of Lǎozǐ and Zhuāngzǐ (Pinyin Romanization). Early Taoist thinkers valued, among other things, absolute harmony and unity between humans and the natural world. A central problem that they felt compelled to confront, therefore, was the apparent incongruity between the transience of human life and the permanence of nature and the cosmos. The ancient Chinese pursued two solutions. One was alchemy, through which they hoped to extend human life indefinitely. The other (which prevailed when it became clear that alchemical concoctions were in fact killing those upon whom they were supposed to bestow immortality) was philosophical and stemmed from the observation that nature is essentially cyclical. Leaves fall from the trees in the autumn, only to grow anew in the spring. Life and death could be understood as a natural cycle, no different from the seasons, the waxing and waning of the moon, or the rising and setting of the sun: in death, human life was in unity with the earth and the cosmos after all. Taoist thought became an important ideological source for

---

[34] Susanne Kelley, '"Der ungeheure Begriff Asien": China and Japan in Fin-de-Siècle Literature, Art, and Culture' (unpublished doctoral thesis, University of California at Los Angeles, 2005), p. 98. On Hofmannsthal, see pp. 93–131, and on Klimt, pp. 44–92.

[35] Mahler met Hirth in New York in the spring of 1908; at the time Hirth had just completed his book *The Ancient History of China* (New York, 1908). See Henry-Louis de la Grange, *Gustav Mahler. Chronique d'une vie*, 3 vols (Paris, 1979–84), III, 301.

[36] Kelley, '"Der ungeheure Begriff Asien"', pp. 25–27.

[37] For an overview of German poets' reception of Chinese poetry in the period, see Ingrid Schuster, *China und Japan in der deutschen Literatur, 1890–1925* (Bern, 1977).

Part 1					
Bar 1	*19*	*27*	*55*	*158*	*166*
Introduction	Recitative 1	Aria 1	Aria 2	Recitative 2	Aria 3
C−	C− (F−)	C+ (C−)	A− F+	(A−) D−	D− B♭+

Part 2					
Bar 304	*375*	*383*	*431*	*461*	
Funeral March	Recitative 3	Reprise of Aria 1	Reprise of Aria 2	Reprise of Aria 3	
C−	C− F−	C−	F+	C+	

TABLE 1. Structure of 'Der Abschied'

writers such as Alfred Mombert, Max Dauthendey, Klabund, Hofmannsthal, and later Hermann Hesse and Bertolt Brecht. The alternatives it offered to western notions of atomized subjectivity and linear time were particularly attractive to Mombert and Dauthendey. As Ingrid Schuster notes, for them '[d]as Leben selbst wurde in allen seinen organischen und anorganischen Erscheinungsformen verabsolutiert; auch der Tod des einzelnen wurde als Teil des allgemeinen Lebens begriffen' [life itself, in all its organic and inorganic manifestations, became one with the absolute, and the death of the individual was also understood as part of life's totality].[38] And Klabund found real solace in the Taoist epistemology of death. A month after his first wife succumbed to complications following childbirth, he wrote to his friend Walther Heinrich:

> Wäre ich nicht ein Jünger des Tao (der *einzigen* Philosophie, die dem Menschen *dieser* Zeit etwas zu sagen hätte: denn es ist eine lebendige Philosophie [...]), ich wäre längst verzweifelt. Wüßte ich nicht, daß die Seele Stern und Sonne *ist*, nicht daß sie bloß Objekte der Augen sind, wüßte ich nicht daß die *Einzel*seele so gut unsterblich wie die *Gesamt*seele (der 'Urtao'), so hätte ich mir längst eine Kugel in den Kopf gejagt.[39]
>
> [Were I not a disciple of the Tao (the *only* philosophy that has something to say to people of *our* time: because it is a philosophy that is alive), I would have lost hope long ago. If I did not know that the soul *is* the sun and the stars, that these are not merely objects for the eye to gaze upon, if I did not know that the *individual* soul was just as immortal as the *complete* soul (the 'primal Tao'), I would have put a bullet in my head long ago.]

Though the poems of *Die chinesische Flöte* (the source for the texts of *Das Lied von der Erde*) are several times removed from the Chinese originals — Bethge mainly reworked Hans Heilmann's German translations of French paraphrases by Judith Gautier and the Marquis d'Hervey-Saint-Denys — such important

---

[38] Ibid., pp. 148–50 (p. 149). See also Christiane C. Günther, *Aufbruch nach Asien. Kulturelle Fremde in der deutschen Literatur um 1900* (Munich, 1988), pp. 26–32. On Hofmannsthal and Taoism, see Kelley, '"Der ungeheure Begriff Asien"', pp. 117–20.

[39] Klabund to Walther Heinrich, 29 November 1918, in Klabund, *Briefe an einen Freund*, ed. by Ernst Heinrich (Cologne, 1963), p. 134; emphasis in original.

Part I – Source: In Erwartung des Freundes
Protagonist speaks

6. *Der Abschied*		
Die Sonne scheidet hinter dem Gebirge.	Recit. 1	
In alle Täler steigt der Abend nieder	'Neutral'/	
Mit seinen Schatten, die voll Kühlung sind.	Nature	
O sieh! Wie eine Silberbarke schwebt	Aria 1	
Der Mond am blauen Himmelssee herauf.	'Reflective'/	
Ich spüre eines feinen Windes Weh'n	Nature's	
Hinter den dunklen Fichten!	beauty	
Der Bach singt voller Wohllaut durch das Dunkel.	Aria 2	
Die Blumen blassen im Dämmerschein.	'Reflective'	
Die Erde atmet voll von Ruh' und Schlaf;		
Alle Sehnsucht will nun träumen,		
Die müden Menschen geh'n heimwärts,		
Um in Schlaf vergess'nes Glück		
Und Jugend neu zu lernen!		
Die Vögel hocken still in ihren Zweigen.		
Die Welt schläft ein!		
Es wehet kühl im Schatten meiner Fichten.	Recit. 2	
<u>Ich</u> stehe hier und harre meines Freundes;	'Neutral'	
<u>Ich</u> harre sein zum letzten Lebewohl.		
<u>Ich</u> sehne mich, O Freund, an deiner Seite	Aria 3	
Die Schönheit dieses Abends zu genießen.	'Reflective'	
Wo bleibst du! Du lässt <u>mich</u> lang allein!		
<u>Ich</u> wandle auf und nieder mit meiner Laute		
Auf Wegen, die von weichem Grase schwellen.		
O Schönheit! O ewigen Liebens – Lebens – trunk'ne Welt!		
Part II – Source: Der Abschied des Freundes		
Narrator speaks		
Er stieg vom Pferd und reichte ihm den Trunk	Recit. 3	'Neutral'/
Des Abschieds dar. Er fragte ihn, wohin		Nature
Er führe, und auch warum es müßte sein.		becomes
Er sprach, seine Stimme war umflort: Du, mein Freund,	Aria 1,	'Farewell'
Mir war auf dieser Welt das Glück nicht hold!	reprise	narrative
Wohin ich geh? Ich geh', ich wand're in die Berge.		↓
Ich suche Ruhe für mein einsam Herz!		↓
Ich wandle nach der Heimat! meiner Stätte!	Aria 2,	↓
Ich werde niemals in die Ferne schweifen.	reprise	↓
Still ist mein Herz und harret seiner Stunde!		↓
Die liebe Erde allüberall blüht auf im Lenz und grünt	Aria 3,	Reflective
Aufs neu! Allüberall und ewig blauen licht die Fernen!	reprise	
Ewig ... Ewig ...		

TABLE 2. Lyrical structure of 'Der Abschied'

Death, Orientalism and Mahler's 'Der Abschied'

Part I – Source: In Erwartung des Freundes
Protagonist speaks

6. *The Farewell*		
The sun departs behind the mountains.	Recit. 1	
Into all the valleys the evening descends	'Neutral'/	
With its shadows, which are full of coolness.	Nature	
Oh see! Like a silver barque	Aria 1	
The moon floats upward on the blue lake of heaven.	'Reflective'/	
I feel a soft wind blowing	Nature's	
Behind the dark spruces.	beauty	
The brook sings, full of pleasant sound, through the dark.	Aria 2	
The flowers pale in the twilight,	'Reflective'	
The earth breathes, full of quiet and sleep.		
All longing now wants to dream,		
Weary men go homeward,		
To learn again in sleep		
Forgotten happiness and youth.		
The birds perch quietly in their branches,		
The world falls asleep!		
A cool breeze blows in the shade of my spruces.	Recit. 2	
I stand here and await my friend;	'Neutral'	
I await him for a final farewell.		
I long, O friend, to enjoy	Aria 3	
The beauty of this evening at your side.	'Reflective'	
Where are you? You leave me alone so long!		
I walk up and down with my lute		
On paths that swell with soft grass.		
O beauty! O world drunk with eternal love and life!		
Part II – Source: Der Abschied des Freundes		
Narrator speaks		
He alighted from his horse and offered him	Recit. 3	'Neutral'/
The draught of farewell. He asked him where		Nature
He was bound and also why it had to be.		becomes
He spoke, his voice was veiled: My friend,	Aria 1,	'Farewell'
Fortune was not kind to me in this world!	reprise	narrative
Where do I go? I walk, I wander into the mountains.		↓
I seek peace for my lonely heart.		↓
I go to my homeland, my abode!	Aria 2,	↓
I will never roam in distant lands.	reprise	↓
My heart is still and awaits its hour.		↓
The beloved earth everywhere blossoms and greens in springtime	Aria 3, reprise	Reflective
Anew. Everywhere and forever the distances brighten blue!		
Forever ... forever ...		

Taoist concepts are nonetheless clearly articulated in a number of them.[40] Indeed, the opening 'Trinklied vom Jammer der Erde' [Drinking Song of Earth's Sorrow] of Mahler's song-symphony poses the central existential problem: the earth is eternal, but humans live 'Nicht hundert Jahre' [not even a hundred years]. Let us now turn to 'Der Abschied', to see how Mahler's finale works through the classical Taoist solution. As Table 1 shows, the piece comprises a series of recitatives and arias, and (following Stephen Hefling and others) may be parsed into two large parts, where Part II (introduced by a substantial funeral march) is a varied reprise of Part I.[41] The text (shown in Table 2) is Mahler's conflation and liberal adaptation of two poems, 'In Erwartung des Freundes' [Awaiting the Friend] and 'Der Abschied des Freundes' [The Friend's Farewell], which furnish the texts for Parts I and II respectively.[42]

These appear on facing pages in Bethge's volume, and their interrelated 'farewell' story-line makes them a natural pair: in the former, the lonely protagonist awaits the arrival of a friend; in the latter, the awaited friend arrives, the final farewell is exchanged and the protagonist departs to await his 'heart's hour'.[43] The point where the two poems meet in Mahler's conflation, however, is a moment of striking disjunction. Throughout Part I, the protagonist speaks (sings) in the first person ('I feel a soft wind blowing'; 'I stand here and await my friend, I await him for a final farewell', and so on). As the underlinings in Table 2 show, however, the point of view abruptly shifts to the third person at the beginning of Part II: 'He [the awaited friend who now arrives] alighted from his horse and offered him [the protagonist] | the draught of farewell. He [the arriving friend] asked him [the protagonist] where | He was bound and why it had to be'. Mahler's text implies that, half way through, 'Der Abschied' becomes a *narrative*, in Carolyn Abbate's restrictive usage of that term (derived from Paul Ricoeur and structuralist narratology as practised by Gérald Genette and others). That is, it becomes a discourse formulated by a narrator, who relates the remainder of the farewell story from a detached and temporally distanced position.[44] The implications of this shift command attention: in Part

---

[40] Hamao Fusako has painstakingly traced the genesis of Mahler's texts through their layers of translation and paraphrase back to their eighth-century originals. See Fusako, 'The Sources of the Texts in Mahler's *Das Lied von der Erde*', *19th-Century Music*, 19 (1995), 83–95.

[41] Hefling, *Mahler. Das Lied*, pp. 88–91.

[42] On Mahler's adaptations of Bethge's texts, see Arthur Wenk, 'The Composer as Poet in *Das Lied von der Erde*', *19th-Century Music*, 1 (1977), 33–47, and Mitchell, *Songs and Symphonies*, pp. 420–25 and *passim*. The text and English translation in Table 2 are drawn from the widely available 1988 Dover (New York) full-score edition of *Das Lied*, the punctuation of the German slightly altered to accommodate inconsistencies between score and prefatory text.

[43] According to Bethge, these poems were an epistolary exchange between Mèng Hàorán ('In Erwartung des Freundes') and Wáng Wéi ('Der Abschied des Freundes'). See Hans Bethge, *Die chinesische Flöte* (Leipzig, 1926), p. 114.

[44] Carolyn Abbate, *Unsung Voices. Opera and Musical Narrative in the Nineteenth Century* (Princeton, NJ, 1991), pp. 1–60; see especially pp. 23–26 and 48–56.

I the protagonist is the speaking (singing) subject, but in Part II his voice has vanished, and his words are merely *quoted* by the narrator. The music, one might say, no longer emanates from him; the protagonist has become an *object*, an Other to the narrator, who now treats the protagonist's final farewell and death as a *topic*. This peculiar structure has spawned a good deal of commentary, most of which attempts to explain it away. Mitchell argues at length that it must be ignored as a manifestation of Mahler's subconscious anxiety over his immanent death that caused him to bungle his conflation of Bethge's poems.[45] Danuser insists that the music's formal continuity trumps grammatical disjunction in the text, and Draughon similarly argues that the appearance of a narrating voice is only apparent; she invokes the trope of the 'outside observer', a contrivance Mahler had first employed in a programme for the Second Symphony's scherzo movement, which tells of a lonely figure watching a festive waltz through a ballroom window, deaf to the music.[46]

These complicated (and in Mitchell's case questionable) arguments reflect high stakes. For if the music no longer emanates from the protagonist in Part II, the cherished notion that the piece's conclusion is a mimetic representation of his ecstatic and triumphant death becomes problematic. Indeed, the abrupt shift to narrative (with its characteristic temporal structure) implies that the protagonist has already died (offstage, so to speak) when the narrator first appears at the beginning of Recitative 3 (see again Tables 1 and 2), an issue to which we shall soon return. In short, if the structure of Mahler's text is read at face value, the hermeneutic core of 'Der Abschied' criticism crumbles. Yet Mahler ultimately gives us no reason not to take the text literally — especially if we acknowledge that its peculiar structure was of his own, deliberate doing: the beginning of Bethge's 'Der Abschied des Freundes' reads 'Ich stieg vom Pferd und reichte ihm den Trunk | Des Abschieds dar. Ich fragte ihn, wohin | Und auch warum er reisen wolle' [I dismounted and offered him the farewell draught. I enquired of him where — and indeed why — he wished to travel]. Had Mahler wanted to retain the first-person perspective of Part I, he could simply have reversed the pronouns.

This structure, moreover, is not merely a matter of grammar, but is also projected (*pace* Danuser) by Mahler's music. The structural voice-leading (the underlying counterpoint that supports the music's surface) in Part I is based on a 5–6 pattern, whereby the fifth of the triad moves up by step to produce a new chord as illustrated in Example 1a.[47] This gesture factors substantially in much of *Das Lied*, but in 'Der Abschied' it derives from the neighbour-note

---

[45] Mitchell, *Songs and Symphonies*, pp. 370–432 *passim*; see especially pp. 416–32.
[46] Danuser, *Gustav Mahler. Das Lied*, p. 104; Draughon, 'Mahler and the Music of Fin-de-Siècle Identity', pp. 200–02. For another reading of the structure of Mahler's text, see Wenk, 'The Composer as Poet', pp. 33–47.
[47] The 5–6 pattern is also an important contrapuntal device in Mahler's Ninth Symphony; on its role in that work see Christopher Orlo Lewis, *Tonal Coherence in Mahler's Ninth Symphony* (Ann Arbor, MI, 1984).

Example 1a: 5–6 intervallic pattern

Example 1b: Neighbour-note motive in Introduction

motive prominent at the outset (see Example 1b), in which the neighbour notes are sometimes incomplete. The neighbour motive is prominent in recitative 1 (Example 1c), and forms the melodic basis of Aria 1 (Example 1d). As an incomplete neighbour note, it subsequently becomes structural (that is, it passes from the music's surface to a deeper level of underlying counterpoint): as Example 1e shows, at the beginning of Aria 2, G, the fifth degree of C, slides up to A, the sixth, to form an A-minor triad, and the same motive quickly converts A minor to F major. Within Aria 2, another 5–6 pattern produces a D-minor triad that launches a cadential progression in C. The relationship between F major and D minor that has been produced through this pattern is subsequently composed out (that is, this local event comes to structure a larger span of music): the conclusion of Aria 2 moves from F major to D minor, with A remaining in the bass. Recitative 2 seems to settle in A minor, but quickly returns to D minor (with A still in the bass); and the composing-out process is completed at the beginning of Aria 3, where the pedal on A resolves to D. D minor then gives way, once again via a 5–6 pattern, to B-flat major, the main key of the aria.

Example 1c: Neighbour-note motive in Recitative 1 (bars 19–26)

Example 1d: Neighbour-note motive in Aria 1 (bars 30–38)

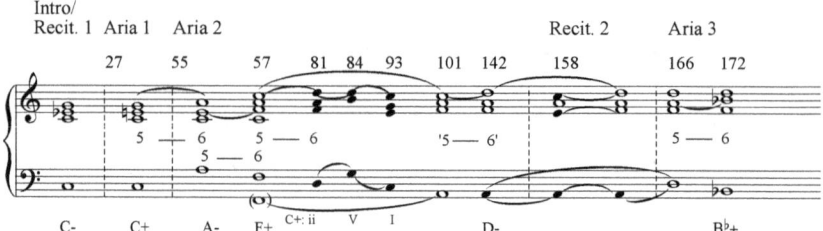

Example 1e: Structural voice-leading in Part I

The next projected tonal area would be G minor. As Example 1f shows, a bass pedal on G does appear at the end of Aria 3, but the structural harmony is an E-flat major triad (the subdominant of B flat), and the music cuts to the C-minor tonality that initiates Part II without ever centring on G minor. The voice-leading that has underlain the middleground tonal structure of the piece up to this point thus *breaks down* at the end of Aria 3 — that is, precisely where the protagonist's voice *vanishes*. And the ensuing funeral march, the initiating C-minor downbeat which Mahler labelled 'Grabgeläute' [death knell] in his short score, reveals his fate: the protagonist does not die at the end of the piece (as the received interpretation has it) but before his funeral march.

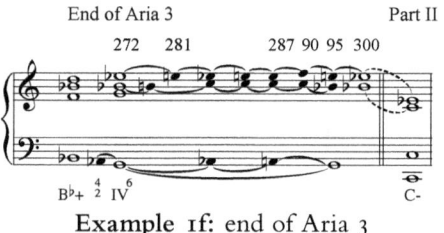

Example 1f: end of Aria 3

Mahler's music also projects the appearance of the narrator, who subsequently recounts the protagonist's final farewell, after the fact and in the past tense. As soon as the protagonist's voice vanishes, an entirely new motive (Example 2a) materializes, and this event is conspicuous since the music has been dominated up to this point by a handful of motives that have all been introduced in the opening bars of the piece. As Example 2b shows, the ensuing funeral march is spun out of the new motive, as though this new presence — the narrator — were the mourner, the singer of the march. The new motive persists in the highly varied reprise of Aria 1, and material it previously generated here inflects the melody of the voice (compare, for example the cadential tag of Example 2b with Example 2c). In other words, the protagonist's music (that is, the original Aria 1) and the narrator's are here juxtaposed, and this juxtaposition of musical materials parallels the layering of narrative voices in the text: for here the narrator is *quoting* the protagonist.

Example 2a: New motive (bars 310–11)

Example 2b (above): New motive in march melody (bars 326–33 and 337–44)
Example 2c (below): New Motive in Rep. of Aria 1 (bars 417–20)

'Der Abschied', to recapitulate, becomes a narrative halfway through; in the process, subject becomes object, and the protagonist's farewell and death become the narrator's topic. The conclusion of the piece takes a further step along this trajectory from drama *of* to discourse *on* death. The narrator concludes the farewell story in the reprise of Aria 2, by quoting the protagonist's final words ('still ist mein Herz', etc.). The scene then dissolves in a wash of whole-tone sonority, out of which emerges the piece's famous climax: the soaring, ecstatic reprise of Aria 3, in the tonic major key. The text here ('Die liebe Erde', etc.) is purely lyrical, and this new discursive register and its contrast with the preceding narrative are reflected and underscored by the new orchestral colour of the music (featuring harps, and then mandolin and celesta) and floating quality lacking metre. The climax of the piece is thus not the climax of the farewell drama and the apotheosis of the subject (as Hefling, Mitchell and others would have it), but the narrator's *meditation* upon the tale he has just told (or at least completed). In other words, the climax of the piece is the moral of the story, which is none other than the classic Taoist worldview, where in death individual subjectivity is folded into nature's eternal cyclicism: just as spring follows winter, the narrator tells us, the earth blossoms anew after the protagonist's death.

It is not only through the words and ecstatic music of the narrator's final meditation that the piece celebrates death as natural beauty, but it also does so by way of a formal process that plays out over its entire span. As Wenk, Mitchell and others have noted, the text of Part I (see again Table 2) swings between more or less neutral descriptions of the protagonist's natural surroundings and his subjective reflections upon them.[48] These segments of text correspond to the recitatives and arias respectively. In recitative 1, we hear about the setting sun, the mountainous background and so on. In the aria, the protagonist reflects on nature's beauty: the moon magically becomes a silver boat floating on a heavenly lake. Aria 2, where the sound of the stream becomes music, is a similar meditation on nature's beauty. Recitative 2 reverts to description (the protagonist tells us he awaits his friend amid the spruce trees), while in Aria 3 the protagonist literally proclaims the beauty of his surroundings: 'die Schönheit dieses Abends'.

Part II maintains and substantially elaborates this rhythm of recitative and aria. Here, the formal labels, 'Reprise of Aria 1' and 'Reprise of Aria 2', are somewhat misleading in that they merely reflect the distribution of material, rather than musical texture as such. Indeed, the reprise of Aria 1, with its fragmentary juxtaposition of material from Aria 1 and the march, is distinctly declamatory and, as Mitchell notes, more closely resembles accompanied recitative than aria.[49] The reprise of Aria 2 becomes slightly more songlike, but it is substantially shortened and its most impassioned passages are omitted. Arioso appropriately characterizes its texture. Mahler's procedure in Part II expresses a growth process, from recitative, through the more 'songful' — but still declamatory — gradients of accompanied recitative and arioso, which culminates in the dramatic reprise of Aria 3, where a true aria texture finally breaks through.

The pairing of speech-like music with primarily neutral, descriptive text and aria with reflection and meditation also persists in Part II. But whereas in Part I the neutral segments of text were the protagonist's descriptions of nature, the neutral, descriptive member of the pair here becomes the narrative of the protagonist's final farewell. This substitution is significant: the structural parallel with Part I has brought the form of the piece to interpret human death as nature in Part II. Yet the sentiment expressed in the ensuing aria remains the same: the narrator finds his story as beautiful as the protagonist found the silvery moon, or the music of the stream. The form of the piece, in short, equates nature with beauty, insists that death is natural and concludes that it, too, is beautiful.

Finally, 'Der Abschied' also embodies the Classical Chinese world-view — which understands life and death as an eternal terrestrial cycle — at a level that

---

[48] Wenk, 'The Composer as Poet', pp. 41–43; Mitchell, *Songs and Symphonies*, pp. 370–73, and pp. 370–432 *passim*.

[49] Mitchell, *Songs and Symphonies*, pp. 401–02.

might be called 'programmatic', where the text simply circumscribes a field of meaning for an underlying formal procedure. The growth process we have just observed in Part II also operates in Part I. The opening of 'Der Abschied' unfolds a *creatio ex nihilo*, where a fragmentary cluster of motives gradually coalesces into Recitative 1. The process of generation and growth continues as the recitative blossoms into Aria 1. And here it reaches its apex: chromaticism invades the C-major tonality, and the aria texture begins to decay, eventually dying away; Mahler marked the final measure of Aria 1 'morendo' — into nothing. The process then recommences when the beginning of Aria 2 emerges tentatively from the silence. The texture becomes something like instrumental arioso, as a halting oboe solo sounds against static harmony, before the music flowers into a formally complex aria. Like Aria 1, Aria 2 then decays and dies away into silence, and the whole process — which has now become a cycle — begins yet again: Recitative 2 grows into Aria 3, which, like the first two, decays into nothing, and the ensuing march follows suit, emerging from, and retreating into, oblivion. With Recitative 3 the cycle begins yet again. And here again the process reaches an apex (the climactic reprise of Aria 3); a dissonance — an added sixth — initiates another disintegration of the texture, which evaporates into the final silence.

Such iterative or paratactic formal patterns had become part of the classical and nineteenth-century symphonic vernacular long before Mahler composed 'Der Abschied'. As James Hepokoski and Warren Darcy have shown, 'rotational form' (whereby an ordered succession of thematic material repeats throughout a composition) is an important structuring principle in the eighteenth and nineteenth centuries;[50] Scott Burnham has elegantly argued that an ongoing rhythm of large-scale upbeats and downbeats is central to Beethoven's heroic-style works (the music builds to great climaxes or grinding impasses, momentarily relaxes and begins to build again);[51] and one thinks of the great 'waves' that characterize the music of Bruckner, or certain of Mahler's own earlier works, particularly the first movement of the Fifth Symphony. But the cyclic rhythm we have observed in 'Der Abschied' differs from all of these in both quality and degree. Mahler's 'rotations' involve not themes or motives, but texture — the material substance of music. And his 'waves' are more fully and consistently contoured than Beethoven's, Bruckner's or those of his own Fifth Symphony: like the moon, the piece's texture gradually waxes to fullness and wanes into nothingness, or like the development of a deciduous tree's foliage over the course of the seasons, it buds, grows, flourishes, dies off and buds again. Ultimately neither the idea of 'rotations' nor that of 'waves' adequately conveys Mahler's practice. 'Der Abschied' embodies — indeed, its

---

[50] James Hepokoski and Warren Darcy, *Elements of Sonata Theory. Norms, Types, and Deformations in the Late-Eighteenth-Century Sonata* (New York and Oxford, 2006), pp. 23–26, 47–50 and 60–84.
[51] Scott Burnham, *Beethoven Hero* (Princeton, NJ, 1995).

Example 3: 5–6 Motion at Conclusion (bars 542–73)

underlying form-building procedure *is* — a perpetual cycle of musical death and regeneration, a cycle that, as we have seen, continues from the piece's start to its finish.

Danuser, among others, has expounded at length upon the 'open' quality of the conclusion of 'Der Abschied'.[52] We might, however, linger on a detail that escapes his attention, which implies that although the piece (of course) ends, this cycle does not. The final sonority, the famous added-sixth chord (shown in Example 3), is particularly ingenious not only because it fuses the two principal keys of *Das Lied* (A minor and C major) or verticalizes the pentatonic scale, but also because it contains a seed of regeneration. For as the example shows, the 5–6 gesture that generates the harmonic structure of Part I reappears here and implies harmonic growth even as the music is dying into silence. And this gesture of re-beginning projects the cycle of musical death and regeneration — let's call it The Song of the Earth — beyond the end of the piece and into the indefinite future.

[52] Danuser, *Das Lied*, pp. 107–11.

Leo Golowski as Minor Key in Schnitzler's *Der Weg ins Freie*: Musical Theory, Political Behaviour and Ethical Action

FELIX W. TWERASER

Utah State University

Arthur Schnitzler's novel *Der Weg ins Freie* [*The Road into the Open*, 1908] is widely recognized as one of the most important artistic and historical documents of turn-of-the-century Vienna. The text depicts late imperial Austrian society in crisis, the anxiety of its Jewish citizens, the indifference and hostility of the dominant culture's representatives, and the salons and institutions of high musical and political culture in which these figures move. Music, both in theory and in practice, becomes an important metaphorical register of the social and political concerns in the text, functioning as a parallel undercurrent to the novel's primary plotlines. In the preface to his English translation of the novel, Roger Byers emphasizes the way music animates the narrative: 'I found myself reading and rereading individual sentences with the same pleasure with which one listens to a finely crafted and expressive melody [...]. It was the music in Schnitzler that captured me'.[1] Schnitzler's novel does indeed engage with musical theory and composition both formally and thematically: its structure suggests Wagnerian compositional techniques at the same time that its protagonist works on an opera with many Wagnerian elements, attends performances of Wagner's operas (including those under the direction of Gustav Mahler at the Opera House in Vienna) and composes his own material in a conventional mode. Marc Weiner argues persuasively that, in spite of his frequent interactions with Jews, in his professional choices and in his relationship to the Wagnerian tradition, Georg acts out an anti-Semitic agenda. For Weiner, a key scene in the novel is Georg's attendance at a performance of *Tristan und Isolde* at the Opera House in Vienna; Georg suppresses any acknowledgement of Gustav Mahler's direction in favour of his own megalomaniacal reverie.[2]

Scholars have recognized the political aspects of the novel's construction, arguing that its critique of rampant Wagnerism complements the extended discussions of the limited political options available to Vienna's Jews and the

---

[1] Roger Byers, 'Translator's Preface', Arthur Schnitzler, *The Road into the Open* (Berkeley, CA, 1992), p. v.
[2] Marc A. Weiner, *Arthur Schnitzler and the Crisis of Musical Culture* (Stuttgart, 1985).

legacy of an increasingly diffuse liberalism at the turn of the twentieth century. Russell Berman, for example, argues that 'the personal (Georg's privacy) and the political (the social panorama) are, if not identical, then, at the very least, backed up against each other, pushing on each other, transforming each other, and it is precisely this tense coexistence of psyche and society, private desire and social change, that epitomizes the Vienna of Schnitzler's time'.[3] A central aspect of the novel is the interaction between Jews and non-Jews; while initial scholarly readings looked at this question, broadly speaking, according to the binary of assimilation and Zionism, with the corresponding assumption that it was a one-way movement of a minority towards or away from the dominant majority, more recent interpretations have productively employed the concept of mutually beneficial acculturation — multifaceted individual interactions, political differentiation and nuance on both sides, and the day-to-day realities of the multicultural empire — to establish the novel's richly complex picture of a society in the grips of seismic change. Frank Stern neatly summarizes this dilemma for Vienna's Jews: 'Das Jüdische in der deutschsprachigen Kultur — so wie jüdische Kulturen überhaupt — ist weder eine dogmengeschichtlich definierte Religion noch eine abgeschlossene eigene Kultur, sondern existiert immer in einer dynamischen Wechselwirkung, sich verändernd, modifizierend, viele Identitäten, regionale und nationale Eigenarten in sich verbindend' [The Jewish element in German-language culture — like Jewish cultures in general — is neither a religion defined by its dogmatic history nor a separate culture, isolated from the rest, but exists rather in dynamic interaction, changing, modifying itself, bringing together many identities, and regional and national singularities].[4]

In a strategy similar to that employed in his play *Professor Bernhardi* (1912), Schnitzler blurs the distinction between public and private action in the late Habsburg Empire.[5] *Der Weg ins Freie* dissects the religious, racial and economic anti-Semitism that animated Austrian political culture following the dissolution of the Liberal coalition in Parliament in 1867, presenting Austria's Jewish community in its historical and ethnic complexity. The Jewish figures in both play and novel present a spectrum of human characteristics, from unapologetic champions of Zionism or ethnic pride, through assimilationists — those who converted to Christianity and those who remained nominally Jews — to crass opportunists who are embarrassed by their Jewishness. In so doing, Schnitzler

---

[3] Russell A. Berman, 'Introduction' to Schnitzler, *The Road into the Open*, p. vii.
[4] Frank Stern, 'Wege ins Freie: Der Dichter der Akkulturation und die Angst vor der Visualisierung des Jüdischen im Werk Arthur Schnitzlers (1945–2007)', in *Die Tatsachen der Seele. Arthur Schnitzler und der Film*, ed. by Thomas Ballhausen et al. (Vienna, 2006), pp. 171–206 (pp. 181–82).
[5] See Szilvia Ritz, *Der Österreich-Begriff in Schnitzlers Schaffen. Analyse seiner Erzählungen* (Vienna, 2006), p. 125: 'Schnitzlers Kritik gilt der Scheinheiligkeit und Unaufrichtigkeit sowohl im privaten als auch im öffentlichen Leben' [Schnitzler's critique is directed at hypocrisy and insincerity in both private and public life].

demystifies the construct of a uniform Jewish identity for a largely non-Jewish reading public, and posits the Jews in Austria as neither better nor worse than any other collective, indeed subject to the same human frailties as the general population. What was rapidly changing, though, for this same reading public, was the political atmosphere, where political anti-Semitism in the manner of Vienna's mayor Karl Lueger invoked a meta-Jew, one that had become a cipher for explaining many of the otherwise complex transformations of modernity and a convenient means to simplify, if not distort the interpretation of social and cultural developments. As Steven Beller points out, 'the anti-Semitism that emerged in the 1880s fed off a real culture clash. A population brought up with a traditional Catholic mindset, disoriented by the modern economy, was all too willing to accept the mendacious accusation that the "Jews" were to blame, for the one group who had completely identified their interests and values with the new modern world was emancipated Viennese Jewry'.[6] Schnitzler wrote against this grain, showing how the Jewish community, no more or less than any other, *reflected* such structural changes in Austrian society. This fundamental emphasis on demystification of social constructions — particularly as applied to the various relationships among its Jewish and non-Jewish characters — inhabits the novel's structure and characterizations, correctly refashioning the 'Jewish Question' to be equally a Christian Social, German Nationalist, Socialist or Austrian one.[7]

The novel chronicles a year in the life of the composer Georg von Wergenthin, a Gentile of noble birth and station. Georg's father has recently died, and the son, in his late twenties, must contemplate the end of his comfortable and relatively carefree existence in Vienna and the necessity of finding work as a composer or conductor. During the year, Georg begins a liaison with Anna Rosner, a singer (who is also not Jewish) from a lower-middle-class background, and socializes with writers, artists and musicians who congregate at a salon hosted by the Ehrenberg family. Here he meets Heinrich Bermann, a Jewish writer with whom he becomes more friendly, and the two begin work on an opera that has more than a little in common with the plot of Wagner's *Tristan und Isolde.* Through his contacts in the Ehrenberg salon, Georg witnesses passionate discussions of contemporary Austrian politics by a diverse array of Jewish figures; topics include nascent political Zionism, at the time one of the most important parliamentary debates. In addition to his association with Heinrich, Georg gets to know Edmund Nürnberger, a writer of the older generation of the liberal era, and Leo Golowski, a young mathematician and musical theorist. These acquaintances take an interest in Georg's compositions and value his company, although it is not clear to what extent Georg reciprocates their interest. Georg ends his relationship with Anna after the child

---

[6] Steven Beller, *A Concise History of Austria* (Cambridge, 2006), p. 175.
[7] See Heidi Gideon, 'Haupt- und Nebensache in Arthur Schnitzlers Roman *Der Weg ins Freie*', Text + Kritik, 138/139 (1998), 47–60.

they conceive is still-born, and leaves Vienna to take a job assisting the Kapellmeister at the court in Detmold. During the year, Georg begins several compositions but does not finish any of them, and the collaboration with Heinrich on their opera comes to naught.

As the novel's protagonist, Georg lacks the virtues Schnitzler prized as essential to coherent political action and social engagement: objectivity, courage and a sense of responsibility. Schnitzler stated in his *Aphorismen und Betrachtungen* [*Aphorisms and Observations*]: 'es gibt nur drei absolute Tugenden: Sachlichkeit, Mut und Verantwortungsgefühl; diese drei schließen nicht nur alle anderen gewissermaßen in sich ein, sondern ihr Dasein paralysiert sogar manche Untugenden und Schwächen, die gleichzeitig in derselben Seele vorhanden sein mögen' [there are only three absolute virtues: objectivity, courage and a sense of responsibility; these three not only encompass all others, in a sense, but their existence even paralyses some vices and weaknesses that might be present in the same soul].[8] Georg's lack of professional direction, the sentimental quality of his compositions, and his general tendency to indolence are prominent features of Schnitzler's characterization, implicitly linking to the other principal plotline, Georg's romantic liaison with Anna Rosner. With two notable scenic exceptions, the action is narrated from Georg's point of view, but Schnitzler is careful to present a gallery of complementary characters who make apparent the limitations of Georg's point of view. These limitations are especially evident in Georg's repression of memory, denial of responsibility and ultimate flight to Germany — in the world of the text, a place safe from Jews — and fit broadly into one of Schnitzler's primary aesthetic concerns: memory.[9] In order to establish Georg's limited point of view, one must tease out cues in the text — how his words and actions resonate with those around him — with which Schnitzler signals the unreliability of Georg's version of events while suggesting alternative roads into the open. The character who attempts to exert the most direct educational influence on Georg, one who encourages him to work harder and harness his musical talent more effectively, is Leo Golowski.

Central to my argument is this key corrective figure of Leo, a Jew, with whom, as John Neubauer points out, Georg shares the closest bond of any character in the novel: 'The bond with Golowski is the strongest, suggesting occasionally even touches of homoeroticism. [...] [I]ndeed, he seems to have an admiration for Golowski's Zionism, not because the idea itself appeals to him but rather because it shows (together with Golowski's duel) that he is a decisive and active person who forges new ideals to replace the outdated ones: Golowski has the determination and commitment that Georg is lacking'.[10]

---

[8] Arthur Schnitzler, *Aphorismen und Betrachtungen*, ed. by Robert O. Weiss (Frankfurt a. M., 1967), p. 48.
[9] See Konstanze Fliedl, *Arthur Schnitzler. Poetik der Erinnerung* (Vienna, 1997).
[10] John Neubauer, 'The Overaged Adolescents of Schnitzler's *Der Weg ins Freie*', in *A*

Georg is also linked to Leo through Anna, who had a crush on him when they were teenagers. In terms of Schnitzler's set of preferred virtues, Leo is all the things Georg is not: as a musician and theorist, Leo preaches and practises an ascetic formal Modernism à la Schoenberg, while Georg's compositions and playing style suggest a sentimentality that compensates for a lack of feeling and discipline, the 'innere Kälte' [inner coldness] that Leo diagnoses.[11] As Anna Rosner's first flame, Leo had conducted himself with honour, and speaks of her musical talents with empathy and insight, while Georg seduces and then abandons her; and as a political actor Leo is a principled Zionist who fights a duel against and kills his anti-Semitic commanding officer, while Georg remains in essence unaffected by the earnest pronouncements about political Zionism made by his numerous Jewish acquaintances — not just Leo — which constitute a large portion of the novel. As Andrew Wisely cogently observes, 'Schnitzler's most gripping account of military anti-Semitism is Leo Golowski's service year in *Der Weg ins Freie* [...]. Leo duels to liberate himself from a frightening status quo, not to preserve it, using a sanctioned vehicle of revenge in the age of mass politics'.[12] Since Georg's point of view dominates, the unfiltered sentiments of secondary characters such as Leo become important markers of Schnitzler's ironic distance from his central character.

Such thematic contrasts are buttressed by Schnitzler's formal introduction and use of this secondary character: Leo's appearances are sudden and surprising, and — suggesting the Wagnerian leitmotif — are compositionally consistent, surprising to Georg and the reader, but all bearing similar characteristics linking one appearance to the next. Leo's diction is brief and direct, in marked contrast to Georg's own often contradictory and rambling ruminations, and Leo's actions correlate directly with his stated principles. Leo's first actual appearance in the novel is choreographed to ensure maximum surprise to Georg and the reader. Heinrich and Georg are spinning out a fantasy of opening hotels in the Vienna Woods, speculating on how much they would cost, 'als plötzlich Leo

---

Companion to the Works of Arthur Schnitzler, ed. by Dagmar C. G. Lorenz (Rochester, NY, 2003), pp. 265–76 (p. 272).

[11] Arthur Schnitzler, *Das erzählerische Werk*, 7 vols (Frankfurt a. M., 1977–78), v: *Der Weg ins Freie* (rpt. 2000), p. 185. Subsequent references will be given in the body of the text simply as page numbers in parentheses (W). The translations are taken from Byers's edition of *The Road into the Open* (R: see note 1), here p. 143. On sentimentality, see Angela H. Lin, 'Resisting "Bad Taste": Sentimentality, "Jewishness", and Modernity in Arthur Schnitzler's *Der Weg ins Freie*', *German Quarterly*, 79 (2006), 366–80. Lin argues that Schnitzler's critique of sentimentality is at the heart of the novel: 'The author criticizes through showing us, unblinkingly, the hyper-reflexivity, the inaction, and the disorientation that sentimentality causes. If this unmediated look into the casualties of sentimentality renders the novel itself fragmentary and meandering, [...] we can nevertheless read it as a strategic comment, seemingly provided without lifting a critical finger that allows the problematic effects of sentimentality to surface on the body of the text' (p. 378).

[12] Andrew C. Wisely, *Arthur Schnitzler and the Discourse of Honor and Dueling* (New York, 1996), p. 195.

Golowski dastand' [when suddenly Leo Golowski was standing there] (W 99, R 76). Leo appears, as it were, embedded within a fantastical reverie — even within the same sentence — and immediately brings his interlocutors back to reality. Here the reader is also introduced to Leo's musical theories:

> Leo glaubte der Ursache auf der Spur zu sein, aus der Dur- und Molltonarten die menschliche Seele in so verschiedener Weise berührten. Gerne folgte Georg seinen klaren und scharfsinnigen Auseinandersetzungen, wenn sich auch etwas in ihm gegen den verwegenen Versuch wehrte, allen Zauber und alles Geheimnis der Klänge aus dem Walten von Gesetzen gedeutet zu hören. (W 100)

> [Leo believed the foundation to lie in the way the major and minor tonalities moved the human soul in such diverse ways. Georg followed the clear and incisive repartee with enjoyment, though something in him also resisted hearing the bold attempt to explain all the magic and all the mystery of the sounds through the rule of laws.] (R 77)

Georg distances himself from Leo's theoretical approach to musical language, preferring a more impressionistic position. While Georg thus bears a familial resemblance to such central characters in Schnitzler's works as Anatol, Dr Gräsler, Willi Kasda and Fridolin, Leo is quite the opposite; his theoretical bent in musical questions informs his ethical action in questions of honour and politics.

Of particular importance to the novel's musical theme is a central scene — one of the main features of the novel's middle chapter — between Georg and Leo. The announcement: 'Sie sprachen beinahe nur über Musik an diesem Abend' [They spoke almost only about music this evening] (W 184, R 142) introduces their dialogue,[13] in which Leo expounds on his own musical theory, tells Georg directly that he is lazy and that his musical compositions reflect this, and encourages Georg to rededicate himself to his craft. Here Schnitzler, through the contrast of Georg's dominant point of view with the minor-key composition of Leo's character, is able to suggest a broader indictment of social relations and political practice at the turn of the century without compromising the narrative construct, which demands that events be filtered through the main protagonist's consciousness. Georg, then, as representative of the dominant culture, is not held to an exacting standard, so his dishonourable actions and mediocre compositions remain, within the text, without consequence, while Leo, who personally represents a more ethical and original road into the open, is fated to a more marginal existence.

From the time of its publication, Der Weg ins Freie met with critical resistance based on the claim that Schnitzler had insufficiently integrated the two primary plotlines, the love story between Georg and Anna and the broad discussions of cultural and political questions. A close look at the composition of the figure of

---

[13] Interestingly, Lin ('Resisting "Bad Taste"') does not analyse the musical criticism in the text, even though it is at these moments that the category of sentimentality finds its most cogent examples in Leo's critique of Georg's compositional technique.

Leo Golowski shows one important way in which Schnitzler connects the two plotlines: he had been Anna's first love interest — Georg finds this by turns disturbing and admirable — and he speaks insightfully about contemporary political and cultural matters, particularly in the extended dialogue on the Sophienalpe with Heinrich Bermann, while acting honourably *vis-à-vis* Anna and with pride in his Jewishness. The novel's central themes, music, politics, and honour in interpersonal relations, find ethical expression, if briefly, in what Leo says and does, and present a counter-example to Georg's much more extensive reflections, which are rarely productive and often contradictory.

When comparing initial drafts of the novel with the final published version, one is struck by the strategic nature of Schnitzler's cuts: what was at first a character given to expansive and pathos-laden orations becomes, in the published version, one whose appearances are brief, whose remarks are to-the-point, and whose presence is ultimately vexing for Georg (and the reader). Particularly in the conception of Leo's character, Schnitzler contrasts ethical action with the more prominent characters' solipsism and creative stasis: while others talk, Leo acts. Konstanze Fliedl, in her broad reflections on the novel, argues that crafting the Georg/Leo contrast in this way is evidence of the discipline and discretion of Schnitzler's narrative technique; Leo's broad indictments in the initial drafts, where he is given to sweeping and emotional generalizations, become lean, principled articulations of his political Zionism, characterized by empathy and engagement (qualities that Georg lacks): 'Schnitzler war, was Georgs Haltung — und die Anklage der jüdischen Figuren — betrifft, von einer unglaublichen Diskretion [...] besonders Leo Golowski kürzt [er] ab' [Schnitzler was unbelievably discreet with respect to Georg's attitude and the charges of the Jewish figures; in particular he makes cuts in the role of Leo Golowski].[14] The scenes where Leo is present come at key points in the novel: the famous discussion of Jews' assimilation versus political Zionism conducted on a bicycle outing to the Sophienalpe; the meeting and musical conversation with Georg at the novel's mid-point; Leo's appearance in Georg's cryptic dream, lecturing on musical theory; and Georg's visit to Leo after the latter's duel (which has been described largely by other figures in the text). In each instance, Leo acts in a didactic capacity with respect to Georg — most clearly in the dream sequence in which Leo is lecturing on musical theory and directing the late-arriving Georg to his seat — suggesting by his actions an example that Georg would do well to heed; that Georg does not learn from Leo and is not penalized for his lapses in judgment, indeed is promoted, is one of the novel's more poignant and prophetic ironies.

One of the key elements of Leo's critique of Georg is the latter's approach to his art. Schnitzler establishes this early in the text, introducing Georg's lack of compositional discipline in a scene where he remembers a conversation

[14] Konstanze Fliedl, 'Nachwort' to Arthur Schnitzler, *Der Weg ins Freie* (Salzburg, 1995), p. 460.

with his now-deceased father:

> Er hatte wieder ein halbes Jahr oder länger nichts Rechtes gearbeitet, nicht einmal das schwermütige Adagio war niedergeschrieben, das er in Palermo, an einem bewegten Morgen am Ufer spazierengehend, aus dem Rauschen der Wellen herausgehört hatte. Nun spielte er das Thema seinem Vater vor, phantasierte darüber mit einem übertriebenen Reichtum an Harmonien, der die einfache Melodie beinahe verschlang; und als er eben in eine wild modulierende Variation geraten war, hatte der Vater, vom anderen Ende des Flügels her, lächelnd gefragt: Wohin, wohin? Georg, wie beschämt, ließ den Schwall der Töne verklingen. (W 7–8)
>
> [He had not really worked again for a half year or longer; not even the melancholy Adagio that he had heard in the roaring of the waves on an agitated morning in Palermo as he walked along the shore had been written down. He had played the theme for his father, in a fantasy of such excessive harmonic richness that the simple melody was almost engulfed; and as he began a new wildly modulating variation, his father had asked, smiling from the other end of the grand piano: 'Where, where?' Georg, as if embarrassed, let the flood of tones die away.] (R 3–4)

In this passage, the reader sees a conventional account of artistic inspiration — one in stark contrast to Leo Golowski's ascetic Modernism, for instance, and it is no coincidence that in a subsequent scene it is Georg's recital of this particular composition for Leo that prompts the latter's withering critique — where the musical piece is prompted by a self-indulgent and uncritical reverie. Leo's verdict emphasizes, however, the lack of compositional discipline that undermines Georg's art: 'Manches ist wie von einem Dilettanten mit sehr viel Geschmack und anderes wie von einem Künstler ohne rechte Zucht' [Some of it is like a dilettante with a lot of taste, and some like an artist without enough discipline] (W 185, R 143). Leo espouses a musical aesthetic that anticipates the formal modernism of Theodor Adorno, specifically linking the ethical and political to compositional principles of innovation and analytical rigour, while Georg perceives such an approach as taking away the magical, Romantic aspect of musical creation. Though Schnitzler goes out of his way to discourage readerly identification with Leo, who remains relatively inscrutable, on the question of the link between creativity, politics and ethics there can be little doubt: Georg's approach valorizes musical kitsch, while Leo's is one of formal rigour.

Georg's compositional practice is also outlined in a brief exchange with Anna Rosner, one which becomes paradigmatic for their relationship as well:

> 'Das Lied hat mir [Anna] heut' noch besser gefallen, als beim erstenmal, wie ich mich selber begleiten mußte. Nur zum Schluß verläuft es ein bißchen ... ich weiß nicht, wie ich sagen soll.'
> 'Ich weiß, was Sie meinen. Der Schluß ist konventionell, das hab' ich gleich gefühlt. Hoffentlich kann ich Ihnen bald was Besseres bringen, Fräulein Anna.'
> 'Lassen Sie mich aber nicht zu lange darauf warten.' (W 38)

['I (Anna) liked the song better today than the first time when I had to accompany myself. Only it seems to drift a little at the end ... I don't quite know how I should put it.'
'I know what you mean. The conclusion is conventional; I felt it myself. Hopefully I can bring you something better soon, Fraulein Anna.'
'But don't keep me waiting for it too long.'] (R 27)

The end of their relationship is foreshadowed here: Georg does not transcend the social conventions attending a noble–petit bourgeois liaison, and nor does he ever intend to, so he breaks with Anna as soon as it is socially acceptable to do so. More importantly, Schnitzler here links Georg's artistic praxis with his approach to interpersonal relationships; Anna, like Leo, engages Georg about the conventionality and sentimentality of his compositions, encouraging him to work harder and go beyond the limitations of artistic convention, and while Georg listens, there is little translation of what he hears into concrete action. Georg's ethical failure is thus drafted in musicological terms: where Georg keeps domains of his personal and professional life distinct and compartmentalized, Schnitzler — through the didactic impulses of secondary figures — shows such compartmentalization to be dangerously illusory and self-deceptive, with ultimately serious political consequences.

Leo is variously described in the novel as mathematician, musical theorist, political activist and one-year man serving in the Imperial army. He has clearly reflected on philosophical matters, the nature of art and creativity, and the relations between Jews and non-Jews in Austria, and is active in a wide variety of disciplines: 'Er hörte Vorlesungen an der Technik, gab Klavierlektionen, plante zuweilen sogar eine Virtuosenlaufbahn und übte dann wochenlang fünf bis sechs Stunden täglich' [He attended lectures at the technical school, gave piano lessons, even planned a virtuoso career for a time, and then would practice five to six hours a day] (W 111–12, R 85). He also takes more than a passing interest in politics, often accompanying his sister, Therese, who is a rising star in the Social Democratic Party, to sessions of Parliament. Leo's political philosophy is equally stringent in its assessment of the gulf between stated purpose and actual political action. The Golowski family as a whole comes to represent the fragmentary nature and tragic fate of Austria's Jewish community: the father's business fails, necessitating a move to a much more modest home; the mother must work but also selflessly helps out during Anna's pregnancy; Therese becomes an activist in the Social Democratic Party, while pursuing Romantic liaisons with members of the aristocracy; and Leo's many talents receive relatively little social echo. Where one might expect diffusion, though, the Golowski family unit actually becomes a site of common purpose, as is evident in Georg's final visit, in which he is surprised to find a commodious family scene.

Throughout the novel, Leo — and particularly his duel — is a preferred topic of conversation among its characters, functioning in the retelling as an example of principled action. Schnitzler emphasizes this in one of the few scenes in which Georg is not present, thus one not narrated through his point of view: Dr Stauber and his son, Berthold, another physician, discuss Berthold's return to Austrian politics after a fellowship at the Pasteur Institute in Paris. Berthold had resigned his parliamentary mandate in disgust because of political anti-Semitism but has returned to rejoin the battle, armed as well with an unfortunate emphasis on eugenics in public health policy. The topic of the conversation between father and son is Leo Golowski, particularly the circumstances surrounding the prosecution of his duel. Berthold is sceptical about whether Leo will receive amnesty: 'Im übrigen leben wir bekanntlich in einem Staat, wo ein Jude nicht davor sicher ist, wegen Ritualmords zum Tode verurteilt zu werden; warum sollten also die Behörden vor der offiziösen Annahme zurückscheuen, daß Juden sich bei Pistolenduellen gegen Christen — vielleicht aus religiösen Gründen — einen verbrecherischen Vorteil zu sichern wissen?' [Besides, it's well known that we live in a country where a Jew is not safe from being condemned to death for a ritual killing; why should the authorities shy away from the official assumption that by pistol duels with Christians — perhaps on religious grounds — Jews know how to secure a criminal advantage?] (W 317–18, R 248). Dr Stauber, on the other hand, compares Leo's actions favourably with Berthold's motivations for political activity: 'Daß einer losschlägt, wie es Leo Golowski getan, das kann ich noch verstehen, so wenig ich es billigen möchte. Aber immer dastehen, die geballte Faust in der Tasche, sozusagen, was hat das für einen Zweck?' [That someone strikes out like Leo Golowski did, I can still understand, however little I may approve of it. But to just stand there, with a clenched fist in one's pocket, so to speak, what's the purpose of that?] (W 319, R 249). By contrasting Leo's conception of individual honour with Berthold's advocacy of sacrificing unhealthy citizens in the interest of the public good, Schnitzler underscores the decoupling of appearance and reality in political action.

Like Leo Golowski, the Staubers are intertwined in both of the novel's plotlines. As a potential suitor for Anna, Berthold loses out to Georg; and as a parliamentarian he is disgusted by political anti-Semitism. His father, who takes a longer view of political questions, represents the liberal belief in social progress through tolerance and deeds, while also serving as the attending physician during Anna's pregnancy. Berthold also provides the important corrective *vis-à-vis* Georg when attempting to explain why the Jewish figures in the text seek his company: 'Nun ja, ein schöner, schlanker, blonder junger Mann; Freiherr, Germane, Christ — welcher Jude könnte diesem Zauber widerstehen?' [Well yes, a handsome, slender, blond young man; Baron, German, Christian, — what Jew could resist this magic?] (W 323–24, R 253). Dr Stauber takes his son to task for not knowing his proper place in the social hierarchy, but takes a different tone in the following encounter with Georg, who has been waiting to meet Dr Stauber during the dialogue between father and son. This tone is overly solicitous and indulgent, given that Dr Stauber has closely witnessed Georg's behaviour *vis-à-vis* Anna, and subtly underscores the validity of Berthold's point. Berthold, Anna and Leo are linked, then, with each other, in a nexus of personal and professional relationships, and with Georg, as figures who, through discussions of musical culture and contemporary politics, attempt unsuccessfully to bring Georg into a more socially engaged and creatively interesting position.

Schnitzler treats these questions through the figure of Leo most expansively in the extended dialogue on art, politics and Zionism between Heinrich and Leo on the Sophienalpe; throughout the dialogue, Georg remains a relatively silent witness. Heinrich dismisses the philosophical underpinnings of the Zionist position, arguing that he feels at home in Austria and in the German language. It has become a commonplace of Schnitzler scholarship to identify Heinrich Bermann as Schnitzler's spokesman in the text,[15] but it may be equally applicable to see aspects of Leo's character as representative of Schnitzler's position. Leo's principled Zionism approximates what Schnitzler articulated when explaining his vote for the Zionist party in the state elections of 1920 ('dass in der National Versammlung einige bewußte Juden sitzen, die sagen, was zu sagen ist' [so that a few self-aware Jews are elected to the National Assembly and say what needs to be said]),[16] and it is clear in the text that Leo embodies the most ethical conduct. After Heinrich asserts that members of a Christian Social youth group have no right to argue that Jews do not belong in Austrian society, and that the Zionist position tacitly approves such an assertion, Leo, while agreeing with Heinrich's premise, passionately refutes Heinrich's solipsistic position:

> Ihr [Heinrichs] Blick in diesen Dingen ist doch ein wenig beschränkt. Sie denken immer an sich und an den nebensächlichen Umstand [...]. Es handelt sich aber in erster Linie gar nicht um Sie und auch nicht um mich, auch nicht um die paar jüdischen Beamten, die nicht avancieren, die paar jüdischen Freiwilligen, die nicht Offiziere werden, die jüdischen Dozenten, die man nicht oder verspätet zu Professoren macht, — das sind lauter Unannehmlichkeiten zweiten Ranges sozusagen; es handelt sich hier um ganz andre Menschen, die Sie nicht genau oder gar nicht kennen, und um Schicksale, über die Sie, ich versichre Sie, lieber Heinrich, über die Sie gewiß, trotz der Verpflichtung, die Sie eigentlich dazu hätten, noch nicht gründlich genug nachgedacht haben. (W 105)

> [Your view in these matters is a little restricted. You always think of yourself and of the incidental circumstance [...]. In the first place it isn't a matter at all of you or of me, nor of a few Jewish officials who are not promoted, a few Jewish volunteers who are not made officers, or of Jewish docents who are never or only late made professors, — those are mere inconveniences of secondary importance so to speak; it is a matter here of

---

[15] See Fliedl, 'Nachwort' to Schnitzler, *Der Weg ins Freie*, pp. 458–59.
[16] Arthur Schnitzler, *Tagebuch. 1920–1922*, ed. by Werner Welzig et al. (Vienna, 1993), p. 98; entry for 17 October 1920.

entirely different people, whom you know little or not at all, and of destiny, about which you, I assure you, dear Heinrich, about which you certainly, despite the obligation that you actually should feel, have not yet considered thoroughly enough.] (R 81)

Leo frames his Zionist position around the principles of empathy and responsibility, going on to recount his experiences at the international Zionist Congress in Basle; he attacks Heinrich's assimilationist position as selfish and egocentric. While Georg witnesses this impassioned argument, and is from time to time engaged by Heinrich and Leo for his opinion, he only follows their discussion at a superficial level. Here Schnitzler's narrative technique is careful simultaneously to evoke the content of the discussion and Georg's inattentiveness: 'Die Sätze stürmten ineinander hinein, verkrampften sich ineinander, schossen aneinander vorbei, gingen ins Leere; — und in irgend einem Augenblick merkte Georg, daß er nur mehr den Klang der Reden hörte, ohne ihrem Inhalt folgen zu können' [The sentences stormed into one another, cramped each other, and, missing their mark, flew out into empty space; — and at some point Georg realized that he could hear only the noise of their argument, without being able to follow the content] (W 109, R 83). Georg distances himself from Heinrich's and Leo's assertions because they make him uncomfortable; in the subsequent discussion of Georg's compositions in the novel's central chapter, it is just this sort of emotional distancing that Leo diagnoses in Georg's artistic production, and the dialogue on the Sophienalpe prefigures Leo's dissection of Georg's musical sensibility.

The specific topics of their discussion of musical matters are Georg's Adagio and the Quintet, compositions that Georg transcribed after being inspired by the physical world. Leo uses this premise to engage Georg on more general musical questions, which prompts a quite direct critique of Georg's work:

'Eigentlich weiß man noch gar nichts,' sagte [Leo]. 'Manches ist wie von einem Dilettanten mit sehr viel Geschmack und anderes wie von einem Künstler ohne rechte Zucht. In den Liedern spürt man noch am ehesten ... aber was ... Talent? ... ich weiß nicht ... daß Sie eine vornehme Natur sind, spürt man jedenfalls, eine musikalisch vornehme Natur.'

'Na, das wäre nicht viel.'

'Es ist sogar ziemlich wenig. Aber da Sie noch so wenig gearbeitet haben, beweist das auch nichts gegen Sie. Wenig gearbeitet und wenig durchfühlt.'

'Sie glauben ...' Georg zwang sich zu einem spöttischen Lächeln.

'O, erlebt wahrscheinlich sehr viel, aber gefühlt ... wissen Sie, was ich meine, Georg?'

'Ja, ich kann mir's schon denken. Aber Sie irren sich entschieden. Ich finde sogar eher, daß ich eine gewisse Neigung zu Sentimentalität habe, die ich bekämpfen muß.'

'Ja, das ist es eben. Sentimentalität ist nämlich etwas, was in einem direkten Gegensatz zum Gefühl steht, etwas, womit man sich über seine Gefühllosigkeit, seine innere Kälte beruhigt. Sentimentalität ist Gefühl, das man sozusagen unter dem Einkaufspreis erstanden hat. Ich hasse Sentimentalität.' (W 185)

['I really can't tell yet,' (Leo) said, 'Some of it is like a dilettante with a lot of taste, and some like an artist without enough discipline. One feels it most in the songs ... but what? ... Talent? ... I don't know. ... In any case one feels that you have a noble nature, a musically noble nature.'
'Well, that's not much.'
'It may seem rather little. But since you still have worked so little, it doesn't prove anything against you. Worked little and experienced little.'
'You think ...' Georg responded, forcing a derisive smile.
'Oh, lived through a lot, perhaps, but felt ... do you know what I mean Georg?'
'Yes, I can imagine. But you're quite wrong. I even feel that I have a certain inclination to sentimentality, which I have to resist.'
'Yes, that's it. Sentimentality is something that stands in direct opposition to feeling, something with which one compensates for one's lack of feeling, one's inner coldness. Sentimentality is feeling that one has bought, so to speak, for the purchase price. I hate sentimentality.'] (R 143)

In Leo's withering indictment of Georg's artistic praxis — one borne out by subsequent events in the text, as Georg brings nothing to fruition — music functions as a safe topic, though one laden with significance, allowing Leo to refer obliquely to Georg's liaison with Anna. As we have seen, Schnitzler links the characters of Anna and Leo on numerous levels, and each acts with Georg's best interests at heart, but Georg does not respond in a way that transcends the inner coldness that Leo diagnoses. It is through the category of sentimentality that Leo links Georg's approach to music, his casual attitude to political questions that are of existential importance to others, and his emotional coldness towards Anna. What Georg tries to keep apart, Leo links in an argument undergirded by ethical concerns and their translation into coherent action.

Leo also plays a prominent role in a troubling dream that Georg has on the train returning to Vienna from a trip that he has taken just days before Anna is due to give birth. The dream — only dimly recalled by Georg — brings together in telescopic fashion characters from the novel and from Georg's opera; the links between Georg, Anna and Leo feature prominently:

Leo hatte seinen Vortrag über Mollakkorde begonnen, hielt inne, als Georg erschien, stieg vom Katheder herab und führte ihn selbst zu einem freien Stuhl, der in der ersten Reihe neben Anna stand. Anna lächelte glückselig, als Georg erschien. Sie war jung und strahlend, in einem herrlichen, dekolletierten Abendtoilette. Gleich hinter ihr saß ein kleiner Bub mit blonden Locken, in Matrosenanzug mit breitem, weißem Kragen, und Anna sagte: 'Das ist er.' Georg machte ihr ein Zeichen zu schweigen, denn es sollte ja ein Geheimnis sein. Indessen spielte Leo oben als Beweis seiner Theorie die cis-Moll-Nocturne von Chopin. (W 273)

[Leo, who had begun his lecture on minor chords, stopped as Georg arrived, came down from the rostrum, and led Georg himself to an open chair which stood in the first row next to Anna. Anna smiled happily when Georg appeared. She was young and radiant, in a splendid, low-necked evening dress. Right behind her sat a small boy with blond hair, in a sailor suit with a broad white collar, and Anna said: 'That's him.' Georg made a sign to be quiet, since it was supposed to be a secret. Meanwhile up front, Leo played the Chopin C♯ minor Nocturne in demonstration of his theory.] (R 212)

Here, in most encapsulated form, Leo performs pedagogically, directing Georg to his seat, but also theoretically informing the wider audience. When Georg awakens, Schnitzler is careful to evoke Georg's inability to recall these details in the dream. Still, the reader sees that Georg has internalized Leo as an educational figure, one who guides him to the place where he belongs. That Georg ignores Leo's musical and ethical recommendations is clear, and is ultimately constitutive of Schnitzler's critique of his central character. The contents of Leo's lecture sketch out his philosophy of complexity in human affairs; Leo functions as a figure in the text as a minor key to Georg's major key.

In their final encounter — one brought about by his desire to congratulate Leo after the latter is released from prison — Georg already begins to distance himself emotionally from Leo. This psychological move, paradoxically, is animated by empathy, something attendant to Leo's philosophy of life, but something which Georg generally lacks in his interpersonal relations. Curiously, Georg finds himself thinking of the duel's victim while he talks to Leo: '[Georg] nickte nur und dachte an den armen jungen Menschen, den Leo erschossen und der eigentlich gar nichts anderes gegen die Juden gehabt hatte, als daß sie ihm so zuwider gewesen waren, wie schließlich den meisten Menschen — und dessen Schuld im Grunde nur darin bestanden hatte, daß er an den Unrechten gekommen war' [Georg only nodded and thought of the poor young man whom Leo had shot, and who actually had no more against the Jews than that they had been as unappealing to him as they were to most other people — and whose guilt at bottom had consisted only in that he had come up against the wrong man] (W 355, R 277). This is one of many instances in the text where Georg's thoughts are much more aligned with the dominant culture's mainstream attitudes than his utterances would betray, given that these are usually governed by politeness, discretion and his audience of the moment. Nevertheless, coming at the end of a novel with many nods to the tradition of the *Bildungsroman*, it is interesting to note how little education and spiritual growth has taken place in Georg. His relocation to Detmold is then the objective correlative to the psychological distance that he requires after each individual encounter with the novel's Jews; just as he soothes his own conscience by banishing troubling thoughts, he flees to a location that ensures that such troubling encounters are kept to a minimum.

Der Weg ins Freie endures as a revelatory psychogram of turn-of-the-century Vienna because it simultaneously evokes the crises of modernity and the indolence of the Monarchy's privileged classes. The rise of the Jewish community and its contribution to economic, political and cultural spheres corresponded to the nobility's inexorable decline in status and economic power, and it is this particular cleavage that is at the heart of the novel's construction. Georg von Wergenthin, a nobleman of apparent good intentions, if ineffectual results, enjoys a free pass politically, economically, ethically and artistically, while the complementary characters, almost exclusively of Jewish origin, are depicted in their day-to-day struggles for acceptance and recognition in an atmosphere characterized by lack of empathy and hostility. Leo Golowski is a key figure in this gallery of complementary characters, a brief photographic negative of Georg von Wergenthin, one who embodies the qualities of objectivity, courage and responsibility in inverse relation to Georg. Even though the text makes clear the bond between the two, their attitudes towards music become an important point of contrast. Georg is comfortable reworking musical conventions in his own compositions, requiring only the atmosphere of his art, while Leo thinks originally about the philosophical underpinnings of music. Similarly, the emotional equation of their relationship is out of balance, as Leo succinctly puts it after a chance meeting: '*Sie* freut es, […] daß Sie mich zufällig wieder zu Gesicht kriegen, und mir war es ein Bedürfnis, Sie noch einmal zu sehen, das ist der Unterschied' [*You* are glad that by accident you found me in person, but for me it was a necessity to see you again, that's the difference] (W 184, R 142). Leo is one of many figures in Schnitzler's text who takes more than a passing interest in the moral education of the central figure; that they fail to move Georg out of creative stasis and emotional frigidity is central to Schnitzler's larger point about the social and political consequences of such inability to empathize with others. Here we find a compelling and poignant illustration of the limits of acculturation in turn-of-the-century Vienna.

The Adventures of *The Cunning Little Vixen*: Leoš Janáček, Max Brod and their Predecessors

GEOFFREY CHEW

Royal Holloway, University of London

I

The image of the composer Leoš Janáček as an unruly genius whose wild ideas sometimes needed taming is an old one; and to some extent his faithful admirer and translator, Max Brod, is to blame, even if Janáček himself began by enthusiastically accepting Brod's help. Brod's relationship with Janáček, and his understanding of the relation between words and music in Janáček's works, in fact depended on complicated issues of personality, aesthetics, religion and politics. I would like to illustrate these here through focusing on the work in which Brod's 'tamings' of Janáček reached their peak in 1925, *Příhody lišky Bystroušky* [*The Cunning Little Vixen*, 'The Adventures of Vixen Sharpears', 1922–23]; and to do this adequately, the genesis of the libretto of that opera, in its various earlier versions, will need to be revisited, as well as Brod's own intellectual development in the 1920s. Much of the material to be quoted is well known in general, but the interpretations offered here are new in a number of respects and will help, I hope, to clarify some aspects of the relationship between words and music in *The Cunning Little Vixen* (and not only in Brod's version of it) that may still seem puzzling.

As is well known, Brod spoke and read Czech, and his engagement with the composer had begun with his translation of the libretto of *Jenůfa* (*Její pastorkyňa*) in 1916–17.[1] Introduced to Janáček's music by Josef Suk, Dvořák's

[1] For substantial recent accounts of the relationship between Janáček and Brod, see Chapter 8 ('Max Brod, Friend and Meddler') in John Tyrrell, *Janáček. Years of a Life*, 2 vols (London, 2006–07), II: *Tsar of the Forests*, pp. 124–31; and Antony Ernst, '"Durch kleine Ritze nimmt man Abgründe wahr". An Examination of Max Brod's Performing Versions of the Works of Leoš Janáček' (unpublished doctoral thesis, University of Newcastle, Australia, 2003). I am grateful to Dr Ernst for making a copy of his dissertation available to me. Earlier discussions include Charles Susskind, *Janáček and Brod* (New Haven, CT, 1985), and influential contributions from Milan Kundera, notably in his *Les testaments trahis. Essai* (Paris, 1993), and several translations, including *Testaments Betrayed. An Essay in Nine Parts*, trans. by Linda Asher (London, 1995). The present article overlaps in minor respects with my own brief (unreferenced) article, 'Is Leoš Janáček's *Příhody lišky Bystroušky* a Rejection of a Romantic Lie?', in the Festschrift for Miloš Štědroň, *Sborník prací Filozofické fakulty Brněnské univerzity / Studia minora facultatis philosophicae universitatis Brunensis*, H 41 (2006), 75–82, but offers fresh perspectives.

son-in-law, Brod was bowled over by its originality, and he resolved to fight the composer's cause, translating texts, publishing the first book on Janáček in 1924, and generally acting as a cultural go-between.[2] All this immeasurably eased the progress of the composer's reputation in Vienna and further afield. But Brod had a sense that Janáček's taste and judgment were not always infallible, at least in the impression his works were likely to make on audiences in the German-speaking sphere. So a pattern of intervention as well as assistance began to emerge in his translations of Janáček's texts, from *Káťa Kabanová* (1921–22) onwards, with Brod increasingly rationalizing elements in them. Such intervention reached its peak in the text for the *Vixen*, referred to by both Brod and Janáček in letters as an *Umdichtung* [recomposition] rather than an *Übersetzung* [translation].[3] Subsequently, it may have been Janáček's increasing fame that enabled the composer, with the support of his publishers, Universal Edition, to resist further sweeping changes proposed by Brod for the translation of the text of *The Makropulos Case* (1926), with Brod retreating to a more conservative and cautious line, though he continued to act as Janáček's translator.

II

Although Brod arguably failed to grasp important aspects of Janáček's aesthetic, an issue to which we shall return, in the case of *The Cunning Little Vixen* there are substantial intrinsic peculiarities, if not problems, which are largely to do with its genre. As Susskind points out, the relatively familiar operatic generic features of the plots of *Jenůfa* and *Káťa Kabanová*, especially that of the latter, with a heroine doomed to die tragically at the end, are dropped in favour of a series of 'nine dreamy episodes [that] follow no particular logic' and have 'perplexed all listeners (beginning with Brod) whose thinking tends to be [...] "linear"'.[4] But this episodic structure, though new in Janáček's output, was not his invention. It derives both from the novel on which the opera is based, Rudolf Těsnohlídek's *Liška Bystrouška* (1921), which was originally serialized in the Brno newspaper *Lidové noviny*, and from an earlier source yet, a series of

---

[2] The book was published first in Czech translation (Max Brod, *Leoš Janáček. Život a dílo* [Prague, 1924]), and the original German version was published the following year.

[3] See Ernst, '"Durch kleine Ritze nimmt man Abgründe wahr"', p. 233. Janáček uses the term in writing to Emil Hertzka of Universal Edition, 22 June 1925: 'ich möchte [...] vor dem Druck gern seine "Umdichtung" lesen' [I would like to read his 'recomposition' before it goes into print]. Leoš Janáček, *Briefe an die Universal Edition*, ed. by Ernst Hilmar (Tutzing, 1988), p. 237.

[4] Susskind, *Janáček and Brod*, p. 71. Janáček intended at one point to drop the division of the opera into acts and instead use named scenes, but though names for scenes remained, he finally settled on a compromise three-act structure. Michael Ewans argues against the opera having an episodic structure at all (Michael Ewans, *Janáček's Tragic Operas* [London, 1977], p. 138), but only because the episodes come in a notionally chronological order.

more than 200 black-and-white drawings by the genre painter Stanislav Lolek (1873–1936).[5]

The status of these pictures and their connection with Těsnohlídek's novel were explained to the Brno public later by Bohumil Markalous, who had been the arts editor of the newspaper and had felt the need of a pictorial feature for it.[6] Visiting Prague, by chance he discovered a portfolio of comic drawings of a fox in Lolek's studio, and persuaded the artist to let him take them to Brno as the basis of a serialized feature which he thought might be in the style of Wilhelm Busch's *Hans Huckebein, der Unglücksrabe* [*Hans Huckebein, the Bird of Ill-Omen*], also first published in serial form more than half a century earlier.[7] Busch's concise rhyming couplets, each accompanied by a drawing, tell of the escapades of a crow, captured as a chick and taken home by a small boy, that wreaks havoc in his aunt's old-fashioned domestic establishment until it hangs itself in her knitting; there is much amoral comic *Schadenfreude* before the sudden tongue-in-cheek, matter-of-fact 'moral' of the final couplet: '"Die Bosheit war sein Hauptpläsier, | Drum", spricht die Tante, "hängt er hier!"' ['Mischief was his main diversion', his aunt proclaims, 'that's why he's hanging here now!']. With this in mind, the general editor of *Lidové noviny*, Arnošt Heinrich, asked Těsnohlídek, a member of the editorial staff at the time, to create a 'Buschiade' by writing verses to accompany Lolek's drawings; the intended genre (a comic versified account of unrelated episodes of catastrophic mischief-making) was clear. Těsnohlídek agreed, but was permitted in the event to expand the narrative into continuous prose, which allowed him much more freedom in reinterpreting the drawings.

Although the original purpose of Lolek's drawings remains unclear, they were well suited to this new use, and their narrative thrust is not difficult to follow. Groups of drawings tell brief, self-contained stories illustrating the behaviour of a fox and other wild forest animals, which are lightly anthropomorphized with unsentimental and gently comic attributes. And traces remain of Lolek's conception in all later versions.

To illustrate the relationship between the versions, it may be worth tracing one of the episodes in detail through them. To this end, I shall select the episode that became the first scene of Act II — one of the more problematic

---

[5] The drawings are all reproduced in the Prague National Theatre production booklet, *Leoš Janáček: Příhody lišky Bystroušky*, ed. by Pavel Petránek (Prague, 2002).

[6] Markalous's first-hand account, published under his pen name, Jaromír John, was written in collaboration with Josef Rejsek and published in the *Divadelní list Národního divadla v Brně* of 5 May 1948; my account of it above is quoted from Jaroslav Vogel, *Leoš Janáček* (Prague, 1963; rev. edn, Prague, 1997), p. 257 (rev. edn); Eng. trans. in Vogel, *Leoš Janáček. A Biography* (London, 1962; rev. edn, London, 1981), p. 269 (rev. edn).

[7] Busch's *Hans Huckebein*, still in print today, was first published in four instalments in the Stuttgart journal *Über Land und Meer*, 10 (1867–68), 1/13, 3/45, 5/77 and 8/125. Markalous also mentions another illustrated story of Busch's as a possible model, his *Pater Filuzius* (an allegorical versified story about ecclesiastical politics).

The Adventures of *The Cunning Little Vixen* 117

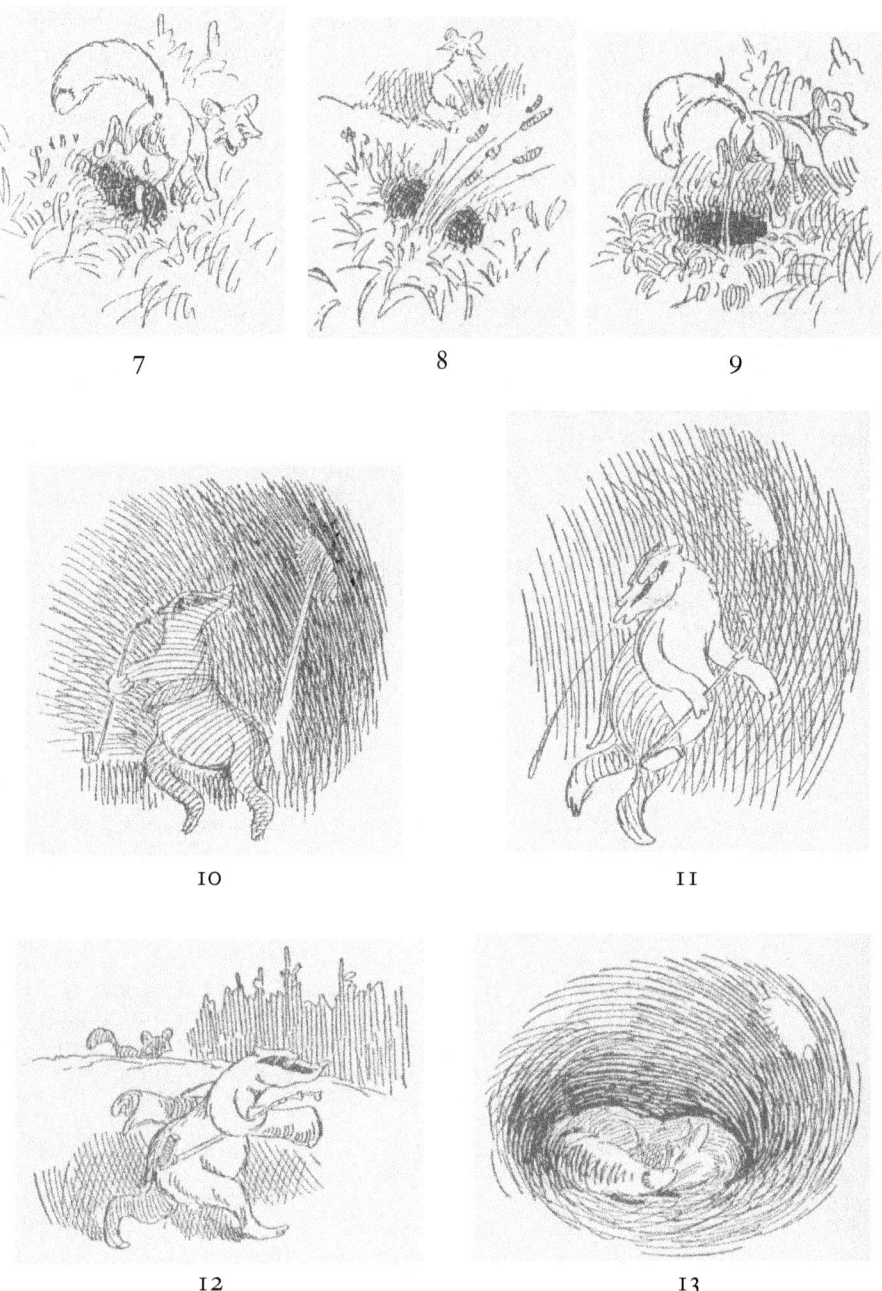

scenes within Janáček's opera, at least from the point of view of a producer, and later one of the most problematic for Brod. This is based on the thirteen successive pictures reproduced here from Lolek's originals, which depict a fox or vixen expelling a badger from its sett by fouling it. They alternate unstably between naturalistic observation and anthropomorphism. The first three pictures launch the narrative, with the fox and badger both reacting to a shower of rain — the badger emerging (picture 2), retreating (3), and thus drawing the attention of the fox to the sett. Next, the animals are shown with human attributes: the badger contentedly smokes a long pipe (4) and repels the intruder with a whip (5), and the fox creates a scene with melodramatic human gestures (6). Anthropomorphism is abandoned, with the fox spraying the sett with a few drops of urine (7), the badger reacting strongly (8), and the fox then fouling the sett with a deluge of urine (9–10), but it returns, with the badger (pipe in hand) spitting disgustedly (11), and leaving the sett with pipe and rolled-up mat (12), watched from a distance by the fox. Finally the fox is installed in the sett (13).

Těsnohlídek brings his version of Lolek's narrative up to date for the readers of the newspaper, and links successive episodes as clearly as possible within a single coherent narrative, while admittedly paying little attention to literary quality — this novel is *Trivialliteratur*, though a model of its type.[8] The fox becomes unambiguously female, a lively, irreverent vixen. She thereby invites self-identification from the implicit readership, young, well-off, unmarried bourgeois girls from 1920s Brno, with an eye to modern fashion, sex and the marriage market; the author compliments them backhandedly at the end of the novel as his 'milé čtenářky' [dear female readers].[9] For comic effect, the authorial voice is that of a slightly racy 'uncle', or at any rate an older man. As Janáček remarked in a letter, this is a *dívčí román*, a girls' novel,[10] though very remote from either *Little Women* or the Disney tradition that has sometimes

---

[8] See, for example, Milan Kundera's comment, 'œuvre charmante mais sans grandes ambitions artistiques' [a charming book but without any great literary ambition], in his article, 'Le plus nostalgique des opéras', here quoted from *Leoš Janáček. La Petite Renarde rusée*, ed. by Patrick Scemoma (Paris, 2008), pp. 39–44 (p. 39). This article was first published in *Le Monde de la musique*, 188 (May 1995), was incorporated in the Paris Opera production booklet in the same year and was subsequently published separately (Paris, 2001). It has also been published in Czech ('Liška Bystrouška, drásavá idyla', in Milan Kundera, *Můj Janáček* [Brno, 2004], pp. 41–55 [p. 43]).

[9] Rudolf Těsnohlídek, *Liška Bystrouška*, 9th edn (Prague, 1972), p. 167: 'Pravíme "milé čtenářky", poněvadž tak galantně a roztomile psávali milí staří spisovatelé, i když mívali čtenářky nemilé' [We say 'dear female readers', because that is what dear old authors used to write, so gallantly and charmingly, even when the female readers they used to have were not dear at all].

[10] Janáček, letter to Kamila Stösslová, 18 March 1922: 'Pracuji již na dívčím románu, Lišce Bystroušce' [I am now working on the girls' novel, *Liška Bystrouška*]. *Hádanka života (dopisy Leoše Janáčka Kamile Stösslové)*, ed. by Svatava Přibáňová (Brno, 1990), p. 97; Eng. trans. in John Tyrrell, *Janáček's Operas. A Documentary Account* (London, 1992), p. 288 (document LB11).

been thought to make his opera suitable for children.

For the parents of the girls, there is some sly political satire: the novel, basically sympathetic to the democratic ideals of the new First Czechoslovak Republic, pokes fun at anarchism and Bolshevism, both voguish at the time. But the author goes further, modelling forest society on the new democracy while implying throughout that both are anarchically uncontrollable. (This is an aspect that was understandably glossed over during the years of communism in Czechoslovakia, even though the authorities never once withdrew the novel from print.) So the frog in Chapter 2 is a Bolshevist, who enthusiastically but laughably explains that the Party does not permit dissidence because it is strictly controlled (in the opera, this nuance was abandoned); the episode in the henhouse (Chapter 5, later a scene in Act I of the opera) has the vixen preaching communist egalitarianism to the hens from patently self-seeking motives.

The episode with the badger (Chapter 6) similarly becomes a satire of the Bolshevist expropriation of feudal property (as it remained for Janáček). Consequently, anthropomorphism is taken further in this chapter than in the Lolek illustrations, even in an episode like this one, where vulgarity can hardly be avoided when human attributes are bolted on to the fouling of a badger's sett. The essential motivation for the scene becomes not the passing shower of rain, though this is mentioned, but the need of the homeless vixen, immediately after she has escaped from the farmyard, to find a place to live in a mysterious forest which makes every wanderer afraid, even though courting couples in the forest, adds Těsnohlídek archly for his readers, might be afraid only of being spied on.

The badger is also transformed, becoming an elderly property-owner physically resembling Emperor Franz Joseph I, with an unhappy love affair behind him, and with laughable social pretensions recalling the obsolete feudalism of the pre-war Austro-Hungarian aristocracy:

> [B]yl to milostpán jezevec, domácí pán, mládenec obstarožní a bývalý císařský rada v lesní říši [...]. Ač v úřadě nesloužil a samotářsky soukromničil, zachoval si podle rodinné tradice licousy, jež jeho tváři dodávaly zdání šlechtického.[11]

> [It was Sir (literally *gnädiger Herr*) Badger, lord of his household, an elderly bachelor and a former imperial councillor in the empire of the forest. Though he did not work in an office and lived alone on private means, he kept up his side-whiskers in accordance with family tradition, and these gave his face the semblance of an aristocrat's.]

The episode is constructed skilfully to build up a quasi-human justification for the expulsion of the badger by the vixen, even though Lolek's drawings do not suggest dependence on anything other than normal animal behaviour. First a shouting match develops, with the vixen using almost impenetrable

---

[11] Těsnohlídek, *Liška Bystrouška*, p. 47.

Brno dialect and the badger speaking with an affected lisp. (Throughout this book Těsnohlídek projects registers of speech for comic effect, as he does in other works, including both his fiction and the regular reports he wrote for *Lidové noviny* about court cases involving people from the lower orders of society brought before the Brno magistrate.[12] These registers are generally maintained by Janáček in the opera, though the lisp disappears.) In this fracas the vixen's rude behaviour is comically ascribed to her bad upbringing, in which she had 'navykla si sprostým nectnostem lidským' [become accustomed to vulgar, foul human habits]; variants of this joke appear several times in the book. Nevertheless, the noise draws a crowd of neighbouring forest birds and animals, making hostile allegations — that the badger had been profiteering during World War I and that he had subjected a poor, defenceless woman to a beating merely for standing outside his house. However, the deluge of urine that clinches the vixen's victory over the badger comes not as a result of this uproar, but is another joke, when the vixen's attractions encourage the badger to consider settling down in marriage:

> 'Což aby ses tak oženil', prohodil mimoděk jezevec [...]. 'Něco tak pěkného ženského by přece neškodilo.' 'Tebe by zrovna někdo chcél', ozvalo se výsměšně nad jeho hlavou. 'Jak seš v kapse kluste, tak seš hlópé hůř než bot. Tadyk máš něco ženského, abys věděl, že su uznalá.' Zkoprněl, a než se vzpamatoval z úžasu, byl mokrý od hlavy až k patě. Za největších lijáků se mu něco takového nepřihodilo.[13]
>
> ['What about my getting married', remarked the badger involuntarily. 'Something so nice and feminine wouldn't hurt, after all.' 'Someone might almost fancy you', came the taunting answer above his head. 'You're as stupid as your pockets are bulging, and worse than an old boot. Here's something feminine from me, so that you'll know how considerate I am.' He stood aghast, and before he could say Jack Robinson, he was wet from head to toe. Even in the most torrential downpours nothing of the sort had ever happened to him.]

III

No doubt the novel was a highly improbable subject for an opera — Těsnohlídek at first thought he was the subject of a practical joke when the rumour began to circulate in Brno that Janáček was intending to use it[14] — but Janáček's conception of the work was very different from his model. Some of the farcical turns of events in the episodes of the original remain. But Těsnohlídek's interpretation of Lolek's drawings in terms of modern society is expanded into

---

[12] Selections of these 'soudničky' [court-room reports] are published in Rudolf Těsnohlídek, *Mrtvý u kříže a jiné soudničky*, ed. by Miroslav Heřman (Ostrava, 1971), and Rudolf Těsnohlídek, *Surovost z něžnosti a jiné soudničky*, ed. by Bohumil Svozil (Prague, 1982).
[13] Těsnohlídek, *Liška Bystrouška*, p. 52.
[14] Těsnohlídek in *Lidové noviny*, 3 July 1924.

a larger vision of humanity, where the vixen's escapades become the misdeeds, without lasting negative significance, that are perpetrated by a 'prostý lid' [simple populace] that is nevertheless also 'capable of noble thoughts'.[15] They become guarantees of authenticity, of humanity, in those who commit them. This quite alters the tenor of the work, and is arguably at the heart of its enduring appeal.

Furthermore, Janáček's approach to the text works to some extent against the structure of Těsnohlídek's narrative, where each episode is constructed as a large-scale joke. According to his usual practice, Janáček drew literally on lines from the novel, both direct speech and third-person narrative, and reduced the number of words to an absolute minimum, even at the expense of the coherence, motivation and logic of the dialogue. Though this seems to indicate slavish conformity to the original, in practice it defamiliarizes it and deprives it of realism. In the first scene of Act I, for example, as I have noted elsewhere, the dialogue is fragmented and allocated to children's voices, so that it lacks the motivation and political awareness it possesses in the novel, and the music confers on the scene a solemnly ceremonious, though also ominous, dance-like atmosphere, as the listeners' first introduction to the atmosphere of the forest, which is very far from farcical.[16]

In the badger scene we have been considering, the final exchange between vixen and badger (at the fouling of the sett) becomes very strange. First, 'Tu máš něco ženskýho, abys věděl, že su uznalá' [Here's something feminine for you, so that you'll know how considerate I am], from the vixen, comes out of the blue rather than being a reply to the badger; so, if understood in terms of normal logic, it is motivated by vulgarity rather than wit. It is followed by 'Ó, jak jsem mravně rozhořčen! Opustím nevděčné stádo' [Oh, how morally indignant I am! I shall abandon this ungrateful herd!] from the badger. These words, especially 'mravně' [morally], are out of character even with the pomposity of the badger, because they are drawn from a tongue-in-cheek authorial third-person comment in the novel: 'Div ho mrtvice v hněvu spravedlivém neranila. Hluboce mravně rozhořčen povstal' [it was a wonder he did not have heart failure in his righteous wrath. He rose in deep moral indignation].[17]

But this technique, of ending a scene with third-person narration converted into first-person speech, though contradicting realism, works rather like a

---

[15] Janáček, letter to Max Brod, 11 March 1923: 'prostý lid béře zlo ne jak věčnou příhanu. [...] I moje liška Bystrouška je takovou: kradla, rdousila, ale vedle toho je zase schopná cítění ušlechtilých' [The simple populace accepts evil, and not as a lasting stigma. My vixen Bystrouška is like that too: she stole, she throttled (chickens), but besides that she is also capable of noble feelings]. *Korespondence Leoše Janáčka s Maxem Brodem*, ed. by Jan Racek and Artuš Rektorys (Prague, 1953), p. 121; Tyrrell, *Janáček's Operas*, p. 295 (document LB55).
[16] See Chew, 'Is Leoš Janáček's *Příhody lišky Bystroušky* a Rejection of a Romantic Lie?', p. 79.
[17] Těsnohlídek, *Liška Bystrouška*, p. 52.

rhyming couplet at the end of a Shakespearean scene. It is found again in the final scene of the opera, in a more radical way yet: the third-person narration (from Těsnohlídek's Chapter 17), which is put into the forester's mouth in the opera, leads him to abandon his usual dialect for literary Czech, allowing an ecstatic mood, otherwise alien to the forester's persona, to be articulated, in which he sings of *rusalky* [water nymphs] weeping for joy, and mankind understanding that a supernatural happiness has passed its way, before the final orchestral apotheosis. The passage, beginning 'Jak je les divukrásný!' [How exquisite the forest is!] immediately features the distinctly bookish word 'divukrásný', 'exquisite', and is drawn directly from Těsnohlídek's passage, beginning 'Kterak byl nyní les divukrásný!' [How exquisite the forest now was!].[18]

In such cases, the sung text is defamiliarized, in a way that was unprecedented in Janáček's work up to that time, and to that extent it renders the narrative surreal, in style if not in content, rather than carrying the plot forward.[19] As Milan Kundera has written, the music takes its place in controlling the narrative:

> Si on les [the two operas, *The Cunning Little Vixen* and *From the House of the Dead*, which Kundera regards as a pair] représentait sans musique, les livrets s'avéreraient plutôt nuls; nuls parce que, dès leur conception, Janáček réserve le rôle dominant à la musique; c'est elle qui raconte, qui dévoile la psychologie des personnages, qui émeut, qui surprend, qui médite, qui envoûte et, même, qui organise l'ensemble et détermine l'architecture (d'ailleurs très travaillée et très raffinée) de l'œuvre.[20]

---

[18] Ibid., p. 131; Janáček, *The Cunning Little Vixen*, Act III, from 4 bars before rehearsal no. 52 to 3 bars after rehearsal no. 54.

[19] Though there is no space here to expand on this point, Janáček's literalism in mining his sources for text is arguably a very important aspect of his late operas: it forces the attentive listener to take them as intertextual commentaries on their models. This notionally sets up their models (unlike, say, Shakespeare's *Othello* when used as the basis for Verdi's *Otello*) as works that ideally should not be left out of account in interpreting them, and makes them, according to Peter Petersen's definition, *Literaturopern*: 'Der Terminus "Literaturoper" bezeichnet eine Sonderform des Musiktheaters, bei der das Libretto auf einem bereits vorliegenden literarischen Text (Drama, Erzählung) basiert, dessen sprachliche, semantische und ästhetische Struktur in einen musikalisch-dramatischen Text (Opernpartitur) eingeht und dort als Strukturschicht kenntlich bleibt' [The term 'Literaturoper' refers to a particular form of music theatre in which the libretto is based on a pre-existing literary text (drama or narrative), whose linguistic, semantic and aesthetic structure is adopted in a musical and dramatic text (an operatic score), and remains recognizable as a structural level within it]: Peter Petersen, 'Der Terminus "Literaturoper" — eine Begriffsbestimmung', *Archiv für Musikwissenschaft*, 56 (1999), 52–70 (p. 60). I have discussed Petersen's article (among other things) in relation to Janáček, though not specifically to *The Cunning Little Vixen*, in '"Literaturoper": A Term Still in Search of a Definition', the introduction to the special number *Janáček and the Literaturoper* of *Sborník prací Filozofické fakulty Brněnské univerzity*, H 42–43 (2007–08), 5–13.

[20] Kundera, 'Le plus nostalgique des opéras', p. 40.

[If *The Cunning Little Vixen* and *From the House of the Dead* were staged without music, their libretti would seem rather pointless, for, from the moment that he conceived the operas, Janáček gave the leading role to music. It is the music that narrates, that reveals the psychology of the characters, that constructs emotion, surprises, meditates, enchants, and organizes the whole piece and constructs its architecture, which is, moreover, very well wrought and refined.]

The music is also in a style new for Janáček, who, not for the first time in his life, rethinks his musical language. John Tyrrell has pointed out that *The Cunning Little Vixen* may represent Janáček's adoption of traits of the music of Debussy; Janáček had only recently (1921) become acquainted with *La Mer* [*The Sea*] and *Pelléas et Mélisande*.[21] The opera has unfortunately not yet been thoroughly analysed in these terms, and it would be out of place to attempt to do so here, but it is no doubt significant that the scene with the badger begins with an extended, static whole-tone passage, perhaps suggested by Debussy's music — although very different from it, and drawing on a method of handling motivic material, already well established in Janáček's output, whose subtlety goes well beyond anything that needs to be said here.[22] A melodic motif (first appearing as Ex. 1a) is heard in various forms through the scene and permeates it; the initial non-tonal passage in which it is first heard may possibly be intended to represent the mysterious, forbidding forest depths into which the vixen is cast once she has escaped from the captivity of Act I.[23]

---

[21] Tyrrell, *Janáček. Years of a Life*, II, 317. Though it has been suggested that Janáček 'probably' encountered Debussy's music as early as 1910, when *La Mer* was performed in Prague by the Czech Philharmonic on 30 January (see Miloš Štědroň, *Leoš Janáček a hudba 20. století* [*Janáček and 20th-Century Music*] [Brno, 1998], p. 82, quoting earlier literature), there is no evidence that Janáček attended this or other early performances. Some years later, there is a brief quotation from Debussy's *Fêtes galantes* in Janáček's harmony manual of 1919 (Leoš Janáček, *Hudebně teoretické dílo*, vol. 2, ed. by Zdeněk Blažek [Prague, 1974], p. 317). His interest in Debussy is very well documented from 1921 in an analysis he made that year of 'Jeux de vagues' from *La Mer* (Brno, Janáček Archive of the Moravian Museum, MS S 64, published in facsimile in Miloš Štědroň, 'Janáček, verismus a impresionismus' [Janáček, verismo and impressionism], *Časopis Moravského musea / Acta musei Moraviae, vědy společenské*, 53–54 [1968–69], 125–54, and again with commentary in Štědroň, *Leoš Janáček a hudba 20. století*, pp. 82–86). For a detailed study of Janáček's analysis, including comparisons with other twentieth-century analyses of Debussy, and the suggestion that the composer made the study as an aid to his composition of *Dunaj* [*The Danube*] (1923–25?), see Paul Wingfield, 'Janáček, Musical Analysis, and Debussy's "Jeux de vagues"', in *Janáček Studies*, ed. by Paul Wingfield (Cambridge, 1999), pp. 183–280 (for the *Dunaj* suggestion, p. 207).
[22] On the complexity of Janáček's motivic technique, see the useful discussion in Wingfield, 'Janáček, Musical Analysis, and Debussy's "Jeux de vagues"', pp. 237–46. On the use of whole-tone scales in this piece, see the tabulation in Nors S. Josephson, 'Musical and Dramatic Organization in Janáček's *The Cunning Little Vixen*', in *Janáček and Czech Music. Proceedings of the International Conference (Saint Louis, 1988)*, ed. by Michael Beckerman and Glen Bauer (Stuyvesant, NY, 1995), pp. 83–91 (pp. 88–89); further on Josephson's analysis, see the comments below in this article.
[23] Vogel, by contrast, thinks the motif of Ex. 1a represents the 'determination' of the vixen once she has escaped (*Leoš Janáček*, 1997 edn, p. 266).

Ex. 1a: Act II, overture, first four bars (woodwind)

As the curtain rises, this same motif is transformed into a triumphant B major (bars 9–12 after rehearsal no. 2), presumably as the vixen spies the badger's sett; it is then sung by the vixen (Ex. 1b) as the first words of the scene:

Ex. 1b: Act II, scene 1, bars 2–3 after rehearsal no. 3

This motif in its various transformations in this scene emphasizes the continuity between the landscape and the sung words; generally, the music of this opera suggests the constant presence of the forest and its inhabitants as something palpable, strong, irrational, and potentially both threatening and tender. This is further emphasized in this scene by Janáček's use of the chorus: the lesní havěť [*Waldgetier*, forest animals, insects and birds] is given a voice very different from that of the noisy neighbours who suddenly intrude in Těsnohlídek's version. Janáček's lesní havěť is present from the outset, watching the incident and making continual threatening comments, as a revolutionary rabble supporting the vixen and demanding vengeance against the badger.[24] Their unsettling effect is very similar to that of the prisoners who intervene towards the end of Act II of *From the House of the Dead*, who are incensed when Gorjančikov dares to drink tea and thereby displays his superior social status, and who finally resort to extreme violence.

IV

Faced with a work so different from its predecessors, Max Brod was clearly nonplussed when Janáček first put his plans for the *Vixen* to him in March 1923.[25] However, it would seem likely that some of the principal themes

---

[24] The BBC's animated version of the opera brought this aspect out visually too, in an outstanding way, with pairs of eyes everywhere scrutinizing the action, throughout the opera (*The Cunning Little Vixen. The Animated Film of Janáček's Opera*, DVD OA 0839 D, London, 2003).

[25] Brod, letter to Janáček, 23 March 1923: 'ich habe Ihren Text gelesen. Offen gestanden mutet er mich sehr fremd an. Ich kann noch gar kein inneres Verhältnis dazu gewinnen, vielleicht deshalb, weil ich Tiere so wenig kenne' [I have read your text. To be frank it seems very strange to me. I cannot yet relate inwardly to it at all, perhaps because I understand animals so little]. *Korespondence Leoše Janáčka s Maxem Brodem*, ed. by Racek and Rektorys, p. 124; Tyrrell, *Janáček's Operas*, p. 296 (document LB57).

of the opera were in the event very congenial to him, for they correspond rather closely with ideas of his own which he had developed in the post-war years and published in 1921, in his two-volume *Heidentum — Christentum — Judentum* [*Paganism — Christianity — Judaism*].[26] This book seems essentially to represent a reaction to the First World War: Brod's acute awareness of the unnecessary suffering caused by the war had led him to think carefully about the nature of suffering and the role of religion in dealing with it, and radically to reformulate his own Judaism as a programme for living. To do so, he draws a fundamental distinction in the book between 'edles' and 'unedles Unglück', 'noble' and 'ignoble' misfortune respectively. 'Edles Unglück' is ontological, the misfortune that is the lot of human beings because they are human with human limitations, inescapably subject to their God-given attributes, which include aging and death, and are driven primarily by passion (particularly sexual passion):

> Motor des edlen Unglücks ist die Leidenschaft. Deshalb ist die Sexualität das zentrale Gebiet, der Mittelpunkt des edlen Unglücks. Von allen Boten Gottes spricht Eros am eindringlichsten. Er reißt den Menschen am schnellsten vor das Angesicht der Herrlichkeit Gottes, er stellt ihn in seiner Kleinheit dem Unendlichen gegenüber, läßt schärfstes Reinheitslicht auf ihn fallen und weist ihm die häßlichen Flecken seines heuchlerischen Tugendmantels.[27]

> [The driving force of noble misfortune is passion, and so sexuality is the central focus of noble misfortune. Eros is the messenger of God who speaks the most insistently and is quickest to wrench human beings into the presence of God's glory, juxtaposing their puniness to the infinite, casting the most unforgivingly pure light on them, and exposing the ugly stains on the veil of their hypocrisy.]

Such 'noble misfortune', 'edles Unglück', requires humility and acquiescence as the only truly appropriate responses. But, by contrast, such attitudes are wholly inappropriate for 'unedles Unglück', the 'ignoble' misfortune that could always have been averted if forethought had been given and care taken. Much of the suffering caused by the war had been 'ignoble'; and ignoble misfortune, paralysing the senses, deserves no acquiescence:

> [Die] Indulgenz gegenüber dem unedlen Unglück ist ebenso frevelhaft wie die Insolenz gegenüber dem edlen Unglück. [...] [Heute glauben] viele, die sich besonders tief dünken, im Krieg eine der Menschheit gleichsam angeborene Geißel sehen zu dürfen. [...] Wirklich? Wir werden ja sehen!

---

[26] Max Brod, *Heidentum — Christentum — Judentum. Ein Bekenntnisbuch*, 2 vols (Munich, 1921).

[27] Ibid., I, 34. Kundera characterizes Brod as afraid of sexuality, in his discussion of Brod's relationship to Franz Kafka — especially in Brod's censorship of some of the more explicit passages in Kafka's diaries when editing them. See Kundera, *Les testaments trahis*, part 2 ('L'ombre castratrice de Saint Garta', especially p. 57; *Testaments Betrayed*, p. 42). This seems just as misconceived as Brod's meddling.

[...] Mir genügt schon heute mein Gefühl der Entrüstung, um den Krieg als unedles Unglück zu agnoszieren. [...] Bei unedlem Unglück ermattet die Phantasie, das Mitleid kann nicht mehr mit. Ich kann mir die Todesqualen eines Verwundeten im Drahtverhau vorstellen, ich kann schlaflose Nächte lang an die Sommeschlacht denken, — aber zwei Tote oder siebzigtausend Tote in dieser Schlacht, das ergibt keinen Unterschied mehr. Es ist so, als weigere sich die Phantasie, in dieses faktisch zwar Geschehende, jedoch immanent Unnotwendige einzudringen.[28]

[Acquiescence in the face of ignoble misfortune is just as sacrilegious as hubris in the face of noble misfortune. Today there are many who imagine themselves especially profound in regarding war as an innate scourge of humanity. Really? We'll see! My sense of indignation today is enough to make me reject war as ignoble misfortune. The imagination is dulled by ignoble misfortune: sympathy dries up. I can imagine the death throes of a wounded soldier caught in barbed wire, I can lie awake all night thinking about the battle of the Somme, but to distinguish between two deaths and 70,000 deaths in that battle becomes impossible. It is as if the imagination refuses to explore such things, which though happening in fact are immanently unnecessary.]

Then he distinguishes the religions of the Western world (explicitly leaving aside the religions of Asia and Africa) under three main headings, paganism, Christianity and Judaism. They are distinguished by their differing attitudes to the relationship between this world and the hereafter, with paganism in principle affirming only this world, Christianity in principle affirming only the hereafter, and Judaism able, rightly understood, to steer a middle course. He defines paganism as the religion of warmongering and nationalism (and includes 'Hakenkreuzleute' [Nazis, literally Swastika people] as well as Marxists, under this heading[29]) and sees it, even in 1921, as the current most likely to dominate Europe's future. He thinks that Christianity, essentially because of its doctrines of original sin and the justification of sinners through substitutionary atonement, cannot adequately distinguish between noble and ignoble misfortune (not only because this has been demonstrated by the glorification of the war in 'millions' of ecclesiastical rites and ceremonies), and is too often unhappily wedded with modern paganism. Judaism, then, though standing aside as a wallflower, has much potentially to offer the West.

In *The Cunning Little Vixen*, it may be 'edles Unglück' in Brod's sense that colours the autumnal 'sad ending' referred to by Janáček,[30] with the forester accepting the inevitability of old age and death, and the renewal of nature.[31]

---

[28] Brod, *Heidentum — Christentum — Judentum*, I, 36–37.
[29] Ibid., I, 12.
[30] Janáček, letter to Kamila Stösslová, 10 February 1922: 'Veselá věc se smutným koncem: a já se do toho smutného konce sám stavím!' [A cheerful thing with a sad ending: and I am taking my place at that sad ending myself!]. *Hádanka života*, ed. by Přibáňová, p. 96; Tyrrell, *Janáček's Operas*, p. 288 (document LB10).
[31] Ernst is the only commentator I know to give an account of *Heidentum — Christentum —*

This is a new theme in Janáček's output, and is far from Těsnohlídek's conception, in which the forester's old age is only a passing episode, and which concludes with a conventional happy ending, the marriage of fox and vixen. This celebration of 'edles Unglück' must have appealed enormously to Brod; but at the same time he must have been dismayed by the fact that it seemed underplayed and undermined by Janáček's odd new approach to his text, and, as I shall suggest below, it seems to have occurred to him that the opera could speak more clearly about 'edles Unglück' if he edited it a little. Most famously, he objected to the appearance, at the end of the opera, of the grandson of the original frog, as an inappropriate intrusion into a moment of exaltation, where he would have preferred the forester to exclaim, 'So kehret alles zurück, alles in ewiger Jugendpracht!' [Thus everything comes around once more, everything, in the eternal splendour of youth!],[32] although this would have been tame compared with the defamiliarized third-person speech the forester in fact uses (already mentioned above).

Janáček understandably resisted this suggestion, pointing out that the music alone says all that needs saying; but merely to quote Brod's proposal shows the gap between the aesthetic of the two men. It shows Brod's inability to grasp the originality of what Janáček had done with the relationship between words and music, coupled with his desire to improve Janáček until the composer matched Brod's notion of him — as a genius infinitely sympathetic to the weaknesses of his 'poor children', but believing ultimately in 'die Unzerstörbarkeit des Lebens' [the inextinguishability of life] as exemplified by the ending of the *Vixen*.[33] Kundera goes much too far in writing of 'le renoncement de Janáček à une affabulation, à une action dramatique' [Janáček's refusal to adopt a plot or dramatic action] in this opera, but he is right that Brod's suggested additions would in this case have turned Janáček's remarkable achievement into kitsch.[34]

Judentum within a discussion of Brod and Janáček, but I remain unconvinced by his attempt to interpret *Jenůfa* in terms of 'edles' and 'unedles Unglück' (Ernst, ' "Durch kleine Ritze nimmt man Abgründe wahr" ', pp. 49–50). Brod was strong-minded enough to regard not only the casualties of war, but even such things as inherited syphilis as examples of 'unedles Unglück'. On his terms, surely hardly any of the misfortune in *Jenůfa* can seem noble, with the possible exception of the ending.
[32] See Janáček, letter to Max Brod, 26 June 1925: *Korespondence Leoše Janáčka s Maxem Brodem*, ed. by Racek and Rektorys, pp. 185–86; Tyrrell, *Janáček's Operas*, pp. 299–300 (document LB65). See Kundera, *Les testaments trahis*, p. 169: 'encore une apothéose' [yet another apotheosis].
[33] Max Brod, *Leoš Janáček. Leben und Werk* (Vienna, 1925), p. 61.
[34] Kundera, 'Le plus nostalgique des opéras', p. 39. The Czech translation ('Liška Bystrouška, drásavá idyla', p. 44) omits the reference to Brod in this passage.

V

Much has been written about the place of anthropomorphism in *The Cunning Little Vixen*, largely because of the role that Brod wished it to play in the opera. To some degree already present in Lolek's drawings, it was well established in Těsnohlídek's novel, though mostly for ironic or comic purposes, presenting unexpected reversals of values between humans and animals. A few typical tongue-in-cheek examples may be mentioned, beyond the joke about the vixen's bad upbringing already quoted above: the predilection of a mosquito for buzzing around sweaty humans on pilgrimages is due solely to his fervent Catholicism and his enjoyment of hymn-singing;[35] when Lapák, the dog, sniffs the vixen's genitals at their first acquaintance, 'očenichával ji kavalírsky a zdvořile, všude, kde se sluší a patří, a Bystrouška si v duchu řekla: "je vidět, že je to vzdělané pán"' [he took account of her gallantly and courteously, in all the places where it is right and proper so to do, and the vixen said to herself, 'Obviously he's a real gent'];[36] Lapák is devoted to the arts and sings melancholy songs of his own composition in the evenings, but his master chastises him 'inhumanly' (*nelidsky*) for them;[37] the vixen tells the fox about her prowling, as the prim constitutional she allows herself every day, and he praises her lavishly as 'prostě ideál moderní dívky' [simply the ideal of a modern girl], even though this activity takes place between midnight and one o'clock in the morning, when walks by respectable female readers might be misconstrued.[38] Some of this anthropomorphism is retained in the opera, also in part for comic purposes: Janáček is by no means averse to Těsnohlídek's jokes.[39]

But there is a complication in the opera: probably for reasons of economy in production, Janáček made some notes drawing parallels, not found in the novel, between some of the animals and some of the human beings. He may have envisaged these merely as an aid to facilitate casting, allowing singers to take more than one part; but in the subsequent history of the piece, they have been taken to justify a kind of allegorical anthropomorphism alien both to Těsnohlídek's original and to Janáček's adaptation of it. For, once Brod

---

[35] Těsnohlídek, *Liška Bystrouška*, pp. 11–12.
[36] Ibid., pp. 27–28.
[37] Ibid., p. 29.
[38] Ibid., p. 144.
[39] There have been interesting differences between productions of the opera from this point of view. Walter Felsenstein's 1956 Berlin production, mentioned below (sect. VI), which first ensured success for the opera outside Czechoslovakia, adopted realistic costumes for the animals, minimizing anthropomorphism; Jonathan Miller's 1975 Glyndebourne production, which marked the *Vixen*'s first success in the English-speaking world, characterized the animals with historic regional costumes devised by Rosemary Vercoe, such as a hussar's uniform for the cock. See Alena Němcová, 'Dvě janáčkovské inscenace v Anglii', in *Janáčkiana '78 a '79. Sborník materiálů z hudebně vědeckých konferencí Ostrava 1978 a 1979*, ed. by Karel Steinmetz (Ostrava, 1980), pp. 19–24 (pp. 21–22).

had started work on the translation in June 1925, he began considering how he might rationalize the relationships between animals and humans more thoroughly than in the Czech libretto, and put these proposals to Emil Hertzka of the Viennese Universal Edition. In a letter to Brod, which he forwarded to Janáček, Hertzka comments:

> Es [...] wäre wärmstens zu begrüßen, wenn es Ihnen gelingen würde, das allerdings schwere Problem der Vermenschlichung der Tiere und das Tierische im Menschen in sinnfälligere Wechselbeziehungen zu bringen, als dies scheinbar im böhmischen Buche der Fall war.[40]
>
> [It would be most welcome if you could succeed in solving the admittedly difficult problem of aligning the humanizing of the animals and the animal element in the humans more clearly than is apparently the case in the Czech libretto.]

To do this Brod was thinking of ways in which the animal and human realms in the opera might be linked symbolically; and, apparently in order to increase the degree of 'edles Unglück' in the plot, he hit on the idea of rewriting the whole libretto, not only highlighting the roles of aging and of the cycle of nature, but also strengthening the role of erotic passion within the plot, and imposing an overall symbolic scheme linking animals and humans. The redundancy of much of Janáček's Czech dialogue (from a logical point of view) made it possible for him to do this, and to introduce new elements of plot, while leaving the music almost completely intact. As for the role of erotic passion, on 13 June 1925 he wrote to Janáček explaining what he had in mind and asking to be allowed a free hand in the translation:

> Ich stelle mir [...] vor, daß die Bystrouška (Füchsin Schlaukopf) für alle Menschen, die in dem Stück auftreten, so etwas wie das Symbol der Jugend, Wildheit, Natur bedeutet. — Schulmeister, Förster und Pfarrer sind alle drei im Leben an ihrem Glück vorbeigegangen. Um die Sache zu vereinfachen [...], will ich es so fügen, daß alle drei die Terynka, ein Zigeunerkind, geliebt haben, aber alle drei haben nicht die Kraft gehabt, sie festzuhalten. [...] So hoffe ich eine gewisse Einheit in den Text hineinzubringen und Verständlichkeit, dramatische Konzentration zu erzielen.[...] Musikalisch wird natürlich nichts geändert — und die Textänderungen werden Sie, wie ich hoffe, willkommen heißen.[41]
>
> [I propose that the Vixen should signify something like the symbol of youth, wildness and nature for all the human characters in the piece. The schoolmaster, forester and priest have all failed to achieve happiness in their lives. To simplify things I would like to make it that all three of them were formerly in love with Terynka, a gypsy child, but all three of them lacked the power to keep hold of her. Thus I hope to introduce a certain unity to the libretto, aiming at comprehensibility and dramatic concentration.

[40] Emil Hertzka, letter to Max Brod, 10 June 1925: *Korespondence Leoše Janáčka s Maxem Brodem*, ed. by Racek and Rektorys, p. 252.
[41] Brod, letter to Janáček, 13 June 1925, ibid., pp. 180–81.

Musically, of course nothing will be altered, and I hope you will like the changes in the libretto.]

In this way Brod invented unfulfilled past love affairs with a mysterious gypsy girl, Terynka, for all three male characters (forester, priest and schoolmaster), and made the vixen a symbol of them; Terynka never appears on stage except in a vision linking her with the vixen. (In the Czech version, she is not a gypsy, but an ordinary woman, worshipped from afar by the schoolmaster, who thinks he is meeting her when, drunk, he sees a sunflower; he sheds a quiet tear when she finally marries Harašta, the poacher; Harašta turns the vixen's pelt into a muff for her.) In promoting Terynka to a Carmen-like (but mute and almost invisible) central role in his German version, Brod undeniably raises the profile of erotic love within the opera; but he does so at the expense of the integrity of both the forester, whose nostalgic recollection of his wedding night at the end of the opera becomes a recollection of a passionate episode with Terynka, and the priest, whose vague memory of a love from student days becomes the seduction of an innocent Terynka during her confirmation classes. Both of these risk appearing sordid rather than noble.

It is with the priest that the principal symbolic link is made between animals and humans: the priest is symbolically paired with the badger, both unsympathetic elderly males. On 22 June 1925, Brod wrote again to Janáček to explain how he wished to treat the first scene of Act II of the opera (the badger scene discussed above), and how Terynka was to be incorporated, with the addition of a very convoluted narrative for the sake of maintaining the scheme:

> [Die Terynka] ist ein Zigeunerkind — der Förster hat sie ins Haus genommen — dann, als sie es dort zu toll trieb, dem Pfarrer zum Unterricht gegeben — den aber hat sie in schlechten Ruf gebracht und deshalb muß er seine Pfarre aufgeben und in eine andere versetzt werden. Nun ist ganz genau mit der Vertreibung des Dachses (B. vyvlastňuje) die Parallele hergestellt. Die Szene mit dem Dachs endet nun nicht mit dem bühnenunmöglichen Pischen — sondern so, daß das Füchslein dem Waldgetier erzählt, wie der Dachs (Pfarrer) es während der Konfirmationsstunde mit unsittlichen Anträgen verfolgt hat. [...] Unter Hallo der Waldtiere küßt das Füchslein ostentativ den empörten Dachs, der mit den Worten abgeht: O, ich bin sittlich entrüstet und weiche der frechen Verläumdung.[42]

> [Terynka is a gypsy child; the forester has taken her in, then, when she became too unmanageable, given her to the priest to teach. But she has brought the priest into ill-repute, so that he has to give up the parish and be transferred. This very precisely establishes a parallel with the expulsion of the badger ('Bystrouška expropriates'). The badger scene now ends, not with the unstageable urination, but with the vixen recounting to the forest animals how the badger (priest) had made improper advances to her during confirmation classes. With derisive cries from the forest animals, the vixen

[42] Brod, letter to Janáček, 22 June 1925, ibid., pp. 183–84.

ostentatiously kisses the indignant badger, who leaves, with the words 'Oh, I am morally outraged, and yield to this impudent slander!']

Janáček's response to this proposal — which might have increased the logic of the scene, but at the expense of both simplicity and comedy — is very well known. On 26 June, in a letter already quoted above, he refused to countenance the 'ostentatious kissing' of the badger in this scene, and equally refused to delete the episode with the frog at the end of the opera, whose originality he emphasised:

> 1. Není možné, aby ta Liška-Bystrouška líbala toho jezevce! Důvod té scény: vyvlastňovací — komunistický je tu jedině možný!
> 2. A konec opery! Vždyť je to roztomilé, když ji ta žábička ukončí! Hudba je na to jako 'ušitá'. A originelní je to — a kolotoč života tak je tím pravdivě a věrně znázorněn!⁴³
>
> [1. It is impossible to have the vixen kiss that badger! The only possible reason for that scene is expropriative and communistic!
> 2. And the ending of the opera! For it's charming to have the little frog conclude it! The music fits it like a glove. And it's original — and the carousel of life is depicted by it truly and faithfully!]

Brod relented as far as the frog was concerned, but in the badger scene he would only compromise to the extent of having the vixen expose her backside to the badger.

VI

One might argue, generally, that seen in the light of his *Heidentum — Christentum — Judentum* Brod's version of the opera is an explicitly Jewish reinterpretation of a story infected (because of Janáček's non-traditional approach to the relationship between words and music) by paganism. It is an attempt to realize the full potential, in wide human ideals, of a narrative apparently too often bogged down in irrelevant detail and therefore limited to the values of this world. And these wider ideals are those of the *via media* between paganism and Christianity offered by an infinitely sympathetic and tender-hearted Judaism. This is the religion able to see and accept the foibles of human beings, driven as they are primarily by sexual passion, and yet to interpret them in religious terms. And, bizarrely, Brod saw this Judaism embodied in Janáček.

It might therefore seem even stranger that Brod should have thought his version the one most likely to succeed in German theatres. But in the event, despite the fate that befell Jewish art and music under the Nazis and later, he was largely correct, and his conception of the opera has had, and still has, astonishingly wide currency, perhaps largely because his German version has been preserved in the edition published by Universal Edition in Vienna.

[43] Janáček, letter to Max Brod, 26 June 1925, ibid., pp. 185–86; Tyrrell, *Janáček's Operas*, pp. 299–300 (document LB65).

Its apparent plausibility may be measured by the fact that it still underlies one of the main analytical essays devoted to this opera in English, by Nors P. Josephson, which (in apparent ignorance of the differences between the Czech libretto and Brod's translation of it) absurdly seeks to show that Janáček himself constructed patterns of motivic and tonal unity that were rooted in Brod's idea of 'edles Unglück':

> Janáček's musical organization of his opera *The Cunning Little Vixen* clearly supports the principal dramatic issues and relationship[s] outlined in the libretto. Just as the two embodiments of the 'eternal feminine' complex — the Vixen and Terynka — are musically interrelated through various subtle permutations of [the allegedly central] motives *x* and *y*, much the same holds true for the principal male characters in Terynka's life, who tend to be associated with erotic metamorphoses of *x*. As the drama progresses, the latter *x* variants tend to assume fatalistically descending, dotted rhythmic patterns set to wh-t I pitches [i.e. pitches drawn from the whole-tone scale based on C rather than that on C sharp].[44]

And in German theatres, Brod's version still holds sway. As the basis for the celebrated production by Walter Felsenstein in East Berlin in 1956, it was the version that fuelled the eventual acceptance of this opera in the wider world;[45] and, amazingly, it still remains the normal German translation, whether in its original form or in subsequent adaptations. (German opera houses now sometimes use a translation by the director Peter Brenner — but Brenner is Felsenstein's son, and even his translation is still strongly based on Brod's.[46]) Whether or not this implies that German theatres respond only to ultra-traditional dramaturgy, it certainly means, as Leon Botstein has testily argued, that we owe a great deal to Brod.[47]

---

[44] Josephson, 'Musical and Dramatic Organization', p. 90. The use of keys which Josephson identifies as unifying the opera might best be understood, perhaps, in terms of Janáček's own longstanding idiosyncratic preferences.

[45] See Ernst, '"Durch kleine Ritze nimmt man Abgründe wahr"', Chapter 9, and *'Das schlaue Füchslein' von Leoš Janáček. 'Und doch ist in der Musik nur eine Wahrheit' — Zu Walter Felsensteins Inszenierung an der Komischen Oper Berlin (1956)*, ed. by Ilse Kobán, Wort und Musik 33 (Anif bei Salzburg, 1997).

[46] The current production (2009) at the Cologne Opera is still using Brod's translation, for example. As for the extent to which Brenner's adaptation remains faithful to Brod's conception, see an extract from Chantal Steiner's review of the 2006 Zurich production (*Vox spectatricis*, 16 October 2006), which used it: 'Der Förster, der Schulmeister und der Pfarrer [sitzen] in der Gaststube und sinnieren über eine junge Frau namens Terynka (die nie auftaucht), die ihr seelisches Gleichgewicht durcheinander gebracht hat' [The forester, the schoolmaster and the priest sit in the inn and reminisce about a young woman called Terynka (who never appears), who has destroyed their spiritual equilibrium].

[47] Leon Botstein, 'The Cultural Politics of Language and Music: Max Brod and Leoš Janáček', in *Janáček and his World*, ed. by Michael Beckerman (Princeton, NJ, 2003), pp. 13–36. Botstein does not, however, confront the nature of Brod's translations or their implications in his article.

'Meine Not ist zu Ende und all meine Qual': Erich Zeisl's Setting of Alfons Petzold's 'Der tote Arbeiter'

KARIN WAGNER

Universität für Musik und darstellende Kunst, Vienna

I

In Vienna between the wars Erich Zeisl (1905–1959) was regarded as one of the most important representatives of moderate modernism.[1] Before he fled Austria in 1938, Zeisl produced a substantial body of work, his particular speciality in the broad spectrum of Viennese music of the time being the song. The press regularly described him as highly gifted, and in 1934 Paul Amadeus Pisk (1893–1990), co-editor of the house-journal of Universal Edition Vienna, *Musikblätter des Anbruch* [*Musical Dispatches of 'Der Anbruch' (A New Day)*], and music editor of the *Arbeiter-Zeitung* [*Workers' Newspaper*] counted him as one of 'die stärksten Persönlichkeiten der noch nicht dreißigjährigen Wiener Komponisten' [the strongest personalities amongst Viennese composers under thirty].[2] Whilst he was in Vienna Zeisl composed nearly a hundred songs; 'Komm süsser Tod' [Come Sweet Death], a song in the tradition of Schubert written in January 1938, was the last he composed in German, a farewell to the world of German *Lieder* that may legitimately be read as an autobiographical statement. The homage to Schubert is especially eloquent in the context of Robert Schollum's thesis that 'the Austrian *Lied* in the twentieth century begins with Franz Schubert'.[3] Zeisl's songs reflect a multiplicity of styles: 'Berückung' [Enchantment], for example, set in 1924, is taken from Richard Dehmel's erotically charged volume *Weib und Welt* [*Woman and World*, 1896], and the sensitively differentiated piano part is in no way subordinated to the voice: 'zitternde Narzissen' [trembling narcissi], 'schwarze Locken' [black locks] and 'rote Kissen' [red cushions], set to semiquavers, lend a note of youthful

---

[1] See Malcolm Cole and Barbara Barclay, *Armseelchen. The Life and Music of Eric Zeisl* (Westport, CT, and London, 1984) and Karin Wagner, *Fremd bin ich ausgezogen. Eric Zeisl — Biografie* (Vienna, 2005).
[2] Paul Amadeus Pisk, 'Erich Zeisel [sic]', *Radio Wien*, 31 January 1934.
[3] Robert Schollum argues that only in the work of Webern and his acolytes does the relationship between words and music in the Austrian *Lied* tradition undergo further fundamental change. Robert Schollum, *Das österreichische Lied des 20. Jahrhunderts* (Tutzing, 1977), p. 9.

agitation to the central section, whilst the late-romantic harmonies of the outer sections suggest dark eroticism. With settings of Otto Julius Bierbaum's 'Jannette' and 'Gigerlette' (both 1925), Zeisl enters the sphere of the cabaret and quite appropriately for the period dips into the world of the gentle muse with the cadences of the *chanson*. In 1928 he evokes the fascinating charms of the moon in the grotesques of his cycle 'Mondbilder' [Images of the Moon] after poems by Christian Morgenstern. Using a favourite technique of conservative modernism, his settings of Wilhelm Busch's 'Der Weise' [The Wise Man, 1931] and 'Der Unvorsichtige' [The Incautious Man, 1931], and of Joachim Ringelnatz's 'Arm Kräutchen' [Poor Little Weed, 1931] and 'Ein ganzes Leben' [A Whole Life, 1931], tend towards parody.

At the same time Zeisl was writing songs that combined 'Wolfsche Geistigkeit mit Straußischer Melodik' [(Hugo) Wolf-like spirituality with (Richard) Strauss-esque melodic fluency][4] and are firmly rooted in traditional modes of text-setting: they deploy acoustic and harmonic devices typical of contemporary conservative modernist stylistic models. These include 'Abendstimmung' [Evening Mood] (E♭ minor, 1931), to a text by Reinhold Wilhelm Kühnel, 'Wanderers Nachtlied' [Wanderer's Song at Night] (D♭ major, 1931), after Goethe, and the voluptuously atmospheric 'Nachts' [At Night, 1931], by Eichendorff, which is marked 'bewegt und verträumt' [animated and languorous] and shifts between F minor, D♭ major and E♭ major. These songs are associated with the nocturnal sphere by being, predictably, cloaked in flat keys, suggesting that the harmonic language bears some symbolic significance. On the other hand, the Nietzsche songs — 'Das trunkene Lied' [The Drunken Song, 1931] from *Also sprach Zarathustra* [*Thus Spake Zarathustra*] and 'Die Sonne sinkt' [The Sun Sets, 1931] from the *Dionysos-Dithyramben* [*Dithyrambs of Dionysus*] — are characterized by a return to extroversion in the more exuberant piano part — together with some reduction in the degree of their motivic and harmonic elaboration. A concentrated, even more taut musical language is achieved via the use of early Expressionist devices in 'Liebeslied' [Love Song, 1935] from *Des Knaben Wunderhorn* [*The Youth's Magic Horn*] and in Mörike's 'Ein Stündlein wohl vor Tag' [About an Hour Before Daybreak, 1935].

The various worlds that Zeisl's songs inhabit have idiomatic characteristics that to some extent indicate the influence of his teachers but were also determined independently in response to the contemporary musical world or established Zeisl's personal musical language, one that was itself subject to change over time. And as is the case with most composers of songs, Zeisl's miniatures sometimes became 'musical diaries' that turned individual biographical situations into modes of expression and communication, via words and music, and thus created narratives that could only be relevant to a particular time. This is echoed by Zeisl's preference for certain poets, a factor that is of special importance for a consideration of the Petzold songs.

[4] [Anon.], 'Konzerte', *Neues Wiener Journal*, 29 November 1931, p. 29.

In 1920, at the age of fifteen, Zeisl became a pupil of Richard Franz Stöhr (1874–1967), who in turn was a member of the circle around Robert Fuchs (1847–1927) and was thus a colleague of Fuchs's pupils Richard Heuberger, Hugo Wolf, Gustav Mahler, Camillo Horn, Alexander Zemlinsky, Franz Schmidt, Franz Schreker, Karl Weigl, Egon Kornauth and Erich Wolfgang Korngold.[5] The *Lied* dominated the work of the teacher, theorist and composer Richard Stöhr, who by his own admission was 'kein Komponist der Gegenwart' [not a composer of the present age] and as perhaps the last Austrian representative of a style of composition that could be called 'romantic individualism' taught the young Zeisl the musical language of late romanticism.[6]

After working with Stöhr, Zeisl became a pupil of the 'out-and-out romantic' Joseph Marx (1882–1964).[7] In a survey of contemporary vocal music published in the *Musikblätter des Anbruch* in 1928, Erich Katz sketches the *Lieder* scene of the time: he places Joseph Marx alongside Paul Graener, Hermann Zilcher and Julius Bittner at the point 'wo der Zusammenhang mit der deutschen Tradition des neunzehnten Jahrhunderts noch als stärkste Komponente [hervortrat]' [where the connection with the German tradition of the nineteenth century stood out as the strongest element].[8] In his songs Marx pursued the aims of Schubert, Schumann and above all Wolf by treating the voice and piano parts equally so as to maximize comprehension of the text. (The development of the piano part in Hugo Wolf sometimes takes on the forms of colourful pianistic fantasy to which the vocal line seems merely to have been appended by way of commentary.) In his fairly free handling of the rhythms of the text, Marx adopted Wolf's principles almost by way of deliberately associating himself with the tradition of the romantic *Deklamationslied* [declamatory song].[9] In 1921 Paul Stefan reported the following about Marx in *Neue Musik und Wien* [*New Music and Vienna*]:

> sein Landsmann Hugo Wolf gab das Vorbild für seine ersten Versuche und schon sie zeigten ein starkes Empfinden für das Wesen des neuen Liedes, Verständnis für Sprache, Dichtung, Betonung, für die Kunst des begleitenden Instrumentes, Melodik und die Kraft des rechten Lyrikers. [...] Marx ist einer der für Wien am meisten markanten Musiker, auch

---

[5] *Lexikon zeitgenössischer Musik aus Österreich. Komponisten und Komponistinnen des 20. Jahrhunderts*, ed. by Bernhard Günther (Vienna, 1997), p. 51.

[6] Hans Sittner, *Richard Stöhr. Mensch — Musiker — Lehrer* (Vienna and Munich, 1965), pp. 32 and 34.

[7] Richard Specht, 'Neue Musik in Wien', *Musikblätter des Anbruch*, 13/14 (September 1921), pp. 245–56 (p. 249).

[8] Erich Katz, 'Vokalmusik im Schaffen der Gegenwart. Moderne Liederkomponisten', *Musikblätter des Anbruch*, 9/10: *Jahrbuch 1929, Gesang* (November/December 1928), pp. 399–408 (p. 400).

[9] See Ernst Decsey, *Hugo Wolf. Das Leben und das Lied* (Berlin, 1921); Andreas Holzer, '"Nicht alles, was tönt, ist auch — Musik." Joseph Marx, Hüter der Tradition', PhD thesis (University of Graz, 1999).

von den Jüngsten wohl gelitten, denen er freilich im Übergang geblieben scheint.[10]

[his countryman Hugo Wolf was the model for his first attempts and even these displayed a strong affinity for the essence of the new *Lied*, an understanding of language, poetry, emphasis, for the art of the accompanying instrument, melody and the force of the true lyric writer. Marx is one of the most notable of Vienna's musicians, looked on well even by the most recent generation, even though they regard him as having remained in a transitional phase.]

The 'guardians of tradition', Stöhr and Marx, were assigned by Stefan to the 'transitional generation' in contrast to composers 'from Schreker to Schoenberg', 'Schoenberg and his followers' and 'another generation'. Marx, although 'looked on well even by the most recent generation', used the language of conservatism and reaction in the 1930s in his opposition to the 'atonals' in order to exacerbate the differences within the various groups of Austrian composers in what ultimately became a form of trench-warfare. Marx's conception of art and his social and political attitudes were marked by a profound conservatism that Zeisl, whose views were more open and tolerant, was unwilling to imitate unquestioningly. It was an interest in song composition that had led Zeisl to Marx, who was at that time the most famous Austrian composer of *Lieder*, but the collaboration between them was short-lived.

In the person of the composer, freelance teacher and philosopher of music Hugo Kauder (1888–1972), however, Zeisl had the opportunity in the early 1930s to work with an innovative teacher who more clearly represented 'Modernism'. His proximity to Karl Weigl establishes a line back to Gustav Mahler but his early style also reflects affinities with Max Reger and Johannes Brahms.[11] In 1924 Pisk mentioned '[die] Bande, welche den Symphoniker Karl Weigl und [...] Hugo Kauder [...] mit Mahler verknüpften' [the bonds that linked the symphonist Karl Weigl and Hugo Kauder with Mahler].[12] Kauder engaged in an intensive struggle to find answers to questions of musical philosophy and musical aesthetics. His theoretical essays were published in 1932 as *Entwurf einer Neuen Melodie- und Harmonielehre* [*Outline of a New Theory of Melody and Harmony*].[13] There he develops a theory of scales that can sit unproblematically alongside traditional views of harmony, cadence and polyphony, but philosophically its roots lie in Rudolf Pannwitz's *Renaissance der Vokalmusik aus dem Geiste und als Schöpfung des Kosmos Atheos* [*The Renaissance of Vocal Music from the Spirit and as a Creation of Kosmos Atheos*, 1926].[14] Pannwitz, who saw himself as a direct intellectual descendant of Nietzsche, founded

---

[10] Paul Stefan, *Neue Musik und Wien* (Leipzig, Vienna and Zurich, 1921), p. 34.
[11] See Otto S. Kauder, *Hugo Kauder — Werkverzeichnis* ([n. p.], 1996).
[12] Paul Amadeus Pisk, 'Wiener Musikleben der Gegenwart', *Melos*, 1 (1924), 28–31 (p. 29).
[13] Hugo Kauder, *Entwurf einer neuen Melodie- und Harmonielehre* (Vienna, 1932).
[14] In this context see Raymond Furness, *Zarathustra's Children. A Study of a Lost Generation of German Writers* (Rochester, NY, 2000), pp. 35–36.

the periodical *Charon* with Otto zur Linde, and Kauder was in close contact with both men. Kauder's choice of texts demonstrates how closely involved he was with the *Charon* circle: Pannwitz and zur Linde are represented as poets, together with the *Charon* sympathizer Rudolf Paulsen. The fact that Erich Zeisl also set works by Paulsen confirms Kauder's influence on him, as does Zeisl's settings of texts by Nietzsche that Kauder himself repeatedly returned to (for example, 'Lieder und Sprüche Zarathustras' [Songs and Sayings of Zarathustra, 1921–26]; three of the six songs from 'Hälfte des Lebens' [Half of Life, 1922–34], namely 'Der Tag klingt ab' [The Day Fades], 'Der Herbst' [Autumn] and 'Der Skeptiker spricht' [The Sceptic Speaks]; and 'Die Sonne sinkt' [The Sun Sets, 1933] — five poems for alto, tenor, baritone, chorus and orchestra). Zeisl's Nietzsche songs were written in 1931: their thinner textures reflect a retreat from previously full sonorities and they do not engage in sweeping melodic development. In a musical language that is briefer and tighter, the atmospheric romanticism inherited from Stöhr and Marx cedes to a simplicity that became typical for Zeisl at this time, a simplicity whose sparing, trenchant and (because diverging from the norm of the period) *individual* harmonic turns communicate modernity to a high degree. Hugo Kauder's aesthetic may have had an effect on Zeisl. Richard Specht (1870–1932) described him in a 1921 article on 'New Music in Vienna' as 'not definitively placeable',[15] and he represented a wholly individual position within the Viennese musical scene. His network of contacts penetrated as far as the Schoenberg circle — in 1919 Kauder participated as a violist under Schoenberg's baton in a concert for the 'Verein für musikalische Privataufführungen' [Association for Private Musical Performances][16] — and thus afforded Zeisl the opportunity to engage with compositional phenomena of a type that Stöhr and Marx could not have shown him. Romantic and impressionist colouring of the kind that Marx exemplified in his songs was neither a model nor a stimulus for Zeisl; however, in Paul Stefan's words once more, Marx's 'Empfinden für das Wesen des neuen Liedes' [affinity for the essence of the new *Lied*] and his 'Verständnis für Sprache, Dichtung, Betonung, für die Kunst des begleitenden Instruments' [understanding of language, poetry, emphasis, (and) the art of the accompanying instrument] were certainly of importance and extended the insights conveyed previously by Richard Stöhr.[17]

In 1931, known as his 'Liederjahr' [year of songs], Zeisl composed nothing but *Lieder*, and thirty examples mark this period as the culmination of his work in this genre. Thereafter, the rate at which he composed songs diminished

---

[15] Specht, 'Neue Musik in Wien', p. 256.
[16] This concert took place on 6 June 1919 and involved, amongst others, Hugo Gottesmann (violin), Hugo Kauder (viola), Eduard Steuermann (piano), Olga Novakovits (piano), Ernst Bachrich (piano), Arnold Schoenberg (conductor). See the Programme Archive of the Wiener Konzerthaus: http://konzerthaus.at/archiv/datenbanksuche.html.
[17] Stefan, *Neue Musik und Wien*, p. 34.

until he ceased completely in 1938. In 1931 and before Zeisl had taken his texts from the *Wunderhorn*, Goethe, Nietzsche, Eichendorff, Lessing, Dehmel, Morgenstern, Bierbaum, Ringelnatz and Busch, and paid particular attention to Austrian authors such as Lenau, Rilke, Schaukal, Gilm and Kühnel. What followed the 'Liederjahr', however, requires closer consideration. In 1932 Zeisl wrote seven songs; in 1933 there were four, none in 1934, four in 1935, one in 1936, none in 1937, and his last song, 'Komm süsser Tod', was written in 1938.[18] Of the seven composed in 1932 four are to texts by the same author: with 'Der tote Arbeiter' [The Dead Worker], 'Die Arbeiter' [The Workers], 'Ein buckliger Waisenknabe singt' [A Hunchbacked Orphan Boy Sings] and 'Wanderlied' [Wanderer's Song] Erich Zeisl had discovered Alfons Petzold.

II

The archetypal Austrian 'proletarian poet' Petzold was born in 1882 in the Fünfhaus district of west-central Vienna and died in 1923 in Kitzbühel.[19] One of the first articles devoted to his work was published in 1909 under the title 'Alfons Petzold. Ein Arbeiterdichter' [Alfons Petzold. A Worker-Poet] by Josef Luitpold Stern (1886–1966), who was a significant figure in the Social Democratic education campaign. Stern's piece appeared in *Der jugendliche Arbeiter* [*The Young Worker*], the journal of the organization of the same name, with which Robert Danneberg (1885–1942) had close associations. Petzold summarized his response thus in May 1909:

> Was die Petzoldnummer im *Jugendlichen Arbeiter* anbelangt, freue ich mich sehr darüber, bin ich doch durch persönliche Erinnerungen mit den jugendlichen Arbeitern verbunden, war ich doch selbst vor 10 Jahren Mitglied der Ortsgruppe 16 und war es da in einem Kreis Jugendlicher, wo ich als 17jähriger Bursche meine ersten Gedichte rezitierte.[20]
>
> [As far as the Petzold issue of *The Young Worker* is concerned, I am delighted because personal memories link me to this group: ten years ago I was myself a member of Local Chapter 16, a member there of a circle of young people for whom as a 17-year-old boy I recited my first poems.]

---

[18] This list refers only to songs that have been clearly dated. There are also ten undated songs currently known to scholars.

[19] See Roman Herle, 'Alfons Petzold. Versuch einer Monografie', PhD thesis (University of Vienna, 1927); Ernst Glaser, 'Alfons Petzold. Ein Beitrag zum Problem der Arbeiterdichtung', PhD thesis (University of Vienna, 1935); Herbert Exenberger, Fritz Hüser and Hans Schroth, *Alfons Petzold 24.9.1882–25.1.1923. Beiträge zum Leben und Schaffen* (Dortmund, 1972); Elfriede Kirschner, 'Die Tagebücher Alfons Petzolds 1904–22', PhD thesis (University of Innsbruck, 1984); Alfons Petzold, *Ich mit den müden Füßen. Texte eines Arbeiterdichters. Ein Lesebuch*, ed. by Ludwig Roman Fleischer (Klagenfurt, 2002).

[20] Quoted from *Alfons Petzold 1882–1923*, ed. by Franz Patzer (Vienna, 1982), p. 14.

On Stern's initiative the *Dresdner Volkszeitung* [*Dresden People's Newspaper*] had published ten poems by Petzold on 27 January 1909, and four of them appeared four days later in the Viennese *Arbeiter-Zeitung* alongside an article on Petzold by the paper's then cultural editor, Stefan Großmann. This was Petzold's first publication in the central organ of the Austrian Social Democrats.

It is important to scrutinize the criteria that underpin the somewhat sweeping term *Arbeiterdichtung* [workers' poetry], especially as applied to Petzold.[21] Must writing with that label actually have been written by a working man? Or is it more important that those to whom it is principally addressed fall into that category? Are political engagement or solidarity with the workers' movement and Socialism indispensable qualifications? Or is it sufficient that the world described is identifiably that of the working class?[22] It is in fact rare for Socialist literature to be the work of figures from the working class, since such writing usually stems from the politically ambitious intelligentsia. Petzold, however, was more than familiar with working-class life, both as participant and observer, and it is this that determines his credentials as a 'worker poet'. In his autobiography, *Das rauhe Leben* [*The Rough Life*, 1920], he describes — doubtless in a somewhat stylized manner — the miserable lives and harsh conditions endured by the industrial proletariat, the experience of operating in a degrading work place, and long-term illness and infirmity under conditions of homelessness and unemployment. Petzold was a 'Taglöhner, Laufbursche, Bäckerlehrling, Schuhmacherlehrling, Aushilfskellner, Austräger, Schneeschaufler, Hilfsarbeiter da und dort, Metalldreher, Gipsschleifer und Fensterputzer, dazwischen immer wieder ohne Arbeit, dem Hunger und der Verzweiflung preisgegeben' [day-labourer, errand boy, baker's apprentice, cobbler's apprentice, temporary barman, delivery man, snow shoveller, occasional navvy, lathe operator, plaster cutter and window cleaner — and in the interstices repeatedly unemployed, starving and desperate].[23] Even as a child he had taken refuge in the world of the poets his mother had introduced him to, and was used to finding in Tieck, Brentano, Uhland, Heine, Schiller and Körner an alternative world with which to console himself. He slaked his thirst for books in the public library of the Wiener Volksbildungsverein [Viennese People's Education Union] in Ottakring.[24] Looking back on his early life in

[21] See Josef Luitpold Stern, 'Alfons Petzold. Ein Arbeiterdichter', *Der jugendliche Arbeiter* (July 1909), pp. 1–2, and his *Der Arbeiter und die Kultur* (Vienna, 1930), *Klassenkampf und Massenschulung* (Vienna, 1930), *Herakles unter den Arbeitern* (Vienna, 1932). See also Josef Weidenholzer, *Auf dem Weg zum 'Neuen Menschen'. Bildungs- und Kulturarbeit der österreichischen Sozialdemokratie in der Ersten Republik* (Vienna, 1981).

[22] See *Mit uns zieht die neue Zeit. Arbeiterkultur in Österreich 1918–1934*, exhibition catalogue, ed. by Helene Maimann (Vienna, 1981).

[23] Franz Krotsch, 'Vorwort', in Alfons Petzold, *Das rauhe Leben* (Graz, Vienna, Leipzig and Berlin, 1932), p. 6.

[24] See Friedrich Slezak, *Ottakringer Arbeiterkultur an zwei Beispielen. 1. Alfons Petzold (1882–1923) und Josef Slezak (1887–1976). 2. Franz Schütze (1882–1943) und sein Kinderfreunde-Orchester* (Vienna, 1982), p. 4.

1922, he writes in a text entitled 'Im Spiegel' [In the Mirror], 'Aus den finsteren Löchern des sozialen Unrechtes komme ich hervor. Dort kauerte ich jahrelang und schrieb im Hunger und Dunkel die Klage und den Haß der Armen in zerbrochenen Versen nieder' [I have emerged from the dark pits of social injustice. I cowered there for years on end and in hunger and darkness recorded the woes and the hatred of the poor in fractured lines of verse].[25] It can truly be said that Petzold lifted himself out of misery through his writing. In what he himself described as a condition of youthful 'Unschuld und Verblendung und in vollständiger Unkenntnis sozialer und politischer Tatsachen' [innocence and blindness, in complete ignorance of social and political truths], like many he had initially been a passionate supporter of the demagogue Karl Lueger (1844–1910),[26] before he joined the Social Democrat Verein jugendlicher Arbeiter [Young Workers' Union], probably at some point between 1899 and 1902. It was via the workers' educational organizations that formed the bedrock of Social Democracy in the early years of the movement that Petzold then found the opportunity to recite his own socially aware poetry. The list of forthcoming events in the *Arbeiter-Zeitung* for 17 August 1902 includes an announcement for a 'Vorlesung von Herrn Petzold, Schriftsteller' [Lecture by Mr Petzold, writer] to be given in the association's meeting room on 20 August.[27]

Whilst travelling in 1905 Petzold met revolutionary Russian emigrés, and once back in Vienna he worked as an editorial assistant on the weekly political and cultural paper *Der Weg* [*The Path*] which came out in 1905–06. His colleagues there included Hermann Bahr, Alfred Polgar and Robert Scheu.[28] In June 1907 he and like-minded friends Josef Mayerhöfer, Josef Slezak and Rudolf Großmann (1882–1942) planned to form a poetical 'Icarus League' or 'Icarus Club', a society of worker-poets which would meet regularly under Petzold's leadership and styled itself a 'philosophical society' and an 'association of thinking and creative minds', but the project was very short-lived. Slezak wrote about it under the heading 'Bahn frei dem Denkergeist!!!' [Make way for the spirit of the thinker!!!] and announced, amongst other things:

> Unser Sammel- und Leitruf in der zu gründenden Vereinigung frei und offen Denkender, fußend auf dem Boden der internationalen Arbeiterschaft! [...] So werden wir trachten, stets eine Pflegestätte zu bleiben für alles Menschliche und Gute, für alle Wissenschaft: Dichtung und Kunst, Literatur und Theater, Musik und Malerei, Politik und kurz alles, was Geist erheischt, aber obenan und über alles Philosophie! Denn: Wir wollen werden wahre Proletarier-Philosophen![29]

---

[25] Alfons Petzold, 'Im Spiegel', in *Gesang von Morgen bis Mittag. Eine Auswahl der Gedichte von Alfons Petzold* (Vienna and Leipzig, 1922), p. 5.
[26] Quoted from *Alfons Petzold*, ed. by Patzer, p. 6.
[27] Ibid., p. 7.
[28] Slezak, *Ottakringer Arbeiterkultur*, p. 13.
[29] Ibid., p. 17.

[This is the rallying cry and clarion call for the association we are to found for free and open-minded thinkers, rooted in the soil of the international working class! We will always aspire to remain a home for everything that is humane and good, for all forms of knowledge: poetry and art, literature and drama, music and painting, politics and everything, in short, that requires the use of the intellect, philosophy first and foremost! We want to become true proletarian philosophers!]

Shortly after this there is an invitation by Petzold couched in the following terms: 'Werther Genosse! Betreffs Gründung eines Sozialistischen Clubs, ersuche ich Sie, Freitag den 28. d.M. sich bei mir bestimmt einzufinden. [...] Mit Parteigruß Alfons Petzold' [Valued comrade! Concerning the foundation of a Socialist Club I invite you to join me on Friday 28 of this month. I greet you in the name of the party, Alfons Petzold].[30]

Petzold's involvement in Austrian anarchism between 1911 and 1913 was more consistent. Like Rudolf Großmann, who wrote under the pseudonym of Pierre Ramus, Petzold concealed his identity when publishing articles in the anarchist press, signing them 'De Profundis' [From the Depths].[31] But after 1912, when he had access to an increasing number of publications, including the Social Democratic ones, his cooperation with the anarchist journals came to an end.[32] Petzold's autobiography records his qualified acceptance of social structures that he had previously rejected and the influence on him in this respect of his friend, the factory worker Robert Schindler, 'ein fanatischer Sozialist, welcher Weltanschauung er mit religiöser Schwärmerei anhing' [a fanatical Socialist, who clung to the Socialist outlook with religious fervour].[33] Schindler's 'evangelisches Wesen übte trotzdem eine große Anziehungskraft auf mich aus, milderte, ohne daß ich es gleich merkte, viele meiner anarchistischen Ansichten, ließ mich das Leben um mich herum durch hellere Gläser sehen' [evangelical presence nevertheless was hugely attractive to me, and without my noticing at first toned down many of my anarchist views and gave me a clearer perspective on the world around me].[34]

Petzold's first volume of poetry, *Seltsame Musik* [*Strange Music*], was published in Philadelphia in 1909; it was not until 1911 that it appeared in Vienna. There followed *Trotz alledem!* [*Despite Everything!*, 1910], a collection of poems whose publication was facilitated by Luitpold Stern: he persuaded the Social Democrat publishing house to accept the volume with an introduction by himself. The first collection of prose writing was *Memoiren eines Auges* [*Memoirs of an Eye*, 1912], a series of sketches in which a move away from social themes can be

---

[30] Ibid., p. 18.
[31] *Alfons Petzold*, ed. by Patzer, p. 10.
[32] Gerfried Brandstetter, 'Sozialdemokratische Opposition und Anarchismus in Österreich 1889–1918', in *Im Schatten der Arbeiterbewegung. Zur Geschichte des Anarchismus in Österreich und Deutschland*, ed. by Karl R. Stadler (Vienna, 1977), pp. 29–97 (p. 86).
[33] Petzold, *Rauhes Leben*, p. 317.
[34] Ibid., pp. 317–18.

detected in the placing of sections devoted to 'Love' and 'Life and Death' alongside the one headed 'Work'. The same shift in subject-matter is evident in the next volume of poetry, *Das Ewige und die Stunde* [*Eternity and the Hour*, 1912]: these 115 miniatures are divided into chapters headed 'Eine Stunde zu Gott' [An Hour with God], 'Der Wanderer' [The Wanderer] and 'Blick in die Welt' [Looking into the World], and show signs above all of Petzold's growing interest in religious questions. This collection already includes a poem on St Francis of Assisi, who was to become extremely important for Petzold later in life. Towards the end of 1913 the novel *Erde* [*Earth*] appeared in book form: it had previously been published as a serial in the *Arbeiter-Zeitung*, which announced its publication as follows: 'Es ist ein Heilstättenroman. Die Menschen und Schicksale, die eine Lungenheilanstalt zusammenführt, schreiten an uns vorüber' [It is a sanatorium novel. The characters and lives that are brought together in a tuberculosis clinic parade in front of us].[35] *Der heilige Ring* [*The Sacred Ring*, 1914] still contains ardent anti-war poems, but the euphorically martial and patriotic tones of *Krieg* [*War*], which appeared undated but is perhaps from 1914, strike a disconcerting note; they certainly unsettled his friend Luitpold Stern.[36] A change is evident here: as the First World War dragged on, emotional and adulatory nationalism swung round into its opposite, sobriety, and prompted radical depictions of the sufferings of war in, for example, *Volk, mein Volk* [*People, my People*, 1915] or *Der stählerne Schrei* [*The Scream of Steel*, 1916]. It is interesting to read *Deutsche Legende* [*German Legend*, 1916] and its counterpart *Österreichische Legende* [*Austrian Legend*, 1916], which respectively foreground Pan-German nationalism and suggest an 'anointed Austria', against the background of the political realities of the day. The compilation of love poems, *Das neue Fest. Verse der Liebe* [*The New Celebration. Love Poems*, 1916] is in complete contrast to this.

Evocations of nature and professions of his own deep religiousness increase in frequency as the subjects of Petzold's later work. St Francis of Assisi comes to represent for Petzold an exemplary synthesis of social engagement and religion. The 1919 collection *Soziale Gedichte — Der Dornbusch* [*Social Poems — The Thorn Bush*] show this most markedly. After an interruption to his poetic output, but in tune with the revolutionary mood after the end of the war, Petzold compiled an anthology of texts on the current social situation, a group of miniatures published by Strache and dedicated to 'My friend Dr Stefan Licht'.[37] Licht was the leaseholder of a bookshop in Kitzbühel run by the poet. *Der Dornbusch* is

---

[35] Quoted from *Alfons Petzold*, ed. by Patzer, p. 19.
[36] Ibid., p. 21.
[37] The publishing firm was founded by Eduard Strache and had its main offices in Warnsdorf in Bohemia, but from 1917 to 1933 it had an office in Vienna and primarily took on works by the representatives of Austrian Expressionism. Alongside book publication, the firm also printed music: Erich Zeisl's first publication (published some time before 1922), *Drei Lieder* [*Three Songs*], appeared as No. 47 in Strache's series. On Strache, see Murray Hall, *Österreichische Verlagsgeschichte 1918–1938*, 2 vols (Vienna, 1985), II, 384–95.

important in the context of the present essay in that the poems by Petzold set by Zeisl are all taken from this volume.

Petzold's poetry offered Zeisl texts that had less literary value than historical significance. They describe social structures and culturally relevant milieus, but are not free from romanticizing pathos either. If Petzold's miniatures show him as a class warrior, their diction sometimes seems oddly stylised and even unworldly. Many of the poems express a form of lament that resolves itself into redemption from earthly tribulations via the transcendence of suffering on a higher plane of reality.

Petzold's prose is worthy of special consideration. Its language is often of exceptional clarity and very skilfully deployed, such as in the novella 'Der Franzl. Geschichte einer Kindheit' [Little Franz. Story of a Childhood], in which the author shows himself a master of a narrative technique that intimately tracks the protagonist. The writing demonstrates an eye for detail, and the reader learns in heart-rending terms of the bleak, shattered, marginal existence of Little Franz, who, scarred by his parents' alcoholism, as a youth can only find consolation in death. 'Lau und zärtlich strich das Wasser über seine Finger und versuchte wie im Spiel höher hinaufzugreifen. Franzl wollte sich noch einmal aufrichten; aber ihm war, als ziehe ihn das Wasser immer liebevoller an sich; ohne Anstrengung glitt er tiefer und tiefer' [balmy and tender, the water trickled over his fingers and almost as if in play tried to reach higher and higher up. Franzl wanted to stand up again, but he felt as if the water was drawing him ever more lovingly towards it. Effortlessly he slid deeper and deeper down].[38] Short portraits such as 'Der Kellnerbub' [The Bar Boy], 'Schneeschaufler' [Snow Shovellers] or 'Fensterputzer' [Window Cleaners] achieve a directness that is in part attributable to the use of Viennese dialect.

From about 1907 Petzold's work began to find an enthusiastic readership amongst ordinary young people in the working-class districts of Vienna, milieus from which many municipal functionaries and people active in the Social Democratic cultural organizations emerged. They contributed in large measure to Petzold's popularity in the First Republic, when the *Arbeiter-Zeitung* and other left-wing publications adopted his work with enthusiasm. He also came to the attention of David Josef Bach, the initiator of the Workers' Symphony Concerts and Director of the Social Democratic Kunststelle (founded in 1919 and active until 1934 under the motto 'Kunst ins Volk' [Take Art to the People]). From 1926 until 1931 Bach also edited the periodical *Kunst und Volk* [*Art and People*], which was based on Wagner's idea of a 'union with the totality of the people'.[39] In February 1923 Bach published *Kunst und Volk. Eine Festgabe*

---

[38] Alfons Petzold, *Ich mit den müden Füßen*, ed. by Roman Fleischer (Klagenfurt, 2002), p. 63.
[39] See Henriette Kotlan-Werner, *Kunst und Volk. David Josef Bach 1874–1947* (Vienna, 1977); Werner Jank, 'Arbeitermusik zwischen Kunst, Kampf und Geselligkeit. Sozialdemokratische Arbeiter-Musikbewegung in der Ersten Republik', PhD thesis (University of Vienna, 1982);

der Kunststelle zur 1000. Theateraufführung [*Art and the People. A Commemorative Volume from the Kunststelle on the Occasion of the 1000th Performance*]. Petzold had died in January of that year, and the *Festgabe*, which was published shortly afterwards, included 'Der einsame Dichter', 'Drei Gedichte: Beethoven, Der Dichter spricht, Bänkel' [The Lonely Poet. Three Poems: Beethoven, The Poet Speaks, Ballad] and 'Der junge Gelehrte und seine Schwester' [The Young Scholar and his Sister]. There was a detailed obituary of Petzold by Fritz Rosenfeld in the January 1924 number of *Der Kampf* [*The Struggle*]; in 1924 a selected volume entitled *Das letzte Mittel* [*The Final Means*] appeared in Reclam with an afterword by Franz Karl Ginzkey. Petzold was strongly represented in working-class newspapers and workers' libraries, often at the instigation of Josef Luitpold Stern: in January 1933 he wrote a commemorative article in *Der Sozialdemokrat* for the tenth anniversary of Petzold's death, and in November Paul Amadeus Pisk seems to have performed a hymn by Petzold set by Josef Frankl in the Wiener Konzerthaus.[40]

Austrian workers' literature only made headway within organized structures after Petzold's death, in the early 1930s. In 1933 authors including Josef Luitpold Stern, Fritz Brügel and Theodor Kramer founded the Vereinigung sozialistischer Schriftsteller [Union of Socialist Writers].[41] In contrast to Stern, whose writing was always closely linked to the concerns of the Party, Petzold also wrote poetry without Party relevance; solidarity with the working class and humanitarian intervention on behalf of the needy from his own background were the central themes of his work.[42] Franz Krotsch, the author of the foreword to the 1932 edition of *Rauhes Leben*, even questioned whether Petzold had ever been 'ein richtiger Klassenkämpfer' [a true class warrior] and thought instead that he had been linked 'mit der Arbeiterschaft [...], deren Leben er lebte, nicht mit der Partei' [with the working class, whose lives resembled his own, rather than with the Party].[43] Petzold's texts can rarely be called didactic or preachy, and rarely have the confrontational, belligerent air that is otherwise typical of

---

and *Austrian Studies*, 14: *Culture and Politics in Red Vienna* (2006). The Social Democratic Kunststelle was one of several organizations providing access to culture for less affluent citizens. However, neither the Kunststelle für christliche Volksbildung (affiliated to the Christian Social Party) nor the Pan-German Deutsche Kunst- und Bildungsstelle achieved comparable levels of support and success.

[40] Slezak, *Ottakringer Arbeiterkultur*, p. 46. According to Slezak, a long-service celebration took place in the Great Concert Hall on that day, although the archive of the Wiener Konzerthaus provides no confirmation of this.

[41] The Bund proletarisch-revolutionärer Schriftsteller [Union of Proletarian-Revolutionary Writers] grouped around Anna Seghers, Friedrich Wolf and Georg Lukács (founded in 1928 and with close links to the German Communist Party) maintained a subsidiary branch in Austria. Catholic writers of workers' literature such as Anton Forcher and Georg Rendl attempted to find an audience via the Viennese daily newspaper, *Die Reichspost* [*The Post*].

[42] Norbert Leser, 'Austromarxismus und Literatur', in *Aufbruch und Untergang. Österreichische Kultur zwischen 1918 und 1938*, ed. by Franz Kadrnoska (Vienna, 1981), pp. 43–68.

[43] Krotsch, 'Vorwort', in Petzold, *Rauhes Leben*, p. 6.

workers' literature. They belong instead to the mystificatory or transcendent styles, and often reflect religious, even redemptive thinking. Whilst is it true that Petzold's poetry often uses the collective as the symbol of unified ideals, it draws its power from the thought of redemption in unity rather than from calls for the use of actual force of any kind. Petzold does strike a combative note, but usually only in the war poems that should in any case be evaluated separately.

One issue worthy of further consideration is the tension inherent in Petzold's wish to establish a reputation both as a 'workers' writer' and as a poet acknowledged by a broader audience. The desire to avoid being pigeon-holed manifests itself in a tendency to reduce the prominence of social themes in his poetry, which is obvious, for example, in the 1914 collection *Der heilige Ring*. A diary entry from the same year underscores this: 'Ich leide noch immer an der Einbildung, einer der größten Lyriker Österreichs zu werden!' [I am still suffering from the delusion that I can become one of Austria's greatest poets!].[44] Such a statement suggests that a poet socialized by the proletariat has ambitions for his poetry that reach beyond it.

Erich Zeisl's socialization was that of a member of the assimilated Jewish middle class in Vienna's Leopoldstadt district. Zeisl came from a bourgeois commercial background: his parents ran the Café Tegetthoff in Heinestrasse. Since the early 1930s he had been close friends with the writer Hilde Spiel (1911–1990) and, although he himself had not been active on behalf of any of the parties on the political scene at that time, in Spiel he had an ardent Socialist amongst his closest friends. In her *Erinnerungen* [*Reminiscences*] we read:

> Schon Jahre zuvor, am 30. Mai 1930, [...] bin ich abends um halb neun in einem sozialistischen Fackelzug auf der Ringstraße mitmarschiert. [...] Nein, in die Partei trat ich nicht ein, noch nicht. Aber ich war, wenngleich nicht 'primo loco' ein politischer Mensch, doch bald schon ergriffen vom Geist der Zeit und von dem meiner Stadt [...]. Emotionelle mehr als rationale Gründe haben uns nach links gerückt. Russische Lieder aus dem ersten Aufstand 1905: 'Zar Nikolai erließ ein Manifest | Den Toten ihre Freiheit | Die Lebenden in Arrest.' [...] Alfons Petzolds Gedicht vom toten Arbeiter, 'Meine Not ist zu Ende und all meine Qual, köstliche Erde hüllt die ruhenden Hände, und mein Leib ist worden ein leuchtender Sonnenstrahl', sehr bald auch die Songs von Bert Brecht, die wir in den *Versuche*-Heften lasen.[45]

> [Years previously, on 30 May 1930, I joined a Socialist torchlight march on the Ringstrasse at 8.30 in the evening. No, I did not join the Party, not yet anyway. But I was a political animal, even if not primarily so, and was soon seized by the spirit of the age and of my city. We were moved leftwards more by emotion than reason. Russian songs from the first uprising of 1905: 'Tsar Nicholas issued a decree | Freedom for the dead | Detention

---

[44] Quoted in *Alfons Petzold*, ed. by Patzer, p. 21.
[45] Hilde Spiel, *Die hellen und die finsteren Zeiten. Erinnerungen 1911–1946* (Munich, 1989), pp. 81–83.

for the living'; Alfons Petzold's poem about the dead worker, 'My misery is over, and all my pain, rich earth encloses my hands at rest, and my body has become a radiant sunbeam'; very soon also the songs of Bert Brecht, which we read in the *Experiments* series.]

From 1933 until the dissolution of the Party after the brief Civil War of February 1934 Hilde Spiel was a member of the Social Democratic Workers' Party of Austria.[46] In 1933 she published her first novel, *Kati auf der Brücke* [*Katy on the Bridge*], which won the Julius Reich Literature Prize of the City of Vienna. When she wrote these words: 'Dann spielte er wieder. Negerchöre und kleine lyrische Lieder, vertonten Morgenstern und Ringelnatz [...]. Und am Ende noch dies, den toten Arbeiter von Petzold: meine Not ist zu Ende und all meine Qual — ' [Then he played again. Negro spirituals and short lyrical songs, Morgenstern and Ringelnatz set to music. And at the end this, Petzold's 'dead worker': My misery is over, and all my pain], she was depicting her friend Zeisl in the figure of the musician.[47] The fact that she pays homage to the 'dead worker' underlines how important Petzold's poems were to them both. Zeisl had only set 'Der tote Arbeiter' as recently as 1932, doubtless having had his attention drawn to it by Spiel. This was also the year in which he set Petzold's 'Die Arbeiter', 'Ein buckliger Waisenknabe singt' and 'Wanderlied', making four of the seven poems set in 1932. He had not engaged with literature of that type ever before.

Since 1934 at the latest, Zeisl had also been in contact with the 'workers-writer' Adolf Unger — born in 1904 in the Leopoldstadt and murdered in Auschwitz in 1942. Unger was connected with the Viennese community colleges and workers' education organizations and had shared the 1933 Julius Reich Prize with Spiel. After the official dissolution of the 'Union of Socialist Writers', in October 1934 Unger found himself in the adult education institute 'Wiener Urania' once more, participating in an event entitled 'Dichtung der Gegenwart — Junge Kunst' [Poetry of the Present — Contemporary Art]. He was a member of the 1930s interdisciplinary cultural group named 'Junge Kunst', which also involved Julius Chajes (1910–1985) and Alfred Farau (1904–1972, at that time still known as Fred Hernfeld),[48] and was also part of the Austrian Workers' Writers Union founded in 1936 by Viktor Matejka, Otto Spranger and Anton Forcher.

Zeisl's focus on Petzold at this time, in the context of ever-widening differences in the positions of the Austrian political parties, underscores not only the importance of the material for him but also his solidarity and empathy

---

[46] 'Hilde Spiel' in *Lexikon der österreichischen Exilliteratur*, ed. by Siglinde Bolbecher and Konstantin Kaiser (Vienna and Munich, 2000), pp. 603–05.

[47] Hilde Spiel, *Kati auf der Brücke* (Berlin, Vienna and Leipzig, 1933), p. 164.

[48] On that evening Zeisl appeared as the composer of Morgenstern songs. See the programme note *Dichtung der Gegenwart — Junge Kunst, Klubsaal der Wiener Urania, 27. Oktober 1934* (Eric Zeisl Archive, University of California, Los Angeles, Performing Arts Special Collections).

with Social Democracy itself, as is suggested by a remark by Gertrud Zeisl concerning the start of work on the 'Requiem Concertante': 'We had a great political upheaval in Austria, in which a man by the name of Dollfuss [...] suppressed the Socialists, and it was like a civil war. There was shooting in the streets, and there were many dead. And that is when Erich began the Requiem.'[49]

III

Der tote Arbeiter

Meine Not ist zu Ende
und all meine Qual, —
köstliche Erde hüllt die ruhenden Hände
und mein Leib ist worden ein leuchtender Sonnenstrahl.

Als ich noch lebte:
O, wie ich da nach Sonne und Erde strebte!
Erde und Sonne! Wie oft habe ich darum gebeten,
mußt ich in Dumpfheit und Schwere die Drehbank treten.
Hob ich den Blick zur Schau auf glühendes Land,
fraß ihn das russige Dunkel der Werkstättenwand.

Nun aber berge
ich Sonne und Erde in meinen trunkenen Blick. —
Brüder, Brüder: erst im Reiche der Särge
blüht empor unser wahres Menschengeschick.[50]

[My misery is over, and all my pain, — rich earth encloses my hands at rest, and my body has become a radiant sunbeam.

When I was still alive: oh, how I was drawn to the sun and the earth! Earth and sun! How often have I pleaded for them when I had to pedal the lathe, numb and heavy. If I lifted my gaze to look at the radiant land, the sooty darkness of the workshop wall consumed it.

Now, however, I harbour sun and earth in my drunken gaze. — Brothers, brothers! Only in the coffins' realm does our true human destiny send its blossoms upwards.]

This poem demonstrates clearly the thoughts of redemption that are typical of Petzold's lyric poetry. The lament, intensified by being couched in the first person, is inverted to become a song of triumph as past suffering is

---

[49] Zeisl began working on the 'Requiem Concertante' in October 1933 and completed it in August 1934. Gertrud Zeisl's dates are therefore not accurate, and Zeisl can only have been *continuing* his work on the Requiem during the political events of 1934. Nonetheless, her remarks still confirm her husband's political concerns at that time. See 'Oral History Malcolm Cole, Gertrud Zeisl 1975': http://www.schoenberglaw.com/zeisl/oralhistory.html.
[50] Alfons Petzold, *Der Dornbusch. Soziale Gedichte von Alfons Petzold* (Vienna, Prague and Leipzig, 1919), p. 39.

transformed using the idea of progress from darkness to light. Once pain has been withstood, misery and affliction grow into the 'true human destiny' of a new, metaphysical reality. The misery that used to characterize life, now observed with the distance of hindsight, stands in sharp contrast to the 'coffins' realm' that is now perceived as the locus of liberation. The text is defined by the confrontation of these two planes. Attaining a quasi-transcendental higher realm resembles a form of apotheosis that repolarizes the text positively and, strengthened by the message of brotherly unity, transforms the fate of the individual into the triumphant collective. Being granted a utopian vision such as this is a common ideal of workers' literature, even though Petzold would have been seen as insufficiently radical in his proclamation of the goals of revolutionary class warfare.

Zeisl's handling of the text in the song setting is interesting. The shortened version of the text below fails to enact the positive, utopian turn of Petzold's original vision of human brotherhood: it lacks the third stanza that establishes the notion of the collective. In order to maintain the tripartite structure, Zeisl repeats the first stanza and thus remains firmly within the singular perspective of the first-person narrator. Zeisl's text also ends positively (with 'my body has become a radiant sunbeam'), but 'true human destiny' and brotherhood cannot be achieved in this version, which omits Petzold's key idea. The second stanza also loses the conscious enactment of retrospection, as the opening words 'When I was still alive' are cut.

> *Der tote Arbeiter* (song text)
>
> Meine Not ist zu Ende
> und all meine Qual, —
> köstliche Erde hüllt die ruhenden Hände
> und mein Leib ist wie ein leuchtender Sonnenstrahl.
>
> Erde und Sonne, wie oft hab ich darum gebeten,
> musste in Dumpfheit und Schwere die Drehbank treten,
> hob ich den Blick zur Schau auf glühendes Land,
> frass ihn das russige Dunkel der Werkstättenwand.
>
> Meine Not ist zu Ende
> und all meine Qual, —
> köstliche Erde hüllt die ruhenden Hände
> und mein Leib ist wie ein leuchtender Sonnenstrahl!

An ostinato system of changing chords in inexorable crotchet beats from beginning to end underpins the song, which is headed *Tempo di Marcia* [in march time].[51] Dotted fanfare motifs and triplets support the feel of a funeral march as constitutive elements of the baritone voice part. The key is, appropriately, G minor, which since the early Baroque has symbolized the realm of death and

---

[51] One manuscript version has the insistent left-hand chords played as arpeggios; Zeisl's tempo marking in this version specifies 'In funeral march time'.

Manuscript of Zeisl's setting of 'Der tote Arbeiter', Eric Zeisl Archive, University of California, Los Angeles, Performing Arts Special Collections. I. Songs: Box 3, Item 9.

the grave.[52] The chord structure that dominates the song is announced in the very first bar, which functions as a condensed introduction with the G Minor added sixth chord. In Mahler's *Lied von der Erde* [*Song of the Earth*, 1908] this chord and the major sixth, which implies several possibilities for progression, supports the idea of a conclusion that is deliberately kept open. George Gerschwin's 'Summertime' (1935) uses the same chord structure (A–C–E–F♯), although the added sixth here is merely for the purposes of colouring. For Zeisl, the minor added sixth chord, which during the genesis of 'Der tote Arbeiter' was no longer regarded as unusual, will have been tonally interesting, although it is doubtful whether he deliberately used it in Mahler's sense. In the context of the song the minor chord with the added major sixth conveys harmonic instability. From the second bar on, 'Der tote Arbeiter' is divided strictly into groups of four bars and within these, into two groups of two bars each. The first stanza occupies eight bars, which in accordance with the sense of the text are divided into two sections, each treated differently. The interlude (marked 'quasi Hymne!' [almost like a hymn!]) is four bars long; the shortened second stanza again takes up eight. The reprise matches the opening in respect of period and harmony, and a four-bar epilogue closes the piece.[53]

Quite in keeping with the poem's 'closeness to the people', the song 'Der tote Arbeiter' is free of complex construction or artificial ornamentation. Zeisl exploits the possibilities of repetition on the same note of the scale, and avoids sequences (repetition at a different pitch), variations or extravagant extensions, and thereby achieves clarity, simplicity and comprehensibility. His usual fidelity to the text is evident in his exemplary adaptation of the first stanza of 'Der tote Arbeiter': only the phrase 'und mein Leib ist worden ein' [and my body has become a] is replaced by the composer with 'und mein Leib ist wie ein' [my body is like a] so as to retain the pairing of notes in the triplet figures that appear here for the first time. Otherwise Petzold's text for this stanza remains unchanged.

Zeisl derives the material for the melody directly from the accompanying chords. At the beginning of the bar he exploits the dotted-quaver-plus-semiquaver figure as the sign of the march. The subsequent tied crotchet, which seems to pick up the momentum of the previous dotted figure, emphasizes the key words 'Not' and 'all'. In accordance with their stresses, 'Ende' and 'Qual'

[52] Hartmut Krones, 'Das Wort-Ton-Verhältnis bei den Meistern der Wiener Klassik', in *Wort-Ton-Verhältnis. Beiträge zur Geschichte im europäischen Raum*, ed. by Elisabeth Haselauer (Vienna, Cologne and Graz 1981), pp. 47–66 and 145–51. See also Bernhard Meier, *Alte Tonarten, dargestellt an der Instrumentalmusik des 16. und 17. Jahrhunderts*, Bärenreiter Studienbücher Musik 3, ed. by Silke Leopold and Jutta Schmoll-Barthel (Kassel, Basel, London, New York and Prague, 1992).

[53] The reprise exists in two versions: one takes over from the opening the piano echo on 'Qual', the other keeps the continuous crotchets and omits the piano echo, although this is most probably a slip rather than deliberate since Zeisl later completed the piano octaves by transcribing in the crotchet chords.

are placed at the beginnings of the following bars and the third that falls heavily into the root is echoed by the piano. There is a relatively restricted melodic range, and the central note is the B♭ that determines the G minor tonality.

Ex. 1: Line 1 of the poem; bars 1–3

After 'Qual' the piano echoes the voice once again, though with altered rhythm, and makes a transition into the new section via the flattened supertonic in the bass of the next chord. The second line of verse, 'und all meine Qual', is harmonically intensified with an F♭ major seventh in inversion (bar 4), which affords a slight relief from the insistent bass G which is reinforced by the ostinato, besides providing an additional underlining of the sense.

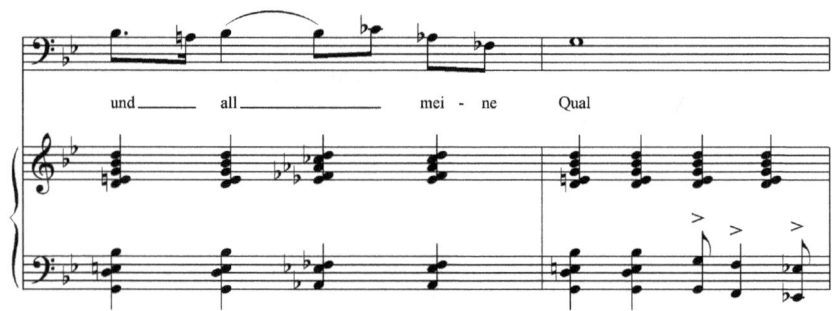

Ex. 2: Line 2; bars 4–5

The characteristic dominant ninth chord in G minor (second beats of bars 6 and 7) determines the setting of the third line of text: the potential of this chord to resolve on to either a major or minor version of the tonic opens up the prospect of new tonal horizons, corresponding to the more consolatory sense of the text. Its minor ninth, functioning as an 'ambiguous' note, permits more than one possibility in the ensuing harmonic progression; like the *sixte ajoutée*, the major sixth added to minor triads, which dominates the texture at the outset of the song, it confers harmonic instability. The new key, G major, emerges for the first time at 'und mein Leib', via the use of the flattened supertonic (end of bar 7), which sounds like a Neapolitan chord, and as usual in Zeisl's work symbolizes sorrow, though at first it is heard as the dominant of C minor. This new tonic is finally established via a cadence that is remarkable in a number of respects, and ends the first stanza in its setting of 'leuchtender Sonnenstrahl'.

Ex. 3: Lines 2–3; bars 6–10

The new tonal area that is opened by the dominant ninth chord permits the baritone to declaim the significant words 'Erde' and 'Hände' in a higher tessitura and more extended range, on E♭ as a recitation note over the open-position chord. A fanfare-like figure (a quaver followed by two semi-quavers) established as a sign of the march is used to set off the minor ninth that dominates the texture; it persists even in the heavy bass progression to the tonic, G. In the following bar the expectation of the major key is momentarily satisfied in that the major third, B♮, is incorporated into the beginning of the line, and emphasized by a new element, a triplet figure; then it is placed immediately at the beginning of the succeeding bar, in a surprisingly pure second-inversion G major triad, decisively colouring the cadence and, with it, the final turn towards the major key. Thus the effect suggested at 'und mein Leib' is further developed by means of a traditional circle-of-fifths progression. The harmonically stable dominant sevenths, presented without any additional notes, produce a striking effect. The idea of a circle-of-fifths progression as a symbol of continuing and permanent constancy might correspond, in terms of the relationship between words and music, to a prospect of a utopia. Apart from occasional melismas introduced for emphasis, Zeisl keeps the song strictly syllabic, but with the brightening of the mood and the change to the major, he alters the style of declamation through an accented lengthening of each note at 'Sonnenstrahl'. In the space of a single bar, the baritone, previously restricted in range, leaps an octave, and reaches the final note in a simple leap of a fifth.

From this point, the piano takes over the function of providing the motivic material in a new register, and initiates the instrumental hymn (*Hymne*), which functions as an interlude (bars 10–11). In this the dotted-quaver-plus-semiquaver element recurs as a means of separating the motives from one another in the second bar of the *Hymne*, but now notated with semiquaver rests (suggesting a contrast between instrumental and vocal performance); the concept of evoking a march through sharp double-dotting is suggested. The important major third, B♯, reached via ascending melody doubled in octaves, leaps down a major sixth to D, which is immediately followed by an E♭ chord superimposed on a G minor triad with an added sixth: the E♮ of the added sixth and the E♭ of the superimposed chord thus contradict one another sharply.

Ex. 4: Interlude; bars 10–11

Precisely at this point (bar 11), the minor third replaces the major third that has previously been established. Within the accented chords played by the left hand, based on G, the upper notes oscillate between B♭ and B♮, the two notes that determine the minor and major modes respectively. The major-minor ambiguity, already manifest in the added-sixth and dominant minor ninth chords, which comes increasingly to represent the leading idea of the song, now characterizes the *Hymne*, and produces false relations through the immediate juxtaposition of major and minor triads. A further musical sign is established in the melodic figure comprising a falling major sixth followed by a chord lying a semitone higher (right hand, bar 11): this suggests affinities with the depictions of marches by Mahler.

With the retrospection of the second stanza (from bar 14), the narrative perspective changes. Nevertheless, the general mood continues to be coloured by 'Dumpfheit und Schwere'. The dynamics sink from *forte* to *mezzo forte*, the chords in the accompaniment sink into the depths of the bass register, the bass G — hitherto constantly offering support both to major and minor harmonies — no longer controls the texture, the vocal line is 'frozen' into the narrowest of ranges, and the oscillation of the chords conveys monotony. Although the harmonic rhythm speeds up at 'musste in Dumpfheit und Schwere die Drehbank treten', the depiction of listlessness thereby becomes yet more extreme. The two-note alternation in the vocal line (first C and B♭) presents the image of the lathe in a mechanical lament at this point (bars 16–17), whereas the 'Blick zur Schau auf glühendes Land' is depicted here merely by the closing ornamental turn (bar 19). The expressive material hardly differs from that of the first stanza; Zeisl depicts the scenario created by Petzold by retaining ostinato chord progressions and the same rhythmic elements, including triplets and dotted-quaver-plus-semiquaver figures and quavers.

Ex. 5: bars 16–19

With the incorporation of the initial march rhythm in the piano part (bar 20) — unlike the vocal line, set in a high register — the *Hymne* resumes; the correspondence to the beginning of the song is established through the use once again of a minor chord with an added major sixth (here F♯ minor with an added D♯), and the march rhythm of the instrumental *Hymne*, within a narrative perspective that remains retrospective, heralds redemption. Except in the *Hymne*, the piano part presents distinctive melodic and rhythmic motives at this point, where retrospection and the image of a utopia are combined. This expressive complexity evaporates, all at once, in the cadence leading to the recapitulation that begins at bar 21, the long G♯ in the vocal part (bar 21) is first the major third in an E major chord, is enharmonically reinterpreted as A♭, the minor third in an F minor chord, becomes a dissonant appoggiatura in a dominant seventh on E♭, and finally resolves (with a crescendo) on to A, the fifth of a chord on D with a major seventh (C♯) which slides down through chromatic semitones to B♭ and thereby stabilizes the home key of G minor.

Ex. 6: bars 20–22

The notation does not show unequivocally whether the return to the *tempo primo* at the recapitulation is preceded by a speeding up or a slowing down. One can assume, nevertheless, that Zeisl intended a *ritardando*. The overlaid complexity imposed by the intrusive recurrence of the march rhythm, and the crescendo in the last bar before the recapitulation, after the combination of accented dotted-note figures and triplets, correspond with the basic idea of retardation through the holding back of energy that can burst forth anew as the recapitulation is launched, *forte*, in the initial tempo. The accents that are specified in the last two bars before the recapitulation also suggest a slowing down.

The vocal line of the song concludes in the vivid allegory of the 'leuchtender Sonnenstrahl' as a vision of the liberation achieved in death. In a mere four bars, however, the epilogue (bars 34 to 37) unexpectedly demolishes the idea of redemption that has been maintained up to that point, and neutralizes it. Its first bar immediately suggests misfortune, with the descending chromatic semitones in the upper voice of the chordal accompaniment, which may be interpreted as a borrowing from the Baroque rhetorical figure of the *passus duriusculus* and hence as a symbol of death.

Ex. 7: Epilogue; bars 34–37

In the shortest possible space, the tessitura of the instrumental *Hymne* drifts down to depths that have scarcely been touched upon hitherto; previously ascending intervals now become descending intervals. The G in the upper voice that was reached at bar 10 as a top note with an ascending perfect fifth from a C, at 'leuchtender Sonnenstrahl', now falls impotently back to C, and is immediately followed by another descending perfect fifth. In this epilogue, the energetic dotted-note figure loses its status as a sign of a triumphal march; for the first time in this song, phrased pairs of quavers appear, bringing the music to a close in this coda.

The tonic chord of G minor is reached via a C minor chord including a minor seventh and a major ninth, followed by the dominant, rendered extremely expressive with a diminished fifth and major sixth, through a crescendo (bar 36). The G minor tonality is unambiguously established — as a significant exception within this entire song — through the final chord, in which there are no notes besides those of the triad. The sole comparable chord in this piece, characterized harmonically as it is by added sevenths, ninths and sixths, occurs before the important cadence in the major: at 'leuchtender Sonnenstrahl' Zeisl makes use of a strikingly simple second-inversion G major triad (bar 9). The march rhythm with which the song began is appended to the final funereal G minor chord and closes the song. Only an impotent twofold sidestep to the neighbouring chord of A♭ minor (final bar) is added, seemingly trapped and confined; the major-minor ambivalence essentially characterizing the song reaches a negative conclusion.

If Zeisl's cuts in the third stanza of the poem had the radical affect of excising Petzold's conception of the collective — 'Brüder, Brüder: erst im Reiche der Särge | blüht empor unser wahres Menschengeschick' — the harmonically unambiguous ending does confirm that the idea of a higher, transcendental reality to succeed earthly suffering present in both poem and song — 'und mein Leib ist worden ein leuchtender Sonnenstrahl' — cannot ultimately be fulfilled. Zeisl remains anchored in the funeral march and in his interpretation; 'Der tote Arbeiter' is a powerful evocation of mourning. Petzold's idea of redemption on several different planes is not taken up in the song version.

In July 1932 Zeisl set 'Die Arbeiter' and 'Der tote Arbeiter' from the *Dornbusch* collection; in August there followed 'Ein buckliger Waisenknabe singt' and 'Wanderlied' from the same volume. Whilst the song version of 'Der tote Arbeiter' is adapted and therefore only partly fulfils the intentions of Petzold, the text of 'Die Arbeiter' is left intact.

> *Die Arbeiter*
>
> Sturm und Gewalt ist in unseren Händen,
> stehn wir im räderdurchdonnerten Raum;
> doch in dem keuchenden Beugen der Lenden
> sind wir gar oftmals nur Andacht und Traum.
>
> In dunkler Berge verlorner Kaverne
> sind wir die Brüder der strahlenden Tage;
> türmen wir Steine im Antlitz der Sterne,
> lebt Gottes Sehnsucht in unserer Plage.
>
> Unser Wille erschüttert die Erde,
> und der heiligsten Unruhe voll
> schenken wir ihr durch die stete Beschwerde
> Ewigkeit, die unserm Schaffen entquoll.[54]

[Storm and violence in our hands, we stand in the space filled with the thunder of wheels; yet in the panting stooping of our loins, we are often only reverence and dream.

In the lost cavern of dark mountains we are brothers to the sunlit days; when we pile up stones in the face of the stars, God's longing lives in our trials.

Our will shakes the earth and, full of the most sacred of discontent, through our constant complaint we grant it eternity, which has flowed from our creation.]

This song, also set for baritone voice and in B♭ minor, is characterized by thunderous ostinato chords in a strident *forte*. Although ostinati and major-minor ambiguity constitute essential elements in both songs — as early as bar 1 of 'Die Arbeiter', the tonic B♭ minor yields to the relative major, G♭ — there are clear differences in their treatment: the vocal line, as a contributor to the ensemble, moves in a wider range in 'Die Arbeiter', and is incomparably richer in motivic development. The sphere of 'Andacht und Traum' is expressed in more distant harmonic regions (F♯ minor, A major, E♭ major, G♭ major, B♭ minor), before the middle section, now in the major version of the initial key and with a surprisingly wide sweep in the vocal line, makes a 'slower!' (*Langsamer!*) expression possible. Petzold's basic idea — 'türmen wir Steine im Antlitz der Sterne, | lebt Gottes Sehnsucht in unserer Plage' — is thus able to become a postulate through stable declamation, via E major, D major, F major and G♭ major. Nevertheless, Zeisl's alteration of the text at this point seems

---

[54] Petzold, *Dornbusch*, p. 33.

arbitrary, and indeed not fully comprehensible; it may indeed be an error for 'türmen wir Steine im Antlitz der Sterne, | lebt Gottes Sehnsucht und Plage'.[55] This song also returns to the minor tonality of the beginning, with the tonal correspondence between the third stanza and the first. However, the funeral-march gestures, which remain stereotypical for the sake of comprehensibility, and the exaggeratedly simple (even stark) harmonic and motivic structure are counterbalanced by features that contrast with the lament — more complex harmonic textures and a significantly increased melodic flexibility — for the freedom of the vocal line has a rhapsodic effect unlike the strictly confined melodic style of 'Der tote Arbeiter'. These elements reproduce Petzold's idealized romantic poem, and the very manner of this romanticization may even find its equivalent in the choice of the key of B♭ minor, which might otherwise be seen as 'over-romantic'.

The setting of 'Ein buckliger Waisenknabe singt' is different again:

> *Ein buckliger Waisenknabe singt*
>
> Sagt mir, wo ich armer Narr
> eine Heimat habe?
>
> Dort nicht, da nicht, nur im Grabe
> wird ein Glühwurm für mich scheinen,
> eine Wurzel, wenn es regnet weinen
> auf mein blondes Waisenhaar.
>
> Schöne Mädchen stehn im Kreis,
> lachen, wenn ich weine. —
> Ach wie sind so brennend heiß
> alle Pflastersteine.
>
> Heiß, daß ich die arge Glut
> weh im Herzen fühle,
> Mutter in der Erdenkühle,
> weißt du, wie das brennen tut?[56]

[Can you tell me where I, poor fool, may find a home?
  Not here, not there, only in the grave will a glow-worm glimmer for me, a root weep on my blond orphan's hair when it rains.
  Beautiful girls stand in a circle and laugh when I cry. — Oh, how all the paving stones are burning hot.
  Hot, such that I can feel the terrible heat as pain in my heart. Mother, in the cool of the earth, do you know how much it burns me?]

This song, now intended for a soprano voice, and in a slow, mournful tempo (*langsam, klagend*), though in E minor, is suspended from the first bar in the veiled dominant of the home key. The minor third determining the mode

---

[55] Otherwise, Zeisl alters extremely little in the original version of 'Die Arbeiter', and does so in order to bring the declamation into conformity with the natural metre of the bar.
[56] Petzold, *Dornbusch*, p. 74.

is lacking and is replaced by a fourth. The soprano begins the lament on F♯, the fifth of the dominant chord. It is only at the key word 'Grab' in the phrase 'dort nicht, da nicht, nur im Grabe' that the complete dominant chord, B major, including the third of the chord, appears, and this is preceded by a C minor chord that can be considered to be its flattened supertonic: Zeisl marks this 'schmerzlich' [painfully], and in this use of a quasi-Neapolitan chord remains entirely within the realm of traditional musical symbolism. The idea of redemption through the grave as a metaphor for death corresponds with the message already established in 'Der tote Arbeiter': Zeisl employs harmonic symbols corresponding to the text — the major variant in 'Der tote Arbeiter', and the use of the major dominant chord in 'Ein buckliger Waisenknabe singt'. However, a correspondence with Petzold's idea of salvation in death is mediated also by the final progression in 'Ein buckliger Waisenknabe singt'. A progression of seventh chords (on F♯ major, D major, B♭ major, D major, G major and A major) ends in stability on a B-major triad — the song ends on the dominant chord, initially anticipated but ultimately reduced to its root, third and fifth. However, quite differently from in 'Der tote Arbeiter', here there is reference to a future 'Heimat im Grabe' [home in the grave] perceived as being far in the distance — and with this glimpse of the future the vision of redemption in death can therefore be maintained.

The last of Zeisl's Petzold settings, the D major song 'Wanderlied', was also written in August 1932.[57] Kept fresh in both character and tempo, a feeling of freedom is evoked that is manifested in the gestures of happily 'walking away' and cheerfully 'turning one's back on one's workplace'. This is expressed musically in fragments, full of associative references and seemingly almost naïve, drawn from folk-song, such as progressions of parallel thirds, fifths and nursery-rhyme rhythms, moving principally in crotchets and quavers.

> *Wanderlied*
>
> Heute noch im Werkstattkleid
> drück' ich Tisch und Diele,
> aber morgen ist die Zeit
> sonntäglicher Ziele.
>
> Eine Straße winkt mir zu
> aus der grünen Weite.
> Liebe Straße segne du

---

[57] Petzold often chose the topos of the wanderer as part of his speculative glorification of romantic poetry. The collection *Gesang von Morgen bis Mittag* (1922) included poems in the first of the sections headed 'Der Wanderer' that directly echo the symbolism familiar from the writings of Wilhelm Müller (1794–1827): these include 'Der selige Fußgänger' [The Blessed Walker], 'Die Straße' [The Road], 'Morgentraum' [Morning Dream], 'Die Linde' [The Linden Tree], 'Sommerstunde' [A Summer Hour], 'Der Brunnen' [The Fountain], 'Der Bettler und der Brunnen' [The Beggar and the Fountain], 'Heimkehr oder Der ewige Wanderer' [Homecoming, or The Eternal Wanderer] — to name but a few.

meine derben Wanderschuh,
wenn ich morgen in der Früh',
fern der harten Drehbankmüh',
singend dich beschreite.

Sause Riemen, glühe Draht —
meine Wiesen tönen —
morgen wird kein schweres Rad
meiner Jugend höhnen.[58]

[Today, still in my working clothes, I shirk the table and the hall, but tomorrow is the time for Sunday's aspirations.
 A road calls to me from the distant green. Dear road, bless my coarse walking shoes when tomorrow, early, far from the harsh toil of the lathe, I walk along you with a song.
 Hurtle belt and smoulder wire — my meadows are resounding — tomorrow no heavy wheel will scoff at my youth.]

The fact that the cheeriness described here is not lasting but is a superficial snapshot of a mood is suggested by the piano introduction on an open-position diminished seventh chord on E♯, demanding resolution on to F♯ as the major third of the home key, for the major third is undermined by the minor third already at the entry of the soprano in bar 7: E♯, F and F♯ occur in the first bar of the voice part in immediate succession. The idea of the collision between different harmonic regions permeates the entire song, though undisturbed by this, elements of ostinato rhythms 'wander' on, up to the end. In the expression of the text, there are variations in the mobility of the vocal line, which occasionally features leaps of wide intervals, and the rate of harmonic change. This structural principle is established by Zeisl right at the beginning, at 'aber morgen ist die Zeit | sonntäglicher Ziele'. Here an alternative world is able to emerge against that of the first line, harmonically and melodically static as it is. The thought of the 'Sunday aspirations' allows the vocal line to rise energetically to the dominant — now strongly supported sonorously by the accented, increasingly widely spaced piano part — and then again to pass to its alternative 'soft' (*weich!*) world with the essentially static image of a street leading into the distance. The 'wandering' along the 'dear' road leading to freedom ends at the first culmination point — a cry, which is celebrated by Zeisl in the repetition (absent in the original text) of the extended central word, 'singend', on the highest note.

This, reached at the tempo indication *'etwas langsamer, aber fest!'* [somewhat more slowly, but firmly], represents a parallel to the 'aspiration' previously visualized in the future, and to the later postulate, in which youth is represented as the opposite pole from the 'heavy wheel' of the lathe. A comparison of these three key passages in the 'Wanderlied' is instructive. If the 'aspirations' clearly

---

[58] Petzold, *Dornbusch*, p. 67.

illuminate the home key on the dominant seventh chord, the word 'singend' is placed in a vague F♯ minor region briefly and transiently drifting towards F major; this F♯ minor region also underlies the important word 'höhnen', but is there strongly and emphatically disturbed and destabilized, in part through markedly disruptive descending chromatic chords.

The poem mediates the vision of an opposition between the world of labour and that of innocent, pure youth, which even defies the dread or horror of the workplace. Zeisl appears to be playing with both worlds, manifestly through harmonic regions that are brought into a power relationship with, and paralyse, one another. Youth is sublime: the ascending progression to 'meiner Jugend höhnen' passes through E♭ minor, the major seventh chords on C and B, E major, G major, F♯ major (with a false relation between E♯ and E), and B major; but it remains a deceptive image. A descent into F♯ minor occurs in all three exclamatory passages ('Ziele', 'singen' and 'höhnen'), which, after a brief encounter with the notes E♭, D♭ and B♭, is incorporated in D major, and then leads into further progressions in ways that differ according to the sense of the text.

In 1933 Zeisl only composed four songs: 'Kein Ton mehr klingt' [No Note Sounds Now], by Rudolf Paulsen, 'Altes Reiterliedchen' [Old Riding Song], by Klabund (Alfred Henschke), 'Lied im Herbst' [Autumn Song], also by Klabund and 'Polnisches Freiheitslied' [Polish Song of Freedom], which was translated from the Polish of Adam Mickiewicz by Klabund. This last song has a political message:

> Wenn ich nach Sibirien trotte,
> Muss ich schwer in Ketten karren;
> Doch mit der versoff'nen Rotte
> Will ich schuften ... für den Zaren.
>
> [...]
>
> Silbergraue Fäden rinnen
> Fest durch meine Hand, in Jahren
> Wird mein Sohn zum Strick sie spinnen ...
> Für den Zaren ... für den Zaren.[59]

[When I trudge towards Siberia, I have to toil along in chains; but with that drunken gang I'll be slogging ... for the Tsar.
Silver-grey threads run stiffly through my hands; in years my son will weave them into a noose ... for the Tsar ... for the Tsar.]

In 1934, a year of civil war, there was literally 'no note' of a Zeisl song sounding, and it was not until 1935 and 1936 that more songs were written, with 'Komm süsser Tod' as the last of them in 1938. For a composer like Erich Zeisl, to whom the composition of songs was always akin to keeping an intimate diary,

---

[59] Eric Zeisl Archive, University of California, Los Angeles, Performing Arts Special Collections. I. Songs (unpublished). Text published as 'Zarenlied (nach Adam Mickiewicz)' in *Dragoner und Husaren. Die Soldatenlieder von Klabund* (Munich, 1916), p. 42.

this meant the onset of silence. Losing the supportive context of his mother tongue in exile meant that after 'Komm süsser Tod' Zeisl was definitively 'linguistically dead'.

> Komm süsser Tod,
> Komm sel'ge Ruh!
> Komm, führe mich in Friede,
> Weil ich der Welt bin müde.
> Ach komm, ich wart' auf Dich,
> Komm bald und führe mich,
> Drücke mir die Augen zu.
> Komm, sel'ge Ruh![60]

[Come sweet death, come blessed peace! Come, lead me in peace because I am tired of the world. Oh, come, I am waiting for you, come soon and lead me, close my eyes for me. Come, blessed peace!]

The song suggests the acceptance of death, too, in its major-minor polarity. Deliberately uniform progression is stressed, as it often is in Schubert or Wolf, by the exclusive use of minims and crotchets; the device of reinforcing the voice with the subsequent imitation in the piano part also sounds typically Schubertian. 'Komm süsser Tod' is a song of mourning for Zeisl's homeland of Austria and a homage to Schubert, and closely reflects Zeisl's own life: faced with the threat of National Socialism he was plunged into deep depression, and the song is thus a deeply personal expression in words and music of this condition. Comparing it with 'Der tote Arbeiter' reveals interesting parallels: both songs are markedly simple in construction, the harmonic structure is kept clear and readily comprehensible, both songs progress with a steady ostinato over which the voice narrates the action from a first-person perspective. Heightened in their expressivity by these techniques, both 'Der tote Arbeiter' and 'Komm süsser Tod' achieve a sustained effect, at the same time conveying a message of a confessional nature. If 'Komm süsser Tod' reflects Zeisl's persecution by the National Socialists, then in the context of its own genesis — when Austria was soon to face civil war, the crushing of democracy and the establishment of an Austro-Fascist dictatorship — 'Der tote Arbeiter' is no less a personal commentary.

---

[60] Eric Zeisl Archive, University of California, Los Angeles, Performing Arts Special Collections. I. Songs (unpublished). Text published in *Musicalisches Gesang-Buch*, ed. by Georg Christian Schemelli (Leipzig, 1736), p. 591.

'Das Erdorchester bedienen':
Epiphany, Enchantment and the
Sonorous World of Peter Handke

MARTON MARKO

University of Montana

Through the five decades of his prolific writing career, music has played a key role in the works of Peter Handke. Tropes, topics and figures related to the perception of sound and to the phenomenon of music have served varied functions in Handke's work, most notably as models of immediacy and connection, in aesthetic, cultural and autobiographic terms. For Handke and his contemporaries, the wave of popular British and American music that permeated Central European culture in the 1960s provided a readily available outlet for social rebellion and cultural critique as well as a framework for subjective expression and introspection. Born in 1942, Handke spent most of his youth in the rural reaches of southern Carinthia, and the pop, rock, folk and blues invasions that flooded Austria from the early 1960s on served as a portal for the young writer, allowing him access to new worlds of cultural and personal discovery, and representing radical forms of articulation that would quickly be reflected in his writing. Accordingly, music has commonly been connected to themes of travel and exoticism in Handke's works. The setting of musical space as a place of otherness, alterity and movement yields a dimension to these works that seeks to point beyond literature. Ultimately, the ubiquity of sound, evolving into music, provides a unifying model on which Handke relies in his frequent treatment of problems related to cultural and subjective fragmentation. This article focuses on musical treatments in Handke's works as vehicles of recurring epiphanic enchantment that serve as an antidote to such disunities.

I

Gaining initial notoriety and success as a playwright with the appearance of *Publikumsbeschimpfung* [*Offending the Audience*] in 1966, Handke's arrival on the Central European literary scene was immediately linked with the rock-'n'-roll rapture that had spread across the continent. Performances of *Publikumsbeschimpfung* were likened to rock concerts, as the rhythmic repetition of litanies, insults and accusations, along with non-stop verbal and conceptual twists and turns, lent themselves easily to stagings that permitted a rock-'n'-

roll-like delivery of the play, bringing to the fore the theatrical nature of the event as such. In an interview with Artur Joseph, Handke comments on the significance of both the formalistic and the rhythmic in his early theatrical work, including *Publikumsbeschimpfung*, as a unifying dimension producing messages and effects beyond the rhetorical aims or achievements to which the text itself could lay claim:

> JOSEPH: The rhythms of your plays provide a strong emotional impact. Is this intentional?
> HANDKE: I can't separate the rational and emotional effects. Doesn't a stunning new thought, a new insight, a new view that is based on Reason, often make you feel wholly emotional effects? I think what happens is that the novelty, the new perspective, removes the rational view, and emotions come into being — a kind of joy that you could call emotional. However, in *Offending the Audience* many spectators didn't even listen to what was being said. They heard the rhythms, and apparently, rhythms somehow reduce the distance between speakers and listeners. These rhythms turn directly into emotion, bringing objects closer.[1]

This appeal to sensory immediacy via the rhythmic and auditory is evident throughout Handke's early theatre work. It is particularly notable in such pieces as 'Geräusch eines Geräusches' [Sound of a Sound, 1969] and 'Wind und Meer' [Wind and Sea, 1970]. The liminal quality of language as both performative medium and communicative instrument is highlighted in 'Geräusch eines Geräusches' where, in textual terms, a relationship is forged between the description of various sounds and the suggestive performance they are to elicit on stage. Stage directions that detail sound effects in the text take on a life of their own as they 'speak for themselves', though still tied to the primacy of the text which invisibly summons them. In this sense, the play functions as an incisive study of text and script *vis-à-vis* performance under the guise of the most simple and elemental of staged sounds. The formal structure of the audio-play is further highlighted by the use of the term 'Pause' [break, pause, rest] as a metrical device, albeit one without any specific indication of duration. Rather than being determined as an interval of specific length, the 'rests' are suggested by the number of 'pauses' listed between sounds.

> Ansage
> Pause.
> Pause.
> Pause.

---

[1] Artur Joseph, Peter Handke, and E. B. Ashton, 'Nauseated by Language. From an Interview with Peter Handke', *The Drama Review: TDR*, 15/i (1970), 57–61 (p. 58). In the interview, Handke further discusses the rhythmic manipulation in *Publiksumsbeschimpfung*: its purpose is to 'transport the words' so as to draw attention to the structured temporal nature of the play, which Handke himself likens to the structures and tempi of rock music.

Coca-Cola, das unhörbar aus der Flasche ins Glas gegossen wurde, braust auf, bis die aufsteigenden Kohlensäurebläschen wieder unhörbar sind.
Pause.
Pause.
Pause.
Pause.
Der Kühlschrankmotor fängt an zu summen und summt so lange, bis er sich wieder ausschaltet.
Pause.
Pause.
Ein Stück weicher Butter fällt aus Tischhöhe auf den Steinboden.[2]

[Address
Pause.
Pause.
Pause.
Coca-Cola, inaudibly poured from a bottle into a glass, foams up until the rising carbonated bubbles are inaudible again.
Pause.
Pause.
Pause.
Pause.
The refrigerator motor begins to hum and hums until it shuts itself off again.
Pause.
Pause.
A stick of soft butter falls from table height on to the stone floor.]

Along with the prescribed number of pauses, the precise qualifications and descriptions of the sounds ultimately comment on the open field in which the most basic of factors are at play in the formation of texts — and ultimately, since the stage allegorizes, in the formation of social realities as well. On the one hand, the text can be recognized as the score of a musical enactment of sorts, with specific parameters that define potential performances. On the other hand, the manifestation of the sounds and pauses amongst the words serves to deconstruct any natural quality we might be inclined to read into or *hear* in the relationship between text and what the text should yield as performance. Those reading the text of the play will see that the author is indeed earnest about his playfulness with the conventions of stage direction, as on four consecutive instances only the partial word 'Pau-' is included rather than the full word 'Pause'.[3] Whether this is intended to suggest that the half-word should only merit half a time interval is a matter of interpretation for directors and readers.

The role of authorial voice and performance can also be witnessed in the 'Regeln für die Schauspieler' [Rules for the Actors] that open *Publikums-*

---

[2] Peter Handke, 'Geräusch eines Geräusches', in *Wind und Meer. Vier Hörspiele* (Frankfurt a. M., 1970), pp. 15–25 (p. 17).
[3] Ibid., p. 18.

beschimpfung. The majority of these 'rules' are instructions to listen to specific acoustic events: Catholic liturgies, the cheers and jeers at football stadiums, the song 'Tell me' by the Rolling Stones, and the spinning wheels of a bicycle turned upside-down on its seat (until they stop), along with the gradual loudening of a cement mixer after its engine has been turned on.[4] The prescribed visual activities of the actors involve further engagement with pop culture, including, amongst other things, the face of Gary Cooper in the film *The Man from the West* and Ringo Starr in the first Beatles film, where, after he has been teased by the others, he smiles and sits back down at the drum set and begins to play.[5] The milieu in which Handke seeks to immerse performers and members of the audience is that of the Anglo-American pop culture that had begun to infiltrate daily life in Central Europe. Handke's preoccupation with these elements goes beyond their pop status. His programme at this early point in his career is dedicated to the overall critical examination of habit, pattern and cliché. Using direct citation and the careful manipulation of rhythm and sound — often in stark minimalist fashion — Handke directs his critical attention to rudimentary aesthetic and social structures. The reductionism of Handke's early plays reveals not only a focus on the relationship between ideas of performance in theatre and in cultural praxis but also how linguistic and literary operations achieve their effects. From these works a trajectory emerges in Handke's treatment of sound in the early 1970s that moves from experiments in acoustic essentialism towards a deeper and more central concern with the musical.

II

A similar move from a deconstructive posture toward one of conscious reconstruction informs the theme and style of Handke's American road novel of 1972, *Der kurze Brief zum langen Abschied* [*Short Letter, Long Farewell*]. Elements of reductionism persist in *Der kurze Brief*, yet the atomized perceptions, descriptions and narrative passages found in the piece function largely as a backdrop against which to gauge the principal focus on connection, affinity and harmonious flow. While Handke's first novel, *Die Hornissen* [*The Hornets*, 1966] involves quasi-cryptic references to travel, *Der kurze Brief* clearly situates the theme of the journey as central to narrative structure and action. The plot construction also involves the appearance of figures characterized in a more or less conventional manner.

Der kurze Brief provides Handke's readers with an introduction to an object prominent in his writing, the jukebox. Handke's use of the jukebox presents an intriguing sequence of vantage points from which to examine the fusing of subject, machine and cultural identity. Following his arrival in Providence,

---

[4] Peter Handke, *Publikumsbeschimpfung*, in *Publikumsbeschimpfung und andere Sprechstücke* (Frankfurt a. M., 1966), p. 9.
[5] Ibid.

Rhode Island, the protagonist of *Der kurze Brief* finds himself in a 'Snackbar' with small individual jukebox devices at each table (called 'wallboxes' or 'bar-boxes'), which customers use to make their selections remotely, 'ohne dafür aufzustehen' [without having to get up].[6] The added element of remote operation here with respect to the already mechanical jukebox suggests a particular type of immediacy for the snack bar customer, one which, in Handke's treatment, remains free from hints of techno-criticism or any critical evaluation of subjective instrumentalization. The protagonist inserts a coin, makes his selection, and sinks into the contemplative strains of Otis Redding's 'Sitting On The Dock Of The Bay' (*KB*, p. 19).

If the automated and hyper-convenient fashion in which the musical product is delivered by the mini-jukebox is mapped onto theoretical approaches to reading and consuming, then the procedure echoes Roland Barthes's observations concerning the intersection of reading, play and interpretation in a culture of mass-produced entertainment:

> In fact, *reading*, in the sense of consuming, is far from *playing* with the text. 'Playing' must be understood here in all its polysemy: the text itself *plays* (like a door, like a machine with 'play') and the reader plays twice over, playing the Text as one plays a game, looking for a practice which re-produces it, but, in order that that practice not be reduced to a passive, inner *mimesis* [...], also playing the Text in the musical sense of the term.[7]

In this regard, Barthes's recognition of the history of music as *practice* is an apt analogy to the notion of text as nodal point of social, linguistic and aesthetic understanding. He alludes to the conceptual evolution of interpretation via musical praxis and listening through a historic trajectory from times of ubiquitous amateur musicianship, where playing and listening were intrinsically linked, to the era of mass automated musical production and consumption in the late twentieth century.

> We know that today post-serial music has radically altered the role of the 'interpreter', who is called on to be in some sort the co-author of the score, completing it rather than giving it 'expression'. The Text is very much a score of this new kind: it asks of the reader a practical collaboration. Which is an important change, for who executes the work?[8]

---

[6] Peter Handke, *Der kurze Brief zum langen Abschied* (Frankfurt a. M., 1972), p. 19. Subsequent references are given in parentheses in the body of the text (as *KB* with page numbers).

[7] Roland Barthes, 'From Work to Text', in *Image, Music, Text*, trans. by Stephen Heath (New York, 1977), pp. 155–64 (p. 162).

[8] Ibid., p. 163. Barthes situates his discourse on reading practice and music specifically in the context of modern European bourgeois history and offers further brief reference to the 'history of the piano' as a societal mark of bourgeois cultivation. Barthes suggests that the 'play' of recorded music as an inherently intersubjective enterprise in a society of mass consumption reflects a logical next step in the shift of acculturating tastes and attitudes.

Barthes's theoretical postulation acutely characterizes the post-war variant of the emerging multi-mediated subject of the twentieth century, when film, television and music radically resituated notions of a centred textual source and definitive socio-cultural readings. The fact that Handke seeks in *Der kurze Brief* to inscribe the narrative of individual identity in such a milieu of mass cultural mediation, and furthermore that he makes such an inscription from a European standpoint, is a noteworthy strategy on the part of the writer. America clearly represents for the author a field for the projection of individual fantasy in the work. Yet the direction of the work is also unquestionably oriented towards heightened social awareness and consciousness.

Christoph Bartmann discusses the marriage of the subjective and collective in the novel as carried out via a particular mythicization and aestheticization of the everyday, witnessed in a number of Handke's works and brought into the narrative spotlight in *Der kurze Brief*.[9] Throughout the novel, elements of American pop culture, music and film are brought together to form an exotic, idealized American public sphere for the protagonist. In the mini-jukebox scene described above, the narrator spots a picture on a T-shirt of the singer Al Wilson (from the rock group Canned Heat), who had recently been found dead in his sleeping bag on the outskirts of Los Angeles (Wilson died on 3 September 1970). The image prompts the protagonist to reflect on how, unlike the deaths of Jimi Hendrix and Janis Joplin 'die mir [...] immer gleichgültiger wurden' [about which I cared less and less], the passing of Wilson had genuinely moved him to sadness, expressed as if he had enjoyed a personal acquaintance with him (*KB*, p. 23). Later the protagonist and his travelling companion, a girlfriend from a previous visit to the States, stay with another couple in St. Louis who serve as an additional model of social mediation and individual connection in the story. Both members of the St. Louis pair work as film poster painters and enjoy a form of communion which is allegorized by the experiences they share via popular music, as the musical records in their home serve as an archive of their lives together (*KB*, p. 140).

These particular encounters with music, myth and collective experience in the story are framed by an anchoring epiphanic scene which takes place on the Mississippi River on a tourist steam boat, *The Mark Twain*. Here, as the narrator talks to his American companions, themes associated with music and the flow of experience throughout his travels are grounded in one sonic burst, that of the ship's steam whistle, described as 'so gewaltig' [so immense] that it brings on a 'Traum von einem Amerika [...], von dem man mir bis jetzt nur erzählt hatte' [dream of America previously known only through 'stories'] (*KB*, p. 121). The moment is conveyed as an 'Auferstehung' [resurrection]:

[9] Christoph Bartmann, *Suche nach Zusammenhang. Handkes Werk als Prozeß* (Vienna, 1984), p. 87. Bartmann provides an extensive examination of Handke's 'quest for connection' in his works up to the early 1980s, focusing in particular on Handke's treatment of the media, especially music and film.

in dem alles ringsherum seine Beziehungslosigkeit verlor, in dem Leute und Landschaft, Lebendes und Totes an seinen Platz rückte und eine einzige, schmerzliche und theatralische Geschichte offenbarte. (*KB*, p. 122)

[in which everything around lost its lack of connection, in which people and landscape, the living and the dead, took their places and one single, painful and theatrical history was revealed.]

A decade later, in the 1983 Salzburg novel *Der Chinese des Schmerzes* [*The Chinaman of Pain*, published in English as *Across*], an epiphanic experience which reinterprets the revelation on the Mississippi appears in an Austrian context. The dimension of the auditory is again central, recognized firstly through the protagonist's surname, Andreas Loser, a name deriving from the verb 'losen', related to 'lauschen' [to listen or hearken]. Loser's story extends the experience of subjective and cultural reconstruction encountered in *Der kurze Brief*. But here we find this reconstitutive move in the setting of Handke's native land, and furthermore, in a setting symbolic of canonical Austrian culture — particularly from a post-war American perspective, Salzburg. While Handke's American epiphany involved the formation of personal revelation via the fusion of pop and epic elements with an emphasis on the former, Loser's allegorical summoning of Austria as still culturally salvageable despite the lingering legacy of Nazism is directed towards the classical and the natural. Loser, a teacher of classical languages and literatures, is on professional leave when we witness him commit a strangely spontaneous and stylized murder, as the pedagogue tracks down the painter of a freshly sprayed swastika in the hills above the city and — not without symbolic suggestiveness — casts a stone at his victim, who falls down dead. In the aftermath of this allegorical clash between categories of violence, between the symbolic and the active, Loser, the listener and teacher turned killer, must find a connection to some source or symbol of solace and redemption in the world around him, now not only for the sake of his nation's past and future, but also for himself.

The search for harmony is extended thematically from the Mississippi River scene in the earlier novel towards models of confluence between the natural order and the musical. The resurrection motif is also reiterated, as the story of *Der Chinese des Schmerzes* takes place during Holy Week and a key epiphanic scene is set on the evening of Easter Saturday as Loser lies awake, anxiously alert to the sounds of his surroundings. The passage describes a path towards literal enchantment, towards the musicalization of the landscape and the world via elements of the natural and the everyday:

Zwischendurch war es so still gewesen, daß in den Bergen die Wasserfälle laut wurden. Später brauste von einem Ende der Ebene zum andern eine eigentümliche sonore Melodie: im Halbschlaf — der eher eine besondere Art des Wachseins war — gaben die Einzelgeräusche einander die Antwort und wurden dadurch zu Tönen. [...] Recht betrachtet, handelte es sich um keine Melodie, sondern um ein sich ins Unendliche fortsetzendes

Leitmotiv. Jedes neu hinzukommende Geräusch spielte das gegebene Motiv, dieses so verstärkend, weiter.[10]

[Meanwhile it had become so quiet that the waterfalls in the mountains became audible. Later a peculiar, sonorous melody boomed from one end of the plain to the other: in half-sleep — which was in fact a particular type of being awake — the individual sounds replied to one another and became tones. Observed closely, it was not a melody but an infinitely continuing leitmotif. Each newly added sound played the motif again and strengthened it.]

The significance of the earthly in the context of the religious framing of the scene set during Holy Week is punctuated by reference to 'other worlds' as well as the particular film mentioned, the American pop science-fiction movie *E. T.* (1982). The ideas of the extraterrestrial and the cinematic both operate as contrasts to the authenticity and primacy of the naturalized musical experience illustrated in the passage.

Einmal hatte ich mit den Kindern einen Film angesehen, in dem Irdische und Außerirdische sich mit einem solchen, ständig wiederholten Motiv untereinander verständigten. Waren auch hier Außerirdische gelandet, und der Tonfall jetzt war ihr Signal? Nein, es tönte vielmehr das Irdische, und ein Irdischer lag und träumte, mit seinem Atem, sozusagen durch ein einziges Mundloch, das Erdorchester zu bedienen.[11]

[Once I saw a film with my children in which terrestrial and extraterrestrial beings communicated with each other with this kind of ongoing, repeated motif. Had extraterrestrials landed here and was this cadence now their signal? No, what produced this sound was earthly, and an earthly being lay there and dreamed that with his breath, through his single port, so to speak, he was serving this earthly orchestra.]

The cohesive capacity of music brought forth in this scene ultimately draws attention to an aspect of cultural and individual participation that is shared on a continuum, a concept also essentially musical. While the constitution of the earthly orchestra clearly relies on a naturalized idea of harmony, the role of this harmony with respect to our sense of the moral place of Loser, the literal assailant not just of Nazi symbolism but also of human life (and signification) through self-determined justification, remains vague. While the passage suggests that a source of resolution is being sought, when perceived together with the musical motifs from *E.T.* referred to, there is a palpable coldness, mechanization and distance in this orchestration as well. And if the epiphanic experience of enchantment we witness is to be read as one that bonds the listener with the heard musical surroundings, the cool detachment of the scene can also be sensed as a lingering indeterminacy in the character of Loser: the involvement of music cannot help but signal a systematic ambivalence, if not self-conscious irony in the novel.

[10] Peter Handke, *Der Chinese des Schmerzes* (Frankfurt a. M., 1983), pp. 194–95.
[11] Ibid., pp. 195–96.

III

Questions of music, mechanization, immediacy and detachment bring us back to the trademark object of the jukebox, an item that features prominently in Handke's book-length essay, *Versuch über die Jukebox. Eine Erzählung* [*Essay on the Jukebox. A Story*, 1990]. While *Der Chinese des Schmerzes* unearths the legacy of fascism and brings into focus a continuity between the Nazi era and the 1980s in Austria and in Central Europe, *Versuch über die Jukebox* represents the other end of an historical trajectory that began with the rise of Hitler, continued with the atrocities of the Second World War and the trauma of the Cold War, and reached its terminus with the fall of the Berlin Wall in 1989. It is, in fact, precisely at the moment when the Wall fell that the essay's narrative begins. The essayist recalls how, rather than accept the invitation of friends to come to Berlin to witness world history allegedly in the making, he chose instead to experience history in an alternative fashion, seeking out a hidden, idiosyncratic locale in which to undertake a project that aims to reveal what an object such as a jukebox can mean not just to him but to a changing world in which such a contraption is becoming ever more obsolete.

The essay starts out in the city of Soria, in the mountains of Northern Spain, a fitting backdrop for the contemplative paths that wind through the author's own life-history as well as for episodes in cultural history from ancient Greece to prohibition-era America and post-war Austria. While the narrative celebrates a myriad of intersubjective contexts in which jukeboxes present the intersection of personal and global histories, the work's setting assumes a strikingly monastic character, preparing readers perhaps for the appearance of a figure such as St Teresa of Avila, whose meditations on the nature of the epiphanic provide a key conceptual guide for the essay. A considerable portion of the work involves thoughts and recollections concerning the role of the jukebox as a phenomenon through which the writer is able 'sich [...] zu sammeln' [to collect himself].[12] He cites in particular the association he made in his youth between jukeboxes and field huts strewn along the rural roads and fields of his childhood, seeing them as places not of refuge but of 'rest' in the context of this idea of transcendence and 'personal collection' (VJ, p. 102). Such an instance is discernible in the anecdote he shares from his evenings in a local café listening to the jukebox as a student in Graz:

> Auf einmal, nach der Plattenwechselpause, die, mitsamt ihren Geräuschen — dem Klicken, dem Suchsurren, hinwärts und herwärts durch den Gerätbauch, dem Schnappen, dem Einrasten, dem Knistern vor dem ersten Takt — , gleichsam zum Wesen der Jukebox gehörte, scholl von dort aus

---

[12] Peter Handke, 'Versuch über die Jukebox', in *Die drei Versuche* (Frankfurt a. M., 2001), p. 107. Subsequent references are given in parentheses in the body of the text (as VJ with page numbers).

der Tiefe eine Musik, bei der er zum ersten Mal im Leben, und später nur noch in den Augenblicken der Liebe, das erfuhr, was in der Fachsprache 'Levitation' heißt. (VJ, p. 108)

[Suddenly, after the pause during which the record changed, with its accompanying sounds — the clicking, the hum of the search back and forth through the belly of the machine, the snap, the lock into position, the crackle before the first beat — which, in effect, were all part of the entity of the jukebox, from its depths rang out a music, hearing which, for the first time in his life, and later on only in moments of love, he experienced what in technical terms would be called 'levitation'.]

Handke here evokes a scene which not only emphasizes the role of music itself in the development of the epiphanic experience of 'levitation' but also sees the incidental sounds of the mechanical operation of the jukebox as part of the event, as part of the orchestration that stages the music. The mechanical sounds function as a kind of integral prelude to the seminal musical event and entry into an enlightened present moment.

As the essayist directs his attention to his present-day thoughts on the processes of personal collection he otherwise describes from earlier years, he cites the writings of St Teresa on a sixteenth-century theological debate about how best to approach communion with the divine. In his discussion of St Teresa we see how Handke has located the terminology he has inscribed into his portrayal of his early years of self-collection and meditation. The dispute which concerned St Teresa involved the so-called *recodigos*, who believed that the appropriate method of approaching God necessitated a process of self-preparation and collection, and the *dejados*, 'the allowers', who believed in leaving themselves open to God to guide them according to divine will. Teresa aligned herself with the latter and presents the writer with a model by which he may find a different approach to his jukebox experiences (VJ, p. 115). Like St Teresa's *dejados,* Handke can recognize his jukebox encounters in more recent years as involving less a 'sich konzentrieren für das Weitertun' [concentration on what was to come] and instead an openness to what his jukebox experiences would bring (VJ, p. 115). Handke describes this as 'ein offenes Ohr' [an open ear], and refers to the jukebox songs as those he would not only choose but also 'play', calling to mind Barthes's discussion of the *inter*play of subject, text and, in the case of the listener in mass industrial culture, the machine.

In their discussion of Handke's discourse on the music machine and its epiphany-producing qualities, Lutz Koepnick and Ulrich Schönherr have both drawn on the concept of the *aura* as presented in Walter Benjamin's 1936 essay 'The Work of Art in the Age of Mechanical Reproduction'.[13] Benjamin

---

[13] Walter Benjamin, 'The Work of Art in the Age of Mechanical Reproduction', in *Illuminations*, ed. by Hannah Arendt, trans. by Harry Zohn (New York, 1968), pp. 217–42. Subsequent references are given in parentheses in the body of the text (as *IL* with page numbers).

associates the concept of the aura with qualities of originality, singularity and authenticity in works of art — the presence of which he viewed as steadily diminishing in the course of time up to the modern era. Aura, Benjamin emphasizes, has less to do with objects than with the social and ritual function of art. As such, aura can be connected to what Benjamin identifies as the original cult value of art (*IL*, p. 223). While Benjamin sees the first significant decline in the ritual basis of art in the secularized 'cult of beauty' of the European Renaissance, he locates the most significant loss of the aura in art in the industrialization of the nineteenth century, where the singularity of the art work becomes challenged by the phenomenon of 'process reproduction' (*IL*, p. 220). Benjamin focuses on the advent of photography in the nineteenth century as the medium whose inherent reproducibility most radically alters the value and function of art in the modern age. The displacement of the cult value of painting by the serialization and objectification of photography, as Benjamin notes, anticipates the emergence of both film and the phonograph record as mechanized reformulations of stage and musical performance respectively, with equally revolutionary effects (*IL*, pp. 220–21). On the one hand, such reproducibility clearly diminishes the notion of authenticity connected to the art object. On the other, this dimension of loss, according to Benjamin, creates a circumstance whereby aura is still discernible as a 'unique phenomenon of distance' between observer and object (*IL*, p. 223). In this regard, according to Graeme Gilloch's interpretation, aura still maintains the power to 'stimulate in the spectator or listener a sense of reverence and wonder'.[14]

Reading Handke via Benjamin, Koepnick identifies the recovery of auratic value for the essayist in *Versuch über die Jukebox* particularly in his delight in marginalia, expressed as in tension with the forces of industrial centralization; an example might be his reverence for the mixed print and various forms of handwriting that grace the playlist labels of favourite jukeboxes cited in the work.[15] Handke contrasts these 'mish-mashes' of script, together with the

---

[14] Graeme Gilloch, *Walter Benjamin. Critical Constellations* (Cambridge, 2002), pp. 182–83.

[15] Lutz Koepnick, 'Negotiating Popular Culture: Wenders, Handke, and the Topographies of Cultural Studies', *German Quarterly*, 69 (1996), 381–400 (p. 394). In his essay, Koepnick discusses Handke's *Versuch über die Jukebox* and Wim Wenders's film *Faraway, So Close!* (1993) — the sequel to Wenders's collaborative project with Handke, *Wings of Desire* (1987) — as meeting points of high and popular culture and as case studies of differing trajectories in critical examination in the fields of Germanic Studies in Central Europe and German Cultural Studies in Britain and the United States. Koepnick identifies aspects of Wenders's film and Handke's essay that illustrate a dual dimension of the legacy of the neo-Marxist Frankfurt School, of which Benjamin was a part. This duality is seen in the 1990s as reflected on the one hand in an insistent focus on classical critical theory in Central Europe and on the other in the more pronounced emphasis on cultural studies in Britain and the United States. While Koepnick sees Wenders as in league with the classical critical component of the Frankfurt School, and poses Handke as reflective of the Anglo-American cultural studies approach, he identifies each as 'clearly devoted to one and the same project, namely the search [...] for a new mythology, for a resurgence of metaphysical meanings and

idiosyncratic musical styles and tastes they signify, with the growing number of so-called 'mafia jukeboxes' he encounters featuring pre-set, pre-printed playlists. While the records and boxes themselves each represent artefacts of Benjaminian mechanical reproduction *par excellence*, Handke's thematic use of these musical mechanisms in service of the formation of his own text points again to the disruption of the traditional divisions between readership and authorship that Barthes allegorizes in reference to the historical development of the concept of 'playing' music.

Schönherr directs attention to the manner in which Handke's jukebox essay resurrects categories of immediacy and authenticity through the redeployment of aesthetic reception, which, he argues, lends an auratic dimension to the technical media of reproduction themselves. Furthermore, Schönherr highlights the transposition of religious codes towards both the jukebox and the musical experiences associated with it as central to this re-appearance of the auratic; these are reminiscent of the strategies used by the Romantics in their appropriation of religious frameworks for the discourse of aesthetic significance and power.[16] This neo-Romantic connection permits a view of Handke as echoing similar Romantic appropriations within the Austrian tradition, most notably at the turn of the previous century, where matters of heightened aesthetic value, immediacy and historic self-consciousness defined a culture that began to witness the fibres of modernity unravelling in what was arguably an anticipatory stage of the post-modern. Paths struck by Handke are visible in this context as reflecting such figures as Hugo von Hofmannsthal, whose language crises directed him towards a re-constituted ideal of 'das Soziale' [the social] and are re-traced in Handke's progression from the formalistic language-intensive works of the 1960s to the utopian themes of social community heralded by *Der kurze Brief*.[17] In a broader musical context, Handke's preoccupation with fusions of classical and popular culture, as displayed in merging tonalities of

---

auratic experiences' (p. 396). In this sense, Benjamin's is clearly a voice that informs Handke (and Wenders) from both a critical and an aesthetic standpoint.

[16] Ulrich Schönherr, 'Die Wiederkehr der Aura im Zeitalter technischer Reproduzierbarkeit: Musik, Literatur und Medien in Peter Handkes *Versuch über die Jukebox*', *Modern Austrian Literature*, 33/ii (2000), 55–72 (p. 64). In his discussion of Handke's religious re-codification in the light of the Romantics, Schönherr draws on the example of Wackenroder's 'aestheticization of religion' and his corresponding sacralization of literature as found in 'Tonkünstler Berglinger', taken as a model of Romantic aesthetic theory that fosters the convergence of the religious and the literary.

[17] Steven Schaber, 'Novalis' *Ein Monolog* and Hofmannsthal's *Ein Brief*. Two Poets in Search of Language', *German Quarterly*, 47 (1974), 204–14 (pp. 212–13). In linking Hofmannsthal with Novalis, Schaber is able to show how Hofmannsthal's turn towards the social in the light of the crisis of language and cognition presented in the so-called 'Chandos Letter' is an example of the reception of the Romantic insistence on understanding language as an autonomous structure. The crisis ultimately brings Hofmannsthal's figure to the point of expressive paralysis. It is against the background of circumstances of critical stasis such as this that Handke's figures can also be seen as presenting a neo-Romantic self-consciousness.

expression and in a self-conscious recycling of motifs, also recalls the drive behind the aesthetics of Gustav Mahler, whose work has been described, for example by Anthony Newcomb, as overtly narrative, preoccupied with the reinterpretation of formal paradigms, and reflecting neo-Romantic modes of circular and spiral journey.[18]

IV

The self-conscious quest for essentialist return, prefigured in Romantic rhetoric and praxis, and revisited by Handke's Austrian *fin-de-siècle* predecessors, can be recognized as the leitmotif that guides his use of the musical in works written or published after the fall of the Berlin Wall, the event which, although not explicitly mentioned, set the *Versuch über die Jukebox* in motion in 1989. While in the German-speaking world (including Austria), the period since 1989 is referred to as post-*Wende*, referring to the political changes following the reunification of Germany, in Handke's career this period can arguably be seen as prefiguring an era which can be labelled 'post-Yugoslavian', and associated instead with national disintegration. Much of the author's attention would indeed focus on the break-up of the Yugoslav confederation, a state which Handke had heralded in his work as a model of multi-ethnic, utopian otherness, in contrast to his native Austria, and one to which he himself had ties through the ethnic Slovene background of his mother's family in the border region of southern Carinthia.

In the course of Handke's public and controversial challenges to what he regarded as the unjust vilification of Serbs and Serb culture during the 1990s, his essays on Serbia can be seen as reflecting an impetus toward investigation, essentialism and authenticity, where music — along with its pronounced absence, in the form of silence — provides a vehicle for underscoring his mission. But musical treatments also serve to connect matters treated in Handke's Yugoslavia essays to concerns outlined in other works which revolve around the disenchantments underlying the Yugoslavia projects. While appropriations of vernacular music play key roles in Handke's main essay on Yugoslavia, *Eine winterliche Reise zu den Flüssen Donau, Save, Morawa und Drina oder Gerechtigkeit für Serbien* [*A Wintry Journey to the Rivers Danube, Save, Morava and Drina or Justice for Serbia*, 1996], the epiphanic moment that provides the axis for the work features not a musical moment as such but a moment of pronounced silence as the Austrian traveller and his Yugoslav guide seek a mythical spot by the Danube purported to be the most silent corner in all of Serbia. The essayist and his companion reach the spot and indeed it yields no sound, 'nicht das leiseste Plätschern, Gurgeln, Gluckern, kein Laut und kein

---

[18] Anthony Newcomb, 'Narrative Archetypes in Mahler's Ninth Symphony', in *Music and Text. Critical Inquiries*, ed. by Steven Paul Scher (Cambridge, 1992), pp. 118–36 (p. 120).

Mucks' [not the slightest splash, gurgle, glug, not a sound, not a word].[19] As America, which Handke had previously idealized, begins to play the role of cultural adversary in the essay — complicit with its Western European NATO counterparts — the counterpoint of the silent Danube to the myth-bearing roar on the American Mississippi from *Der kurze Brief* becomes telling in its protected voicelessness.

Handke's motivation in these essays is to investigate the landscapes, the culture and the people of Serbia for himself and to create a mode of intercultural inquiry that the writer wishes to present as poetic. He endeavours to establish this approach in contrast to the 'unmusikalische Fraglosigkeit' [unmusical questionlessness] of the present referred to by a character in Handke's play *Die Kunst des Fragens* [*The Art of Asking*, 1989], which has the alternative title 'oder Die Reise zum Sonoren Land' [or Journey to the Sonorous Land].[20] It is towards modes of the dialogic that Handke seeks to move his musical paradigm in the later stages of his career, as symbolized by the halted tirade of the blues-singing figure of the 'Wild Man', in the play *Untertagblues* [*Underday Blues*, 2003], which can be seen as continuing the diatribes of *Publikumsbeschimpfung* nearly forty years later. At the end of the play, after passengers have been hurled about on what is almost literally a 'Stationendrama' [drama in stations] consisting of a subterranean journey from one random global subway stop to another, the Wild Man is ultimately silenced by his nemesis, the Wild Woman, who reduces the anti-hero to a level of self-aggrandizing meaninglessness with her final lines:

> Du... du... du Monolog du. Und in Wahrheit müßte meine Rolle hier dreimal so lang sein wie die deine.[21]
>
> [You... you... you monologue, you. And in truth, my role here should be three times as long as yours.]

This move towards a feminized dialogization of the male voice can be witnessed most recently in Handke's novel *Kali. Eine Vorwintergeschichte* [*Kali. An Early Winter's Tale*, 2007], which features as its protagonist a figure simply named 'Die Sängerin' [The Songstress]. Here we may note how Handke's thematic treatments of the figure of the singer — found, for instance, in a passage featuring a stage performance in the novel *Langsame Heimkehr* [*Slow Homecoming*, 1979], clearly modelled on Van Morrison, and in an entire chapter of the novel *Mein Jahr in der Niemandsbucht* [*My Year in No-Man's Bay*, 1994], which is devoted to a figure also unquestionably based on Morrison — give way to a female character.[22] As Handke revisits themes of travel, the exotic and

---

[19] Peter Handke, *Eine winterliche Reise zu den Flüssen Donau, Save, Morawa und Drina oder Gerechtigkeit für Serbien* (Frankfurt a. M., 1996), p. 69.
[20] Peter Handke, *Die Kunst des Fragens* (Frankfurt a. M., 1989), p. 150.
[21] Peter Handke, *Untertagblues. Ein Stationendrama* (Frankfurt a. M., 2003), p. 77.
[22] Peter Handke, *Langsame Heimkehr* (Frankfurt a. M., 1979), pp. 125–28, and *Mein Jahr*

auratic retrieval, drawing on the genre of the fairy tale in *Kali*, Barthes's play of reading and listening is highlighted by a narrator who recounts events from the outset as first heard and then seen, focusing again on the primacy of the auditory in this enchanting landscape of fusion and harmony:

> Allmählich setzt das Gedächtnis ein, und ich höre sie, noch ohne sie zu sehen. Und was höre ich von ihr? Ist das ihre Stimme? Oder ein Instrument? Der Ton, eher der Klang, hat etwas von beidem. Es ist eine Art von Zusammenklang, von Instrument und Stimme.[23]
>
> [Gradually my memory sets in and I hear her without yet seeing her. And what do I hear from her? Is it her voice? Or an instrument? The tone, or rather the sound, has something of both. It is a kind of coming together of instrument and voice.]

In this 'coming together', the themes of voice, self, enchantment and journey found in the works by Handke discussed above resonate here yet again. And in this way readers are invited once more to engage in the epiphanic meeting points of word, music and world — in effect, to play along in their formation.

---

in der Niemandsbucht. Ein Märchen aus den neuen Zeiten (Frankfurt a. M., 1994), pp. 261–83. Handke's chapter provides an intriguing fictitious scenario of a singer figure found neither in Morrison's native Northern Ireland nor in England, where he currently lives, but on a lengthy walking tour through the Scottish Highlands. The figure usually meditates on Handkean issues more than on what one imagines Morrison himself might be concerned with or on what appears in his songs. The fusion of writer and imagined singer nonetheless sheds further light on the applicability of the musical paradigm to Barthes's theories concerning identity, reading, interpretation and (musical) play.

[23] Peter Handke, *Kali. Eine Vorwintergeschichte* (Frankfurt a. M., 2007), p. 7.

'Schreiben und Komponieren': Elfriede Jelinek's *Rosamunde*

GILLIAN PYE AND SIOBHÁN DONOVAN

University College Dublin

This discussion will consider ways in which Elfriede Jelinek's writing, exemplified in the dramolet *Rosamunde*, one of the five 'Prinzessinnendramen' [Princess Plays] which form the cycle *Der Tod und das Mädchen I-V* [*Death and the Maiden I-V*], may be construed as musical. It will examine the relationship between Jelinek's *Rosamunde* and its Romantic intertext, written by Helmina von Chézy (1783–1856), and will explore how Jelinek exploits the discourses of words and music in order to give voice to a female subject who is more spoken than speaking.

Helmina von Chézy's praise for Schubert's incidental music to her play *Rosamunde* (1823) is remarkable for several reasons:

> Ein majestätischer Strom, als süß verklärender Spiegel der Dichtung durch ihre Verschlingungen dahin wallend, großartig, *rein melodiös*, innig und unnennbar rührend und tief, riß die Gewalt der Töne alle Gemüther hin. [...] *dieser* Strom des Wohllauts hätte *alles* besiegt.[1]
>
> [A majestic stream, sweetly reflecting and transfiguring the poetry, swelling as it twists and turns on its way, magnificent, *purely melodic*, fervent, indescribably moving and deep, the power of its tones sweeps all souls from their feet. *This* stream of beautiful sound would have conquered *all*.]

Striking here are the singling out of the music, the most fleeting reference to her own creation, and the choice of figurative language and word play in her description of the music. For *Rosamunde* is a conventional, even formulaic Romantic drama about the triumph of the female titular protagonist — the reluctant Cypriot princess and challenger to the tyrannical male incumbent, Fulvio — set against a stormy coastal backdrop. Chézy's play itself was lacerated by the critics and, coming at the same time as the negative reception of her libretto for Weber's *Euryanthe*, this tarnished her reputation. Schubert's Op. 26, D. 797, of course, is still one of the most frequently performed pieces of

---

[1] Cited in *Rosamunde. Drama in fünf Akten von Helmina von Chézy. Musik von Franz Schubert. Erstveröffentlichung der überarbeiteten Fassung. Mit einer Einleitung und unbekannten Quellen*, ed. by Till Gerrit Waidelich (Tutzing, 1996), p. 79. This is Chézy's considerably reworked version of the 1823 original and the version used by Jelinek.

incidental music.² As Schubert took centre stage, Chézy sank into obscurity,³ and the manuscript for *Rosamunde* did not receive attention again until the early 1990s, remaining unpublished until 1996, when it appeared as part of the *Schubert-Studien*.⁴

The controversial author Elfriede Jelinek and her irony-laden, experimental œuvre have had many storms to weather, and her trademark language with its so-called 'language planes' is undoubtedly (in)famous for its dissonant sonorities and crass wordplays rather than for its dulcet tones.⁵ Violence generally — but usually patriarchal violence (both intellectual and corporal) committed against the dominated female — is a favourite Jelinek hobbyhorse.⁶ In one of her many provocative statements on the topic of female subjugation and male hegemony, Jelinek comments: '[D]ie Gebiete, aus denen die Frau am gründlichsten ausgeschlossen ist und war, sind: das Denken und die Musik' [the areas from which women were and are most thoroughly excluded are thought and music].⁷ A professionally trained organist who came to writing via music,⁸ having previously tried her hand at composition, Jelinek describes her writing as 'kompositorisch', effectively a hybrid of composing and writing.⁹ As a librettist, she has worked with composers such as Hans Werner Henze and Olga Neuwirth.¹⁰ It is therefore not surprising that many critics comment on the musicality of her language, with one concluding that Jelinek's theatre *is*

---

² On the genre of incidental (or 'stage') music, see Roger Savage, 'Incidental music' (especially 5: 'Afterlives'), *Grove Music Online. Oxford Music Online*, http://www.oxfordmusiconline.com/subscriber/article/grove/music/43289 (correct on 17 June 2009). Given the financial and logistic complications, it is hardly surprising that scenic reprises (i.e. with live music) after the first run are the exception rather than the rule. Thus, that Schubert's music has enjoyed its own concertante afterlife is nothing unusual. However, in general, the incidental music still heard today is for plays that are famous in their own right and are frequently performed (without the music), for example Felix Mendelssohn Bartholdy's incidental music to *A Midsummer Night's Dream*.

³ See *Rosamunde*, ed. by Waidelich, p. 79.

⁴ Ibid., p. 59.

⁵ See particularly Christina Schmidt, 'SPRECHEN SEIN. Elfriede Jelineks Theater der Sprachflächen', *Sprache im technischen Zeitalter*, 153 (2000), 65–74.

⁶ See Hans-Jürgen Heinrichs, 'Gespräch mit Elfriede Jelinek', *Sinn und Form*, 65/vi (2004), 760–83 (p. 768).

⁷ '"Man muss sogar immer scheitern, wenn man denkt". Elfriede Jelinek über ihre Prinzessinnen-Zwischenspiele', Email interview with Matthias Dreyer in programme (for *Prinzessinnendramen I-III* premiere), Deutsches Schauspielhaus, Hamburg, Heft Nr. 29 (2002–03) [last page of interview in unpaginated programme].

⁸ Heinrichs, 'Gespräch mit Elfriede Jelinek', p. 764.

⁹ Elfriede Jelinek, Sabine Treude and Günther Hopfgartner, '"Ich meine alles ironisch". Ein Gespräch', *Sprache im technischen Zeitalter*, 153 (2000), 21–31 (p. 24).

¹⁰ With Hans Werner Henze, Jelinek created the opera *Robert der Teufel* (1984); with Olga Neuwirth, the mini-operas *Körperliche Veränderungen* and *Der Wald* (1991), *Bählamms Fest* (1999) and *Lost Highway* (2003). On her collaboration with Olga Neuwirth see Barbara Basting, 'Drastische Töne', *du. Die Zeitschrift der Kultur*, 10 (1999), 22–25 (pp. 22–23).

music;[11] and when Jelinek was awarded the Nobel Prize for Literature in 2004 homage was paid to 'her musical flow of voices and counter-voices in novels and plays that with extraordinary linguistic zeal reveal the absurdity of society's clichés and their subjugating power'.[12]

Despite the acknowledged centrality of music to Jelinek's œuvre, Larson Powell and Brenda Bethman argue that this aspect of her work has, until recently, been somewhat neglected.[13] As they imply in their analysis, which focuses on examples from the novels *Lust* and *Die Klavierspielerin* [*The Piano Teacher*], the 'Prinzessinnendramen' would particularly lend themselves to a discussion of the relationship between music, writing and subjectivity in Jelinek's work.[14] Described on the back cover of the 2003 DTV edition as the 'parodistic pendant' to Shakespeare's 'Königsdramen' [history plays based on the lives of English kings], the female protagonists of all five 'Prinzessinnendramen' are either literary or historical princess-type or iconic figures who suffer a real or allegorical murder at the hands of a sadistic male oppressor.[15] The cycle's title, *Der Tod und das Mädchen*, of course, alludes to the poem by Matthias Claudius from 1775,[16] which was set to music by Schubert in 1817 and subsequently re-worked by the composer in 1825–26, emerging as his famous String Quartet in D Minor. In a similar fashion, Jelinek's *Rosamunde* adapts, re-works, re-forms — or rather, parodies, distorts or, as she herself says, 'autobiographically' and 'parasitically' 'abuses' — Chézy's ill-fated pre-text.[17] Jelinek is an avowed devotee of Schubert, but the stimulus for writing the play was actually an external one: she was invited to

---

[11] Ulrike Haß, 'Grausige Bilder. Große Musik. Zu den Theaterstücken Elfriede Jelineks', in *Text + Kritik*, 117: *Elfriede Jelinek*, 2nd rev. edn, ed. by H. L. Arnold (Munich, 1999), 35–43 (p. 43).
[12] Press release by the Swedish Academy, 7 October 2004, http://nobelprize.org/ nobel_prizes/literature/laureates/2004/press.html (correct on 15 June 2009).
[13] Larson Powell and Brenda Bethman, '"One must have tradition in oneself, to hate it properly". Elfriede Jelinek's Musicality', *Journal of Modern Literature*, 32/i (2008), 163–83. As Powell and Bethman point out, a small number of recent studies have begun to take up this issue, notably Pia Janke's survey, 'Elfriede Jelinek und die Musik. Versuch einer ersten Bestandsaufnahme', in *Sprachmusik. Grenzgänge der Literatur*, ed. by Gerhard Melzer and Paul Pechmann (Vienna, 2003), pp. 189–207.
[14] Powell and Bethman, 'Elfriede Jelinek's Musicality', p. 171.
[15] The first three dramolets had appeared separately between 1999 and 2002, the first (subsequently subtitled *Schneewittchen* [*Snow White*]) appearing alongside two other dramas with Schubert song titles: *Erlkönigin* and *Der Wanderer*. For details of these early editions see Elfriede Jelinek, *Der Tod und das Mädchen I-V* (Berlin, 2003), p. 154. The dramolets in this edition are *Schneewittchen*, *Dornröschen* [*Sleeping Beauty*], *Rosamunde*, *Jackie* [= Jacqueline Kennedy Onassis] and *Die Wand* [*The Wall*, referring to Marlen Haushofer's 1963 novel, and featuring protagonists identifiable as Ingeborg Bachmann and Sylvia Plath]. Further references to this edition, including references to the *Rosamunde* dramolet (pp. 40–61) will be given in parentheses in the text as DTM with page numbers.
[16] Matthias Claudius, *Sämtliche Werke*, ed. by Jost Perfahl (Munich, 1984), pp. 86–87.
[17] See p. 2 of email interview with Matthias Dreyer.

write a text to accompany a performance of Schubert's *Rosamunde* music by the Berlin Philharmonic.[18]

In a deliberate perversion of Chézy's Rosamunde, whose purity and inability to hate are praised by a repentant and reformed Fulvio in the final scene, Jelinek turns her princess into a frenzied, tormented, contradictory and vindictive female speaker whose tirade of hate is unleashed at the end.[19] Jelinek's Rosamunde is not only a thinker, but also a writer, and here one is reminded of another of Jelinek's statements: 'Für eine Frau ist schon das Schreiben ein gewalttätiger Akt, weil das weibliche Subjekt kein sprechendes ist' [For a woman, writing is itself an act of violence, because the female subject is not a speaking subject].[20] Chézy's female protagonist certainly has a voice — with which she opens and closes the drama (in addition to appearing in practically every scene) — but, although there are several opportunities in the text, intriguingly enough she is given nothing to sing.[21] Imitating an operatic exchange, Jelinek's Rosamunde (who sarcastically refers to herself as the 'Königin der Welt' [queen of the world], DTM, p. 44) and her 'prince' Fulvio intone Jelinek's familiar theme: although, here too, it is the female voice that opens and closes the play, while the male voice attempts to control discourse.[22]

> FULVIO: Eine Stimme. Eine Stimme. Eine Stimme. Eine Stimme. Sagt. [...]
> ROSAMUNDE: Meine Stimme. Meine Stimme. Meine Stimme. Meine Stimme. Sagt nichts. (DTM, pp. 60–61)
>
> [FULVIO: A voice. A voice. A voice. A voice. Says.
> ROSAMUNDE: My voice. My voice. My voice. My voice. Says nothing.]

He tries to affirm, assert, voice his centrality, typically in a series of paratactic statements, such as: 'Du bist dein eigenes Recyclingprodukt. Du warst eine Dose. Du warst der Schrecken der Macht. Dich hab ich gedacht, dich hab ich gemacht. Mein mußt du sein!' [You are your own recycling product. You

---

[18] In her interview with Dreyer Jelinek instances Schubert as the composer who 'means the most' to her (p. 2). Her website contains an essay on the composer (1998): http://www.elfriedejelinek.com/ (correct on 17 June 2009).

[19] *Rosamunde*, ed. by Waidelich, p. 149, DTM, p. 60.

[20] Riki Winter, 'Gespräch mit Elfriede Jelinek', in *Elfriede Jelinek*, ed. by Kurt Bartsch and Günther A. Höfler, Dossier 2 (Graz, 1991), pp. 9–19 (p. 14).

[21] The only setting for soloist is the famous melancholic romance for Axa, Rosamunde's foster mother. This is also the only long and completely unchanged quotation from Chézy in Jelinek's drama, trivialized with the subtitle 'Kindermilchschnitte fürs Zwischendurch' [Children's Chocolate Bars for in between Meals] (DTM, p. 48).

[22] We have to presume that the unnamed female who opens Jelinek's text is Rosamunde. However, as Bärbel Lücke notes, this is left open. See Bärbel Lücke, 'Denkbewegungen, Schreibbewegungen — Weiblichkeits- und Männlichkeitsmythen im Spiegel abendländischer Philosophie: Eine dekonstruktivistische Lektüre von Elfriede Jelineks "Prinzessinnendramen" *Der Tod und das Mädchen I–III*', in *Weiblichkeit als politisches Programm? Sexualität, Macht und Mythos*, ed. by Bettina Gruber and Heinz-Peter Preußer (Würzburg, 2005), pp. 107–36, cited here from the 36-page PDF version on Lücke's website: http://www.vermessungsseiten.de/luecke/denkbewegungen.pdf, p. 24 (correct on 17 June 2009).

were a tin can. You struck fear into power. I thought you, I made you. You shall be mine!] (DTM, p. 49). Conversely, while Jelinek's female speaker talks incessantly, she does not appear to be fully in control of her voice. Instead she is subjected to the noise, not only of the contemporary social environment (represented by fragments of the language of TV talk- and quiz shows, holiday brochures and women's magazines) but also of the literary-historical and philosophical intertext. Large portions of Chézy's dialogue, along with many of her main themes, are creatively appropriated in Jelinek's pastiche. In this way, in the manner of modern sound-engineering, Jelinek 'lays down' a number of 'tracks', which together create a complex discursive 'noise'. This takes Roland Barthes's notion of intertext, as the 'stubborn after-image, which [...] drowns the sound of my own present words' to its logical (feminist) conclusion.[23] Thus, at the opening of the piece we hear Rosamunde voice the following:

> Mir ist da leider Wasser in den Körper eingedrungen. Obwohl ich nur meine Bilder ein wenig tränken wollte. Ich bin ziemlich betroffen, daß ich davon gleich ertrinken muß. Auf Gottes schöner Erde zerreißt der Tiger das Lamm. Nur ich kann mir nicht helfen. Bin von allem betroffen, auch von dem, was mich nichts angeht. So bin ich und so bleibe ich, nur Neues, Trübes seh ich an der Welt. Man sagt es mir tausendmal, was soll ich machen, auch das hat mich dann schon wieder betroffen! Die Feder führ ich unermüdlich, keine fremden Sprachen red ich und wenn, dann falsch. Eine Badende im scharfen Bikini wär ich gern, die Schmerzensschreie ausstößt, süßes Gift auf ihrer eignen Zunge. Doch aus der Badenden wird plötzlich Ernst, bloß weil ich sie darstellen muß. (DTM, p. 43)

> [The water has unfortunately seeped into my body. Although I only wanted to soak my pictures a little. I am quite affected by the fact that I will soon drown as a result of this. On God's beautiful earth the tiger tears apart the lamb. Only I can't save myself. I am affected by everything, even by things that have nothing to do with me. This is how I am and how I will remain, I see nothing but the new, the dismal, in the world. They tell me a thousand times, but what can I do, even that has affected me again. My pen moves tirelessly, I speak no foreign languages and when I do, then incorrectly. I would like to be a bathing girl in a sexy bikini, crying out in pain, with sweet poison on her own tongue. But suddenly the bather is getting serious, only because I have to portray her.]

These opening lines serve as an example of the way in which Jelinek creates a soundtrack that produces a cacophonous mix of the multiple discourses seeking to define and contain the female subject. From the topos of the drowning Ophelia, 'forever framed by someone else's story',[24] and epitomized by John

---

[23] 'From *Writing Degree Zero*', in *Roland Barthes. A Reader*, ed. and introd. by Susan Sontag (London, 1993), pp. 31–81 (p. 37).
[24] Elizabeth Bronfen on Millais's *Ophelia*: www.tate.org.uk/tateetc/issue3/microtate3.htm (correct on 12 December 2009).

Everett Millais's 1851–52 painting, to the biblical imagery of the tiger and the lamb as contrasting creations (taken up perhaps most famously in the poetry of William Blake, but also quoted directly here from Chézy's drama), to the late-twentieth-century cliché of the screeching, bikini-clad cover-girl, Jelinek's composition is defined by the 'stereographic plurality of its weave of signifiers'.[25] This performs the drowning out of the female voice, her circumscription by generations of male words and images, but yet simultaneously aims to create a free space in which, amongst the din, this voice might — albeit in a fragmentary fashion — nevertheless be heard.

As Powell and Bethman note, it is perhaps something of a cliché to refer to Roland Barthes's influence on Jelinek. Nevertheless, this essay argues that his writing on music offers ways of approaching the relationship of words, music and the female voice in Jelinek's text.[26] In his essay 'Musica Practica', Barthes argues that both music and written text are 'composed', and to compose, means '*to give to do*, not to give to hear but to give to write'.[27] He sees music as a manual activity that is actually 'very little auditory', involving the body transcribing 'what it reads, making sound and meaning, the body as inscriber and not just transmitter, simple receiver.'[28] This confirms Jelinek's work as 'kompositorisch': the text is composed to be 'played' by its recipients as one plays music. This means, obviously, that as post-dramatic theatre — which offers neither plot nor coherent figures, featuring instead a series of discursive tracks — this text, like Jelinek's other dramas, requires that its recipients engage actively in its inscription. Moreover, Jelinek also 'plays with' composition as the basis for bodily inscription, turning this on its head: if, conventionally, the dramatic text is the basis for performance — having obvious implications for the female figure, defined predominantly by her physical body[29] — then here, in a manner which is consonant with her well-documented love/hate relationship to the theatre, Jelinek performs the partial dematerialization of this 'body'. By demonstrating the way in which it is constructed in discourse, Jelinek presents a body defined by the sound-bite.

In addition, Jelinek's texts may also be seen as musical in their repetitive sampling of particular words and phrases, in ways that emphasize their phonetic

---

[25] Roland Barthes, 'From Work to Text', originally published as 'De l'œuvre au texte', in *Revue d'esthétique*, 3 (1971), reprinted in translation in *Image, Music, Text*, trans. by Stephen Heath (London, 1977), pp. 155–64 (p. 159).
[26] See Powell and Bethman, 'Elfriede Jelinek's Musicality', p. 179. They argue that to refer Jelinek's musicality to Barthes's 'rustling of language' may do little more than slightly modernize interpretations which tend towards those 'hermeneutical metaphors of meaning and Utopianism that music conjures up' (p. 164).
[27] Originally published in *L'Arc*, 40 (1970) and reprinted in translation in *Image, Music, Text*, pp. 149–54 (p. 153).
[28] Ibid., p. 149.
[29] See for example Jill Dolan, *The Feminist Spectator as Critic* (Ann Arbor, MI, 1988) on the issue of the significance of the female body in theatrical performance.

qualities. However, according to Powell and Bethman, moving beyond a description of her writing as musical 'sampling' can be problematic.[30] Here, Barthes's essay 'The Grain of the Voice' may prove useful in considering how Jelinek composes a text that aims to create space for the female, or at least to disrupt the totalizing effect of male-controlled discourse, by playing with the materiality of language.[31] In this essay Barthes explores the contact between music and language as two distinct, yet overlapping signifying systems. Although, as he observes, the special quality of language is that it is able to interpret other (non-verbal) signifying systems, he finds that language has not been very successful in interpreting music. Specifically, he argues that music criticism tends towards deadening adjectival description, along the lines of the formula 'the music is *this*, the execution is *that*' (Grain, p. 179). Barthes's solution is not, in the first place, to suggest that language be altered, but rather that the musical object itself should change the way 'it presents itself to discourse' (Grain, p. 180). In other words, he seeks a means of better understanding music as a semiotic system in order to open it more fully to language. In so doing, he aims to illuminate 'the fringe of contact between music and language' (Grain, p. 181).

In order to achieve this aim, Barthes borrows from Julia Kristeva, whose work he himself influenced.[32] Here he takes Kristeva's terms 'pheno-text' and 'geno-text', turning them into 'pheno-song' and 'geno-song'. Kristeva employs 'geno-text' to refer to 'language's underlying foundation', the domain of potentiality engendered by 'semiotic processes'. For Kristeva such processes include drives, ecological and social systems surrounding the body, and pre-Œdipal relationships with parents. The 'pheno-text' denotes 'language that serves to communicate, which linguistics describes in terms of "competence" and "performance"' and which 'obeys rules of communication'.[33] In his essay, Barthes adapts these terms using 'pheno-song' to refer to the communicative aspects of performance: 'everything which it is customary to talk about, which forms the tissue of cultural values' (Grain, p. 182). With the term 'geno-song', Barthes describes a source of potential, 'the space where significations germinate "from within language and in its very materiality"' (ibid.). Here, it is the relationship between the two semiotic systems which is at stake, for the geno-song 'works at the language — not at what it says, but the voluptuousness of its sound-signifiers, of its letters'. This manifests itself particularly in the

---

[30] Powell and Bethman, 'Elfriede Jelinek's Musicality, p. 179, n. 2.
[31] Originally published as 'Le grain de la voix', in *Musique en jeu* (1972), reprinted in translation in *Image, Music, Text*, pp. 179–89 (p. 182). Further references will be given in parentheses in the text as 'Grain' with page numbers.
[32] Leon S. Roudiez describes how, at Kristeva's PhD *viva voce* defence in 1973, Barthes declared that her work had encouraged him to shift 'away from a semiology of products to a semiotics of production', in Julia Kristeva, *Revolution in Poetic Language*, trans. by Margaret Waller and introd. by Leon S. Roudiez (New York, 1984), pp. 1–10 (p. 10).
[33] Kristeva, *Revolution in Poetic Language*, pp. 86–87.

'grain of the voice', which is language made material in vocal music. This is where the voice operates 'in a dual posture, a dual production — of language and of music' (Grain, p. 181) thus unpicking, by means of 'the materiality of the body' (Grain, p. 182), the seam between the two systems.

Here Barthes is addressing the cliché of music as a signifying system with direct access to human passions. He echoes Kristeva's understanding that, although language differs from music because the latter is a 'nonverbal signifying system' that is 'constructed exclusively on the basis of the semiotic' (in other words heavily indebted to pre-linguistic drives and energies), this exclusivity is nevertheless 'relative': music cannot be seen to operate independently from language.[34] In Barthes's discussion of pheno- and geno-song the nature of this relativity is explored. First, he shows that the pheno-song is dependent on the linguistic horizon, 'what in music *can be said*: what is said about it, predicatively, by Institution, Criticism, Opinion' (Grain, p. 185). Second, he asks how, by reconfiguring the way in which it receives musical performance, language may open itself up to the potentiality of the geno-text. This is the role of the geno-song, manifest in the 'grain' of the voice. Thus, Barthes approaches, from another angle, Kristeva's interest in the revolutionary potential of poetic language as a means of accessing the power of the semiotic.[35] Acknowledging both Kristeva and Jonathan Dunsby's comment that Barthes's idea of the 'grain of the voice' has been somewhat overused, particularly in writing about music,[36] here we argue that it may nevertheless provide a fruitful jumping-off point for this discussion. Specifically, taking Barthes's description of the 'grain' as that instance where the voice operates in a 'dual posture' may help to generate an understanding of how and why Jelinek's writing might be said to be musical.

Significantly for this present discussion, Barthes's example of typical pheno-song practice is the singer Dietrich Fischer-Dieskau, of whom Barthes claims, '[i]f you like Schubert but not FD, then Schubert is today *forbidden* you' (Grain, p. 185). What Barthes criticizes is the subjection, in Fischer-Dieskau's performance, of Schubert's music to a set of 'average' expectations, specifically, in a performance that 'translates' emotion, and represents the 'meaning' of a poem (Grain, p. 185), suggesting an artistic autonomy and harmonious transcendence, which in some ways typify the Romantic ideal of the fusion of words

---

[34] Kristeva explains as follows: 'Because the subject is always *both* semiotic *and* symbolic, no signifying system he produces can be either "exclusively" semiotic or "exclusively" symbolic' (ibid., p. 24, emphasis in original). Kristeva's concern here, however, is with language and her comments on music in this instance are therefore not developed.

[35] In *Revolution in Poetic Language*, Kristeva's aim is to consider the role of poetic language as a potential source of revolution for the subject. Here, as Roudiez points out, she suggests that certain avant-garde writers may come close to the geno-text (ibid., p. 5).

[36] Jonathan Dunsby, 'Roland Barthes and the Grain of Panzéra's Voice', *Journal of the Royal Musical Association*, 134/i (2009), 113–32 (p. 113).

and music in the *Lied*.³⁷ Barthes contrasts this with the lesser-known French singer Charles Panzéra's performance, in which the 'geno-song' is shown at work in the friction revealed between words and music. Briefly, Barthes suggests that this occurs in Panzéra's very vocal technique, which betrays the physical operation of the mouth and throat (as opposed to the swelling of the breath in the lungs), suggesting the fleshy, bodily aspect of the music. In addition, as Dunsby argues, such friction may also be revealed in the structure of the performance. Analysing Panzéra's performance of the Schumann *Lied* 'Ich will meine Seele tauchen' [I want to dip my soul], Dunsby shows how the singer pays attention to the contact between music and words, for instance by employing an 'unmistakable glottal intake of breath' in such a way as to emphasize the word 'hauchen' [to breathe], thus giving Heine's text physical form. At the same time, in the adoption of a strategy which is, according to Dunsby, 'counter-intuitive' to the musical structure of Schumann's score, Panzéra works along the fringe of contact between language and music.³⁸

It can be argued that Jelinek likewise works with the friction between music and language in *Rosamunde*, which, as a text ostensibly intended to be performed, and in its emphasis on apparently random juxtapositions and phonetic associations, could be described as 'writing aloud'. For Barthes, such writing aloud 'belongs to the geno-text', 'it is carried not by dramatic inflections, subtle stresses, sympathetic accents, but by the *grain* of the voice. [...] its aim is not the clarity of messages, the theater of emotions; what it searches for [...] are the pulsional incidents, the language lined with flesh, a text where we can hear the grain of the throat, the patina of consonants, the voluptuousness of vowels, a whole carnal stereophony: the articulation of the body'.³⁹ Again, skirting along the fringe of contact between music and words, Barthes invokes echoes of the normative performance he ascribes to Fischer-Dieskau as the model interpreter of the Romantic *Lied*, rejecting this in favour of a disrupted performance in which the body may materialize. Here, it is argued that, by mimicking the Romantic *Lied* cycle in *Der Tod und das Mädchen*, Jelinek's approach is similar. This is shown most clearly in *Rosamunde*, where Romantic poetry and patriarchal discourse, with their emphasis on transcendence and harmony, are disrupted by a text made fleshy, both in its subversion of Romantic tropes and in its insistence on phonetics.

Turning to the question of the insistence on sound, a brief analysis of the

---

³⁷ Powell and Bethman note the inextricable link between Romantic art and poetry and the ideal of autonomy and emphasize the importance of this concept in many of Jelinek's works ('Elfriede Jelinek's Musicality', p. 164). Their perceptive analysis of an excerpt from *Lust* also looks at textual strategies that may be deemed to be musical, although there the discussion focuses much of its attention on comparisons to Kafka, Joyce and Freud (ibid., pp. 166–70).
³⁸ Dunsby, 'Roland Barthes and the Grain of Panzéra's Voice', pp. 123–26.
³⁹ Roland Barthes, *The Pleasure of the Text*, trans. by Richard Miller (Oxford, 1975), pp. 66–67.

opening section cited earlier may illuminate Jelinek's musical strategy here: this stereographic piece relies on wordplay dependent on the imagery of water and drowning ('Wasser [...] eingedrungen / tränken / ertrinken / Badende im [...] Bikini' [water / seeped / dip / drown / bathing girl in a bikini]). Here, the image of the drowning woman is eroded and debunked, partly by comic relativization. This can be seen, for example, in the use of 'leider' [unfortunately] and the idea of just being 'betroffen' [affected] by an impending death by drowning. The repetition of 'betroffen' too — itself an ambiguous indicator of the precarious situation of the female who, like Ophelia, forever framed by someone else's story, cannot avoid being affected by everything — allows the text to trip along from one idea to the next. Moreover, she plays with — tears apart even, as the tiger does the lamb (Rosamunde thus unwittingly presaging her expected fate) — Chézy's drama to create a pastiche, taking quotations seemingly at random and stitching them together in a way that either perverts their original meaning (Chézy's Rosamunde can speak foreign languages), or shuffles them around almost in the manner of nonsense poetry, to comic effect. As throughout the dramolet, sound-bites from Chézy's *Rosamunde* are numerous.[40] Finally, and this perhaps relates most closely to the idea of the geno-song, a dense pattern of repeated sounds, which emphasizes the phonetic qualities of the words — their materiality — carries the text. For example, the 'ch', 'sch' and 's' sounds in the sequence 'ich / ziemlich / gleich / muß / Gottes / schöner / zerreißt / mich nichts / Neues / Trübes / sagt es / tausendmal' create a 'rushing' effect, which recalls the sound of the water — a recurring theme in this text, as in Chézy's — but does not fit neatly into a coherent semantic context. Rather, Jelinek creates a veneer of musical cohesion, a *Wortmusik* [word music] — in this example the 'rushing' sound — that plays upon the idea of the fusion of words and music as the Romantic *Lied* idealizes it, only ultimately to refuse this. By pairing such *Wortmusik* with semantic dissonance — the sequence of discursive fragments which follow one another with no pretence at constructing a credible dramatic character — Jelinek adopts a technique that appears to play with the idea of the grain of the voice as a stance of dual production, able to work along the 'fringe of contact' between words and music.

Moreover, taking the musical analogy further, it could be argued that, just as the female speaker here rarely speaks foreign languages and, if so, she does it badly ('wenn, dann falsch'), as a 'player' of the text, in the traditional sense at least, Jelinek shows the female playing it 'out of tune' or badly. Aside from direct references to her inability to express herself, as noted earlier the

---

[40] Jelinek is quoting here in the main from Act I, scene v, part of Rosamunde's self-characterization (*Rosamunde*, ed. by Waidelich, p. 92). For a summary of Chézy's play and comparison to Jelinek's adaptation, see Britta Kallin, '"Die Feder führ ich unermüdlich": Helmina von Chézy's *Rosamunde* as Intertext in Elfriede Jelinek's *Der Tod und das Mädchen III: Rosamunde*', *Glossen*, 26 (2007), http://www2.dickinson.edu/glossen/heft26/article26/kallin26.html (correct on 15 August 2009).

female speaker also produces comic relativizations, which, not being attached to 'irgendwelche Gedankengänge eines Bewusstseins oder eines sprechenden Wesens' [any kind of train of thought of a consciousness or a speaking entity] and reflecting ironically on the female situation, cannot be construed as intentional on the part of the speaking voice.[41] Rather, the female voice reveals herself to be more spoken than speaking, clumsy amateur rather than virtuoso performer, puppet rather than sovereign subject.[42] In this way, Jelinek's female speaker in *Rosamunde* mimics and debunks the virtuoso player, subverts a sort of pheno-song with geno-song. This mimicry manifests itself in the playing of 'wrong notes', which appear as discords and as the explicitly emphasized lack of control the speaker exercises over the text. This takes Barthes's concept of the grain of the voice one step further, subverting the notion of the masterful performance in the figure of the ineptly spoken female voice.

That Jelinek's text itself is a virtuoso performance, however, is clear. The creation of the geno-song is achieved in a consummate mastery of her material, playing with its form.[43] This is nowhere clearer than in her plundering of Chézy's moralistic text and its Romantic themes (love, death, intrigue, mistaken identity, disguise, deception, hypocrisy and patriarchal tyranny), imagery (land- and water-based nature, day/night and personification) and even rhetoric (apostrophizing). By disrupting the flow of this discourse, refusing the smooth surface of the pheno-song and its appeal to 'average' expectations, Jelinek draws attention to the materiality of its language. This procedure may be illustrated by comparing the final two stanzas of the opening wistful poem of Chézy's play with a section taken from the second page of Jelinek's *Rosamunde* (following on from the section analysed above). Chézy's text reads as follows:

> Hätt' ich Flügel, mich zu tragen,
> Hin, wo blaue Klippen ragen,
> Scharf gezackt im Purpurstrahl,
> Daß ich säh von ihren Zinken,
> Wipfel ragen, Fluthen blinken,
> Sanft geschwungen durch das Thal.

---

[41] Allyson Fiddler, 'Im Netz der Moral: Monologe, Massenmedien und Mythologie in Elfriede Jelineks "Babel"', in *Das Analoge sträubt sich gegen das Digitale?*, ed. by David Barnett, Moray McGowan and Karen Jürs-Munby, Theater der Zeit Recherchen 37 (Berlin, 2006), pp. 101–12 (p. 103).

[42] Fulvio's later vindictive dismissal of her as a puppet is thus not wide of the mark: 'Ein Bild von Zucker, eine Gliederpuppe' [a sugar-sweet picture, a jointed doll] (DTM, p. 56), a direct quotation from Act III, scene 7 of Chézy's play (*Rosamunde*, ed. by Waidelich, p. 116).

[43] Jonathan Dunsby points out that, in the case of the French singer Panzéra, Barthes's chosen example of geno-song performance, 'it is precisely because Panzéra was a complete master of the pheno-song that his geno-song can come through' ('Roland Barthes and the Grain of Panzéra's Voice', p. 128). This underscores Dunsby's point that Barthes perhaps somewhat disingenuously takes what are, in Kristeva's thinking, complementary terms and makes them appear as alternatives to one another (pp. 128–29).

> O, wer thut mir kund, ob jene
> Thale bergen, was ich wähne;
> Still ersehnet, — o, wo blüht
> Fern ein Glück in goldnen Räumen,
> Wie es oft in süßen Träumen
> Stürmisch meine Brust durchglüht?[44]

> [Had I but wings to carry myself there, where blue crags jut out, zigzagging sharply in purple rays of light, so that I could see from their heights mountain tops soaring, torrents flashing, softly flowing through the valley! Oh, who can tell me if yonder valleys shelter what I imagine. In silent yearning, — oh, where does distant joy in golden spaces blossom, as oft in sweet dreams it sets my breast tempestuously aglow?]

Jelinek's Rosamunde also speaks of a mountainous landscape and tumultuous waters, but here it is quite different:

> Bitte geben Sie mir ein Paar Schwimmflügel, mich zu tragen! Wer unterbricht den grünen Wogenfall, von dem ich derzeit noch nicht weiß, daß er von Wogen herrührt? Jawohl, jetzt kommts, hier, plötzlich, das Blinklicht von Fluten, die nicht für mich gebremst haben, obwohl sie es sogar für Tiere tun. Und da bohrt sich doch glatt dieser Zinken von einer Flut in meinen Kühlergrill. Scharf gezackt, neinnein, nicht ich in meinem Zweiteiler, wo ich meine Formen abgestellt habe! Nicht ich! Im Purpurstrahl leuchtet meine Motorhaube noch einmal auf, sanft schwingt sich das Tal drüber weg, in elegantem Sprung. Das Tal, von Bergen eingekesselt, hätt auch mich noch bergen sollen, doch, blöde Betroffenheit, du wirfst mich immer wieder raus, wo ich ja froh sein könnte in der Laube meines lieben Landes. Fern ein Glück in goldnen Räumen, ja oder nein? Entscheiden Sie sich jetzt! (DTM, pp. 43–44)

> [Please, give me a pair of water-wings to carry me! Who interrupts the green wave-fall, of which I currently don't yet know that it comes from waves? Oh yes, here it comes, here suddenly, in the flashing light of floods, which didn't brake for me, even though they would do for animals. And this pointed flood is drilling into my radiator grill. Sharply zigzagged, no no, not I in my two-piece, where I have cast off my shapes. Not I! In the purple rays of light my car bonnet lights up once again, softly the valley runs over it with an elegant leap. The valley, enclosed by mountains, could have sheltered me too, but, stupid dismay, you throw me out over and over again, when I could be happy in the bower of my beloved land. Distant joy in golden spaces, yes or no? Decide now!]

Chézy's opening verses function as a kind of 'overture', introducing themes and key terms which are reprised throughout the play. In this example, Chézy's 'music' is apparent in the regular verse patterns (couplets with enclosed rhyme, and with a predominance of feminine rhyme) and metre. Sound, sight and meaning are intended to be harmonious, as the verses flow, running from the peaks of the mountains down into the valleys, expressing the yearning and

---

[44] *Rosamunde*, ed. by Waidelich, p. 83.

dreaming of the melancholic and lyrical Romantic self. Although Jelinek's text depends on recurring words and images, it deliberately undermines the type of closed drama anticipated in an overture. It operates by debunking the fabric of the Romantic intertext and, far from soaring on Romantic flights of fancy, it mimics an uncontrolled speaking aloud, voicing a sequence of disjointed images. This is not least because Chézy's verses are highly stylized and derivative (for example, the obvious reference to Gretchen at the spinning-wheel in the opening lines of the play), lending themselves to parody. As Birgit Tautz explores in her analysis of *Der Tod und das Mädchen* I and II, this reflects Jelinek's interest in the Early Romantic preoccupation with flux and (gender) mobility, and with the subsequent ossification of female identity, particularly in the fairytales of the Brothers Grimm.[45]

Jelinek's text replaces the rhyme and metre of the Romantic original with a chaotic prose, in which the phonetic emphasis is, instead, placed on repeated sounds and words (such as 'Wogen', 'Flut/Fluten', 'Bergen/bergen'). Also, the images taken over from Chézy's text are degraded as they are modified in puns and 'mixed up'. One example of this is the use of the term 'Flügel' [wings]. While Chézy's heroine wishes for wings, Jelinek's speaker wishes rather for '*Schwimm*flügel' [water-wings]. Here the Romantic is undermined by the modern, the pragmatic, but also by the *incompetent* ('Schwimmflügel' for the incompetent swimmer, itself a degraded image of the Romantic longing for an often watery 'Liebestod' [love-death]). Another example is the transformation of 'Fluthen blinken' [torrents flashing] into 'das Blinklicht von Fluten' [the flashing light — also: car indicator — of the torrents], suggesting again, the 'helplessness' of the female, not in the face of a raging passion reflected in nature, but rather of a road traffic accident.

A further example from these extracts shows the way in which Jelinek's 'remix' refuses unified meaning and simultaneously exposes the way in which Chézy's text is ideologically determined. Taking up Chézy's mountain imagery, Jelinek's text reads, '[u]nd da bohrt sich doch glatt dieser Zinken von einer Flut in meinen Kühlergrill. Scharf gezackt, neinnein, nicht ich in meinem Zweiteiler'. The terms 'Zinken' and 'Zacke/zacken', torn from their Romantic context and mixed with the recurring images of the car, defy interpretation. Instead the words are combined in a way that suggests incoherence, underlining the 'incompetence' of the speaker. The metaphors are flattened — literally, in the amalgamation of peaks and valleys, water and rock in Jelinek's lines — but this also draws attention to the power of the original imagery. Specifically, in this example the new combination plays with its phallic and blatantly sexual nature, already glaringly obvious in the original Romantic text, with its recurring reference to mountaintops and peaks ('Zinken', 'Zacke') and lush,

---

[45] Birgit Tautz, 'A Fairy Tale Reality? Elfriede Jelinek's *Snow White, Sleeping Beauty* and the Mythologization of Contemporary Society', *Women in German Yearbook*, 24 (2008), 165–84.

wet valleys.[46] Jelinek's 'remix' takes the metaphors out of a coherent context but nevertheless manages to inflate their sexual content. In other words, there is little doubt, despite the obscurity of phrases such as 'Und da bohrt sich doch glatt dieser Zinken von einer Flut in meinen Kühlergrill', that the 'Zinken/Flut/Kühlergrill' [peaks/torrent/radiator grill] stand for penis/semen/vagina. At the same time, this metonymically marks by extension the patriarchal control of signification, to which the female is subjected. That this has material consequences for female identity is echoed in the description of the female body as 'scharf gezackt': it appears to have been shaped by the action of a (literally) phallically shaped discourse. That the female has become complicit in this process, however, is reflected throughout the text in references to the relationship between the female and her body. In dismantling Chézy's text, Jelinek draws attention to the materiality of words, not only in a phonetic sense, but also to their ideological materiality.

This could be described as the 'grain of the voice' written into a piece such as *Rosamunde*: Jelinek's cacophonous music works at the materiality of the language, demonstrating its complicity with discourses of (phallocentric) power, to which the female speaker is subjected. By playing Chézy 'out of tune' Jelinek mocks the (patriarchal) pretensions of the Romantic intertext, with its reputation as the product of an incompetent female writer. At the same time, Jelinek reveals the extent to which Chézy herself is not only 'overwritten' by the Romantic music that sonorously drowned out and outlived her drama, but also by a clichéd Romantic discourse, replete with a language that seeks to define and contain female identity.

Jelinek's text resounds with intertext in a way that is ultimately cacophonous rather than dissonant because it refuses semantic, dramatic and lyrical resolution. Just as the grain of Panzéra's voice works at the language, unpicking the seam between words and music, so Jelinek's musical text 'plays' Chézy's drama, working it in a way that tears at the tissue of our cultural values.

---

[46] This is confirmed in Act III, scene 16 of Chézy's play, when Fulvio delivers Rosamunde an ultimatum: death or a life of voluptuousness at his side (*Rosamunde*, ed. by Waidelich, p. 127). See also Kallin, '"Die Feder führ ich unermüdlich"', on the sexual nature of Chézy's imagery.

Reviews

Joseph II. Volume II: Against the World 1780–1790. By DEREK BEALES. Cambridge: Cambridge University Press. 2009. xix + 733 pp. £80. ISBN 978-0-521-32488-55.

The second and final volume of this superlative biography of Joseph II appears some twenty years after the first, which encompassed Joseph's upbringing, apprenticeship and co-regency with his mother. The present volume covers the ten years of personal rule in seventeen chapters, interleaving thematic and narrative sequences, almost like a sequence of musical variations, with the whole rounded off with an introduction and substantial coda, which expound and then ultimately rework the main themes. Even just shortly after publication we can already see that the completion of this massive project represents a major event in Habsburg and indeed early modern European historiography: now that the two volumes can be read side by side it is clear that Beales has written a study of enlightened Europe's most ambitious and energetic ruler which will stand as the leading account in any language for many years to come. Moreover, the sheer range of Joseph's territories and hyperactive commitments ensures that these two volumes can on one level be read much more widely as a running commentary on the challenges and opportunities of enlightened monarchy and the evolution of new regional power blocs in Central and Eastern Europe in the later eighteenth century. For all these reasons this book transcends the narrowing of focus implicit in any biographical approach, and will become an indispensable point of reference for all historians of the period. Readers will appreciate too the easy, often elegant style and the many touches of slightly mischievous humour along the way.

There are so many new interpretations offered here or corrections to received wisdom that it is particularly difficult to single out individual sections; yet early readers have rightly highlighted the weight given to Joseph's impact on the cultural history of the Monarchy, to religion conceived broadly as far more than just the Toleration Patents and the monastic closures programme, and the key roles played by Belgium and Hungary within the maintenance of the imperial framework and — conversely — its near unravelling in Joseph's final years. For the general reader the chapters on foreign policy provide a masterly and lucid guide through the intricacies of Joseph's vision and the responses, suspicions and feints of his fellow rulers, with Joseph's overlooked successes in the final war against the Turks providing a fine denouement. While this is a genre of historical writing to which Beales has made many distinguished contributions, there are surprises too — for example a venture into microhistory in Chapter 6, devoted to the Pope's month-long visit to Vienna in 1782. Here the author takes advantage of an unusually rich survival of records in the form of Joseph's 'diary' and detailed reports from the papal nuncio to take us as close as possible to Joseph's negotiating style.

As so often in this work, we find that the emperor's political stance in close-up was wiser and more shrewd and flexible than the popular image of him would suggest.

For readers of *Austrian Studies* the particular rewards of this book are perhaps to be found in the accounts of Joseph's policies which carried over a decisive legacy and influence into the nineteenth century, and also in those sections which describe Joseph's impact on the city of Vienna, and his relations with musicians, and with Mozart above all. The sparkling Chapter 13 provides the most concentrated focus on these last themes, though there are important reflections scattered throughout the volume. Beales has written with distinction on Mozart before now, but here presents in much greater detail his case that 'Mozart was fortunate in finding in the emperor, for all his quirks, a warm admirer and a steady supporter' (p. 459). The discussion in this chapter and elsewhere across the huge canvas of this study digs deeper than before, especially into the performance history of *The Marriage of Figaro*, and it is to be hoped that Beales will do full justice to his many insights into Mozart's own works, his milieu and Joseph's patronage policy in a separate monograph. Again, it is invidious to select it but one neglected aspect of Joseph's domestic legacy that receives its proper due for the first time is the promulgation of the first volume of the Civil Code, whose originality and importance are described in detail (pp. 544–54): Beales demonstrates convincingly that Joseph's much criticized insistence on pressing ahead with codification at a great pace was in fact essential to its completion. This was more than other contemporary European rulers achieved, and much of the *Gesetzbuch* is still in force today.

In his conclusion Beales confronts himself and the reader with a number of incisive questions — was Joseph despotic, was he enlightened, was he revolutionary, what was his legacy, and how important was his personality in determining those outcomes? Each of the answers provided is both judicious and carefully nuanced, as one would expect, but ultimately his verdict is clear and uncompromising: 'he [Joseph] stands out as incomparably the most innovative ruler the Monarchy ever had, and one of the most original that any country has known' (p. 690). As a result of this book, the product of over thirty years of research and reflection, we are now able to assess this thesis for ourselves with the benefit of a new understanding of both reign and era that has matched Joseph's own reach in leaving no area of foreign or domestic policy untouched.

LONDON SCHOOL OF ECONOMICS AND POLITICAL SCIENCE   TIM HOCHSTRASSER

Vienna in the Age of Uncertainty. Science, Liberalism and Private Life. By DEBORAH COEN. Chicago and London: University of Chicago Press. 2007. 352 pp. $45. ISBN 978-0-226-11172-8.

The subtitle of this wide-ranging study by no means covers all of the topics it deals with: at the very least, Coen could also have added aesthetics, pedagogy, literature and public institutions with impunity. Cast as a milieu study of the multifaceted, multitalented Exner family and its spheres of influence, *Vienna in the Age of Uncertainty* defines itself in contrast to Schorske's analysis of the Viennese *fin de siècle*. Coen sets out to challenge the idea that a 'crisis of rationalism' signalled the end of an Austrian liberalism unable to cope with modernist innovation. Tracing the development of scientific theories of probability and anti-determinism over three generations of Exners, she claims that, far from being wedded to dogmatic rationalism, scepticism was one of the central values of Austria's bourgeois liberals and an important source of their moral and political authority. Rather than finding themselves in unresolvable conflict with the *fin de siècle*, she argues, their willingness to doubt, combined with an openness to empirical experimentation, helped usher in reforms and radicalism both at mid-century and at the century's end.

Coen begins with an account of the life and times of the founder of this academic dynasty, Franz Exner (1802–1853), to whose early years and career as a philosopher and education reformer she dedicates a whole discrete chapter. Later family members are not given such detailed coverage: it is the author's stated intention not to produce a comprehensive group portrait. Instead, what follows is a roughly chronological whirl of academic achievements and debates, during which 'the Exners' and 'Exner' stand for a variety of groupings and individuals. Two of Franz Exner's four sons, Adolf, Karl, Sigmund and Serafin, became Rectors of the University of Vienna, and all of them held a series of prestigious professorships in their respective subjects (law, physiology and physics). They influenced a number of talented students, including such luminaries as Sigmund Freud and Erwin Schrödinger. However, 'the Exners' is also used to refer to the family as a whole and its domestic life. Coen's analysis concentrates in particular on the role played by the rustic idyll they constructed for themselves at Brunnwinkl on the Wolfgangsee. She proposes the bourgeois *Sommerfrische* as the cradle of a distinctly Austrian approach to science and scientific experimentation, conditioned by the Alps and a free-and-easy holiday atmosphere. This emphasis enables her to reassess the contribution of the family's women to its scientific standing. Marie Exner von Frisch, also the offspring of Franz Exner, founded and planned Brunnwinkl in the 1880s; another guiding spirit was Emilie Exner, writer and wife of the physiologist Sigmund. Quotations from Emilie Exner's fascinating unpublished correspondence with Marie von Ebner-Eschenbach provide some of the most vivid insights into the family's doings throughout the book.

In the 1890s, the physiologist Sigmund Exner described causal thinking as a 'mental habit' that he hoped would be overcome by evolution (p. 15). Coen traces the implications of this basic premise in her accounts of experiments in colour theory, molecular physics, animal behaviour and statistical meteorology, just some of the fields in which Exners made pioneering advances. The scientific detail is mostly accessible to the non-specialist, and the implications of anti-determinism as a stance are examined in many related and not so obviously related spheres. The volume is particularly illuminating on how the natural sciences were understood as a political and social tool in late-nineteenth-century Austria. Following studies such as Werner Michler's *Darwinismus und Literatur* (Vienna, 1999), Coen provides another convincing layer of evidence that the dominant liberal current saw the natural sciences not primarily as utilitarian disciplines but as an integral part of a humanistic world-view.

The advantages, but also the dilemmas, of using a family history to comment on the development of Austrian liberalism become especially clear in the volume's brief concluding chapter, 'A Family's Legacy' (pp. 333–52). The family's German nationalist and elitist sentiments took an ugly turn in the case of several of Franz Exner's grandchildren, who welcomed the *Anschluss* in 1938 (the physicist Robert Exner for example, but also Marie's son, Karl von Frisch). In earlier chapters, Coen emphasizes the Exners' support for universalism in education; the nationalist and class-bound assumptions that underlay this ideal in practice would perhaps have merited closer examination throughout. In her otherwise thorough analysis of the Exners' self-appointed models of 'farmer' and 'hunter' in their research, for example, Coen does not mention the potentially reactionary nature of these models except in passing. However, her conclusion tackles these issues head-on, and by leaving the family's Nazi skeletons in the closet until the very end, she also avoids any suggestion of teleology.

Coen is sensitive throughout to the mixed nature of her sources. She sets out to question the boundaries conventionally drawn in the history of science between the private and public spheres, and marshals an impressive array of published and unpublished documentation to do so. One minor criticism must nevertheless be left to stand: quotations are entirely in English, and only rarely is the German supplied for individual concepts. Given that the scientific theories discussed here are complex, and the educational theories politically and culturally loaded, a little more original text would have been very helpful.

LUDWIG BOLTZMANN INSTITUT FÜR GESCHICHTE UND THEORIE DER BIOGRAPHIE,
VIENNA   DEBORAH HOLMES

Wien und die jüdische Erfahrung 1900–1938. Akkulturation — Antisemitismus — Zionismus. Ed. by FRANK STERN and BARBARA EICHINGER. Vienna, Cologne and Weimar: Böhlau. 2009. xxv + 529 pp. €49. ISBN 978-3-205-78317-6.

In the spring of 1946, the former Austrian Socialist Fritz Flesch, now settled in Detroit, sat down to write a commentary on the events of February 1934 and plead with the Austrian Socialists. 'Die Zeit der agnostischen Juden ist in der Politik der Partei vorbei', he argued, and the Socialists needed to find a way to gain Catholic support. In the US there was such a thing as liberal Catholicism, Flesch explained. In fact, he had only just spoken to a Catholic academic who expressed his amazement 'dass es sogar unter Katholiken Antisemiten gibt'. 'Ich sagte ihm,' Flesch wrote, 'er soll nach Wien kommen und den dortigen Katholiken das sagen, die wuerden sich wundern, dass es in Amerika Katholiken gibt, die keine Antisemiten sind' (IISG Amsterdam, Collection Fritz Flesch, Folder 29).

Were one to take seriously the stark claims to originality propounded by the editors of the volume under review, one would have to assume that a similar chasm still gapes between the rich Anglophone historiography dealing with Austrian and (especially) Viennese Jewry and the horizon of the likely (Austrian) readership of this (for the most part) German-language collection. It seeks to emancipate Viennese Jewish history and culture proper from the history of antisemitism and contribute to a perception of Vienna 'nicht nur als "Hauptstadt des Antisemitismus" [...], sondern auch als ein kulturelles, politisches, soziales und wirtschaftliches Zentrum österreichisch-jüdischer Akkulturation und Integration' (p. xxiv).

Even by the standards of an edited collection, the contributions in this volume are unusually disparate and uneven, both in their quality and in terms of the audience at which they seem to be pitched. They range from the introductory to the highly specialized and include a significant number of largely antiquarian pieces that seem material-driven rather than argument-driven and/or read like over-long encyclopaedia entries. The overall impression is hardly aided by the all-too-conventional and, for the most part, purely ornamental use of illustrations. Virtually no effort is made to clarify how the illustrations tie in with the discussion in the text, what exactly it is they supposedly illustrate, let alone how they do so. Alas, this is hardly unusual but it is all the more irritating in a book that makes so much of the centrality of cultural studies for an understanding of Jewish life and culture and Jewish/non-Jewish relations.

Steven Beller and Eleonore Lappin have provided solid and readable introductory discussions of Jewish life and Jewish/non-Jewish relations in interwar Vienna that offer few surprises. Albert Lichtblau's chapter charting the development of antisemitism in Vienna until 1938 demonstrates an outstanding ability to present an introductory account that is both succinct and accessible yet also conceptually acute and crisp. Gabriele Anderl's discussion of Zionism adds another solid and elegantly crafted survey, although the way in which she utilizes individual recollections on a par with other sources without offering any sort of methodological reflection is perhaps slightly troubling.

Among the more specialized contributions I would recommend Sander Gilman's reworking of two earlier articles on Kraus, Mahler and Richard Strauss's *Salome*, Bettina Riedmann's piece on Schnitzler, Michael Miller's discussion of Hungarian Jewish students in interwar Vienna, and Hanno Loewy's account of Béla Balázs's sojourn in Vienna between 1920 and 1926. Klaus Hödl's methodological piece on the uses of the concept of performativity for the study of Jewish identity formation and Jewish/non-Jewish relations is thought-provoking and exemplary in its clarity. Wolfgang Müller-Funk reflects on the divergent Jewish identities of Soma Morgenstern and Joseph Roth, and Siegfried Mattl offers a perceptive discussion of the 'weak' Zionism of Felix Salten (think 'Bambi'!). Werner Hanak's comparative discussion, '*Frau Breier aus Gaya* meets *The Jazz Singer*', is not only intriguing and thoughtful but also enormous fun to read. Yet all this makes up little more than a third of what is a fairly hefty tome, and much as individual scholars will doubtless be able to mine the remaining contributions for information on specific issues, the volume as a whole is not a success.

THE CENTRE FOR THE STUDY OF JEWISH-CHRISTIAN RELATIONS, CAMBRIDGE
LARS FISCHER

Pour une autre vision de l'histoire littéraire et théâtrale. Karl Kraus lecteur de Johann Nestroy. By MARC LACHENY. Paris: Presses Sorbonne Nouvelle. 2008. 328 pp. €23. ISBN 978-2-87854-436-7.

In Nestroy, Karl Kraus championed a precursor of his own linguistic satire who was underrated in the context of the traditional canon. Kraus's key role in the resurgence of interest in Nestroy is of continuing interest and importance because of the joint influence they exercised on twentieth-century Austrian literature and theatre, notably on the distinctive preoccupation with language.

The centrality of Nestroy to Kraus's work is subtly brought out on the front cover of Marc Lacheny's book by one of the familiar photographs by Julius Scherb of Kraus's study, which prominently features two framed photographs of Nestroy by Hermann Klee, both dating from 1861, one a studio portrait, the other in costume as Knieriem. Nestroy specialists and Kraus specialists have not, however, established a consensus on the link between the two satirists. Nestroy specialists can no doubt overstate the importance of Nestroy for Kraus, Kraus specialists can assume too readily that Kraus's is the most important voice in our understanding of Nestroy. Lacheny's book, a reworking of his doctoral dissertation, provides a full and impressively balanced account of the interaction between the two. Recognizing that Nestroy frequently functions as the 'motor' of Kraus's creativeness (p. 12), he argues that detailed exploration of Kraus's use of Nestroy leads the reader to the heart of Kraus's satirical strategy. What is particularly unusual in Lacheny's work is that it combines thorough treatment of Kraus's work with sound knowledge both of Nestroy's plays and of up-to-date Nestroy scholarship.

The main part of the book is organized chronologically, following the development of Kraus's reading of Nestroy in four stages. The argument is informed throughout by reception theory, notions of intertextuality and Pierre Bourdieu's concept of 'fields'; but there is no obscure abstract theorizing, and the writing is entirely jargon-free. In his early writings Kraus established the position of Nestroy's language as a standard tool in his polemical criticism of the press and of contemporary theatre, underpinning his attack on the corrupting debilitation of cultural and intellectual life. This first period culminates in an essay of 1901, which Lacheny identifies as a key text, treating under the stylized subtitle 'Herzl versus Nestroy' misinterpretations of Nestroy, notably under inappropriate political criteria. The second stage, in which Kraus developed his polemical critical contrast between Nestroy and Heine, culminates in the landmark lecture 'Nestroy und die Nachwelt' which explores the very nature of satire and which he delivered and published in 1912 to mark the fiftieth anniversary of Nestroy's death.

The longest section in Lacheny's study is the one concentrating on the years 1912–26. It is in this period that Kraus coined his description of Nestroy as 'der im Sprachwitz tiefste, bis zur Lyrik unerbittlichste satirische Denker Deutschlands'. The section centres on Kraus's regular performances of Nestroy in his public readings, his published adaptations of two plays, and the many additional stanzas he composed updating Nestroy's satirical songs (*Couplets*). The fourth section covers the final years of Kraus's life (1926–36). The only previous monograph, *Karl Kraus und Nestroy. Kritik und Verarbeitung* by Helmut Rössler (Stuttgart, 1981), presented Nestroy's role in Kraus's work as being essentially taken over at this stage by Offenbach; in fact, as Lacheny shows, Nestroy remained a constant and much invoked presence to the last.

Lacheny has succeeded in reducing an exhaustively documented dissertation of 724 pages to a lucidly written book of less than half the length, a splendid example of how revising and paring an academic thesis can benefit book publication. The result is both thorough and admirably readable, with all quotations given in the original Geman. Lacheny has considerably shortened the bibliography (the dissertation, now lodged in the library of the Sorbonne Nouvelle [Paris III], has a voluminous bibliography that could serve as a useful reference source). He has added as an appendix a 'glossary' of names, a last-minute addition designed as an aid for the general reader (signs of haste here in unreliable details are a small blemish in an excellent book); and there are useful indexes.

In a convincing conclusion, Lacheny sums up how Kraus's revaluation drew on a cultural reassessment of Nestroy in the context of several 'fields', Nestroy being 'not just a barb but one of the very bases of Kraus's satire' (p. 277). He spells out that Nestroy scholarship is no longer tied to Kraus's interpretation; to accord the comedy of language priority over stage production is, he observes, to labour an obsolete distinction. One might add that while Kraus's advocacy was decisive in driving the 'Nestroy renascence' of the early twentieth century and remains an inspiring voice, the total novelty of his insight should not be overestimated; the sharpness of Nestroy's satire and the power of the language through which he worked were not lost on his contemporaries. 'Nestroy's greatness', as Lacheny reminds us, is 'based on the indissoluble unity of the writer and the man of the theatre' (p. 279). A corollary of this defence of his theatrical vitality — spelt out in the blurb on the back cover of the book — is the potential for further translations and productions of Nestroy in France, the country from which, after all, he drew so many of his sources.

UNIVERSITY OF EXETER   W. E. YATES

Aus großer Nähe. Karl Kraus in Berichten von Weggefährten und Widersachern. Ed. by FRIEDRICH PFÄFFLIN. (Bibliothek Janowitz 16). Göttingen: Wallstein. 2008. 480 pp. €39,90 [D], €41,10 [A]. ISBN 978–3–8353–0304–1.

Friedrich Pfäfflin, for many years inspirational as curator of exhibitions of the treasures of the Schiller-Nationalmuseum in Marbach, has for just as long been the prime mover in assembling invaluable biographical material on Karl Kraus from the writer's fragmented archive. The monumental revised and enlarged edition of the *Briefe an Sidonie Nádherný von Borutin 1913–1936* (Göttingen, 2005) is not the least of his labours of love that have been devoted to documenting the writer's network of personal friendships (unknown to readers of *Die Fackel*; see my review 'Love, Distance, Bereavement: New Sources for Karl Kraus's Relationships' in *Austrian Studies*, 11, 196–202) and his attachment to the idyllic landscape of the Nádherný family's estate, Janowitz in Bohemia, which is also commemorated in the series name for these compilations and bibliophile editions. The new project partly draws upon these and other recent editions of correspondence. Documents included in the 1999 Marbach exhibition catalogue, *Karl Kraus*, co-edited by Pfäfflin and Eva Dambacher, also revealed more of the history of *Die Fackel* and Kraus's literary relations. (See their compilation *Der 'Fackel'-Lauf*, [Marbach a. N., 1999] and Pfäfflin's *Vom Verglühen der 'Fackel'. Karl Kraus und sein Verlag, 1930–1936* [Warmbronn, 2004]; also *Zwischen Jüngstem Tag und Weltgericht* [Göttingen, 2007], his new edition of Kraus's correspondence with the publisher Kurt Wolff).

Aus großer Nähe assembles some 360 extracts from a vast range of sources, both known and previously unpublished (like Franz Werfel's dissection of Kraus in a letter to Willy Haas from 1916). Of the many eye-witness accounts, anecdotes and memoirs (such as Berthold Viertel's fine portrait) some are familiar, others are from quite remote sources, and their juxtaposition creates a multi-faceted mosaic of the man, his process of working, his impact and his varied reception. The first of the thematic chapters is rather diffuse, comprising sketches of the personality, entitled (after an early remark of Alma Mahler-Werfel's) 'Der Kraus hat was' — but thereafter the material is organized solidly in biographically chronological sequence, reflecting his youth, his encounters with *Jung Wien* and Zionism, the founding of *Die Fackel*, his circle of contributors and literary admirers, and also more sceptical responses (Musil, Manès Sperber, Ernst Gombrich) and apostasies. The selection traces the extension of Kraus's influence beyond Vienna to Munich (the Albert Langen Verlag and *Simplicissimus*), Prague (Werfel, Haas and Kafka), Innsbruck (Ludwig von Ficker's *Der Brenner*) and Berlin (Herwarth Walden's *Der Sturm* and Expressionist circles; later Brecht, the Theater am Schiffbauerdamm and Walter Benjamin). Particular attention is paid to the impact of his brilliant public readings on audiences across Germany and Central Europe and to the impact of his courageous stand against wartime butchery and propaganda on a new generation of readers and a new working-class audience — before dispute with the Social Democratic leadership during the 1920s was followed by his allegiance to Dollfuss in the Civil War of February 1934, for him a last resort to save Austria from National Socialism. This decision cost him most of his support, both working-class and intellectual.

The shadow cast by Kraus's authority over dissenters and the shrillness of some opponents are documented. Pfäfflin samples some of their verbal mockery of Kraus, but notes that polemicists like Albert Ehrenstein and Robert Müller retrospectively modified their views of him. (For more on hostile polemics see *Die Belagerung der Urteilsmauer. Karl Kraus im Zerrspiegel seiner Feinde*, ed. by Franz Schuh and Juliane Vogel [Vienna, 1986].) The chronological line drawn by Pfäfflin is complemented by further facets of Kraus's activity, whether only in glimpses of his use of legal processes or his involvement in avant-garde theatre production, or, more substantially, his virtuoso performances of a repertoire of spoken classics, his 'Theater der Dichtung'. While *Dritte Walpurgisnacht*, his *magnum opus* from 1933, remained unpublished until after the war, we learn how his readings of *Macbeth* suggestively diagnosed the Nazi terror. The despairing and accusatory responses to his perceived silence and to his reaction to 1934 are well represented (for example, Canetti's furious letter to his brother). Elsewhere we find passing references to

Kokoschka's portraits of him and to Franz Marc, but the American 'Blue Rider', Albert Bloch, is a key figure, a sensitive Kraus reader who became an important contact for the community of friends after the satirist's death. New details emerge of the disarray of his devotees over his testament, of their failed plans to continue *Die Fackel* posthumously, and of the salvaging and fragmentation of his archive after the *Anschluss*.

'Der stets Bewaffnete beeindruckt auch unbewaffnet' [Always armed, but even unarmed he is disarming], says the editor. The anecdotes about lifestyle and daily routine form a superficially contradictory picture — some claim Kraus as a creature of the coffee-house (whether affable or domineering), others know a warm private man far from that scene, anything but the misanthropic 'Fackelkraus'. (There is a chapter on his love of nature and animals, but also Ficker's sardonic comparison of his friend's intellect to a 'flesh-eating plant'.) Of the essays and letters of Kraus's life-long companion, Helene Kann, her informative testimony to his deep anxieties after 1933 and her moving record of his last days are of particular value. Another close friend who figures briefly is Mary Gräfin Dobrženský (see Edward Timms, *Karl Kraus. Apocalyptic Satirist*, volume 2), who, we learn, assisted Thomas Theodor Heine's flight into exile in 1933 — just as Kraus assisted Brecht's (a fact recorded obliquely in Lothar Wolf's derogatory 'report' to the Central Committee of the German Communist Party). It is some achievement to have focused such very diverse testimonies in such a comprehensive picture of key issues, not just of 'Karl Kraus privat'. The annotations and appendices are meticulous. The subjectivity of some contemporaries is laconically corrected, as when Ehrenstein claims the initiative for Kraus's poetry volumes. The note on the phrase 'Der Kaiser schaut zu' [The Emperor is watching] as symptomatic of Austrian mentalities is worthy of inclusion in the Austrian Academy of Science's *Wörterbuch der 'Fackel'*. (Minor errors include 'Rudolf Lothar', p. 116, for 'Ernst Lothar', and 'Schiller', p. 175, for 'Schüller'.) Friedrich Pfäfflin's biographical source-book forms an invaluable corpus that complements that public 'diary of the epoch', as he calls *Die Fackel* — a welcome addition to the libraries of both Kraus scholars and readers interested in twentieth-century literary relations and literary politics.

TRINITY COLLEGE DUBLIN   GILBERT J. CARR

Rainer Maria Rilke / Norbert von Hellingrath. Briefe und Dokumente. Ed. by KLAUS E. BOHNENKAMP. (Castrum Peregrini new series 1). Göttingen: Wallstein. 2008. 241 pp. €29,90. ISBN 978-3-8353-00363-8.

Rainer Maria Rilke first met the literary scholar Norbert von Hellingrath, thirteen years his junior, at the salon of Hugo and Elsa Bruckmann, Hellingrath's uncle and aunt, in Munich in 1910. The encounter led to a friendship, developed through occasional meetings and sporadic correspondence, and maintained until Hellingrath's death at Verdun in December 1916. Hellingrath's achievement as a scholar was the discovery of Hölderlin and his work: when he first met Rilke, he had recently been awarded his doctorate for a thesis on Hölderlin's Pindar translations, and by 1916 he had completed three volumes of a pioneering complete edition of the poet's works. Here lies the significance of Hellingrath for Rilke's development as a poet, for the acquaintance with Hellingrath's scholarship inspired in Rilke an intense interest in Hölderlin's life and works in the years leading up to the First World War, and Hölderlin remained one of the most important influences on Rilke's poetry and poetics up to the completion of the *Duineser Elegien* in 1922.

Klaus E. Bohnenkamp's important edition of the correspondence between Rilke and Hellingrath will be of interest to Rilke scholars above all for its documentation of the poet's engagement with Hölderlin, as mediated by Hellingrath. We can trace the development of this interest through the sixteen letters which make up the correspondence, published here in full for the first time. In May 1911 Hellingrath sent Rilke Hölderlin's translation of and commentary on the Pindar fragment, 'Das Belebende', to help him with his translation of Maurice Guérin's 'Le Centaure'; Rilke gratefully acknowledged this help, writing to Hellingrath on 23 January 1912, 'Mich würde es freuen, Ihnen [...] zu erinnern, dass Sie an der Entstehung dieser Übertragung nicht ohne einige Schuld sind' (p. 65). By July 1914 Rilke had read the first two published volumes of Hellingrath's Hölderlin edition 'mit besonderer Bewegung und Hingabe' and was eager to acquire the latest volume, writing to him — with an enthusiasm rarely found in his comments on other poets — that '[Hölderlins] Einfluss auf mich ist groß und großmüthig wie nur der des Reichsten und innerlich Mächtigsten es sein kann' (p. 97). As he reported in a letter to Hellingrath's mother, Marie, in October 1914, reading volume IV of Hellingrath's edition had provided the inspiration for the poem 'An Hölderlin' (p. 115). In February 1915 Rilke attended Hellingrath's lecture, delivered in aid of the war effort, on the topic of Hölderlin's madness, subsequently commenting on it enthusiastically to a variety of correspondents.

While Hölderlin was at the heart of Rilke's friendship with Hellingrath, Bohnenkamp's edition offers so much more than just a documentation of his growing interest in the poet. The two correspondents share thoughts on a variety of other subjects, most notably their impressions of Paris, a city which presented both men with difficulties, and their responses to the outbreak and development of the war. Besides the relatively sparse correspondence with Hellingrath himself, the volume also contains Rilke's correspondence with his mother and, after Hellingrath's death, with his fiancée, Imma von Ehrenfels. The largest part of the work, however, is made up by the editor's explanatory texts and footnotes. The gaps between letters are filled in by accounts of the two men's meetings and independent activities. Far from distracting the reader from the correspondence itself, this documentation enables the latter to be understood in context, as one element in a relationship which, like almost all human relationships, can never be fully captured by the epistolary traces it has left. The extensive and meticulously researched footnotes add to the value of the volume in other ways too. We gain a fuller picture of Hellingrath's life beyond his friendship with Rilke, the only context in which he now tends to be remembered. Bohnenkamp's documentation of his other social and academic contacts provides valuable insights into the German and French academic establishments at the beginning of the twentieth century, and cultural and scholarly networks in Munich — in particular, the George circle, with whom Hellingrath was associated. The volume also provides a wealth of detail concerning Rilke's biography and connections. Bohnenkamp's painstaking research using primary sources results in new evidence and, quite frequently, in the revision of assumptions made in the critical literature hitherto. The sheer detail of the documentation makes this volume a gift for scholars: every reference, every name, every event is explained in full and set in relation to other relevant sources; full details of the physical appearance and location of each of the letters reproduced are provided. In short, this is a volume that has been designed to facilitate further scholarly work on this chapter in literary history. It has also been beautifully produced, incorporating photographs of Rilke, Hellingrath and selected manuscripts, and using different fonts for the letters, footnotes and commentary text to make what could have seemed like an overwhelming amount of information entirely reader-friendly. With this volume Bohnenkamp has set new standards for the scholarly editing of Rilke's correspondence.

UNIVERSITY OF EXETER   HELEN BRIDGE

Stimmen zur Unterhaltung. Operette und Revue in der publizistischen Debatte (1906–1933). Ed. by MARION LINHARDT. (Quodlibet 9). Vienna: Lehner. 2009. 336 pp. €24,90. ISBN 978-3-901749-76-6.

Marion Linhardt's *Habilitationsschrift*, published in 2006 under the title *Residenzstadt und Metropole. Zu einer kulturellen Topographie des Wiener Unterhaltungstheaters (1858–1918)*, is a landmark in Viennese theatre history, exploring in meticulous detail the seemingly irresistible rise of operetta, which by the turn of the twentieth century had become the dominant form of popular, commercial entertainment in the Austrian capital. The texts assembled in the current volume take up the story in the first third of the twentieth century, presenting the journalistic debates engendered by what was increasingly perceived as the decline of operetta, superseded in the inter-war period by visually spectacular American-style revues that combined music, dance and variety acts. That these could be infused with both eroticism and striking local colour is highlighted by the cover illustration, taken from the Viennese revue *Alles aus Liebe* (1927), which features a bare-armed female performer in costume as St Stephen's Cathedral.

Stimmen zur Unterhaltung comprises some fifty-one texts, authored by journalists, musicologists, composers, librettists, directors and other theatrical practitioners, together with twenty-six pages of introduction and an index of names and works. Despite the choice of cover illustration, the focus is not exclusively Viennese, but the city features strongly, having continued throughout the inter-war period to exert decisive influence on the production and reception of operettas, even if the works themselves had broader Central European and transatlantic appeal. All originally published in German-language journals, newspapers and magazines, the texts vary considerably in their nature, scope and intended audience. Brief responses to questionnaires and articles from newspapers such as the *Neues Wiener Journal* and *Berliner Lokal-Anzeiger* sit alongside more substantial reflections that originally appeared in specialist publications such as *Die Scene* or the *Musikblätter des Anbruch*. The list of authors includes some familiar names — Karl Kraus, Felix Salten, David Josef Bach, Ernst Křenek, Emmerich Kálmán, Oscar Straus, Gustav Charlé, Louis Treumann and Arthur Kahane — but also many who will be known only to specialists and a few for whom Linhardt can provide only incomplete biographical data.

The volume's point of departure is Lehár's *Die lustige Witwe* (1905), reviewed under the title 'Die neue Operette' (pp. 39–45) by Salten, who immediately recognized its originality and international appeal. The first few articles sample responses to the 'Silver Era' of Viennese operetta, registering parallels with American musical theatre and highlighting the impact of *Vertrustung*, whereby impresarios would secure exclusive rights to publish and produce the work of particular composers, thus exerting enormous influence on the repertoire. Although this system had many drawbacks, interviews with Kálmán, Straus and Victor Hollaender show that, especially pre-1914, successful composers enjoyed glamorous, globetrotting lifestyles.

Articles bemoaning the eroticization of operetta, the artistic decline of the genre and its corrupting influence on public morality are most strongly represented during and in the immediate aftermath of the First World War. Under the title 'Die Operettenseuche' the later cultural editor of the *Völkischer Beobachter*, Josef Stolzing, attributes its continued popularity to 'eine krankhafte Massenpsychose' (p. 125), while several commentators question whether operetta has any place in programmes of cultural education sponsored by the new democratic republics.

The 1920s indeed see profound changes in the entertainment sector, as commercial pressures become ever more urgent, American influence intensifies, theatres face growing competition from film and radio, and audiences become more insistent in their demand for escapist fare. From mid-decade on, the proliferation of American-style revues, with jazz-inspired music and a strong emphasis on displaying the female form, not least in high-kicking chorus lines, is intensively debated. While respondents to an opinion poll organized by the conservative Bühnenvolksbund are predictably scathing, a Viennese survey asking 'Operette oder Revue?' finds considerable enthusiasm for the latter, which is almost universally recognized as emblematically modern: 'Wie das Leben dieser Zeit ist die Revue ein Durcheinander von Nummern, eine chaotische Mannigfaltigkeit, die sich gegen jede Einheit sträubt' (Erik Reger, 1925, p. 166). This modernity was not, however, welcomed by the NSDAP, and the final text in the collection appeared in 1933.

Stimmen zur Unterhaltung is flawlessly produced, and the introduction provides an excellent framework within which to read the articles themselves. In making them available, Marion Linhardt has done a service to the scholarly community.

UNIVERSITY COLLEGE LONDON   JUDITH BENISTON

Joseph Roth. Eine Biographie. By WILHELM VON STERNBURG. Cologne: Kiepenheuer & Witsch. 2009. 560 pp. €22,95. ISBN 978–3462055559.

Joseph Roth. Im Exil in Paris 1933 bis 1939. By HEINZ LUNZER. (*Zirkular* Sondernummer 68). Vienna: Dokumentationsstelle für neuere österreichische Literatur. 2008. 224 pp. €16. ISBN 978-3-900-467-68-5.

The two volumes under review here can only sensibly be considered with reference to a publication that is now thirty-five years old but remains indispensible to researchers working on Joseph Roth: David Bronsen's biography of Roth, first published by Kiepenheuer & Witsch in 1974. It is not an exaggeration to describe this as a landmark contribution to scholarship. Bronsen's extraordinary achievement was to penetrate decades of misinformation and misunderstandings about the life and work of Roth, to which the author himself — Bronsen labelled him a 'mythomaniac' — had energetically contributed, and whose final years and death in exile, in 1939, had further complicated the task facing any would-be biographer. Bronsen spent more than a decade on his project, and was able to interview almost every remaining family member, friend and acquaintance of the famously gregarious Roth, travelling extensively around Europe and America to do so. By the early 1970s Roth's work as a novelist, and as an extraordinarily prolific and original journalistic voice, was gradually being rediscovered and appreciated again after a period of neglect in the post-war years; the resultant biography, largely as a result of the use to which he put the first-hand accounts, presented for the first time a compelling portrait of Roth the human being and a narrative that made some sense of a chaotic and troubled existence. Writing in the 1970s Bronsen could not necessarily assume the acquaintance of his readership with the full extent of Roth's achievements as a writer — he was still chiefly remembered only for *Radetzkymarsch* — and the mammoth first edition was republished in 1993 in a sensibly abridged version that took account, amongst other things, of the republication, in the intervening period, of the greater part of Roth's output as a writer. This edition has, however, been out of print for a number of years, and readers interested in Roth's life as well as his work have had to rely on the handsome *Leben und Werk in Bildern* compiled by Heinz Lunzer and Victoria Lunzer-Talos (Kiepenheuer & Witsch, 1994; reissued in paperback in 2009). 2009 is the seventieth anniversary of Roth's death and has seen commemorative events, conferences, exhibitions and publications in various countries. With both popular and scholarly interest in Roth's work at something of a high water mark, Kiepenheuer & Witsch, the publisher of Roth's work (a relationship dating back to Roth's contract and personal friendship with Gustav Kiepenheuer in the early 1930s), clearly feels that the time is right for a new biography.

Whereas Bronsen's meticulous approach reflected his academic training (he was Professor of German at St Louis University) and the expectations of a largely scholarly readership, the author of this new biography, Wilhelm von Sternburg — not an academic Roth specialist but a journalist and professional biographer — is clearly addressing a broader readership. The biography does not claim to have uncovered much (if any) new information about Roth's life and work — needless to say the sort of interviews conducted by Bronsen in the 1950s and 1960s are no longer possible — but instead sets out to synthesize the available data in a readable, clear narrative, and to offer appropriate contextual information on the numerous stations in Roth's life and career as he moves from Galician childhood and student years in Vienna to publishing success in Weimar Germany, travels around Europe, and the final years of exile in France and Holland. Sternburg writes well and the volume is, judged as a whole and with the intended readership in mind, a success. Perhaps mindful of the status of Bronsen's biography and the need to mark out his own approach if he is not to be accused of redundantly treading in another's footsteps, Sternburg makes sparing use of Bronsen's interviews, which he recorded in transcriptions and notes that are now lodged with the rest of the late researcher's *Nachlass* in the Dokumentationsstelle für neuere österreichische Literatur in Vienna. Rather defensively, after quoting from one of Bronsen's interviews, Sternburg asserts: 'Solche, Jahrzehnte später gemachte Äußerungen sind zweifellos interessant, aber auch mit Zurückhaltung zu bewerten. Menschen aus seiner Jugendzeit, die sich nach dem Zweiten Weltkrieg über ihre frühen Begegnungen mit Roth äußern, tun dies schon mit dem Wissen, dass sie über einen inzwischen berühmt gewordenen Schriftsteller urteilen' (p. 113). One might object here that at the point when Bronsen was conducting his interviews Roth had fallen once again into relative obscurity and was by no means truly 'famous'; but even given the basic validity of the note of caution that Sternburg strikes here it is still, at least to this reviewer, incomprehensible that there is no proper introduction to this volume acknowledging Bronsen's achievement, making clear Sternburg's own methodology, and perhaps explaining why a new biography is necessary at all.

The long-time director of the Dokumentationsstelle, Heinz Lunzer, together with his wife Victoria Lunzer-Talos, have, after Bronsen, done more than anyone else to publicize Joseph Roth's work and, in particular, to deepen our understanding of the context in which it was produced. Lunzer's latest volume, *Joseph Roth im Exil in Paris*, stands in marked contrast to Sternburg's biography, for, far from marginalizing and downplaying the significance of Bronsen's interviews and correspondence with contemporaries of Joseph Roth, the volume uses them, alongside the biographical research conducted for a never-completed dissertation by Senta Zeidler during the 1950s, as the springboard for a volume that offers new depth of insight into, and helps to bring to life, the period of exile that concluded Roth's short life. The meticulously documented volume reproduces the transcriptions of some of the most significant and revealing interviews conducted by Bronsen, including those with Roth's female companions Andrea Manga Bell and the novelist Irmgard Keun, along with his accompanying notes and glosses (which make very clear that Bronsen himself was very aware of the limitations of memory and of this type of oral history); it includes previously unpublished letters to and from Roth, as well as correspondence relating to Bronsen's and Zeidler's research (many letters are reproduced in accompanying photographs); and presents numerous, fascinating documents of the period of exile, such as facsimile reproductions of newspaper reports, documents relating to the activities of the exile presses, countless unfamiliar photographs of Roth and contemporaries, and many of the sketches and caricatures of Roth produced by Bill Spira, only a handful of which have accompanied previous publications. Spira's drawings are often signed by Roth with scurrilous, self-mocking comments such as this observation, accompanying a 1938 sketch of Roth with the patrician moustache he cultivated towards the end of his life: 'Nietzsche hatte einen, Rainer Maria Rilke hatte ihn, ich bin der letzte Erbe dieses Schnurrbarts' (p. 102). The pleasure and lasting value of this volume is to be found in such little details. Admittedly, it has a rather patchwork character that reflects the concept of the exhibitions that some of the material documented has, under Lunzer's curatorship, contributed to during in 2008 and 2009 (exhibitions in Vienna, Ljubljana and Paris), but this is not really a criticism, for this is a volume that can be dipped into and read out of sequence if a reader so wishes.

The publications under review here, then, appeal to slightly different constituencies and will certainly please these readers. Scholars and specialists will, needless to say, find more in Lunzer's volume but the publication of such a readable, and often insightful new biography, even if it cannot be said to 'replace' Bronsen's, is also something to be celebrated. Both reflect and play a role in the continued renaissance of Roth not only as an Austrian author but, as the destinations of Lunzer's exhibitions indicate, as a major figure in modern European literature.

ROYAL HOLLOWAY, UNIVERSITY OF LONDON   JON HUGHES

Joseph Roth's March into History. From the Early Novels to 'Radetzkymarsch' and 'Die Kapuzinergruft'. By KATI TONKIN. Rochester, NY: Camden House. 2008. 236 pp. £40. ISBN 9781571133892.

As point of departure to her study, Kati Tonkin questions the widely held assumption that Joseph Roth's works can be divided into an early 'socialist' and a later 'monarchist' phase. She especially challenges the view that Roth's novels of the 1930s present a nostalgic picture of a Habsburg Empire as he would have liked it to have been — an escapist 'backward-turned utopia', as Magris and others have called it. Tonkin argues that this is not the case, reading Roth's novels as very political attempts to address the present while grasping reasons for the failure of the Empire. In the first chapter, she refutes the theory that Roth's works are fruits of an ongoing identity crisis that ought to explain his 'metamorphosis from socialist to monarchist' (p. 17). She situates 'his own sense of doubleness [sic] and ambivalence as an Eastern Jew' (p. 26) within the wider parameters of the interwar era, a time when uncertainty about identity was a problem shared by many. Identity and ideology make a dangerous combination — Tonkin states that Roth consistently resists the appeal thereof. Using his essay *Juden auf Wanderschaft* as an example, she highlights the polemical intent of the text with its 'deliberately elusive narrative voice' (p. 25), reading it as an implicit rejection by Roth of the stereotypical dichotomy of Eastern and Western Jewry. In the tale of the Jewish clown from Radziwillow, Tonkin recognizes a 'lack of contradiction in the clown's dual loyalty', being assimilated while maintaining a Jewish identity (p. 34). Tonkin recognises parallels drawn between freedom of movement and self-determination, with Roth defending the idea that nationalism inhibits the free expression of individual identity (p. 37). In voicing criticism of Jewish nationalism and Zionism, he is said to reject ethnic nationalism as a doctrine privileging one nation over others and attaching territory to national status. For Tonkin it is Roth's preoccupation with questions of nationalism and identity ascription that finds expression in much of his work, from the early novels to *Radetzkymarsch* and *Die Kapuzinergruft* (p. 37).

Chapter Two demonstrates that the early novels do not support a socialist stand by their author. 'Roth's refusal to succumb in these novels to a simplistic solution in order to achieve some form of literary resolution is an early indication that he would continue to seek the appropriate literary form with which to understand his time in its diversity' (p. 37). Tonkin sees the ethnic nationalist solution rejected (*Das Spinnennetz*) along with the socialist revolution (*Hotel Savoy*). She argues that Roth turns his attention to the question of individual responsibility for the perpetuation of social injustice (*Die Rebellion*), and in doing so once again rejects absolutist forms of thinking. Tonkin questions labels such as 'socialist' with regard to Roth (p. 47) and sees his motivation in the early novels in the desire 'to understand and reveal the sources of contemporary social and political problems, not to provide solutions' (p. 91). The distinct lack of optimism in Roth's first three novels, as well as their literary style, is indicative 'of his struggle at this stage in his career as a novelist to find a form that would give adequate expression to an exploration of the problems of contemporary Central Europe' (p. 92). Thus after three further novels which Tonkin refers to as belonging to a 'transitional period' (p. 92), Roth turns to the historical novel: 'Roth has realized that it is not possible to make sense of the present without writing about the past, and it is for this reason, not in order to take flight from reality, that he turns to the portrayal of the Habsburg Empire in *Radetzkymarsch*' (p. 92). After a brief discussion of the genre in the third chapter, Tonkin classifies Roth's masterpiece as a historical novel conforming to the criteria proposed by Lukács. In her view, Roth's perception has not changed dramatically: 'To an extent previously unrecognized, Roth's concern with the problems of the post-Habsburg order, which was so clear in his early novels, remains in *Radetzkymarsch* and *Die Kapuzinergruft*. In both novels he looks back to the Habsburg Empire in an effort to understand the roots of contemporary problems' (p. 111).

Tonkin's interpretation of *Radetzkymarsch* shows how the Habsburg 'myth' is uncovered through contrasts between appearance and reality: 'The discrepancy between what is said, written, or believed and what is true is not restricted to the depiction of historical events in school readers but extends throughout society and manifests in the gap between professed morality or codes of behaviour and what actually happens behind closed doors' (p. 115). She argues convincingly that this discrepancy triggers the crisis of Carl Joseph, who falls prey to the myth of the Hero and of Austria, just as Max Demant similarly falls prey to anachronistic ideals. In Tonkin's view, Roth suggests critically that 'an excessive, almost pathological orientation toward the past' prevented a response to changed circumstances and the realization that Austria needed to adapt (p. 152). Similarly, Tonkin tells us, he regards a proper examination of the relationship between past and present as vital to the understanding of what ails his society — an aspect he feels is being disregarded by his contemporaries and which he reiterates in Die Kapuzinergruft. 'This, rather than nostalgia for better times, is the implication of his criticism [...] and it is this that makes Radetzkymarsch a historical novel rather than a backward-turned utopia' (p. 153). Tonkin's viewpoints are not altogether new but she delivers clear, perspicacious examples in a strong argument. The final chapter is dedicated to Die Kapuzinergruft or, as Tonkin puts it, to the confrontation with the past through the extension of 'the dialogue between past and present begun in Radetzkymarsch' (p. 173). Here Tonkin neatly closes the circle opened in the first chapter: Heimat and identity are not found in a place of physical borders and ideology; 'Roth exposes the unreality of this experience [the search of the fatherland] in the serial loss of Heimat Franz Ferdinand narrates' (p. 190). For Tonkin this proves that 'it is not Roth who has been searching vainly for his fatherland in the lost world of the Habsburg monarchy but his narrator' (p. 191).

Tonkin's lucid book is a must-read for anyone interested in Roth but also for readers wanting to learn about the political and socio-cultural environment of the times and places he lived in.

UNIVERSITY OF STELLENBOSCH   ISABEL DOS SANTOS

Gina Kaus. Schriftstellerin und Öffentlichkeit. Zur Stellung einer Schriftstellerin in der literarischen Öffentlichkeit der Zwischenkriegszeit in Österreich und Deutschland. By HILDEGARD ATZINGER. Frankfurt a. M.: Lang. 2008. 309 pp. €51,50. ISBN 978–3631577875.

Gina Kaus, born in Vienna in 1893, was a celebrated member of the interwar literary scenes in both Vienna and Berlin and a best-selling novelist often (and mostly favourably) compared to Vicki Baum. Her career abruptly finished when her books were banned under Nazi rule, and although she was able to establish herself successfully as a script writer in American exile, the memory of her work in Austria and Germany soon all but faded. Since the 1970s, however, academic interest in her work has been rising again. This initially occurred in the context of the study of exile writing, and since the publication of Kaus's memoirs and the re-edition of some of her novels by Ullstein in the early 1990s, critical attention has extended to include her prose and journalistic work of the interwar period. Kaus has come to be regarded not only as a best-selling author and exile writer but also as one of the most important female German-language writers of the interwar period.

Hildegard Atzinger's monograph stands in this research context. Concentrating on the interwar years, she aims to show 'dass die festgeschriebene Etikettierung Unterhaltungsschriftstellerin zu kurz greift und damit Kaus' Position in der literarischen Öffentlichkeit nicht ausreichend charakterisiert ist' (p. 251). Thus in this socio-literary study Atzinger sets out to analyse Gina Kaus's position (and self-positioning) in the Austrian and German literary movements and markets. In particular, she is interested in the question 'aufgrund welcher inneren

Voraussetzungen (Charaktereigenschaften und Fähigkeiten), Intentionen und Ambitionen und aufgrund welcher äußeren Gegebenheiten und Möglichkeiten (in Literaturbetrieb und kulturellem Markt) sie diese Position in der literarischen Öffentlichkeit der Zwischenkriegszeit einnahm' (pp. 11–12). This dual research interest determines the book's structure. After an introduction to the literary public sphere in Germany and Austria 1918–38, which includes a research survey and a short biographical sketch of Kaus, she divides her study into two main chapters concerned respectively with Kaus's personal and artistic development and her position in the contemporary literary scene.

The study shows very successfully the impressive range and variety of Kaus's sphere of activity. A rounded picture emerges of her not only as a successful novelist, but also as a prolific journalist, a talented salonière and member of the literary café circles in Vienna and Berlin, the editor of a journal on mothering and, connected with this, the organizer of an advice centre on issues of mothering. Added to this are references to her activities in exile as psychological therapist and as an active member of various exile organizations.

Atzinger's focus on Kaus's journalistic work in particular opens up new aspects for the re-evaluation of the writer. She places that work within a well-informed and detailed survey of the contemporary Austrian and German press markets and shows how, finding that there was hardly any opportunity for her to publish in Austrian newspapers and journals, Kaus cleverly and pragmatically positioned herself in the publications market in Berlin, and in particular within the opportunities created by the wide geographical reach of the Ullstein publishing house. Atzinger's description is supported by the exploration of fascinating sources, including, most notably, the correspondence between Gina Kaus and her fellow writer Alice Rühle-Gerstel.

There are, however, a few problems with the book. With its careful — at times over-careful — mapping of the general background (on contemporary writers, the situation of women, literary movements and conditions of literary production) and step-by-step comments on the book's structural progress, it betrays its character as a largely unrevised MA dissertation. The structure is a little clumsy, leading to redundancies and repetitions. Alfred Adler's theories, for instance, are treated both under the heading of 'Selbstverständnis als Frau' (4.2.2) and under that of 'Selbstverständnis als Schriftstellerin' (4.3.2.2.1). More generally, this distinction and that between 'Selbstverständnis' and 'Stellung in literarischer Öffentlichkeit' are not clearly maintained in the text. This may not be a fault of the author, but rather an indication of how closely interlinked these ways of (self-)positioning were for Kaus, thus calling the structural division into question.

There are a number of minor irritations facing the reader. The excessively detailed numbering of sections is distracting (section 5.3.1.2.2 consists of nine lines and one word) and the symbol [!] to mark spelling irregularities in quotations is vastly overused and mostly unnecessary (it appears 13 times in a 23-line quotation on pp. 125–26). It is also unclear why Kaus's works are listed twice in the back of the book: once in the section 'Werküberblick' and again in the bibliography, under the heading 'Texte von Gina Kaus'.

More seriously, the study does not always maintain a high standard of critical rigour. It contains some rather sweeping statements which remain unsupported by Kaus's own texts or other critical writing. Examples of these are the statements that no-one expects any intellectual substance of a woman writer (p. 54) and that modernism in the Berlin of 1923 is synonymous with Americanism (p. 71). Assessments of Kaus's character (e.g. p. 86 or p. 145) and speculations on the reasons for her views (p. 87) are at times presented as facts. This is especially problematic when Atzinger relies for support on Kaus's autobiography, i.e. on the image of herself that Kaus herself has created. A more critical and analytical attitude to the memoirs is required here.

The book would also have benefited from a greater awareness and inclusion of research literature on women's writing and on German-Jewish identities. Kaus's early use of the male pseudonym Andreas Eckbrecht is tentatively explained by reference to her status as adopted daughter of the wealthy financier Josef Kranz, while her texts attack the existing economic and social order. This is convincing up to a point, but it would have been useful here also to consider the context and tradition of female authors writing under (sometimes multiple) male pseudonyms, as described by Barbara Hahn and Susanne Kord among others.

Similarly, it is surprising that a study that sets out to analyse, among other aspects, Kaus's 'Selbstverständnis' does not address her Jewishness. Even if Atzinger's focus is on Kaus's identity as a woman and a writer, the question of her attitude to her Jewish identity cannot justifiably be ignored, in view of the contemporary climate of anti-Semitism and of the subsequent burning of Kaus's books and her enforced exile. Atzinger uses the term 'Jüdin' for Kaus (p. 247), but it is unclear whether this means any more than just the fact she was born to Jewish parents. She states that Kaus placed a remarkably high number of texts in the *Deutsche Zeitung Bohemia*, a journal characterized by its 'großdeutsch-jüdischer Leserkreis', but does not question whether this might be to do with any identification of the writer as Jewish.

Finally, Atzinger remains curiously general about Kaus's writing itself, about the style, the quality and the individuality of her texts. In the section on 'Die neue Sachlichkeit' (4.3.2.2.2), for instance, Kaus's texts are described in terms of their themes and their cool, sober tone, but we have to rely on the author's judgements here as she provides no significant stylistic analysis of individual texts. Close readings of particular text passages would have been helpful to provide the reader with a clear understanding of the nature of Kaus's work and would have allowed Atzinger to attain more convincingly her declared aim of proving that the term 'Unterhaltungsschriftstellerin' does not sufficiently describe Kaus's work.

Despite its shortcomings, this remains a valuable contribution to the study of a writer who has been neglected for far too long. It provides new insights into the breadth of Kaus's work and its position in the literary market both in Vienna and in Berlin.

INSTITUTE OF GERMANIC & ROMANCE STUDIES, UNIVERSITY OF LONDON
GODELA WEISS-SUSSEX

Poetry in a Provisional State. The Austrian Lyric 1945–1955. By ANTHONY BUSHELL. Cardiff: University of Wales Press. 2007. 188 pp. £75. ISBN 978–0–7083–2080–8.

Twentieth-century Austrian literary history knows in principle four dates that figure as important caesuras for the differentiation of aesthetic tendencies and paradigms: 1918 (the end of the First World War), 1938 (the year of Austria's *Anschluss* to the Third Reich), 1945 (the year of Nazi Germany's unconditional surrender) and 1986 (the year of Kurt Waldheim's problematic inauguration as Austria's president).

Anthony Bushell has chosen one of these historical milestones as the starting point for his project — the year 1945, a date that is rather misleading in its global inflationary prominence in historical, political and aesthetical analyses as the beginning of an era that has seemingly been thoroughly and sufficiently explored. But most analyses across disciplines, not only in German Studies, usually go on to cover the 1950s *and* 1960s in order to understand the shifts between values and in the world's economical, political and philosophical *status quo* between 1950 and 1968. Anthony Bushell, however, focuses on the period between 1945 and 1955 in Austria (the year of the State Treaty, premised on permanent neutrality), knowing well that his approach requires a slightly different set of questions that only peripherally touch on the usual topics examined in connection with the post-war period in Europe.

Bushell's informed and enjoyable study thus focuses on an era in Austrian literary history that is known for the emergence of conflicting ideologies and aesthetic tendencies and for its paradoxical reliance on and simultaneous rejection of traditions. The social climate in the Second Republic of Austria that emerged after the end of the war was a direct result of Austria's role in the Third Reich and was dominated by a peculiar confusion as to how and to what extent the recent past had to be dealt with. Bushell's aim is to discuss Austria's post-war identity formation and ambivalent attitude to its recent past by looking at lyric poetry, thus putting himself in the tricky situation of having to account for the inextricable link between form and content when looking at a poem's contexts. It's a challenge he tackles elegantly by structuring the book as an overview of the Second Republic's phases of identity formation, using the phenomenon of literary journals, which functioned after 1945 as programmatic cultural authorities, as a framework for his discussion of individual poets. One of the volume's merits is that Bushell bases his study on the historically ambivalent relationship between Austria and Germany and keeps coming back to this problematic relationship that is reflected in both the non-literary (e.g. the publishing situation, see. p. 48) and in the literary (e.g. canon-building).

Bushell's book is divided into six chapters, some of which have rather lengthy headings that seem to reflect the complex nature of his project. The first chapter, entitled 'The Task Ahead: Political and Cultural Reconstruction in Early Post-war Austria', looks at Austria's unprecedented historical situation after 1945, which allowed her to appear as both perpetrator and victim before the world's eyes. The chapter sets out to give a more detailed account of the socio-political facts that led to Austria's refusal of any joint responsibility for the course of the war, politically as well as culturally. Bushell, in line with previous research, describes Austria's cultural development after 1945 as stifled by a strong desire for continuity, which facilitated the re-establishment of conservative writers like Alexander Lernet-Holenia, who became the leading aesthetic authorities in the post-war years. Most of the first chapter recounts research findings from the past twenty years, and, indeed, the study sports an impressive bibliography that shows a balanced approach to the research in the field, including scholarly works of conservative as well as left-wing, progressive origin. But this survey is needed to understand the prominence of some literary traditions (e.g. neo-realistic writing) and the absence of others (e.g. avant-garde poetry before the 1950s). Bushell also looks beyond the narrow perspective of an Austrian literary scholar and offers fresh insights. For example, he refers to Adorno's dictum of writing a poem after Auschwitz being an act of barbarism (p. 67) in the Austrian context and discusses the reception of German writers such as Wolfgang Borchert at greater length to illustrate the Austrian public's refusal to develop a sense of responsibility for the war. This informed, international academic viewpoint proves to be refreshingly distanced and to be an advantage in the discussion of national aesthetic identities.

In the remaining five chapters the study develops around the phenomenon of continuity, the absence of a sense of responsibility, the notion of radicality and the strong presence of Catholic traditions, all embedded in a new Austrian post-war identity, and he connects it with the emergence of new poetic traditions. Bushell illustrates the 'one step forward, two steps back'-development of poetry, often discussing less-known authors like Martina Wied (p. 116). Thus his study becomes much more of an overview than any other study that only looks at names that have remained well known to the present day. It is an asset of this examination of the 'field' (Bourdieu) that even peripheral phenomena and texts of lesser aesthetic quality are considered, because they exemplify the qualms and problems in Austria's identity-formation process. It is interesting that Bushell credits the existence of a real post-war spirit in poetry to a woman writer, Christine Busta, of whom, referring to her poem 'Am Kammerfenster eines Verschollenen', he asserts: 'Busta achieved [...] something that remained elusive to most poets in early post-war Austrian poetry: a fusion of traditional and understood forms with the topical and intense reality of the times in which she and her readers were living' (p. 104).

It is certainly a challenge to discuss all aspects that contribute to this peculiar sense of identity: exiled authors and authors who had remained in the country have to be included; the Austrian situation has to be read against the general situation of literature in Europe after 1945; subversive and peripheral tendencies have to be discussed as subtexts to the conservative programme of state-sponsored art. Austrian literary history of the period between 1945 and 1955 is a history of covering up, replacing and omission, underpinned by a sense of identity based on repression. If Anthony Bushell's study does not really provide new, surprising insights into Austria's immediate post-war literary history — which, in all fairness, would be a little much to ask, as the period in question has been examined extensively within research on the *Wiederaufbaujahre* — and if some examples seem a bit redundant at times, the book nevertheless combines detailed analyses with an eloquent overview of the relationship between national identity and art from the distanced expert perspective of a British scholar. Furthermore, it manages to address most of the diverse tendencies that become part of the Second Republic's new identity, thus inspiring still more interest in this period of Austrian literary history and its heterogeneous ways of expressing the cultural climate through text.

QUEEN MARY, UNIVERSITY OF LONDON   HEIDE KUNZELMANN

'von einen sprachen'. Poetologische Untersuchungen zum Werk Ernst Jandls. By MICHAEL HAMMERSCHMID and HELMUT NEUNDLINGER. Innsbruck: StudienVerlag. 2008. 226 pp. €24,90. ISBN 978–3–7065–4411–5.

Ernst Jandl was probably best known in his day for his visual-cum-acoustic concrete poems and witty 'surface translations': i.e. as the author of *mai hart lieb zapfen eibe hold* (1963), *Laut und Luise* (1966), *der künstliche baum* (1970), and such powerful *Sprechgedichte* as *schtzngrmm* and *ode auf N*. Yet as his prize-winning radio play *Fünf Mann Menschen*, written in collaboration with Friederike Mayröcker in 1968, suggests, there were more sides to this ever-metamorphosing writer than the received image reflects. One of the achievements of Hammerschmid's and Neundlinger's poetological investigations is to have established the parameters for a clearer appreciation of the range, diversity and ingenuity of Jandl's various phases of intense creativity, from *Andere Augen* (1956) to his swansong: the rigorously constructed *stanzen* in dialect (1992). The early poems of his transitional period in the 1950s, Chapter 2 argues, need to be seen in historical context as 'ein Innehalten und Bestandsaufnahme der Verhältnisse' (p. 57). After a brief evaluation of the early work, Hammerschmid and Neundlinger offer a likewise brief account of Jandl's concrete poetry in order to proceed to the bigger picture presented in their introduction: 'Während in der experimentellen Poesie die Sprache selbst auf dem Spiel steht, um in Laut und Schrift permanent erweitert und in ihren Ausdrucksmöglichkeiten ausgelotet zu werden, leitet die heruntergekommene Sprache zu einer poetisch-spielerischen (Selbst-)Kritik des Schreibens als Tätigkeit über' (p. 13). The first half of their study fleshes out this claim by offering a series of evaluative and contextualizing 'Untersuchungen zur heruntergekommenen Sprache und zu ihren Querverbindungen innerhalb von Jandls Werk' (p. 15).

The allusion in the present study's deliberately ungrammatical title to what Jandl called 'die heruntergekommene Sprache' reflects the authors' thesis that this inventive form of quasi Austro-German pidgin, with its often misunderstood echoes of *Gastarbeiterdeutsch*, offers a key to all the ensuing paradigm shifts in Jandl's 'Poetik des existentiellen und literarischen Nullpunkts' (p. 11). As the authors point out, the afterword to *gedichte an die kindheit* (1977) already emphasizes the programmatic importance of Jandl's interest in 'fehlerhaftes, widersprüchliches in der Sprache' for his ongoing experiments with poetry and related genres. The present study demonstrates this through close readings of his principal works written in 'die heruntergekommene Sprache' (*tagenglas* [1976], *die bearbeitung der mütze* [1978] and *der gelbe hund* [1980]), as well as his play *die humanisten* (1976), the

Sprechoper in 7 Szenen: Aus der Fremde (1978), and the *stanzen* cycle which brought to an abrupt conclusion the systematic experimentation with new linguistic possibilities and literary sub-genres.

Hammerschmid and Neundlinger highlight many of the advantages of 'die heruntergekommene Sprache' as a major breakthrough after Jandl's anxiety that with concrete poetry his writing had somehow reached a dead-end. They present his work written in such a seemingly dysfunctional discourse as essentially a deliberate dual strategy: 'Man muss sie gleichzeitig als elaborierten, hochliterarischen Code *und* als antiliterarische Ketzerei untersuchen' (p. 15). Their interpretations bring out the individuality, thematic range and linguistic diversity of Jandl's poems in 'heruntergekommene Sprache', where the protagonist of each *Rollengedicht* becomes unique in terms of diction, predicament and response. The medium is shown to illuminate various facets of the general human condition, while at the same time offering Jandl a new way of compensating for various personal and artistic crises.

As any reader of the present study soon discovers, Jandl's innovative deployment of 'heruntergekommene Sprache' is a source of both amusement and language renewal, the resultant poems being characterized by a vein of social criticism as well as functioning as an indirect form of artistic introspection. The same holds true of Jandl's later poems on ageing, sexual impotence, the collapse of other basic bodily functions and impending senile dementia in the taboo-breaking cycle *idyllen* (1989). 'Heiter verfallen' is the title of the chapter on this, the most disturbing yet amusing of the poet's works on the problems of ageing and self-disgust (again a metaphor for the condition of the waning poetic self). The terms Jandl uses to explain his various experiments with 'die heruntergekommene Sprache' are revealing. References to 'die konsequente Dekomposition souveränen Schreibens/ Sprechens', 'Zustände der Angst, der Flüchtigkeit und Unsicherheit', 'eine eigene Sprache der Sprachkrise' and 'Extremzustände des Sichabhandenkommens' (pp. 16–47, *passim*) make painfully clear that the source of the problems invoked is both artistic and existential, as indeed are some of the poet's short-termist solutions.

Apart from its dedication to detailed close reading, *'von einen sprachen'* possesses many other virtues too numerous to be more than mentioned here: a recognition of the need to do justice to Jandl's work within its full spectrum of literary, historical and national contexts, an enviable ability to explain complex points to readers coming to such material for the first time and the knack of bringing out concisely and clearly similarities and differences between Jandl's work and that of various contemporaries with whom he has often been too loosely compared. Some readers may take issue with some of the associative readings of certain poems (e.g. that of *deutsches gedicht* in Chapter 2), but the often speculative approach is challenging, as is the decision to discuss Jandl's experiments against the backdrop of the contemporary avant-garde, rap, pop culture and numerous other cultural phenomena of the time.

While *'von einen sprachen'* is generally a highly informative study, there are places where readers might occasionally be grateful for further clarification. It would have been helpful, for example, to hear more about why concrete poetry had become such a creative impasse in Jandl's eyes and whether his published work justified such a harsh verdict. Or to learn why Jandl, having abandoned one paradigm, chose the particular genres he then concentrated his creative energies on. Or to hear what role the collaborative work with Friederike Mayröcker played in offering solutions to the crises Hammerschmid and Neundlinger identify. In what sense, to take another example, did the *stanzen* represent the logical pinnacle of Jandl's creative span (in a way that Artmann's parallel *med ana schwoazzn dintn* could never have been for his *œuvre*)? Or was some form of desperate self-delusion at work in Jandl's later changes of direction? In the case of the *stanzen*, some non-native readers would probably have welcomed more assistance at both linguistic and exegetical levels with the dialect material. But this is not to detract from the value of Hammerschmid's and Neundlinger's excellent study as a whole.

KING'S COLLEGE LONDON   JOHN J. WHITE

Elfriede Jelinek. Eine Einführung in das Werk. By BÄRBEL LÜCKE. Munich: Fink. 2008. 169 pp. €12,90. ISBN 978–3–8252–3051–7.

Bärbel Lücke's concise overview of Jelinek's literary work to date enthusiastically sells itself as 'ein roter Faden durch das Werk der Nobelpreisträgerin!' that aims to provide an accessible introduction to the author whilst at the same time explaining the intellectual framework underlying her writing. Although there has been a flurry of scholarly publications on Jelinek in various languages since she won the Nobel Prize for Literature in 2004, there has been no single-authored contender to update the genuinely accessible and insightful overviews offered by Allyson Fiddler (1994) and Marlies Janz (1995) for those trying to orientate themselves in Jelinek's work. The author's subsequent prolific output alone has made the need for a sequel acute. Lücke's offering, however, falls short of the mark.

Following a brief but useful introduction, Lücke organizes her material into six main chapters, four of which deal with prose writing and two with dramatic output. Within the two distinct genres, texts are ostensibly dealt with in a chronological manner, although there is an irritating tendency for interviews and political statements to be inserted anachronistically, particularly in the two theatre chapters which tend to jump around bewilderingly from one decade to the next. While Jelinek's intertextual tendencies are certainly such that one work often points to another, precisely because of this the order in which the individual works were written should be more strictly adhered to before any wider conclusions are drawn and overarching concerns worked out.

In this respect, perhaps the real problem with Lücke's book is that she mixes the form of an introductory overview with the ambition of drawing together Jelinek's collected and eclectic works, but in doing so does neither properly. Her actual discussion of the primary texts is uneven. Some works, such as *Die Liebhaberinnen* (1975) and *Die Ausgesperrten* (1980), receive comparatively in-depth treatment, others have to make do with little more than a couple of pages of superficial statements, as is the fate of *Gier* (2000), *Neid* (2007) and virtually the entirety of Jelinek's later dramatic *œuvre*. An obvious reason for this is that some pieces simply fit better into Lücke's chosen overarching categories than others: of the four texts mentioned above, the first two work well within a discussion of 'deconstruction of Heimat, family and society' (Chapter Two), while the later texts are perhaps not best approached through the kind of thematic lens offered by either this socio-historical angle or her subsequent attempt in Chapter Three to unveil psychoanalytical structures in Jelinek's work. Lücke, however, remains convinced of her poststructuralist, deconstructionist approach to the exclusion of all else. Thus, while she is unquestionably right to highlight Jelinek's sophisticated linguistic play and grotesque critique of power structures — aspects, incidentally, which are not always sufficiently explored in the earlier volumes on Jelinek, but are certainly made accessible here — by repeating this reading in every chapter and attaching it to little more than cursory descriptions of the works themselves, she falls into the very same trap that some critics have discerned with regard to Jelinek herself: her discussion of the literary work becomes abstract, showing little appreciation of its wider context. Yet some sense of this context — the contentious reception of many of Jelinek's works, for example, and her subsequent response to this, not least within the very works themselves — is an important aspect of Jelinek's authorial presence which anyone being introduced to the writer should be made aware of.

Even if we stick with what Lücke sets out to achieve, shortcomings are in evidence. Where one critical approach is repeated across all of the chapters, one might reasonably expect some clear sense of how the techniques this approach lays bare are developed within or varied across Jelinek's lengthy career. The fact that none emerges should not be taken as a reflection on Jelinek. Lücke appears determined to emphasize constants and continuities, yet in the case of a writer whose work has so repeatedly evoked incomprehension and rejection, a focus on the subtle changes within her overall trajectory that have helped her to remain topical might be more helpful. It is sadly characteristic of this slim volume that its bibliography lists a limited number of German-language sources only, and the index includes only proper names. As an introductory overview, it fails to provide some of the most basic apparatus for introducing the author and her work; for anything more ambitious than this, it is simply too superficial.

UNIVERSITY OF LIVERPOOL   REBECCA BRAUN

Obituary
Peter Branscombe (1929–2008)

Peter Branscombe, who died on the last day of 2008 after a long battle against cancer, was an active member of the Advisory Board of *Austrian Studies* from the foundation of the yearbook in 1990. Born in Sittingbourne, in Kent, he was educated at Dulwich College, where he established himself as a fine cricketer; cricket would remain a lifelong interest. After two years' National Service he went on to Worcester College, Oxford, to read Modern Languages, combining his studies with his interest in music, in particular with extended involvement with the Oxford University Opera Club, of which he would eventually become President; productions included in 1951 the world première of *Incognita* by Egon Wellesz, who had escaped continental Europe after the *Anschluss* and been elected to a Fellowship of Lincoln College in 1939.

Peter's interest in Austria had been established before Oxford; he had the good fortune to be posted there as a National Serviceman in the Intelligence Corps, first to Carinthia, and then to Vienna (his posting was to Hietzing), where he was to enjoy not only theatre visits but, even more memorably, performances given by the State Opera company — then in one of its finest periods — in the Theater an der Wien, where the equivalent of four old pence bought a *Stehplatz* in the grand circle, to which a programme could be added for a further twopence. Peter never forgot the instructive pleasure of regularly hearing singers such as Sena Jurinac, Irmgard Seefried, Maria Reining and Julius Patzak — occasionally with great names including Josef Krips and Karl Böhm conducting.

Peter's interest in music and theatre in Vienna would bear research fruit in a dissertation entitled 'The Connexions between Drama and Music in the Viennese Popular Theatre from the Opening of the Leopoldstädter Theater (1781) to Nestroy's Opera Parodies (*c.* 1855), with Special Reference to the Forms of Parody', which was eventually submitted to the University of London in 1976. Even for those times, when there was less pressure than there is now to finish doctoral theses in three or four years, this was a long gestation (Peter had been lecturing in St Andrews since 1959); but he was never one to rush his work, and only this year a German musicologist wrote to me that it was still an incomparable treasure trove for research on musical theatre of the time, and lamenting that it had not been published in book form.

Peter remained in St Andrews for the rest of his life, devoted to his happy marriage and family life, and surrounded by his impressive collection of books, music, recordings, theatre and concert programmes and other memorabilia, which reflected the catholicity of his cultural and scholarly interests. In 1979 he was appointed to a personal chair as Professor of Austrian Studies. His scholarly publications were not confined to Austrian subjects, as users of his Penguin edition of selected Heine poems (1967), for example, will be gratefully aware. But Austria remained central. 1978 saw the appearance of a volume *Austrian Life and Literature 1780–1938*, edited by Peter and containing articles that had appeared the previous year in the St Andrews-based journal *Forum for Modern Language Studies*; and in the musical field he was one of the translators of Otto Erich Deutsch's 'documentary biography' of Mozart, first published in English in 1965; a volume *Schubert Studies. Problems of Style and Chronology*, co-edited with Eva Badura-Skoda, was published by the Cambridge University Press in 1982, followed nine years later by Peter's celebrated study *Die Zauberflöte* in the Cambridge Opera Handbooks series. Over and above his books and articles in journals, he contributed many entries to standard reference works (*New Grove Dictionary of Music, New Grove Dictionary of Opera*), including authoritative articles on leading composers of the nineteenth-century Viennese commercial stage. He was also a prolific reviewer. He began to review concerts and operas for the *Financial Times* in the late 1950s; he also reviewed gramophone records and CDs widely, in his later years especially in the *International Record Review*. The journals for which he would review works on literary and theatre history included *Germanistik, Modern Language Review* and *Nestroyana*, and for many years he contributed anonymous succinctly judicious short notices to *Forum for Modern Language Studies*.

The twin interests of music and theatre are reflected in his contributions to *Austrian Studies*, both in articles (on 'Music, Theatre and Performance in Vienna around 1800' in Vol. 4, on 'Nestroy and Schiller' in Vol. 9) and in reviews, which appeared in most issues. We also owe to him an outstanding recurring feature of the yearbook in the form of review articles providing comprehensive and always impressively knowledgeable surveys of publications stimulated by anniversaries: 'The Mozart Bicentenary' in Vol. 2 (1988 — so in advance of the bicentenary itself), 'The Schubert Year in Retrospect' (Vol. 10, 1999) and 'The Nestroy Year' in Vol. 11 (2003). When the Mozart year came, Peter gave a paper at a symposium in London which appeared in 1993 under the distinctively stylish title 'Mozart the Arch-Englishman'. That symposium was one of a series of conferences on Austrian matters originally launched by Bernhard Stillfried at which Peter was a regular speaker, from 1979 (a Hofmannsthal conference at Bedford College, at which he discussed sources of libretti for Richard Strauss operas, including *Ariadne auf Naxos*) to the Oxford conference on 'Austrian Theatre' in September 2000, at which he spoke on the 'beginnings of parody' in Viennese popular theatre, a topic on which he must have known more than anyone else alive. In Vienna he attended several of the annual sun-drenched Nestroy conferences in Schwechat. In January 1986 he had fallen on black ice in the centre of Vienna and spent three months in hospital there with a broken hip (visitors recall his skill in identifying the songs of over thirty birds outside his window — his ornithological knowledge was encyclopaedic); when he appeared for the first time in Schwechat in 1987, he was still limping but undaunted. The eight papers he would give there included one in 1997 on the transmission and authorship of the version of Offenbach's *Orpheus in the Underworld* in which Nestroy starred as Jupiter in 1860, a topic on which Peter was still working in the last years of his life; the last was a paper on festivities in Nestroy (2001), which he would rework for publication in a *Festschrift* for Jürgen Hein (2007).

Other conferences in which Peter took part in Vienna included a series of editorial meetings (1992–2000) organized within the *Wiener Vorlesungen* in support of the Nestroy edition. Peter had been signed up as one of the prospective editorial team by the beginning of 1978; the four volumes he edited, *Stücke 35–38*, appeared relatively late (1996–2001), but he played an important, if largely unsung, part in the edition in that most of the volume editors depended on being able to draw on his knowledge of the musical background; the preface to the collected addenda (2007) included a note of special thanks to him for his help, especially on Nestroy's parodistic medleys ('Quodlibets'), and recommending one of his last essays in *Nestroyana*, a detailed catalogue of the first printings of Adolf Müller's music to Nestroy songs.

Peter's kindness in helping fellow-scholars was remarkable: many must treasure letters, always courteous, always generous with his knowledge and patient with detailed queries answered at the expense, it must often have been, of his own work. Together with his humour, his breadth of interests, his energy in travelling to musical, theatrical, or commemorative social events and his rare gift for friendship (he kept up long friendships going back to his schooldays, to the army and Oxford and to his cricketing connections), this immense generosity of spirit was one of his essential and unforgettable characteristics.

UNIVERSITY OF EXETER   W. E. YATES

Abstracts

Setting the Tone: Austria's National Anthems from Haydn to Haider
By ANDREW BARKER

Composed in 1797 to bolster support for the **Habsburgs** during the **Napoleonic Wars**, **Haydn**'s setting of **Haschka**'s 'Gott erhalte Franz, den Kaiser' formed the first Austrian **national anthem**. Haydn's melody later became famous (and notorious) as the vehicle for **Hoffmann von Fallersleben**'s 'Lied der Deutschen' (1841). Until 1918 Haydn's melody then served as the basis for several Austrian anthems. For the new Republic **Karl Renner** and **Wilhelm Kienzl** created a new anthem which was replaced in 1929 by one written by **Ottokar Kernstock**, again utilizing Haydn's tune. With the creation of the **Second Republic** arose the need for yet another anthem. This resulted in a poem by **Paula Preradović** to a melody by **Johann Baptist Holzer** which has survived until the present day.

Mit **Haydns** Vertonung 1797 von **Haschkas** 'Gott erhalte Franz, den Kaiser' entstand die erste österreichische **Nationalhymne**. Ihr Zweck war die Unterstützung der Habsburger während der napoleonischen Kriege. Später wurde Haydns Melodie als Vehikel für **Hoffmann von Fallerslebens** 'Lied der Deutschen' (1841) berühmt und berüchtigt. Bis 1918 diente Haydns Melodie als Basis für verschiedene österreichische Nationalhymnen; für die neue Republik Österreich schufen **Karl Renner** und **Wilhelm Kienzl** eine Hymne, die 1929 durch eine von **Ottokar Kernstock** verfasste Hymne ersetzt wurde, die Haydns Melodie wieder benutzte. Für die **Zweite Republik** benötigte man noch eine neue Hymne; das Ergebnis war die bis heute bestehende Nationalhymne (Text von **Paula Preradović**, Musik von **Johann Baptist Holzer**).

Mozart's Words, Mozart's Music: Untangling an Encounter with a Fortepiano and its Remarkable Consequences
By JOHN IRVING

In October **1777 Wolfgang Amadeus Mozart** encountered for the first time the **fortepianos** of the Augsburg maker, **Johann Anton Stein**. Close reading of **Mozart's letters** to his father, explaining the sound worlds opened up to him following this discovery, afford an insight into the composer's existing preferences in the realm of piano music and his creative responses to new possibilities. These, in turn, are applied interpretatively to a brand new **sonata in C major, KV309**, written immediately in the wake of his new discovery.

Im Oktober **1777** begegnete **Wolfgang Amadeus Mozart** zum ersten Mal den Fortepianos des Augsburger Klavierbauers **Johann Anton Stein**. Eine genaue Analyse der **Briefe Mozarts** an seinen Vater, welche die ihm seit dieser Entdeckung zugänglichen Klangwelten beschreiben, gewährt Einblick in Mozarts Einstellungen zur Klaviermusik und in seine schöpferische Reaktion auf die damit verbundenen neuen Ausdrucksmöglichkeiten. Das wird wiederum für die Interpretation einer neuen **Sonate in C Dur, KV309**, eingesetzt, die aus dieser Begegnung entstanden ist.

'Ausgleichs-Abende': The First Viennese Performances of Smetana's *The Bartered Bride*
By DAVID BRODBECK

The early Viennese performances of **Bedřich Smetana**'s opera *The Bartered Bride* (1866), took place in 1892–93, during a time of great tension between the **Austro-Hungarian Monarchy**'s German and Czech middle classes. The uniformly positive critical reception of the work across the political spectrum suggests that it could serve as all things to all people: for the Czechs, as a source of national pride; for traditional **German-liberal nationalists**, as an artistic product of an enduring supranational **Austrian state** that seemed to exemplify superior German culture; and for the city's *deutschnational* critics, as a salutary model of national consciousness of what might be accomplished by properly 'German' composers in *Deutschösterreich*.

Die frühen Wiener Aufführungen von **Bedřich Smetanas** Oper, *Die verkaufte Braut* (1866) fanden 1892–93 statt, d.h. in einer spannungsreichen Zeit für das deutsche bzw. tschechische Bürgertum der **österreichisch-ungarischen Doppelmonarchie**. Das Werk wurde einheitlich positiv aufgenommen, egal zu welcher politischen oder nationalen Lage der jeweilige Kritiker sich bekannte. Es konnte also jeden zufriedenstellen: den Tschechen galt es als Grund zum Nationalstolz, den traditionsbewussten **deutsch-liberalen Nationalisten** als künstlerisches Erzeugnis eines dauerhaften übernationalen österreichischen Staates, das die Überlegenheit der deutschen Kultur beispielhaft darzustellen schien. **Deutsch-nationale** wiederum sahen in Smetanas Oper ein lehrreiches Vorbild nationalen Bewusstseins und ein Beispiel dafür, was ein echt 'deutscher' Komponist in Deutschösterreich leisten könnte.

Arnold Schoenberg's Wounded Work: 'Litanei' from the String Quartet in F sharp minor, Op. 10
By DARLA M. CRISPIN

The 1908 premiere of **Arnold Schoenberg's** Second String Quartet in F sharp minor, Op. 10, culminated in the so-called **Scandal in the Bösendorfer Saal** and sealed Schoenberg's reputation as one of the most difficult exponents of musical **Modernism**. Through analysis of early press responses, the article explores the reception of the **'Litanei'** movement, and posits that Schoenberg uses this vocal setting as a means of challenging the music and ideas of **Richard Wagner**, as presented in both *Tristan and Isolde* and *Parsifal*. This argument is counterpointed with an examination of **Theodor W. Adorno's** reading of Act III of *Tristan*, which closes his text *In Search of Wagner*.

Im Jahre 1908 gipfelte die Erstaufführung von **Arnold Schoenbergs zweitem Streichquartett (fis-Moll), Op. 10**, im sogenannten **Bösendorfer-Saal Skandal**, welcher Schoenberg seinen Ruf als einen der schwierigsten Exponenten der musikalischen **Moderne** sicherte. Unter Verwendung ausgewählter Pressestimmen der Zeit untersucht dieser Beitrag die Rezeption des 'Litanei'-Satzes und legt nahe, dass Schoenberg mit dieser Vokalfassung sowohl die Musik als auch die Ideenwelt von **Richard Wagners** *Tristan und Isolde* und *Parsifal* in Frage stellen wollte. Dieser Analyse wird **Theodor W. Adornos** Deutung vom dritten Akt des *Tristan*, die seinen *Versuch über Wagner* abschließt, gegenübergestellt.

Mahler's Farewell or The Earth's Song? Death, Orientalism and 'Der Abschied'
By ANDREW DERUCHIE

According to the received interpretation, 'Der Abschied', the finale of Gustav Mahler's exotic and valedictory *Das Lied von der Erde*, depicts the intrinsic subject's farewell to life and ecstatic, quintessentially romantic death. Cultural and anthropological historians of death, however, agree that by Mahler's day, encroaching modernity had rendered such a 'belle mort' a vanishing ideal. This article juxtaposes close musico-poetic and formal analysis against contemporary orientalist discourses to propose that 'Der Abschied' articulates a fresh epistemology of death whereby individual identity becomes subsumed in nature's eternal cycles.

Laut der allgemein akzeptierten Deutung des Schlusssatzes von Gustav Mahlers exotischem Abschiedswerk, dem *Lied von der Erde*, stellt 'Der Abschied' das Lebewohl des immanenten Subjekts an das Leben und seinen ekstatischen ur-romantischen Tod dar. Sich auf die Geschichte des Todes spezialisierende Kulturhistoriker und Anthropologen sind sich aber darüber einig, dass die fortschreitende Moderne bis zu Lebzeiten Mahlers das Ideal eines solchen 'schönen Todes' immer weiter schwinden ließ. Dieser Beitrag stellt eine detaillierte musikalische und poetologische Analyse neben zeitgenössische Orientalismus-Diskurse, um die These aufzustellen, dass 'Der Abschied' eine neue Erkenntnislehre des Todes darstellt, in der die Identität des Einzelnen in den ewigen Naturkreislauf subsumiert wird.

Leo Golowski as Minor Key in Schnitzler's *Der Weg ins Freie*: Musical Theory, Political Behaviour and Ethical Action
By FELIX W. TWERASER

The author argues that Arthur Schnitzler's novel *Der Weg ins Freie* [*The Road into the Open*, 1908], in the depiction of its secondary characters, evokes Vienna's crisis of modernity, the indolence of the Austro-Hungarian Monarchy's privileged classes, and the oft-frustrated attempts of Vienna's Jews to gain acceptance by the dominant culture. Leo Golowski is a key figure in this gallery of complementary characters, a brief photographic negative of the novel's central character, Georg von Wergenthin; while Georg is comfortable reworking musical conventions, Leo thinks originally about the philosophical underpinnings of music. Leo's inability to move Georg out of creative stasis and emotional frigidity supports Schnitzler's broader articulation of the limits of acculturation in turn-of-the-century Vienna.

Der Verfasser vertritt die These, dass die Gestaltung der Nebenfiguren in Arthur Schnitzlers Roman *Der Weg ins Freie* (1908) die Krise der Wiener Moderne, die Trägheit der privilegierten Schichten der österreichisch-ungarischen Monarchie und das oft frustrierte Verlangen nach Akzeptanz unter den Juden Wiens evoziert. Leo Golowski ist eine Schlüsselfigur in der Galerie der Nebenfiguren, ein flüchtiges Negativbild von der Hauptfigur des Romans, Georg von Wergenthin; während Georg der musikalischen Konvention verfallen ist, denkt Leo auf originelle Weise über die philosophischen Grundlagen der Musik nach. Leos Unfähigkeit, Georg aus kreativer Stasis und innerer Kälte zu befreien, deckt sich mit Schnitzlers Betonung der Grenzen der Akkulturation während der Wiener Jahrhundertwende.

The Adventures of *The Cunning Little Vixen*: Leoš Janáček, Max Brod and their Predecessors
By GEOFFREY CHEW

Max Brod, as translator of **Leoš Janáček's** libretti, increasingly sought, up to 1925, to rationalize elements he thought arbitrary in them, especially in Janáček's *Cunning Little Vixen*. Its particular characteristics are illustrated in a comparison of one scene of the opera with the equivalent sections in the novel by **Rudolf Těsnohlídek** on which it is based and in the drawings by **Stanislav Lolek** on which the novel is based: Janáček's sung text is defamiliarized, allowing the music to control the narrative. Brod found that themes of the opera corresponded with his own idealistic interpretation of **Judaism**, and his revisions seem to heighten the correspondences; it is this 'Jewish' version that remains influential in very many later productions, especially in Germany.

Als Übersetzer von den Libretten **Leoš Janáčeks** versuchte **Max Brod** bis 1925 zunehmend diejenigen Bestandteile, die er für willkürlich hielt, zu rationalisieren, vornehmlich in *Das schlaue Füchslein*. Die besonderen Merkmale dieser Oper werden herausgearbeitet, indem eine Szene mit den Teilen des Romans von **Rudolf Těsnohlídek** verglichen wird, auf die sie sich bezieht, aber auch mit den Zeichnungen **Stanislav Loleks**, auf denen wiederum der Roman basiert. Brod entdeckte, dass die Themen der Oper weitgehend seiner eigenen idealistischen Auslegung des **Judentums** entsprachen und seine Überarbeitungsvorschläge scheinen die Ähnlichkeiten zu unterstreichen. Diese 'jüdische' Fassung der Oper bleibt maßgebend für zahlreiche spätere Inszenierungen, insbesonders in Deutschland.

'Meine Not ist zu Ende und all meine Qual': Erich Zeisl's Setting of Alfons Petzold's 'Der tote Arbeiter'
By KARIN WAGNER

In **inter-war Vienna** the **art song** became an important aesthetic medium for **Erich Zeisl**, a representative of moderate modernism who trained with **Richard Stöhr**, **Joseph Marx** and **Hugo Kauder**. In 1932 his settings of the **workers' poet Alfons Petzold** marked a distinctive phase in the career of a composer not otherwise known for his political outspokenness, effectively a political statement on the eve of the **February uprisings** in Austria. Zeisl encountered Petzold via **Hilde Spiel**, who was connected with the **Social Democratic Workers' Party**: alongside three other unpublished settings of songs by Petzold ('The Workers', 'A Hunchbacked Orphan Boy Sings' and 'Wanderer's Song'), the march-like **'The Dead Worker'** is analysed as a case-study of the relationship between **words and music** in Zeisl's works.

Im Wien der **Zwischenkriegszeit** ist das Kunstlied für **Erich Zeisl**, dem bei **Richard Stöhr**, **Joseph Marx** und **Hugo Kauder** ausgebildeten Vertreter moderater **Moderne**, wichtigste Ausdruckssphäre. 1932 zeigen sich die Vertonungen des **Arbeiterdichters Alfons Petzold** als Besonderheit im Schaffen des in politischer Äußerung ansonsten reservierten Komponisten und sind am Vorabend des Bürgerkriegs in Österreich als Statement zu werten. Durch die der **Sozialdemokratischen Arbeiterpartei** verbundene **Hilde Spiel** wird Zeisl auf Petzold gestoßen: Neben drei weiteren unveröffentlichten Petzold-Liedern ('Die Arbeiter', 'Ein buckeliger Waisenknabe singt' und 'Wanderlied') liegt das in Marsch-Typik gehaltene Lied **'Der tote Arbeiter'** als Fallbeispiel zur Analyse des **Wort-Ton-Verhältnisses** vor.

'Das Erdorchester bedienen': Epiphany, Enchantment and the Sonorous World of Peter Handke
By MARTON MARKO

Musical models and themes have been essential features in the work of **Peter Handke** from his rock-concert-like **'language plays'** of the 1960s and early 1970s on. As a temporal medium, music connects directly with a hallmark of Handke's writing, namely the narrative feature of **epiphany**. These pronounced moments of connection between self and world set amid narrative flow are in turn linked to a thematic model of **enchantment** rooted in both **neo-Romantic** and **modernist** aesthetic and critical traditions in Austria and Central Europe. Particular attention is paid to Handke's motif of the **jukebox**, a globalizing musical mechanism that advances both a collective reading of cultural narrative and a subjective critical construction of it.

Seit seinen rockkonzerthaften **Sprechstücken** der 1960er und frühen 1970er Jahre spielen Vorbilder und Themen aus der Sphäre der Musik in der Schreibkarriere **Peter Handkes** bis heute eine bestimmende Rolle. Als zeitverbundenes Medium schließt sich die Musik unmittelbar an einem Grundkennzeichen handkeschen Schreibens an, und zwar dem **Epiphanischen**. Jene inmitten narrativer Bewegung ausgesprochenen Augenblicke des miteinander Verbundenseins zwischen Ich und Welt verknüpfen sich mit dem thematischen Modell der **Verzauberung** — einer Thematik, die in ästhetischen und kulturkritischen Traditionen der österreichischen **Neuromantik** und der **mitteleuropäischen Moderne** tief verwurzelt ist. Weiterer Schwerpunkt des Beitrags bezieht sich auf das handkesche Motiv der **Jukebox**, die als globalisierender Musikmechanismus dient, der sowohl kollektives Ablesen als auch subjektiv-kritische Konstruktionen kultureller Narrative fördert.

'Schreiben und Komponieren': Elfriede Jelinek's *Rosamunde*
By GILLIAN PYE and SIOBHÁN DONOVAN

The Nobel Prize-winning author **Elfriede Jelinek** has described her writing as 'composition', and critics frequently refer to her work as **word-music**. Taking as a case-study *Rosamunde*, one of Jelinek's five **Princess Plays**, this article asks how Jelinek's texts could be construed as musical. Adopting **Roland Barthes's** concept of '**The Grain of the Voice**', we examine how Jelinek treats her Romantic intertext, **Helmina von Chézy's** *Rosamunde* (1823), for which **Schubert** wrote the incidental music. Showing how she 'remixes' Chézy's text, this discussion explores the way in which Jelinek works along the 'fringe of contact' between words and music.

Die österreichische Autorin und Nobelpreisträgerin **Elfriede Jelinek** bezeichnet ihr Schreibverfahren als 'kompositorisch', während Kritiker oft auf ihre **Wortmusik** hinweisen. Dieser Aufsatz widmet sich der Frage, inwiefern Jelineks Texte als musikalisch zu verstehen sind. Das von **Roland Barthes** entwickelte Konzept der '**Körnung der Stimme**' dient als Ausgangspunkt für eine Analyse des 2003 im Dramenzyklus *Der Tod und das Mädchen I-IV* veröffentlichten '**Prinzessinnendramas**' *Rosamunde*. Insbesonders untersuchen wir Jelineks Verarbeitung ihrer romantischen Vorlage, **Helmina von Chézys** Drama *Rosamunde* (1823), das von **Schubert** vertont wurde. Des weiteren zeigt der Aufsatz, wie Jelinek Chézys Text demontiert und neu gestaltet, um an der Schnittstelle zwischen Wort und Musik der Oberfläche der Sprache entgegenzuwirken.

www.ingramcontent.com/pod-product-compliance
Lightning Source LLC
Chambersburg PA
CBHW062204080426
42734CB00010B/1785